D1521148

Russian rightists and the revolution of 1905 examines the emergence of right-wing organizations in Russia during the political crisis of 1905–1907. As the first comprehensive study of rightist activity throughout the country, it focuses not only on such nationally prominent parties as the Union of the Russian People, but also on provincial organizations. Professor Rawson demonstrates how the rightists attempted to resolve the impasse between autocracy and constitutionalism that Russia had reached by the end of 1905. These defenders of the old order sought to counter the liberal and radical forces arrayed against the autocracy, sometimes by force, more often by campaigning in elections to the State Duma. The study concludes that the rightist organizations, while never a match for the opposition parties, mobilized a substantial segment of public sentiment and helped induce the autocracy to reassert its authority.

RUSSIAN RIGHTISTS AND THE REVOLUTION OF 1905

Cambridge Russian, Soviet and Post-Soviet Studies

Series list continues on page 284

RUSSIAN RIGHTISTS AND THE REVOLUTION OF 1905

DON C. RAWSON
Iowa State University

CAMBRIDGE
UNIVERSITY PRESS

Published by the Press Syndicate of the University of Cambridge
The Pitt Building, Trumpington Street, Cambridge CB2 1RP
40 West 20th Street, New York, NY 10011–4211, USA
10 Stamford Road, Oakleigh, Melbourne 3166, Australia

First published 1995

Printed in Great Britain at the University Press, Cambridge

A catalogue record for this book is available from the British Library

Library of Congress cataloguing in publication data

Rawson, Don C.
    Russian rightists and the revolution of 1905/Don C. Rawson.
        p.   cm. – (Cambridge Russian, Soviet and post-Soviet studies; 95)
    Includes bibliographical references and index.
    ISBN 0 521 46487 0
    1. Political parties – Russia – History. 2. Russia – Politics and
government – 1904–1917. 3. Russia – History – Revolution, 1905–1907.
I. Title. II. Series.
JN6598.A1R38 1995
324.247′03′09041 – dc20   94–8850 CIP

ISBN 0 521 46487 0 hardback
ISBN 0 521 48386 7 paperback

CE

To Shirley

Contents

x   **Contents**

Illustrations

Tables

Acknowledgements

In pursuing this study, I have appreciated the generous help of various persons: Donald Treadgold, who first encouraged me to investigate the rightist movement; Roberta Thompson Manning and Robert Edelman, who shared information on sources and offered valuable advice based on their own research; and Andrejs Plakans, Hans Rogger, and Terence Emmons, who read parts or all of the manuscript and commented appropriately.

I am also indebted to the staffs of the Central State Archive of the October Revolution of the USSR (now the State Archive of the Russian Federation) in Moscow; the Central State Historical Archive of the USSR (now the Russian State Historical Archive) in St. Petersburg; the newspaper collection at the Saltykov-Shchedrin Public Library in St. Petersburg; the Slavic Division of the Helsinki University Library; the Butler Library of Columbia University; the Slavonic Room of the New York Public Library; the Hoover Institute; and the Parks Library of Iowa State University.

Map Provinces of European Russia in 1906–1907

Introduction

As Russia entered the twentieth century, few observers anticipated the crisis that soon would engulf the old political order, threatening its very existence. Within half a decade, the autocratic regime, already straining to keep pace with the pressures of modernization, found itself facing a broader, more persistent opposition than any it had encountered in the past. Only reluctantly, it came to recognize the severity of the confrontation and the need for a resolute defense.

The political drama, however, was not limited to the contest between the autocracy and its opponents. During the crisis a new phenomenon appeared: a political movement in support of the faltering autocracy. The resulting maze of parties, unions, and other related groups soon became known collectively as the "right," a designation contrasting them with the revolutionaries on the "left" and the "liberals," "progressives," and "moderates" in between. Admittedly, these terms were imprecise, but they served most contemporary observers – and participants – as a practical means of indicating the extent to which political activists supported or opposed the old regime. Over the years, they have also delineated appropriate areas of historical inquiry.

Unlike the liberals and revolutionaries – those forces most dramatically pitted against the autocracy – the rightists have received little scholarly attention. Yet, in 1905–1907, the opposition parties and the government both regarded them as major determinants in Russia's new political structure. If in retrospect one is to appreciate the complexities of the struggle during those critical years, especially the advent of partisan politics, it is imperative to take into account the entire political spectrum, including its rightist components.

Fortunately, several recent studies have contributed to our knowledge of the rightist movement, particularly the role of rightist parties in St. Petersburg and Moscow, and rightist deputies in the State Duma.[1] But as yet there has been no comprehensive investigation of rightist activity throughout the country.

The present book seeks to meet this need. It examines not only such nationally prominent rightist parties as the Union of the Russian People, Union of Russian Men, Russian Monarchist Party, and Russian Assembly, but also regional and provincial rightist organizations, those that affiliated with the national parties and those that remained independent. This study also explores programmatic and behavioral distinctions within the rightist movement that differentiated moderate and extreme rightists, and that separated special interest groups from those that sought a popular following.

In probing these characteristics, the study emphasizes that the essential nature of the rightist movement lay in its attempt to resolve the impasse that the old political order had reached by the end of 1905. Understandably, staunch monarchists welcomed the autocracy's acknowledgement that, for the sake of survival, it must suppress the revolutionaries and reestablish order in the country; but they were dismayed by how the autocracy chose to handle the reformers, who were demanding parliamentary government. Most monarchists recognized that when Nicholas II conceded legislative powers to the newly created State Duma while at the same time maintaining that Russia was still an autocracy, he had identified, perhaps inadvertently, the political deadlock confronting Russia. Any attempt to depict the tsar as a "constitutional autocrat" added to the confusion. Imbued with a sense of urgency, the rightists took on the troublesome task of dealing with this critical state of affairs.

Among the rightist responses, one can distinguish two general persuasions. Some rightists assumed a primarily defensive stance. They reluctantly accepted the political changes that had already occurred but endeavored to prevent further damage. Others emphasized the work of restoration. They longed to return Russia to the steadfast rule of Alexander III or even to the lost but presumably golden age of Muscovite autocracy, in which the tsar and his people enjoyed a filial bond of trust and cooperation. In this study, I analyze these orientations and, in doing so, treat both the practical and ethereal aspects of the rightist movement. Most of all, I seek to demonstrate how rightist organizations mobilized a substantial segment of public sentiment into a viable political force during the Duma elections, particularly in the socially troubled central agricultural provinces and the ethnically diverse western borderlands. Overall, I hope this study may add to our understanding of the 1905 Revolution, the major defects and dilemmas of the old regime, and the ways in which rightist politics affected the course of events.

1 The advent of the rightist movement

Cast in the context of 1905, the appearance of rightist organizations in Russia may be seen as essentially a reaction to the mounting turmoil. Certainly, many Russians who clung to traditional principles and institutions, especially the autocracy, viewed the ferment with alarm. But more significantly, this rightist activity reflected a growing apprehension among loyalists that the tsar no longer possessed the ability – and perhaps the will – to withstand the forces threatening his authority. In fact, it was a signal of distress from the tsar himself that aroused the heretofore silent supporters of the old regime to action. After months of indecision over the most effectual means of maintaining order in Russia, Nicholas II finally issued a curious combination of imperial acts in February 1905, which incorporated elements both of conciliation and of repression. Bowing to the moderate opposition's call for a representative assembly, the tsar at the same time beckoned his faithful subjects to assist him in fighting the forces of sedition. At once, opponents and loyalists alike comprehended that Russia had reached a turning point in its political life, and both sides began to mobilize. By year's end it had become apparent that in addition to the wave of oppositionists a genuinely right-wing movement was beginning to emerge.

Sources of discontent

There seems little dispute that although the circumstances that persuaded Nicholas and his government to act had long been accumulating, only after the turn of the twentieth century did they become paramount concerns. For years the autocracy had labored under the illusion that popular unrest was but an inherent facet of traditional Russian life. Nicholas himself, hardly an astute observer, tended almost completely to overlook these adverse aspects. Some of his ministers, however, were able to discern two disquieting levels of discontent: on the one hand, a somewhat vague but increasingly emphatic array of economic and social grievances from industrial workers and peasants; on the other, a more sharply focused set of political demands from liberal and radical intellectuals. Both boded ill for the regime.

It took no great perceptiveness to recognize that the workers and peasants, who usually aimed their dissatisfactions at industrial management or the landed nobility, were also impatient with the government for failing to alleviate their plight. Most workers endured the deprivations of a rapidly industrializing society: long, arduous hours at their jobs, low pay, and often wretched living conditions. Generally, the government had responded slowly to the workers' needs. Willing to provide a modest supply of inspectors to hear workers' complaints and help settle disputes between labor and management, the government seemed far more disposed toward the entrepreneurs, whom it considered central to industrialization, than toward the workers. Intent also on preserving social stability and autocratic control, the government had declared labor unions illegal, thus frustrating nascent hopes that the workers could take collective action in their own behalf. Nonetheless, during the 1890s some workers had achieved a sufficient sense of solidarity to engage in sporadic strikes for better working conditions and higher wages. According to statistics published by the government, strikes during the decade prior to 1905 occurred fairly frequently, as shown in Table 1. While no more than 3 or 4 percent of the labor force struck in any given year, both the workers and the government were beginning to realize the potential effectiveness of these walkouts.[1] An unexpected incident made the point. A strike among oil workers in Baku in July 1903 quickly spread to Tiflis, Odessa, Nikolaev, Kiev, and several other cities in southern Russia. Obviously, a strike in the Baku oil fields could cut off practically all of Russia's petroleum production; shutdowns of a few metallurgical factories in the Ukraine could deprive the country of most ferrous metal products; and a walkout in the Tiflis railway repair depot could tie up southern Russia's rail transportation. In sum, a few thousand strikers could seriously affect the nation's economy.

Moreover, the government found during these strikes in 1903 that the workers were both persistent and unpredictable. In several cities they clashed with police or government troops – episodes that only increased the workers' hostility, particularly when fellow workers

Table 1 *Strikes in Russia, 1895–1904*

Year	Number of strikes	Number of strikers	% of total workers
1895	68	31,195	2.01
1896	118	29,527	1.94
1897	145	59,870	3.99
1898	215	43,150	2.87
1899	189	57,498	3.83
1900	125	29,389	1.73
1901	164	32,218	1.89
1902	123	36,671	2.15
1903	550	86,832	5.10
1904	68	24,904	1.46

These figures were for the European provinces and probably represented about 70 percent of the workers in the empire.
Source: D. Kol'tsov, "Rabochie v 1890–1904 gg.," in L. Martov and others, eds., *Obshchestvennoe dvizhenie v Rossii v nachale XX-go veka*, II, 224–225.

were injured or killed.[2] More and more, political agitators from the radical parties circulated among the workers, endeavoring to educate them politically. This meant convincing them that their economic problems stemmed largely from a repressive, unresponsive autocratic government that was committed to upholding the interests of the industrialists.

However acute the grievances of the urban workers, a growing ferment among the country's predominantly peasant population portended an even greater challenge. For years, poverty had plagued rural Russia, partly due to overpopulation but also to inefficient land usage. The peasant commune, which had been the primary form of land tenure since the end of serfdom in 1861, perpetuated the antiquated three-field farming system and the continual repartitioning of small and scattered land strips, all of which diminished agricultural productivity. Many peasants also regarded their financial obligations to the state as a contributory cause of their economic woes. It would be a mistake to suppose that the government made no attempt to remedy the situation, but its efforts remained feeble in view of the enormous problems. Although the government had repealed the poll tax in 1886, it still required redemption payments on the land allotted to the peasants at the time of emancipation. The government's need for revenues to help finance its industrialization program in the 1890s also placed extremely burdensome taxes on such peasant staples as sugar, tea, kerosene, tobacco, and liquor. In imposing these taxes, the policy makers in St. Petersburg reasoned, perhaps correctly, that industrialization would eventually benefit the entire population, thus compensating the peasants for their temporary deprivation; but in the meantime many peasants failed to appreciate the government's economic logic.

Inadequate data make it difficult to assess the general economic status of the peasants in the late nineteenth and early twentieth centuries. Apparently, peasants in some areas maintained a reasonably satisfactory level of living; but others, particularly in the more densely populated central regions, experienced serious economic reverses, especially in years of poor harvests or low market prices for grain.[3] In 1902, riots erupted in Poltava and Kharkov provinces, during which peasants burned estates and looted grain stores, livestock, and equipment. Spasmodic disruptions wracked adjoining provinces. In no substantive sense a peasant rebellion, these disorders did not pass unnoticed by the government. Yet, neither the tsar nor his ministers were unduly disturbed at what they regarded as typical peasant outbursts, quite in keeping with Russia's rural traditions. Speaking to a peasant delegation in Kursk at the end of August 1902, Nicholas informed his listeners that those guilty of the disorders in Poltava and Kharkov provinces would be punished, and that the peasants could best improve their economic situation through hard work, thrift, and obedience to God's commandments. More sympathetically, he promised that honest and loyal peasants could rest assured that he would never cease to care for their needs.[4] Actually, the government was giving some attention to agrarian affairs. In 1899, 1901, and 1902, Nicholas authorized commissions to investigate the economic problems of the peasantry. But these efforts, and even the manifesto of 26 February 1903, announcing that the government would reexamine all legislation on rural conditions, provided little impetus toward fundamental agrarian reform.

Adding to the already ominous signs of peasant and worker discontent was the fact that the autocracy's political adversaries were seeking popular support against the existing social and political order. The government might not become exercised over peasant or worker dissatisfaction in itself; but it could hardly help sensing the latent danger in a coalition of the masses and dissident intellectuals. Indeed, the tsar and his ministers were aware that both the Social Democrats and the Socialist Revolutionaries, recently organized into underground parties, advocated revolution as the most effective means of producing radical social and political change. Although both parties were agitating among the masses – the Marxist Social Democrats among the industrial workers, the populist-inspired Socialist Revolutionaries primarily among the peasants – no one knew in 1904 whether either party had yet acquired a substantial following. But the government increasingly recognized that the revolutionaries posed a serious problem, particularly when the Socialist Revolutionaries authorized their semi-autonomous Battle Organization to carry out political assassinations. Directed at gendarmes, military officers, local officials, provincial governors, and ministers of the central government, the SR terror quickly became an intrusive facet of Russian political life. In 1902 the terrorists assassinated the Minister of Internal Affairs, D. S. Sipiagin; in 1903 the governor of Ufa province, General N. M. Bogdanovich; and during this period scores of lesser figures. In response, the government brought the perpetrators of the crimes to trial, hoping that long prison terms or deportation with hard labor, along with the death sentences imposed by military tribunals to which some of the cases were assigned, would deter future assassins. But events had begun to show that harsh punishments were having little effect on the terrorists, who continued to mete out their own brand of justice to "enemies of the people." Unfortunately for the government, many educated Russians seemed more offended by the severe punishments given political offenders, especially the death sentences, than by the assassins.

By the end of 1904, moderate opponents of the autocracy were also becoming more strident in their demands. From a handful of progressive gentry activists in the zemstvos during the 1870s, calling cautiously for constitutional government, the liberal movement in Russia had grown by 1900 to include lawyers, educators, physicians, engineers, and other professionals. In September 1903, the movement's leaders organized the Union of Liberation, and in their program the following January they proposed a constituent assembly, elected by universal suffrage, that would transform Russia into a constitutional monarchy. In addition, the Union recommended compulsory redistribution of landed estates to the peasants (although with compensation to the former owners), and an eight-hour day and other improvements for workers. While the Union did not regard itself as a revolutionary party, it continued to exert pressure on the autocracy to submit to fundamental reform.

The Union of Liberation seemed to be moving away from the liberals' traditional use of the zemstvos in airing their political objectives, but its emergence actually coincided with a revival of zemstvo activity, compounding the government's concern about the reform movement. Although the government valued the zemstvos as organs of local administration, it now feared that political activists in these assemblies might stir up oppositionist sentiment among the rural population, with which the zemstvos had close contact. As Minister of Internal Affairs from 1902 to 1904, Sipiagin's successor, V. K. Pleve, unwittingly pushed the zemstvo leaders to greater opposition by constantly criticizing their activities. He further fueled their discontent by refusing to confirm the election of D. S. Shipov – probably the most respected of the zemstvo leaders – to his fifth three-year term as chairman of the Moscow provincial zemstvo board. Pleve charged unconvincingly that Shipov had failed to keep unreliable persons out of the zemstvos.[5] Amidst increasing friction, Pleve was assassinated by an SR terrorist on 15 July 1904. This quieted the zemstvo opposition momentarily, as did the announcement that Prince P. D. Sviatopolk-Mirskii would succeed Pleve, since Mirskii said he would inaugurate moderate reforms and pursue a conciliatory policy toward the zemstvos. However, by this time the zemstvo leaders had become both more precise and more insistent. In the hope that Mirskii would listen to their proposals, they convened a zemstvo congress in St. Petersburg on 6 November 1904. At what turned out to be a momentous occasion for the reform movement, the delegates almost unanimously approved a set of eleven resolutions requesting broader civil rights; the end of arbitrary arrests and other violations of personal freedom; and, above all, a popularly elected national assembly. On this last point, a majority of the delegates endorsed the concept of a *legislative* assembly; a minority – the more moderate "Slavophile current" led by Shipov – did not specify the nature of the assembly but implied its preference for a *consultative* body.[6] Despite these differences, the zemstvists had taken a politically historic step by joining the Union of Liberation in calling for constitutional government.

When Shipov discussed the resolutions with Mirskii shortly after the congress, Mirskii seemed sympathetic, siding with the moderate minority on the question of a national assembly.[7] Apparently, he himself had been considering a consultative body, possibly elected from the zemstvos. According to S. E. Kryzhanovskii, then an assistant to Mirskii, the latter suggested to the tsar that he issue a manifesto announcing that elected representatives either be included in the State Council or act under it as a separate body. This body would discuss legislation and submit recommendations to the tsar for his approval.[8]

Predictably, action generated reaction. Both Sergei Witte, Chairman of the Committee of Ministers, and K. P. Pobedonostsev, Chief Procurator of the Holy Synod and a close adviser to Nicholas II, cautioned the tsar against the projected measure, saying that it would only open the way to constitutionalism. Torn between both sides of the debate, Nicholas accepted their advice, which encouraged him to declare that "I will never agree, under any circumstance, to a representative form of government, for I consider it would be harmful to the people that God has entrusted to me."[9] The ukase of 12 December 1904, which Witte drew up for the tsar, instructed the Committee of Ministers to draft legislation granting greater freedom of the press and of religion, more rights to the peasants, and government insurance for the workers – measures proposed by both Mirskii and the zemstvists; but the ukase said nothing about an elected assembly.[10] Clearly, the tsar and most of his ministers were not prepared to accede to the basic demands of the reformers.

More severe reaction was to come. The hints of concessions in the 12 December ukase preceded by only a week a harsh government announcement criticizing the zemstvo assemblies for interfering in the affairs of state and contributing to public unrest. Charging that zemstvo leaders were acting not for the good of the country but for its enemies, the announcement warned that "any violation of order and tranquility, and any assemblages of an anti-government character, should and will be halted by all legal means at the government's disposal, and those guilty of these violations will be held legally responsible and prosecuted." Henceforth, the announcement concluded, the zemstvos were not to deal with questions outside their legal authority.[11]

New problems and the need for action

Unable to formulate a consistent set of policies and instinctively trying to squelch any manifestations of popular initiative, the government left the liberal opposition frustrated, uncertain what to do next. Nonetheless, the question of reform was by no means dead. Soon a succession of events began to turn public sentiment against the government. The course of the war against Japan, begun in January 1904, continued to worsen. Far from uniting opinion behind the government, as some ministers had anticipated, it degenerated into a

series of disasters that served to invigorate the opposition. The fall of
Port Arthur to the Japanese on 20 December, after a prolonged siege
and several bloody battles, brought a wave of criticism that focused
narrowly on the government's deficiencies in its conduct of the war
and broadly on the fact of the war itself.

There followed the tragic spectacle of Bloody Sunday on 9 January
1905, when government troops fired on crowds of workers approaching the Winter Palace to present their grievances to the tsar.
The estimates of more than a hundred killed and several hundred
wounded incensed many Russians who previously had confined their
criticisms to the government's inept war policy. Now they charged
that the autocracy was callous to the fundamental needs and
aspirations of the common people. The replacement of Sviatopolk-
Mirskii on 15 January with A. G. Bulygin as the new Minister of
Internal Affairs failed to silence the critics, despite Bulygin's apparent
willingness to follow a conciliatory course. Few believed such changes
would address the core problems of Russian society.

During January, the opposition grew more shrill and disturbances
multiplied. The Union of Liberation stepped up its political demands,
as did many provincial zemstvo assemblies. At St. Petersburg
University, several thousand students joined in anti-government
demonstrations, often supported by faculty. In the capital, a statement
by 342 professors and members of the Academy of Sciences called for
an assembly of freely elected representatives. Simultaneously, worker
unrest grew. Following strikes in St. Petersburg and Baku at the end
of December, work stoppages occurred in January in Moscow,
Warsaw, Vilna, Riga, Kiev, Ekaterinoslav, Saratov, Tiflis, and other
cities. In one month about 500,000 workers went on strike, more than
the total number of strikers during the entire previous decade.[12]

Amidst the mounting turmoil, some members of the government
began to urge the tsar to take conciliatory action. Nicholas seemed
inclined to go along. Within a week after Bloody Sunday, he directed
Sergei Witte to convene the Committee of Ministers, along with
department heads from the State Council, to discuss measures for
calming the country and possibly introducing reforms beyond those
envisioned in the 12 December ukase. At the meeting, held on 18
January, Witte limited the discussion mainly to the question of issuing
a manifesto in the tsar's name. This document would commend the
Russian people for their wartime loyalty, while reminding them that
dissidents had been creating unrest among the workers, which had
led to Bloody Sunday. The manifesto would also express the tsar's

sorrow over that unhappy event and note that the "rapidity and unexpectedness" of the situation had prevented him from forestalling the confrontation in the streets. Measures would nonetheless be taken by the government to improve the workers' lot.

The debate at the meeting revealed deep divisions. Some believed the manifesto would show that the tsar was sensitive to his people's needs. Others thought a manifesto was too broad an instrument for the intended purpose, especially if its promises of reform could not be underwritten by government action. A rescript would be better, the opponents of a manifesto contended; it would simply provide aid for workers and others who were in distress. With a vote of fourteen in favor of a manifesto and nine against, there seemed not enough consensus to proceed with specific measures. Discussions were to resume later.[13]

During this period, Nicholas's ministers and other advisers continually prodded him to act. Probably the most notable advice came from the Minister of Agriculture and State Domains, A. S. Ermolov, who had long enjoyed the tsar's confidence. In a fervent conversation with Nicholas on 17 January, the usually reserved Ermolov warned that "Russia is currently experiencing a serious situation, unparalleled in its history, the consequences of which are impossible to foretell." Ermolov painted for the tsar an alarming picture of problems requiring attention. The catastrophe of 9 January, he said, was heightening disaffection among the workers. Terrorists would likely continue their assassination attempts, perhaps targeting Nicholas himself. Opposition to the government among the landed nobility, the traditional bulwark of the autocracy, was spreading. The 12 December ukase had raised expectations of reform, but nothing substantial had resulted. It was imperative that the tsar listen to "the voice of the people," and swiftly bring together a popularly elected assembly to participate in the affairs of state.[14] On 31 January, Ermolov submitted a detailed memorandum, reiterating the points he had made in his initial conversation and sounding an even more forceful warning. "The state finds itself on the brink of destruction," he wrote prophetically, "from which neither the military nor energetic government administrators can save it." To quell the turmoil and prevent the autocracy's demise, the tsar must issue a manifesto announcing the convocation of a representative assembly drawn from all estates in society. This body, Ermolov contended, could serve as a much-needed basis of tsarist authority.[15]

Impressed by Ermolov's plea, but still undecided on the most effective alternative, Nicholas met with his Committee of Ministers on 3 February. The Chairman of the State Council, D. M. Solskii, Grand Prince Aleksandr Mikhailovich, and a few other advisers also attended. Discussion centered on the appropriateness of issuing a document that would go further than the manifesto considered on 18 January by dealing not only with the war and domestic turmoil generally but with arrangements for a representative assembly. Ermolov, Bulygin, and S. S. Manukhin, the Minister of Justice, spoke in favor of an assembly as a means of resolving Russia's domestic conflicts. V. N. Kokovtsov, the Minister of Finance, also argued that an assembly was crucial if Russia hoped to obtain the loan it was seeking from French financiers. The French, Kokovtsov said, were concerned that the Russian government was unwilling to make reforms that would stabilize the internal situation sufficiently to remove undue risk in offering a loan.[16] Although Witte and some others at the meeting declined to endorse an assembly, the tsar tentatively agreed to issue a rescript, if not a manifesto, instructing the Minister of Internal Affairs to begin planning a representative assembly. He also asked Bulygin to draw up a draft document for further discussion.[17]

While the drafting proceeded, another traumatic event caused the tsar to consider decisive action against the political opposition. On 4 February, a bomb thrown by a Socialist Revolutionary terrorist killed the tsar's uncle, the Grand Prince Sergei Aleksandrovich, until recently the governor-general of Moscow. Shaken by the assassination, Nicholas decided to admonish the Russian people that they must bring a halt both to these disturbing acts of sedition and to the dissension over the war. While his ministers continued to discuss a rescript concerning a representative assembly, Nicholas put personal aides to work on a manifesto that would have a far more admonitory tone than the one considered earlier.[18]

On 18 February, as Nicholas's ministers were on their way to Tsarskoe Selo to discuss the draft rescript, they learned that the manifesto had been published that morning, along with a ukase that also related to current political issues. No one had notified the ministers that these documents were being prepared or consulted them about the contents. Chagrined, the ministers hurriedly approved the rescript, almost without comment, and Nicholas signed it.[19] Thus, in a single day the tsar issued three important acts, which would have pronounced effects on both the oppositionists and the supporters of the throne.[20]

The message in each document was brief. The rescript, in accord with previous discussions, officially directed Bulygin to prepare procedures for bringing together "worthy persons, invested with the confidence of the people and selected from the populace, for participating in the preliminary examination and discussion of legislative proposals." The body would be a consultative assembly, without the power actually to pass legislation. But it was still a major concession to the moderate opposition.

In the ukase, which was probably initiated by D. F. Trepov, a confidant of the tsar and newly appointed governor-general of St. Petersburg,[21] Nicholas instructed the Council of Ministers to examine suggestions by private persons or groups for "the improvement of the organization of the state and the betterment of the public welfare." In effect, the tsar was offering the assurance that anyone could be heard and heeded by his ministers: a new phenomenon in Russia.

The manifesto carried a sterner message. In it Nicholas reminded his people that in the Far East the sons of Russia were giving their lives for their faith, tsar, and country. At home the country seethed with sedition, a situation obviously satisfying to Russia's enemies. The tsar noted, sorrowfully, the assassination of the Grand Prince. These trying conditions, he said, were surely God's way of testing the endurance of the Russian people. As their sovereign he summoned loyal Russians to help him restore order and tranquility – an unprecedented appeal by a Russian monarch, who presumably had no need to plead for loyalty. Without spelling out the specifics, Nicholas called upon "persons of good will from all estates and statuses, everyone to his calling and in his place, to unite in harmonious assistance to Us, by word and deed, in a great and holy endeavor to overcome the persistent foreign enemy and to eradicate the sedition in our land."

Responses to the acts of 18 February

The three acts immediately provoked a hot debate among both Nicholas's ministers and the public. What exactly was the intent of the documents? Did they supplement one another, or did they contain basic contradictions? What would be their effect? Sergei Witte states in his memoirs that the manifesto came as a complete surprise to him and the other ministers and that it contradicted the rescript (and the ukase as well), since they called simultaneously for expression of the popular will and reaffirmation of the autocratic prerogative. However, according to Witte, when some of the ministers questioned Nicholas about the documents, he replied that he saw no discrepancy. All three were meant to bring peace to Russia.[22]

More significant was the way the acts affected the public. Suddenly, dissidents and loyalists alike had to reassess their political positions. What the liberal oppositionists found was only partly to their liking. Most rejected the patriotic message of the manifesto while discerning some value in the rescript and the ukase. But, like Witte, they agreed that the acts were contradictory. V. A. Maklakov, an eloquent spokesman and legal expert for the Union of Liberation, noted that what the rescript accepted as a commendable "readiness of the people to provide their strength in improving the state order," the manifesto condemned as a "seditious movement." Similarly, even though the rescript envisioned that elected representatives would participate in formulating legislation, the manifesto labeled this prospect as "an encroachment on the foundations of the Russian state." In Maklakov's opinion, "the threats of the manifesto were obliterated by the rescript, while the hopes provoked by the rescript were undermined by the manifesto."[23]

Still, during the next several weeks, zemstvo assemblies, municipal dumas, and professional organizations inundated the Committee of Ministers with petitions calling for reform, all directed at limiting the power of the tsar.[24] On 22–24 April, zemstvo leaders convened a second congress in Moscow, which endorsed the Union of Liberation's program and requested elections to a national assembly that would establish a "legal order" – that is, a rule of law that entailed a constitution.[25]

Intentionally or not, the acts of 18 February helped divide the moderate opposition, particularly driving a wedge between the Shipov faction and the more adamant constitutionalists. Admitting that discrepancies among the acts raised doubts about the tsar's sincerity, Shipov nonetheless interpreted the rescript as indicating a new governmental course. In a telegram to the tsar – one approved by a majority at a meeting of the Moscow provincial zemstvo assembly – he lauded the rescript for promoting unity between the tsar and the people and for attempting to bring tranquility to domestic life.[26] Shipov and his followers were not, however, prepared to go as far as most zemstvo constitutionalists. At the April zemstvo congress, they comprised a decided minority. When the majority voted to press their constitutional demands, the Shipov group walked out. At the next zemstvo congress, held on 24–26 May in Moscow, the split was completed; subsequently many zemstvo constitutionalists, with others in the Union of Liberation, joined in forming the Constitutional Democratic Party – the Kadets – in August 1905. The Shipov group became the nucleus of the Union of 17 October – the Octobrists – later in the fall.[27]

And what of the monarchists? How did they react to the acts of 18 February 1905? By all accounts, they too recognized that major changes were in store for Russia's political structure. A. S. Suvorin, editor of the St. Petersburg daily *Novoe vremia*, spoke as judiciously as any monarchist about the consequences of the three documents. Contending that the acts contained no essential contradictions, since each was intended to uphold the autocracy, Suvorin argued that as the manifesto summoned the Russian people to unity with the throne, so the rescript could improve Russia's political life. Dutiful citizens would assist the tsar in the onerous task of legislating. The ukase would benefit the Russian people by granting them access to the throne, thus bypassing the bureaucracy, a perennial barrier to close relations between tsar and people.[28]

Other monarchists differed somewhat in their interpretation of the imperial acts, their responses indicating the two main emphases that soon characterized the emerging rightist movement. Some responded primarily to the manifesto's emphasis on militant action, with a return to the autocratic firmness and strict governmental control that typified the reign of Alexander III. Others, while acknowledging the need for vigilance, welcomed the possibility raised by the rescript and the ukase that dedicated Russians might participate in an advisory body to the crown – a restoration of what many saw as an ideal political structure in old Muscovy, when a representative assembly, or zemskii sobor, faithfully counseled the autocratic tsar.

V. A. Gringmut, editor of the ultraconservative Moscow newspaper *Moskovskiia vedomosti*, epitomized the first of these responses. On reading the acts of 18 February, Gringmut predicted that "the blabberers and charlatans" in the zemstvos and municipal dumas would hasten to use the rescript to press their own selfish concerns. The result, Gringmut predicted, would be chaos. Nor did he like the ukase. If the Council of Ministers tolerated a flood of private opinions, he warned, the same special interest groups would bombard the government relentlessly; they would turn the zemstvos and municipal dumas into political clubs. In Gringmut's judgment, the concessions made in the rescript and ukase could only lead to further autocratic immobility. A lone hope remained: heed the manifesto's call to unite loyal Russians against the foreign enemy and seditionists at home. Reforms, for what they were worth, could come later. Regarding 18 February as a turning point for Russia, Gringmut declared that the acts drew the battle lines between those who would corrupt Russia with western liberalism, constitutionalism, and democracy, and the true heirs of Russia's autocratic tradition. Henceforth, the latter must join ranks as militant defenders of the throne.[29]

By contrast, Count Pavel Sheremetev, leader of a prominent circle of conservative Muscovite gentry, expressed what would become the "Slavophile" current in the rightist movement. This current stressed a kind of popular autocracy, with the Russian people freely offering their opinions and advice. The events of the past several months had convinced Sheremetev that decisive steps were needed to end Russia's turmoil. The manifesto, he agreed, was a timely call for unity and possibly a means of reconciling tsar and people. The road to such unity, he said, was best indicated by the rescript and the ukase, both of which would enable the sovereign to hear the voice of the people. It was necessary, of course, to ensure that the rescript did not become a first step toward limited monarchy and a parliamentary system of government. But if the representative assembly served to strengthen autocratic power, not to weaken it, and if the assembly only offered counsel to the tsar, without encroaching on his decision-making power, it could transcend the artificial constraints of bureaucratic government that had long alienated Russia from its true political heritage. What Sheremetev anticipated was, in effect, a reinstatement of the zemskii sobor as the basis for participatory autocracy.[30]

Both Gringmut and Sheremetev were correct in their assessment that 18 February had inaugurated a new era in Russia's political life. Certainly, their own responses to the three acts signaled an unprecedented outburst of activity among supporters of the throne. In March, Sheremetev and his circle formed the Union of Russian Men; in April, Gringmut and some colleagues organized the Russian Monarchist Party. That same month, the Patriotic Union appeared in St. Petersburg, and other monarchist associations began to spring up around the country. Some groups came during the fall, including the Union of the Russian People, which rapidly developed into the largest and most influential rightist organization.

Sensing the vulnerability of the tsar, these rightist associations determined, each in its own way and often in cooperation, to bolster the autocracy. They would publicize the dangers threatening traditional Russian institutions, help restore law and order, and most of all campaign against the oppositionists in the forthcoming Duma elections. Generally reluctant to become "political," the rightists soon formed an integral part of Russia's new political system.

Part I

The formation of national rightist organizations

2   The Russian Monarchist Party

Originating soon after the tsar's appeal for assistance in February 1905, the Moscow-based Russian Monarchist Party (*Russkaia monarkhicheskaia partiia*) served as a striking manifestation of the rightist sentiment emerging in Russia. The Party's principal founder and chairman, V. A. Gringmut, editor of Moscow's foremost daily newspaper, *Moskovskiia vedomosti* (*The Moscow News*), was among the first monarchists to envision a national political organization designed to marshal public support for the crown. In this endeavor Gringmut defined an important variant in how rightists would conceptualize Russia's autocracy. He differed, for example, from such groups as the Union of Russian Men, which appeared in Moscow concurrently with his own party. Sharing little of the Union's Slavophile ideal of popular autocracy, epitomized by a zemskii sobor – an elected advisory body to the tsar – Gringmut emphatically called for highly centralized power, a competent bureaucracy, and unencumbered personal rule in the mold of Alexander III. Anything less imperiled Russia's future.

With only a vague notion of how to build an organization capable of contributing to this objective, Gringmut proved less adept at attracting a following than the more demagogic monarchists, like those in the Union of the Russian People. Still, Gringmut, knowledge-able and articulate, contributed much to the monarchist cause. From the inception of his party in April 1905 until his death in September 1907, he acted not only as the party's driving force but as a leading spokesman for the rightist movement and mentor for loyalists throughout the country.

The making of a monarchist

In creating the Russian Monarchist Party, Gringmut imbued it with his personal brand of Russian patriotism, which had developed over the past several decades. Born in 1851, he was a second-generation Russian, the son of a German teacher who had moved to Moscow and a paradigm of those displaced persons who express a stronger devotion to their adopted land than many of its native citizens. He graduated from Moscow University in 1870, after achieving an impressive scholastic record, then took a position teaching German and classical languages at the Lyceum of Tsarevich Nicholas, which one of his professors, P. M. Leontiev, and the influential editor of *Moskovskiia vedomosti*, M. N. Katkov, had founded in Moscow two years before in honor of Tsar Alexander II's late son. During the next quarter-century Gringmut pursued a distinguished academic career at the Lyceum. An excellent teacher – "a true master of his craft," according to a former student – he discharged his increasing load of administrative responsibilities so professionally that in 1894 he was named the Lyceum's director.[1]

During this time, Gringmut became a "true Russian." In 1875, he married a devoutly Orthodox young woman, and three years later converted to Orthodoxy himself. Conservative by upbringing and strengthened by his association with Leontiev and Katkov, he developed a firm devotion to Russia's cultural traditions. In articles he wrote for *Moskovskiia vedomosti* he extolled the worth of classical studies and lamented Russia's new school of naturalist writers for succumbing to the influence of Zola and others in the West and publishing what to him was an unnecessarily vulgar depiction of life.

After Katkov's death in 1887, Gringmut expanded his association with the paper. He joined the editorial staff under Katkov's successor, S. A. Petrovskii, and gradually broadened the scope of his articles to include governmental affairs and contemporary social questions. In order to devote more time to *Moskovskiia vedomosti*, he finally resigned his directorship at the Lyceum in 1895 and became editor of the paper the following year. In the Katkov tradition, he consistently espoused extremely conservative editorial positions, patriotically supporting the state, the autocracy, and especially the "high ideals" of Alexander III.

Gringmut became still more apprehensive after 1900, as domestic unrest continued to spread. When he learned about the new Russian Assembly in St. Petersburg, he wrote to one of its founders, V. L. Velichko, suggesting that the Assembly or a similar organization dedicated to preserving Russia's traditional ideals be established nationwide.[2] Disappointed by the Russian Assembly's rather lethargic leadership and its reluctance to expand beyond St. Petersburg,

Gringmut began to think about creating a new organization based in Moscow. He did not decide to do so, however, until publication of the acts of 18 February 1905, a date that for Gringmut marked a political turning point. He lauded the manifesto as the "alpha and omega of Russian state and public life," and noted again the compelling need to unite loyal Russians around the throne. The rescript impressed Gringmut less. He predicted that opportunists would take advantage of a national assembly to make exorbitant demands on the government. Most importantly, Gringmut concluded that the time had come for him to form a new organization. It appeared shortly as the Russian Monarchist Party.[3]

Gringmut's critique of politics

The name that Gringmut chose for his organization was in itself significant: it became one of the few monarchist groups in Russia to be called a "party." To most monarchists this term was too western, too indicative of the partisan conflicts found in parliamentary systems, and inappropriate for any association that was uniquely Russian. Most organizations preferred Russian names: *soiuz* (union), *sobranie* (assembly), or *obshchestvo* (society). But to Gringmut *partiia* seemed appropriate. Strictly a political term, even if Russia lacked a "political" tradition, it suggested an impending struggle that was political indeed.

Gringmut had been thinking in terms of parties for some time. In an article in 1896, he raised the question, "Are there parties in Russia?" In reply, he held that Russia, unlike the parliamentary countries of the West, should have no political parties. Traditionally, he said, Russia projected an image of a united people joined in bonds of harmony under an autocratic tsar. But he admitted that this image of unity was an ideal, one inconsistent with present realities. In effect, there were two "parties" in Russia, clearly distinguished from each other and irreconcilable. One comprised those who supported the autocracy, the other those who dreamed of constitutions and parliaments, thus rejecting Russia's traditional institutions in favor of western forms. "We did not create these parties in Russia," Gringmut concluded; "they created themselves." They were the unhappy consequence of western ideas infiltrating Russia and automatically dividing the populace into competing political camps.[4]

After the February 1905 manifesto, Gringmut extended his argument. The parties that had previously existed *de facto* were now *de jure*, he said, since the tsar had formally acknowledged the bifurcation of Russian society. Moreover, the conflict had intensified. One party, liberal, constitutional, and cosmopolitan, was determined to overthrow the autocracy. The other, conservative, monarchist, and truly Russian, was dedicated to preserving it. In between lurked illogical and irrational political groups that muddied the waters by interjecting such self-contradictory notions as "constitutional autocracy" – a phrase that Gringmut later criticized the Octobrists for using.

Previously, Gringmut said, the party conflict had been casual, even unconscious, without clearly defined goals or programs. Now, fueled by a rising political consciousness and coupled with the discontent generated by the war with Japan, the conflict had become open and pervasive. From a debate between opposing opinions in the local zemstvos, a larger struggle had evolved, with parties organizing for combat at the national level. D. N. Shipov, for example, a moderate critic of the autocracy, had joined his zemstvist colleagues in calling a unification congress in St. Petersburg for the purpose of forming a national political organization. This action by the oppositionists, Gringmut declared, forced monarchists across Russia to unite in organizing their own party.[5]

The contradiction in Gringmut's argument was quickly noted by Prince B. S. Meshcherskii, editor of the conservative newspaper *Grazhdanin* (*The Citizen*), himself a loyalist. Gringmut's concern was laudable, Meshcherskii conceded, but his intention to lead an independent movement, directed at strengthening the autocracy, meant interference in tsarist affairs. The result would be to debase the image of autocratic power, which by its very nature did not depend on external support. In England and Germany, Meshcherskii added, there were no monarchist parties, since everyone accepted the principle of monarchy. Gringmut might be right about Russia's divided political allegiances, but a monarchist "party" would accentuate basic divisions and weaken the concept of autocracy as much as would the opposition parties.[6]

Although Meshcherskii failed to acknowledge that the tsar himself had issued the appeal for support – or that neither the English nor the Germans lived under an *absolute* monarchy – his criticism pointed up a dilemma that Gringmut must have recognized: how to reconcile popular politics and autocratic power. That dilemma would confront all of Russia's rightist organizations. While advocating a broad-based monarchist movement, Gringmut had reservations about public participation in politics. He knew that independent action could be interpreted as infringing on the principle of autocratic rule. Writing in *Moskovskiia vedomosti*, he contended that surely the imperial rescript did not really suggest general elections. The "worthy persons" designated by the rescript to work on preliminary legislation would be chosen *from* the people, not *by* them. The tsar would make the selections "with the help of God," since elections would in no way guarantee the choice of reliable or capable persons. To build a railway, Gringmut pointed out, one needs engineers; to practice healing, physicians; to administer justice, jurists. Why then permit elections to catapult forward those who had neither the intellect, aptitude, nor training – to say nothing of the moral qualities – that would make them trustworthy aides to the tsar in directing Russia's destiny?[7]

Gringmut was probably aiming this argument at Nicholas himself, hoping that the tsar would reconsider the matter of elections. But he tried in vain. On 6 August, the tsar issued a manifesto announcing a popularly elected assembly, a step that Gringmut was hardly able to accept.

Gringmut found it equally vexing that the proposed assembly was essentially a revived zemskii sobor, a notion promoted by some emerging monarchist organizations. No matter that a zemskii sobor had its roots in Russian history, or that it was a consultative body, not a legislative one; it still seemed tainted with the parliamentary concept of elected "representatives of the people." Gringmut also believed that a sobor would contribute to widening the breach between the tsar and his subjects, not to unifying them. Rejecting the old Slavophile adage of "opinion to the people, decision-making to the tsar," Gringmut argued that "either the tsar will be obliged always to agree with the opinion of the people, in which case he would cease to be an unlimited autocrat; or he will at times have opinions contrary to those expressed by so-called representatives of the people, thus violating the harmony of thought between tsar and people – a schism boding terrible consequences."[8]

Gringmut thus rejected both a western-style parliament and a consultative assembly based on Russia's old zemskii sobor. For that matter, he disavowed any kind of shared political responsibility. In effect, he was criticizing the government, and Nicholas himself, for issuing the February rescript. In Gringmut's view Russia clearly and simply needed a restoration of the tsar's autocratic power. While conceding that an elected national assembly might be at hand, he continued to deny that this innovation could ever become a real parliamentary system. A monarchist party was imperative, not to emulate the political parties of the West, but to struggle against those nascent Russian parties whose aim was to diminish the monarchy.

Party program and objectives

Having defined his basic intentions, Gringmut launched his Russian Monarchist Party on 24 April 1905. Most of the thirty-eight founding members came from his staff at *Moskovskiia vedomosti*, including Baron A. E. Nolde, who became editor after Gringmut's death in 1907, B. V. Nazarevskii, M. P. Lukin, and others who shared Gringmut's views. By mid-summer the membership had increased to about eighty, as Gringmut and his colleagues gathered disciples, primarily landed nobles living in Moscow, government officials, merchants, clerics, and occasionally lawyers, academics, and other professionals.[9] Growth continued slowly, as did organizational work, but Gringmut insisted that a small, articulate nucleus could leaven the whole of Russian society. Still, he recognized that if his party was to counter the opposition effectively, it would likely have to engage in many of the same political activities. Finally, on 9 September, the party leadership met to discuss a "militant" Duma campaign and to appoint a committee to draft a political program.

During the rest of September, the growing sense of urgency turned to alarm. Gringmut and his colleagues watched apprehensively as the 19 September typesetters' strike at the Sytin printing plant in Moscow spread to other cities. By early October most of the country was engulfed by a general strike, with calls not only for better wages and a shorter working day but for civil liberties, an amnesty for political prisoners, and the convocation of a constituent assembly. Demonstrators marched through the streets carrying red flags and singing revolutionary songs. Gringmut reacted instinctively by demanding that the government take immediate action. In a *Moskovskiia vedomosti* editorial he called for martial law in the most disrupted localities. A military commander with dictatorial authority should suppress the unrest, make possible a return to civil rule, and place the sovereign once more in control.[10]

Spurred by events, the Party's program committee completed its task. On 15 October, it presented a document that summed up and elaborated the principles Gringmut had been advocating and that now characterized the Russian Monarchist Party. Even though the program did not reiterate Gringmut's call for a military dictatorship, it clearly reflected the Party leaders' concern over the disruption in Russia. It stated first that the most important task facing Russia was to restore order. Reforms could come later.[11]

For the Russian Monarchist Party and other rightist organizations, the relationship between order and reform was crucial. RMP leaders particularly criticized Count Witte, who argued that reforms should precede the restoration of order, and really were the primary means of pacifying the country. When Witte became Chairman of the Council of Ministers in October 1905, Gringmut had welcomed him, predicting that through his unbending strength of will he could reimpose order. However, Gringmut's expectations – and support – soon began to wane. Witte was not working miracles; in fact, Gringmut claimed that the freedom of speech and press that Witte incorporated into the October Manifesto was serving the opposition as a license to distribute its seditious propaganda. As the disorders continued, Gringmut increased his criticism. Especially after the Moscow uprising in December, he declared that Witte's concessions had not only failed to conciliate most of the liberals but had encouraged the revolutionaries. Instead of restoring monarchical authority, Witte was handing Russia over to its destroyers. By January 1906, Gringmut was charging that Witte's lack of political judgment, coupled with his inflated love of power, made him incapable of heading the government, and it would be best if he resigned.[12]

When the tsar finally dismissed Witte in April 1906, Gringmut and other RMP leaders expressed their relief; they were even more pleased in July, when, after I. L. Goremykin's brief, ineffectual tenure as Chairman of the Council of Ministers, Peter Stolypin took over. While governor of Saratov province, Stolypin had already won the respect of many loyalists for the dispatch with which he suppressed disorders there in early 1906. Now, as the tsar's chief minister, Stolypin made it known that he regarded pacification as a prerequisite to fundamental reform.

Important too was the kind of reform that Gringmut and his party envisioned after the restoration of order. Certainly, they did not want reform in the liberal sense of constitutional innovations designed to lessen the tsar's authority, but reform in terms of revitalized policies and structural overhauling that would produce a stronger, more efficient government. They recommended, first, that the State Council, previously an advisory body to the tsar, which presumably would soon be given the right to approve or veto legislation passed by the State Duma, should be reconstituted to include "more capable" members. Since the present Council consisted mainly of mediocre retired bureaucrats, appointed in recognition of their years of service, the RMP hoped that a more energetic body would act effectively as a counterweight against the Duma and provide instructive counsel to the tsar.[13]

Actually, reform of the State Council, announced in February 1906, came sooner than anticipated, but to the RMP's chagrin it specified that half of the Council members would now be elected instead of being appointed by the tsar. The only consolation was that most of the ninety-eight elected members – chosen primarily by provincial zemstvos, special landowner congresses in areas where zemstvos did not exist, and assemblies of the nobility – proved to be loyal supporters of the crown. But it was still dismaying to find that eight belonged to the liberal Kadet party or other progressive groups. For Gringmut and many monarchists the way in which the State Council had been reconstituted seemed a needless concession to the opposition.

On some matters, the Russian Monarchist Party and the autocracy were in closer accord. While not enamored with the present autocrat, Gringmut could uphold those policies that had not yet been appreciably altered. He emphatically endorsed the russification program of Alexander III, recommending that Russian as the state language, Orthodoxy as the state religion, and Russian culture generally be maintained throughout the empire. Local use of non-Russian languages and customs, he said, should be permitted only if they did not infringe on the unity of the state and had no political significance. It seemed natural that the minority nationalities should defer to Russian preeminence, for the Russians were "the master of the house." They had built the empire and should continue to manage its affairs.[14]

This chauvinism not only denoted a certain insensitivity on Gringmut's part but it drove him and his Party to the conclusion that the non-Russian minorities posed a serious threat to the empire's stability. In Gringmut's opinion, the minorities cared only about their own self-interests and by nature were disloyal to the Russian state. Worst were the Jews; the government would err grievously if it granted them civil equality, which they would misuse to further their own selfish purposes. Gringmut also charged that the Jews were bringing pogroms and other misfortunes on themselves because of their "seditious instincts," which aroused the Russian people's wrath. In October 1905, the Russian Monarchist Party proposed as its first candidate for election to the Bulygin Duma one of its members, A. S.

Shmakov, a noted Moscow lawyer and convinced antisemite. Shmakov had written several books against the Jews and acted as counsel for the defense in the Kishinev pogrom trial in 1903. Gringmut and his colleagues hailed Shmakov as "a noble and fearless warrior," who would defend the Russian people against Jewish domination.[15] While the Party broadcast its antisemitism less stridently than the Union of the Russian People and the Union of Russian Men, it made its disdain of the Jews and its milder discrimination against other non-Russian minorities an integral part of the political struggle.

The Russian Monarchist Party's concern about order and tranquility prompted it to emphasize the need not only for proper relationships among the various minorities but among the traditional social estates. Social equality, it said, was a revolutionary lie, one detrimental to a well-ordered society. Each estate had its proper function, and each must recognize the others' integrity. Granted that the peasants were suffering severe economic problems, but the solution lay not in the socialists' demand for redistributing the nobility's private estates. Arguing that private property was inviolable, the RMP recommended instead that the government should extend more credit through the Peasant Bank for peasants to purchase land. It also urged the government to help peasants resettle in such less densely populated areas as the Caucasus, Siberia, Central Asia, and the southern provinces of Russia proper, before Armenians, Germans, and Jews bought up all the available land. In general, the peasants should receive help in preference to non-Russians but not at the expense of other estates.[16]

Strategies and action

Having approved its program on 15 October 1905, the Russian Monarchist Party was jolted into action two days later, as the October Manifesto announced that the Duma would not simply be a consultative body, but a legislative one. Far from the militant reimposition of order that Gringmut had advocated, the crown had made its greatest concession yet, which was sure to evoke from Gringmut a new round of criticism. The Duma, he complained, should not have been created in the midst of chaos. Echoing Edmund Burke and other conservatives of the past, he asserted that if one's house is engulfed in flames, the first task is to put out the fire. The Russian autocracy seemed to be adding to the conflagration.

Disturbed by the turn of events and facing the question of what to do next, Gringmut and his colleagues reluctantly, but irrevocably, determined a new course of action. When they met in special session on the evening of 18 October, they could see crowds marching with red flags and singing the *Marseillaise*.[17] Two nights later, they decided that they must turn to the people and entreat them "to pledge their faithfulness to the tsar." This seemed a nebulous proposal, but it was a significant one. It meant that Party leaders realized that they could no longer expect to sway the tsar and his government on their own. Gringmut could never hope to be another Katkov. Circumstances were pressing his Party to create a groundswell of public support for the autocracy that could inspire it to withstand its opponents.

To enlist this support, the Party adopted new strategies. Aware that *Moskovskiia vedomosti* was not reaching a broad enough audience, Gringmut began publishing brochures for wider distribution; and while the Party continued its weekly gatherings for members only, it also arranged meetings to which it invited the public. *Moskovskiia vedomosti* reported happily that over 800 persons attended the first such open meeting, held at the Historical Museum in Moscow on 5 February 1906.[18] In later issues, it noted that crowds attended subsequent meetings, listening attentively to Party notables, singing folk hymns, and applauding telegrams to the tsar that proclaimed their devotion and implored him to grasp firmly the reins of power.

Fortunately for the Party, it had several outstanding orators. Gringmut himself was an excellent speaker with a deep voice and impressive bearing; his colleague B. V. Nazarevskii was also eloquent and persuasive. Probably, the most effective speaker was Archpriest Ioann Vostorgov, a Party founder and tireless preacher, who proved unusually proficient in attracting all levels of society. A favorite orator at Party meetings and rightist conferences, Father Vostorgov also addressed workers' groups and preached at religious services throughout Moscow province. Speaking as a spiritual shepherd, Vostorgov admonished ordinary Russians to cling to the traditional principles of Orthodoxy and autocracy. He reminded them that Jesus's parents were workers – a carpenter and a homemaker – and his closest disciples were simple fishermen. Never had Jesus or his apostles preached revolt against legal authority, Vostorgov declared, or encouraged slaves to disobey their masters. Down the centuries Christian leaders had urged humility and conciliation, and taught that true freedom was not the absence of authority but liberation from the bonds of sin. In Russia, the Christian tsars had always taken care of the common people. They had emancipated the serfs, given them land, and more recently provided such benefits as old-age insurance for industrial workers. Now the peasants and workers were achieving political equality with other Russian citizens through participation in elections to the Duma. Yet, false prophets were stirring up discontent among the populace and inciting them to rebellion. "Do not offend Christ the Lord," Vostorgov warned, "by betraying his teachings. Do not make your situation worse by agitating and striking. Do not obstruct the tsar and the government from caring for you and acting in your behalf."[19]

The positive response to his party's public meetings and to the literature it was distributing encouraged Gringmut to set about building a broader political organization. Even though he had no clear concept of how to proceed, he meant to use Moscow as a hub for opening nearby branches, gradually extending into more distant regions. In this task he was hampered in several ways. He lacked contacts, such as the Russian Assembly had among government officials posted in provincial capitals, who were invaluable in establishing local branches. He also had a limited reserve of personnel to travel as organizers, in contrast, for example, to the Union of the Russian People, which sent dozens of functionaries into the provinces. Most important, Gringmut's party did not possess the URP's popular appeal, which enabled the latter to entice local monarchist groups to affiliate with its central organization. For these reasons, expansion moved slowly. In March 1906, Gringmut presided at branch inaugurations in the towns of Bogorodsk, Sergiev Posad, Bronnitsy, and Egorevsk, all within 60 miles of Moscow. Later in the year, the Party opened several other branches in Moscow and Riazan provinces, and eventually in Voronezh, Tambov, Vladimir, and a few other provincial cities. But overall, its attempts at expansion were not very effective. The claim of some Gringmut supporters that the Party opened over 450 branches seems a vast exaggeration, quite unsubstantiated by available evidence.[20] The Party's influence focused on Moscow and its environs, where indeed it did enjoy considerable recognition.

Judging from their actions in late 1905, it becomes apparent that Gringmut and his associates had by then begun to weigh the merits of collaborating with other monarchist organizations. After the October Manifesto, they realized that an alliance might be the only strategy sufficient to minimize the new Duma's role. Gringmut had criticized the Union of Russian Men and others for promoting a consultative assembly, but he knew that the Union at least opposed a legislative Duma and wished to curtail its authority. Intent on demonstrating that the autocracy had wide support, despite the concessions it had made, Gringmut and other Party leaders joined representatives of the Union of Russian Men and some smaller Moscow groups in an audience with the tsar on 1 December 1905. Together they pledged their devotion and beseeched Nicholas to hold fast to his autocratic prerogatives, despite whatever pressure the upcoming Duma might bring to bear.[21] To Nicholas this may have been a heartening gesture; for Gringmut it was an affirmation that joint action among the monarchist associations was essential.

Assured that he should pursue this course, Gringmut sought out other rightist confederates. During his visit to St. Petersburg, he met with A. I. Dubrovin, chairman of the Union of the Russian People, satisfying himself that they shared common objectives. When the URP opened its Moscow branch in January 1906, Gringmut welcomed it and became friends with the branch chairman, N. N. Oznobishin.[22] In some respects, Gringmut's association with the URP reflected his own inclination toward political extremism. Like Oznobishin and other URP leaders, Gringmut often used inflammatory rhetoric in admonishing "true Russians" to combat the forces of sedition. However, he did refrain from the URP's tactic of inciting the populace to violence against Russia's "enemies" – liberals, radicals, and Jews. Consequently, the Monarchist Party and the URP cooperated primarily in the realm of legitimate political action. Along with the Union of Russian Men and some smaller monarchist groups, they campaigned in the Duma elections, becoming a major political force in Moscow.[23]

As part of their quest for collaborative action, Gringmut and his associates also tried to bring cohesion to the rightist movement as a whole. Both he and Vostorgov served as featured speakers at various monarchist congresses. At the first congress, meeting in St. Petersburg in February 1906, Gringmut identified a circumstance that would continue to thwart efforts at unification, when he urged that "any enmity between St. Petersburg and Moscow be put aside." This was a reference to the rivalry that had long separated the inhabitants of the two cities. Gringmut admitted that Muscovites, sheltered in the heart of Russia, had remained somnambulant as the forces of sedition mounted elsewhere in the country; but now aroused, they were eager to join forces with other loyalists.[24] Gringmut thus discerned the minor jealousies that impeded a genuine rightist unification. What he did not yet perceive was that this sense of exclusiveness existed not only between rightist leaders in the two capitals but also among provincial leaders, who were reluctant to relinquish their prerogatives to a central organization. While rightist parties in St. Petersburg and Moscow contributed to unification by establishing branches around the country, it is significant that many provincial organizations continued to operate quite independently.

By early 1906, the Russian Monarchist Party had defined its role in the rightist movement, guided by Gringmut's dominant leadership and reflecting his assessment of Russia's current political and social turmoil. An ardent monarchist and advocate of state power, Gringmut can be credited as one of the first to perceive the magnitude of Russia's political crisis – the escalating contest between liberals and conservatives, the erosion of autocratic power, and, at the moment, the government's apparent inability to mount an adequate defense. Understandably fearing that the autocracy would continue to temporize, Gringmut hoped to prevail on the tsar to act more resolutely. When this tactic proved ineffective, Gringmut set his newly organized Party to the broader task of rallying public acclaim for the autocracy and campaigning for rightist deputies to the Duma. Both endeavors indicated a fundamental break with Russia's political past, as traditionally immobile loyalists entered the emerging realm of partisan politics.

Politically, the Russian Monarchist Party was only marginally successful. It made a substantial impact in and around Moscow, although even there it did not gain as large a following as did rightist parties in other parts of the country. Lacking organizational ability, Gringmut and his associates also found that their insistence on preserving Russia's estate-oriented society hampered their efforts to arouse enthusiasm among workers and peasants, and, for that matter, among the middle class. Probably, Gringmut's greatest contribution came not through his party's political activities but through his personal stature in the rightist movement. While not the *vozhd'*, or supreme chief, of Russia's monarchists, as some of his followers claimed, Gringmut served as an eminent spokesman for rightists everywhere.

3   The Union of Russian Men

The spring of 1905 witnessed the emergence of the rightist organization most deeply rooted in Russia's cultural, social, and political past: the Union of Russian Men (*Soiuz russkikh liudei*). Drawing freely on Slavophile antecedents, the Union regarded itself as a catalyst for regenerating a society that had lost contact with its own identity. In February 1905, when Nicholas II announced that he would convene a consultative assembly, the Union welcomed this prospect as a step toward linking tsar and people in a body reminiscent of the old Muscovite zemskii sobor. What the Union wanted was not a bureaucratic but a patriarchal autocracy. The tsar would again listen to the "voice of the land," expressed through representatives of the traditional estates – a truly "popular" form of government. Forced by the October Manifesto to acknowledge that Russia was taking a different course, the Union proved less able than many rightists to accommodate the changes occurring in the country's political life. It continued to promote its Slavophile principles, but for practical purposes it remained at the edge of politics.

Organization and membership

The central figure in creating the Union of Russian Men was Count Pavel Sheremetev. A district marshal of the nobility in Moscow province, Sheremetev came from a respected landowning family well known for its Slavophile persuasion. At the turn of the century he joined the Beseda Circle, a group of zemstvo figures that had formed in December 1899 to discuss the political role of the zemstvos and nobles' associations, along with ideas for moderate reform. By late 1904, most of the Beseda Circle had moved toward constitutionalism: F. A. Golovin, A. A. Stakhovich, Prince E. N. Trubetskoi, Prince D. I. Shakhovskoi, Princes Pavel and Peter Dolgorukov, and at least fifteen others later joined the Kadet Party; while D. N. Shipov, N. I. Guchkov, Count P. A. Geiden, and several others, who were more conservative, became Octobrists. Increasingly isolated in his conviction that the Beseda group should work to strengthen the autocracy, Sheremetev left to form his own circle.[1]

Sheremetev's positive response to the February 1905 rescript indicated the general attitude of his circle. "In these historical days for Russian society," he wrote, "it is necessary more than ever to unify all the fundamental forces of the country." He predicted that the proposed consultative assembly would lead to "a strong and living unity between throne and people, an intimate and lasting communion between the Supreme Power and the land through locally elected people." This Slavophile rhetoric meant that what he anticipated was in effect a revived zemskii sobor, which would provide "all-estate representation – the wider, the better." The rescript, he cautioned, must not be seen as a step toward limiting the autocracy, as the liberals intended, but toward affirming it.[2]

With a national assembly in view, the Sheremetev circle moved quickly to establish a firmer institutional base. In late March, it launched the Union of Russian Men, with Sheremetev as chairman. Most founding members came from Sheremetev's immediate social milieu of titled aristocracy, as did those who shortly joined. By May, the Union, now several dozen strong, included at least fourteen princes, eleven counts, and three barons. Most notable were Prince A. G. Shcherbatov, one of the country's largest landowners; Prince P. N. Trubetskoi, marshal of the nobility for Moscow province; Prince V. M. Urusov, marshal of the nobility for Smolensk province; Prince B. S. Meshcherskii, editor of the Moscow newspaper, *Grazhdanin* (*The Citizen*); Princes V. D., V. A., and P. P. Golitsyn, scions of an old Muscovite family; and two other members of Sheremetev's clan, Counts D. S. and B. S. Sheremetev. Non-titled nobles and prominent professional persons also entered the Union. The latter included several professors and private-docents from Moscow University, one of whom was D. N. Ilovaiskii, the noted historian and editor of the political–literary journal *Kreml'* (*The Kremlin*). An even better-known publicist, Sergei Sharapov, editor of the weekly newspaper *Russkoe delo* (*The Russian Cause*) and the monthly agricultural journal *Pakhar'* (*The Plowman*), became a member, as did A. V. Buryshkin, who served on the Moscow city duma, and L. A. Georgiaevskii, director of the Lyceum of Tsarevich Nicholas. Appropriately for the Union, Dmitrii Khomiakov, son of the famous nineteenth-century Slavophile, Aleksei Khomiakov, also joined.[3]

Declaring that it welcomed persons of "all estates and statuses," the Union hoped also to attract small landowners, peasants, merchants, workers, and other townspeople, so as to establish a base from which "true representatives of the people" could be chosen to assist the tsar in the forthcoming national assembly. The assumption, not yet verified, was that the general populace would respond to an organization dominated by the privileged classes.

Principles and political reality

While sharing an underlying sense of urgency in addressing Russia's problems, Union leaders moved slowly in formulating any kind of official position. This seeming contradiction between attitude and behavior had a certain internal logic, however, inasmuch as Sheremetev and his associates never regarded the Union as a political party, such as Gringmut's Russian Monarchist Party. Therefore, they did not believe they needed a formal program. They perceived nothing in Russia's heritage to justify their contributing to the divisiveness that partisan politics entailed. Theirs was to promote a renewed rapport within Russian society and between society and the crown. Consequently, the Union issued only a generally worded manifesto, stating that it would use all legal means to unify church, state, and people; to ensure that worthy persons were elected to the consultative assembly proposed by the tsar's February 1905 rescript; and to help restore peace, law, and order to the troubled country.[4] These goals implied an activism in disseminating the Union's message but not actual political campaigning.

Although the Union chose not to adopt a program, it did proceed to elaborate the Slavophile principles that gave coherence to the group. It arranged public meetings in Moscow, gradually expanding these activities into speaking tours of surrounding villages. It issued thousands of brochures, some for educated Russians on such topics as the theoretical basis of autocracy and the incompatibility of Christianity and socialism, but others along more popular lines, stressing native patriotism, family values, and the improvement of peasant life.[5] During 1905 and 1906, it also established branches in Kolomna, Tambov, Kozlov, Odessa, some smaller towns, and a few villages in the central provinces, from which it could make more direct contact with the people.[6]

One of the most articulate spokesmen for the Union's Slavophile persuasion was Dmitrii Khomiakov. Sharing his father's nostalgic longing for a simpler, more fulfilling way of life, Khomiakov emphasized the spiritual aspects of Russian society, particularly the bonds of love, harmony, and voluntary association that he perceived as uniquely Russian. These bonds needed strengthening, he said, in order to unite the people and join them as a family with the tsar. In the political sphere, Khomiakov admitted that autocracy had its faults, and other forms of government had certain advantages in some countries, but only autocracy was suited to the Russian temperament. The Russian people were inherently apolitical; they shunned the burden of governing, preferring to live quietly and leave authority in the hands of the tsar. This idealized concept of the *narod* was, of course, standard Slavophile doctrine.[7]

True to his father's views, Khomiakov saw Orthodoxy as the key to Russian political and social relationships; the union of tsar and people, and of the people themselves, rested on spiritual values that only Orthodox believers could fully appreciate. Religion was thus even more important than nationality. In translating Orthodox preeminence into practical policy, Khomiakov maintained that non-Russians in the empire, as long as they were Orthodox, should have the same rights as Russians. But non-Orthodox persons should not expect to participate completely in the country's cultural, political, and social life. This cautious discrimination meant that Khomiakov objected to equal rights for Jews. Yet, by saying only that the Jews lacked a spiritual kinship with Orthodoxy, he differed from those outspoken nationalists who claimed that the Jews were trying to subvert the foundations of the Russian state.[8]

Some Union publicists, dwelling on the emotion-laden question of Jewish rights, conveyed a more flagrant antisemitism than did the genteel Khomiakov – a reminder of how readily discriminatory notions could be carried to extremes. Sergei Sharapov condemned the Jews as parasites and haters of humanity, historically antipathetic to other peoples and resistant to any efforts of their neighbors to treat them with respect. At present they were attempting to monopolize Russian public life, control the professions and the press, gain ownership of the land, and put a stranglehold on industry and commerce. If they were given equal rights, Sharapov predicted, they would use their position to destroy those who had been so generous to them.[9] Other Union spokesmen also indulged in this kind of antisemitism, especially when addressing workers and peasants. On such occasions their oratory frequently took on a demagogic quality, a feature that was fast becoming a Union hallmark.

On other contemporary issues, Union leaders, particularly Sharapov, sought to incorporate Slavophile principles into usable political concepts and concrete plans of action. Already in the spring of 1905, Sharapov was writing on Russia's nascent political crisis in *Russkoe delo* and *Pakhar'*. He contended that not only had a gulf developed between tsar and people, and that subversive forces in Russia were sharpening that division, but that the political system itself might be at fault. In good Slavophile fashion, he distinguished the exemplary autocracy of old Muscovy from the tarnished imperial absolutism that had developed since Peter the Great. The difference lay between *sobornaia* rule, in which the tsar relied on the counsel of a zemskii sobor, and modern *bureaucratic* rule, in which the ruler drew his advice from government officials. It was the classic contrast between Moscow and St. Petersburg: an intuitive, personal form of governing versus a mechanistic one, in which the bureaucracy stood between the people and their tsar.[10]

Sharapov saw in the 18 February rescript the seeds of a revived zemskii sobor, which would transcend these bureaucratic barriers and reestablish the lost relationship between the tsar and his faithful subjects. The immediate question was whether representatives to this assembly would be chosen on the basis of the traditional estates, like the old zemskii sobor, or through popular elections, as rumors intimated. A popular vote, Sharapov predicted, would involve western-style parties, campaigning, and political agitation, resulting in the election of a hodge-podge of lawyers, journalists, capitalists, and Jewish bankers – all with vested interests – instead of true representatives of the people, devoted to the welfare of Russia.[11]

Sheremetev and other Union leaders shared Sharapov's concerns and cautious hopes, particularly on the question of estate representation versus popular vote. They were especially bothered when, on 6 June 1905, Prince S. N. Trubetskoi, the brother of fellow Unionist P. N. Trubetskoi, speaking for the third zemstvo congress in an address that catapulted him to fame, implored the tsar to ensure that representation to the assembly be such "that all your subjects, equal and without difference, feel themselves to be Russian citizens ..." Trubetskoi insisted that "the Russian tsar is not a tsar of the nobility, or the peasantry, or the merchants, that is, not a tsar of the estates, but of all Russians; likewise those persons elected from the entire population, so that they may act in accord with you, Your Majesty, should serve not the estates but the interests of the general public."[12]

The Union could not endorse this recommendation for obliterating boundaries between the estates, and it endeavored to bring its own influence to bear upon the tsar. On 14 June, Sheremetev met with Count A. A. Bobrinskii, chairman of the St. Petersburg provincial zemstvo assembly, whom he had known in the Beseda Circle. Bobrinskii had already broken with his liberal zemstvo colleagues and was now chairman of the Patriotic Union, which had formed in April. Like Sheremetev, Bobrinskii wished to build an "all-estate" organization, although certainly not a "non-estate" one. Together the two arranged an audience with the tsar. On 21 June, they led a delegation to Tsarskoe Selo, consisting of themselves; A. A. Narishkin, chairman of the Orel provincial zemstvo assembly; Count V. F. Dorrer, marshal of the nobility for Kursk province; and General A. A. Kireev; along with a prominent Moscow merchant, a townsman from Novgorod, and three peasants from the central provinces – a group carefully chosen to convey to the tsar the acceptability of estate representation. At the audience Sheremetev recalled that in old Muscovy people from all the estates met before the tsar in harmony and love. Sheremetev urged that, in like manner, elections to the modern assembly should proceed only on the basis of estate representation.[13]

Very likely, neither Trubetskoi nor Sheremetev had much effect on Nicholas's intentions for the elections. In contradictory statements the tsar assured them both that he approved their recommendations. But in the end, primarily on the advice of his ministers, Nicholas issued the ukase of 6 August, indicating that elections to the assembly would be by electoral curiae – landowners, peasants, urban property owners, and workers – not by estate representation.

The imperial decision came as no great surprise, since reports of it had already been circulating, but it deeply disturbed the Union. Sharapov, caught in the dilemma facing all monarchists who supported the crown despite its vacillations, remarked in *Russkoe delo* that efforts to prevent popular elections were now over; it was necessary simply to accept the new law and hope for the best. Sharapov added gloomily, however, that one should also be prepared for the worst, because the liberals would interpret this latest concession as only the first step toward the eventual abolition of the autocracy.[14]

The October Manifesto alarmed the leaders of the Union of Russian Men even more. Clearly, the forthcoming Duma would not be a consultative body but a legislative one. That, it seemed, could not help but limit autocratic power. Sharapov wrote that the Manifesto was "the second terrible warning to the House of Romanov" – the first had been the assassination of Alexander II in 1881 – for it presaged the end of the dynasty. Strictly speaking, Sharapov remarked, Nicholas had already yielded part of his autocratic power. His last act as absolute monarch had been to appoint Sergei Witte to negotiate the Portsmouth Treaty ending the war with Japan. If Nicholas had acted like a tsar in old Muscovy, he would at once have summoned a great zemskii sobor to advise him on the question of war or peace; and having heard the voice of the people, he would then have consulted his conscience for the final decision. But Nicholas relied neither on the people nor on his conscience; rather he empowered a single minister to resolve the issue of the war. The tsar, Sharapov admonished, if he acts like a constitutional monarch, rules but does not govern. His cabinet becomes the head of state. Having already delegated his own authority to his ministers, the tsar would find the new Duma restricting his prerogatives still further.[15]

With Sharapov's somber appraisal in mind, Union leaders attempted, even at this late date, to forestall a legislative Duma. On 24 November 1905, the Union arranged a joint meeting of the various Moscow rightist organizations. Over 300 persons attended, representing the Union, Gringmut's Russian Monarchist Party, the Society of Banner Carriers, and the newly created Union of Landowners. Despite Gringmut's belief that even a consultative assembly was too great a concession to popular government, the conference endorsed a zemskii sobor as an alternative to the Duma. Out of the conference came a delegation that met with the tsar on 1 December. After pledging his loyalty, the Union's Prince Shcherbatov implored Nicholas to reconsider his plans for the new Duma and convert it into a zemskii sobor. In reply, the tsar only thanked the delegation for its concern and affirmed that the provisions of the October Manifesto would be implemented.[16] All too clearly, the Union realized that its hopes of controlling the political damage already inflicted on the autocracy were proving futile.

Frustrated by the Union's inability to influence the tsar, Sharapov, a member of the 1 December delegation, resumed his criticism of Nicholas's actions. In a sharply worded article in *Pakhar'*, Sharapov complained that the tsar was remiss in his duties. Although he was God's Anointed, he was still a mortal person, who had erred in authorizing the Duma. That body would not truly represent the Russian people, and therefore would have no moral authority. Worst of all, Sharapov predicted, the tsar, following the pattern of western parliamentarianism, would probably soon accept Duma leaders as ministers. The present bureaucratic order was bad enough, but a bureaucracy under a parliament would be even worse. "Parliamentarianism," lamented Sharapov, "like syphilis, is incurable." It would defile the people's soul and create animosities in a population that desperately needed reconciliation and peace.[17]

What then to do? Some rightist groups, coming to terms with political realities, reluctantly adopted the view that, if they could not prevent a legislative assembly *de jure*, they would at least do so *de facto* by getting loyalists elected to the Duma. These deputies might discuss legislation, but they would not encroach on the tsar's power of decision-making. Within the Union of Russian Men, Sharapov himself considered this possibility. Late in 1905, he drafted a program for a proposed Russian People's Party (*Russkaia narodnaia partiia*), which he apparently wanted the Union to form in preparation for the Duma campaign. However, nothing came of his proposal. Other Union leaders, despite the impasse they had reached, objected to the Union's participating in partisan politics. They would continue to emphasize *sobornost'*, not *partiinost'* – community, not division.[18] Unlike the Russian Assembly, for example, which evolved from a cultural association into a political party, the Union of Russian Men never made the transition. The most it was prepared to do was help awaken loyalist sentiments among the Russian people, trusting them to vote for Duma candidates put forth by those rightist organizations that had become actual political parties.

Other concerns

The Union intended not only to shape emerging attitudes toward the Duma but to influence opinion on other pressing issues as well. In keeping with its Slavophile persuasions, it focused on agrarian affairs. Its principal spokesmen were Sharapov, who already had been writing on land issues in *Russkoe delo* and *Pakhar'*, and Prince Shcherbatov, former president of the Moscow Agricultural Society. Both assiduously upheld the interests of the landed nobility, but they were also sympathetic to the needs of the peasants. In fact, for Sharapov, the overarching agrarian question was how to solve the peasants' economic plight. Like many rightists, Sharapov advocated greater government aid, particularly low-interest loans through the Peasant Bank to assist in buying non-commune land. He also favored government programs for resettling peasants in less populated areas of the empire. But he believed adamantly in the inviolability of private property, opposing any program of compulsory expropriation of estate land, either with or without compensation. Basing his argument on historical precedents, Sharapov explained that in Muscovite times the tsar issued land grants in return for military or administrative service. The recipients were given tenure but not ownership. Although service obligations eventually ended, successive tsars did not retrieve the land. Over the centuries, most estates changed hands, and the new landholders purchased the land upon which they lived. Since they paid money for their property, they had a claim of outright ownership to it. This principle of inviolability, Sharapov concluded, must under no circumstances be violated.[19]

Sharapov undoubtedly knew that his position ran counter to that taken by the All-Russian Peasants' Congress, organized by the newly formed Peasant Union, which met in Moscow in November 1905. The Congress called for the abolition of private property, the expropriation of private estates without compensation, and redistribution on the principle "land to those who till it," the amount to be what a peasant family could cultivate without the use of hired labor.[20] Still, it was not clear that the Congress represented a peasant consensus. Sharapov and others in the Union of Russian Men contended that government aid in purchasing could satisfy the peasants' hunger for land without violating the nobility's property claims. In fact, Union spokesmen warned the peasants that if the law did not protect the estates, the peasants might also lose whatever land they had or might acquire. Any principle pertaining to land rights must hold for everyone.

Prince Shcherbatov took a slightly more moderate stand in his booklet *The Land Question* by stressing that equal attention must be given to the rights of estate owners and the needs of the peasants. Charging that the government had been unduly slow in addressing this crucial issue, he recommended that bureaucratic red tape be circumvented by creating local land commissions consisting of both noble and peasant representatives. The commissions would handle questions of land tenure and productivity. Shcherbatov insisted that no inherent conflict divided the peasants and the estate owners, adding that expropriation was not the key to raising the economic level of the peasants. Russia needed large landowners to keep the gulf between countryside and city from widening; without the landed nobility there would be no balance between urban residents with education and capital and their counterparts on the land.[21]

Shcherbatov also argued that the key to relieving peasant poverty lay in raising the productivity of land already cultivated. Drawing on a wealth of statistics, he pointed out that the average size of peasant holdings in European Russia was already greater than in most of western Europe. The average grain yield per unit area, however, was much lower: a third of that in Sweden, a fourth of that in England. The land commissions, he said, could help raise productivity by utilizing marginal land — marshy fields in the north could be drained, dry crop land in the south could be irrigated. Russia's inefficient three-field system of farming also needed change. At present, fields were rotated among winter grain, spring grain, and land left fallow to restore fertility. Shcherbatov argued that far too much land lay fallow: 39 percent in Russia compared with less than 5 percent in much of western Europe, where farmers were better utilizing animal manure and beginning to use mineral fertilizers. A major problem in Russia, Shcherbatov maintained correctly, was that more and more meadowland was being put under cultivation, leaving little land for pastures and fodder crops. To relieve this deficiency, he suggested a four-field system, which would convert some fallow land to hay for livestock. Such a plan would improve meat and milk production and supply more animal fertilizer for the grain fields. Introducing more productive varieties of grain and more profitable breeds of livestock would increase overall productivity even more.[22]

More than most of Shcherbatov's critics would concede, his analysis got to the heart of the land issue. The basic question was productivity, and on this score Shcherbatov's statistics were reliable and his recommendations sound, offering a substantial challenge to those single-issue reformers who saw in land redistribution the answer to the peasant question. Unfortunately, by approaching the matter so narrowly from the other direction, Shcherbatov severely limited his own argument. Never did he suggest that a real solution might require a combination of increased productivity and land reform. Nor, of course, did he propose any challenge to large landowners, asserting instead that private land must be guaranteed as an incentive to production.

While Union leaders agreed on the inviolability of private property rights, they differed on the structure of peasant land ownership. The crux of the question was whether the peasant commune should be dissolved, opening the way for more private peasant holdings. Since the emancipation in 1861, the government and many nobles had assumed that the peasant commune was a desirable means of maintaining social stability in the countryside. But the peasant disorders of 1905 had eroded such assumptions. In its January 1906 deliberations, the Congress of Marshals of the Nobility endorsed the right of peasants to withdraw from the communes and establish private farmsteads. The marshals were not enthusiastic about the prospect of greater peasant independence, but they preferred the acquisition of private property to having the peasants remain in the commune, increasingly a fertile setting for socialist agitators, who called for an end to private property altogether.[23] Many nobles, including some Union members, had begun to hope that, if the peasants had greater opportunity to acquire private property, they would be more inclined to respect the ownership rights of others, peasants and nobility alike.

Still, many members of the Union opposed the dissolution of the peasant commune. Some invoked the old Slavophile idea that the commune embodied the essential Russian values of harmony and mutual support, its members constituting a sort of "moral alliance." Others, such as Sharapov, saw a pragmatic advantage in helping peasants purchase small holdings in addition to their communal land, but affirmed that it was essential to preserve the communes for the sake of social stability. In November 1906, when the government, concerned about the peasant unrest, announced Stolypin's program for dissolving the communes, Sharapov responded sharply. The plan, he warned, was a "giant bomb" that would destroy the principle of inalienability of communal land and put Russia in mortal danger. Sharapov's apocalyptic scenario depicted drunken peasants at village meetings, demanding their portions of the land as private property and prodigally selling these acquisitions to unknown buyers – most likely Jewish speculators – who would destroy village unity and exploit the rural population through their stranglehold on land ownership. Meanwhile, peasants who had exchanged their land for a few miserable rubles would flee to the cities, join the ranks of the proletariat, and await the revolution. The best way to maintain the inviolability of all land ownership, Sharapov said, was to keep it out of the hands of speculators, which meant: preserve the communes.[24] While other Union leaders hesitated to express such an alarmist view as Sharapov's, most protested the alienation of any land, private or communal, fearing that such a move would destroy the social stability they regarded as essential to the countryside.

The Union's views on the land issue point up one of the organization's fundamental characteristics. True to the Slavophile dream of social harmony, the Union, more than any other rightist organization, emphasized the presumed commonality of interest among the estates, particularly the landed nobility and the peasantry. Referring to itself as an all-estate organization, the Union hoped to act as an agent of regeneration, not just for educated society but for the entire populace. Yet, impeded by its elitist origins, it displayed a rather paternalistic attitude toward the peasantry, whom, on the one hand, it tended to idealize, but, on the other, as Sharapov inadvertently admitted, it did not really trust. Despite its lofty intentions, the Union failed to elicit the broad popular response it anticipated, or that the more genuinely all-estate organizations, like the Union of the Russian People, achieved.

The Union of Russian Men encountered similar difficulties as it sought to adapt to Russia's rapidly changing political climate. Steeped in the Slavophile notion of the inherent unity of tsar and people, it might have welcomed the announcement of a consultative assembly, regarding it as a revived zemskii sobor. But faced with the prospect of a legislative body, the Union experienced more distress than most rightist groups in deciding how to respond. Unsuited by temperament to participate in the partisan politics that the new Duma implied, it lingered at the periphery of the emerging rightist movement. Instead of acting as a standard bearer for the populace as a whole, the Union served more appropriately as a forum for those educated Russians already drawn to Slavophilism – a testament to the longevity, if not the efficacy, of that doctrine.

4   The Russian Assembly

One of the major participants in the rightist movement – the Russian Assembly (*Russkoe sobranie*) – had existed in a somewhat different guise well before the imperial pronouncements of 18 February 1905. Originating in St. Petersburg in 1901 as a "cultural association," the Assembly worked initially to counter the growing cosmopolitanism it perceived in Russian life, particularly among the upper strata of society. Not until the crises of 1905 did it become "political," a transformation occasioned by the recognition that, while cultural regeneration remained important, the crucial issue was the future of the autocracy. Warily, the Assembly entered the political arena, armed with typical monarchist concepts and rhetoric, but still hesitant to reach beyond its own upper-class milieu. Although the Assembly cooperated with the more dynamic rightist groups, it is hardly surprising that it never became as effective in attracting a popular following. Primarily, it helped bring cohesion to the rightist movement in its early stages, and it continued to serve as a respected senior partner in the crusade to save the autocracy.

Origins and membership

The initial impetus for founding the Russian Assembly came from a group of prominent St. Petersburg conservatives, led by Prince D. P. Golitsyn. Born into the old aristocracy in 1860, Golitsyn had been educated at the Imperial Academic Lyceum. Subsequently, he held various posts in the State Chancellery and Ministry of Education. Possessing a modest literary talent, he also became a minor novelist. His most ambitious work was *Days of Turmoil* (*Ot smutnykh dnei*), written in 1900, which appeared serially in the journal *Russkii vestnik* early the following year.[1] In his books he firmly opposed the naturalist currents entering Russia from the West during the late

Table 2 *Membership of the Russian Assembly*

	April 1901 (434 members)		January 1903 (1441 members)	
Government and court personnel	140	32%	391	21%
Military officers, active/retired	74	17%	272	19%
Scholars, professors, teachers	25	6%	61	4%
Publicists, journalists	23	5%	26	2%
Writers, poets	18	4%	24	2%
Artists, musicians, actors	15	3%	43	3%
Physicians, dentists, veterinarians	19	4%	49	3%
Lawyers, judges	9	2%	26	2%
Engineers, scientific personnel	8	2%	46	3%
Business executives, merchants	7	2%	34	2%
Clerics	3	1%	16	1%
Peasants	2	0.5%	3	0.2%
Wives and women not included above	34	8%	234	16%
Unspecified	57	13%	216	15%

Source: *Letopis' Russkago sobraniia* (May 1901), 32–34; (January 1903), i–xlii.

nineteenth century, upholding instead traditional Russian values. Golitsyn envisioned the formation of "a new Russian communion" – an *obshchenie* – dedicated to the propagation of "a consciousness that being a Russian citizen is an honorable calling." Too long, he said, had Russians deprecated themselves, assuming that native cultural impulses were no match for western influences.[2]

These views Golitsyn shared with a circle of friends: S. N. Syromiatnikov, the writer; V. L. Velichko, editor of *Russkii vestnik*; A. A. Suvorin, soon to be editor of the influential conservative daily *Novoe vremia*; and others. In January 1901, the group organized the Russian Assembly, with Golitsyn as chairman, Syromiatnikov and Suvorin as vice-chairmen, and a founding membership of forty persons.[3]

In designing the Assembly its originators had few precedents upon which to draw. In some respects the association they created resembled the St. Petersburg clubs frequented by fashionable society. While not meant to be as exclusive as the prestigious English Club or professionally oriented like the clubs for businessmen, physicians, or engineers, it was a decidedly selective private organization, which catered to upper-echelon bureaucrats, military officers, scholars, artists, and other professionals, as indicated in Table 2.[4]

Further examination shows the Assembly's elitism to be even more pronounced. Among the many government and court personnel listed in January 1903 were five members of the State Council, eight members of the Senate, and several high-ranking ministerial officials including V. K. Pleve, the Minister of Internal Affairs, and P. D. Sviatopolk-Mirskii, the governor-general of Vilna, Kovno, and Grodno, and soon to be Pleve's replacement. Among the military officers were five full generals, twenty-one lieutenant-generals, and fifty major-generals. Titles also abounded: twenty-three princes and eight princesses belonged, as did twenty-two counts and three countesses, eight barons and three baronesses. As the table shows, the Assembly drew only moderately from middle-class professionals, and scarcely at all from the commercial middle class, lower classes, or clergy. Moreover, the Assembly remained essentially urban, making little attempt to attract the landed nobility (except some who had entered government service or the military). A number of women belonged, most of them wives or daughters of prominent men who had joined. A few others – eight in 1903 – became members by virtue of their standing as musicians, writers, teachers, or physicians.[5]

The Russian Assembly also shared some features with the literary, artistic, and charitable societies common in St. Petersburg. These societies promoted creative activity in particular fields or engaged in public service and beneficent work. Some critics reported that the Assembly had simply resulted from a split in the Slavonic Benevolent Society, which had become prominent during the late nineteenth century in promoting closer cultural relations between Russians and Balkan Slavs. While the Assembly's founders acknowledged their debt to the Slavonic Benevolent Society, they contended that hardly any of their members had come out of the Society and that no competition existed between the two groups.[6] Moreover, it soon became evident that their objectives differed: the Russian Assembly was less interested in promoting the Slavonic Society's Pan-Slavism than in reviving a sense of uniqueness among the Russians themselves.

As the Assembly grew, it attracted persons from locations outside St. Petersburg, usually officials in the provincial administrations who had earlier been posted in the capital or who kept close connections with events there. Within months the Assembly had several members in Moscow and one or two in each of the provincial cities of Kiev, Odessa, Kursk, Smolensk, Pskov, Warsaw, Vilna, Novgorod, Riazan, Tula, Kostroma, Kaluga, Omsk, and Irkutsk.[7] In 1902, A. S. Viazigin and several other professors at Kharkov University, all members, requested permission to establish a Kharkov branch. Despite the Assembly's growth ambitions, the central council responded reluctantly. It apparently feared that autonomous branches might "distort the Assembly's principles." When the council finally granted the request, it required that the Kharkov charter acknowledge the council's final authority; if the new branch departed from the rules of the central organization, it could be closed.[8] With Viazigin as chairman, the fledgling Kharkov branch maintained close relations with the parent body in St. Petersburg while building a thriving local organization. By 1905, it had over 250 members, evidently without any of the adverse consequences anticipated by the central council.[9]

Having established the feasibility of branches, the Assembly cautiously proceeded to charter several more. In 1904, it opened branches in Kiev, Kazan, Perm, Orenburg, Vilna, and Warsaw, and, in 1905–1907, branches in Odessa, Saratov, Ufa, and Irkutsk, as well as in a few smaller towns.[10] This expansion, however, did not result in what could be considered a nationwide organization; total membership never exceeded a few thousand. Although some branches, particularly those in Kharkov, Irkutsk, Kiev, and Kazan, proved quite active, the Assembly always feared that if it became too "public" it would run the risk of admitting contaminating elements. This congenital exclusiveness precluded the likelihood that the Assembly would ever promote a truly popular movement in Russia.

From cultural to political concerns

Whatever the shortcomings of its elitist character, the Russian Assembly distinguished itself in promoting Russian cultural nationalism. It pledged to "strengthen the public consciousness" by encouraging an appreciation of Russia's distinctive traditions, especially in literature and the arts, and by revitalizing the creative spirit of the Russian people. It devoted its weekly literary–musical evenings to reading the works of Russian masters, performing scenes from Russian operas, and reciting poetry or prose written by Assembly members. Occasionally, the Assembly sponsored art exhibits featuring typical Russian works and lectures on subjects ranging from Pushkin's poetry to the social effects of the Crimean War.[11]

United in their general outlook, Assembly members varied in explaining Russia's distinctiveness, often mixing cultural and political arguments. Some emphasized Slavophile principles. An Assembly founder, A. V. Vasiliev, extolled the Russian people's unrestricted

"freedom of spirit" and "unity of mind" – the *sobornost'* treasured by
the early Slavophiles. Specifically, he cited Khomiakov, the Kireev-
skiis, the Aksakovs, and Samarin, members of the original Slavophile
circle, as spiritual precursors of the Assembly.[12] Other members dwelt
on the trilogy of autocracy, Orthodoxy, and nationality, long popular
among Russian conservatives, often adding that these singular
attributes had enabled Russia to become a great state. "We are the
sons of a world power," General M. M. Borodkin declared at a
meeting in 1903. "But around us we find little love of our native land.
The Russian intelligentsia lacks a sense of self-esteem, a feeling of
national pride." True Russians must genuinely believe in their
country, he admonished, if Russia intended to preserve its unity and
strength.[13]

The circumstances of the next two years heightened the Russian
Assembly's political concerns. Public discontent over Russia's ill-fated
war against Japan, liberal demands for popular representation, the
government's vacillation in dealing with the mounting unrest, all
contributed to the Assembly's growing apprehension about Russia's
political future. When rumors began to circulate that the tsar might
create an elected advisory body that would participate in affairs of
state, the Assembly voiced its first real doubts about government
policy and conduct. On 31 December, 1904, an Assembly delegation
advised the tsar that such a body could easily drive Russia toward
western parliamentarianism and eventually anarchy.[14] At an
Assembly meeting in January 1905, Boris Nikolskii, a lecturer at St.
Petersburg University and a member of the Assembly's council,
asserted that convening an elected body would be a "most dangerous
and regrettable step," even if it was confined to an advisory role, like
the old zemskii sobors. In Muscovite times, he said, Russia was united
and representatives of the people met in harmony. Now there was
discord. Ideally, the convocation of a sobor might be appropriate, but
practically such a move could lead to disaster.[15]

After Nicholas's 18 February rescript, sanctioning a representative
body, Nikolskii warned the Assembly that the tsar could well be
playing into the hands of his opponents. "The liberal ducks are
crying, the radical geese are cackling, the nightingales are singing of
spring," lamented Nikolskii. "This uproar of the senseless crowd is
not at all Russian."[16] Increasingly disturbed, Nikolskii and the
Assembly were becoming conscious of the dilemma facing the
loyalists: How to uphold an autocracy that apparently lacked the will
to preserve its own prerogatives? In allegiance to the throne, the best

the Assembly could do was acquiesce and trust that the tsar had the fortitude to avoid further concessions.

In August 1905, when the government announced elections to the projected Duma, the Assembly debated whether or not to involve itself politically. Some members urged that the Assembly remain a strictly cultural association; others proposed that it prepare to support loyalist candidates in the elections. A few of the newer Assembly members criticized the leadership for its indecisiveness and apathy, and during the fall A. I. Dubrovin, V. M. Purishkevich, A. A. Maikov, and others left to form the Union of the Russian People. Still others made the exodus, as an Assembly chronicler put it, "to the left," where they joined centrist parties. The Assembly's membership, which had reached more than 2,300 in 1905, dropped to about 1,750 by early 1906. Nonetheless, amidst these disruptions the Assembly did finally vote to draft a political program and participate in the Duma elections.[17]

This was an important step. When first organized, the Assembly had drawn up statutes, designed to serve the membership as a statement of the Assembly's objectives, structure, and procedures. Essentially, the statutes had an internal function. Now, by formulating a program, the Assembly was declaring publicly its position on contemporary issues for the purpose of gaining popular support. Implicitly, the program indicated the stand that Assembly candidates would take on these issues if elected to the Duma. Publishing a program was becoming standard practice for the new political parties; for the Russian Assembly, it was an especially difficult task, marking as it did a major departure from the Assembly's subdued self-image.

In its program the Assembly expressed a rather conventional set of rightist principles, centered on the traditional autocracy–Orthodoxy–nationality formula with an emphasis on state power. It claimed that Russia must have a staunch autocracy to fulfill its "Christian world mission," a reference to the messianic vision that had entranced many Russian nationalists during the late nineteenth century and an echo of the Assembly's chauvinistic concept of the state. Adding that Russia needed a strong army and navy to compete internationally, it touched on a sensitive point in view of Russia's dismal performance during the recent war with Japan. Orthodoxy, the Assembly affirmed, should continue to hold a dominant position in Russian life and have a voice in the affairs of state. Non-Russians deserved cultural autonomy but only if this autonomy did not impair the unity of the empire and if the minorities would support the Russian majority in achieving state goals. Like other rightist organizations, the Assembly adopted the catchphrase used by Alexander III: "Russia for the Russians."[18]

The Assembly also joined other rightists in devoting special consideration to the "Jewish question." While not as antisemitic as the Union of the Russian People or the Union of Russian Men, the Assembly clearly displayed its prejudices. It argued that the Jewish question must be handled separately from policies toward other minorities because of the Jews' traditional antagonism toward Christians and their plans for world domination.[19] Later, the Assembly elaborated on its attitude toward the Jews, asserting that equal rights would result in even greater Jewish exploitation of the Russian people.[20]

Thoroughly oriented to the upper strata of society, the Assembly paid scant attention to the concerns of Russia's workers and peasants. Briefly, it spoke to the land issue, insisting that private ownership of land remain inviolable, protected against those who advocated expropriation. For the peasants, the Assembly recommended only that the government extend credit to those who wished to purchase land and provide greater incentives for peasant handicrafts.[21]

Unexceptional in content, the Assembly's program differed little from the usual rightist attitude toward Russia's political and social crises. More than some rightist organizations, the Assembly upheld the autocracy without alluding to the tsar's inability to protect his own prerogatives. But like other rightists, it recognized that it must join in defending an ailing autocracy against those who threatened its existence. The Assembly's pronouncements on the "Jewish question" amply demonstrated that antisemitism had pervaded the upper reaches of Russian society and that this issue was rapidly becoming politicized. One can hardly doubt that the Russian Assembly took these attitudes for granted, perceiving them as a sound and adequate basis for political action.

A role in the rightist movement

Having put itself on record as a political contender, the Russian Assembly embarked on another significant initiative by attempting to unify the nascent rightist movement. On 9–12 February 1906, it hosted the first congress of monarchist associations, whose representatives gathered in St. Petersburg to explore the possibility of coordinating their activities. Attended by over 350 delegates, the congress represented some thirty organizations, including the

Assembly and its branches in Kharkov, Odessa, Kiev, and Warsaw; the Russian Monarchist Party and the Union of Russian Men, both from Moscow; the St. Petersburg-based Union of the Russian People and some of its newly formed branches; and various minor groups.[22]

Convinced that these organizations constituted the genesis of a national movement, congress delegates debated the crucial question of whether they should form some sort of working amalgamation. While the delegates expressed a commonality of purpose, they differed on procedural matters. Those who disliked the notion of partisan politics rejected any hint of founding a national party. Many agreed with Prince Shcherbatov of the Union of Russian Men, who maintained, "We are not parties; we are spokesmen for the spirit of the people."[23] Others, dissatisfied with such ethereal sentiments, advocated doing what the Constitutional Democrats and Octobrists had already accomplished, that is, create a central executive body expressly for the purpose of political campaigning. However, those who favored this route still found themselves impeded by minor jealousies over leadership and personal prerogatives. Wrestling with the problem of how much autonomy existing associations must relinquish to central authority, the delegates postponed any organizational decisions until the next congress, scheduled to meet in Moscow in April. Clearly, the monarchists were as yet ill-prepared for joint action. What they failed to foresee was that the antipodal forces of unification and separatism would continue to plague their endeavors, never enabling them to become a really cohesive movement.

The St. Petersburg congress addressed another issue, one confronting all political contenders – the forthcoming Duma. Denying that the October Manifesto should in any way be construed as a constitution or a limitation on autocratic power, the congress insisted that, despite the wording of the Manifesto, the Duma must serve only as a advisory body. Under no circumstances should it be turned into a constituent assembly. Invoking a traditional Slavophile tenet, the congress affirmed: To the tsar be the power of decision, to the Duma the right of opinion.

Conceptual differences among the congress delegates kept them from deciding exactly how they should be involved in the Duma elections. Delegates who refused to regard the monarchist associations as political parties questioned whether they should even enter the campaign. Those who did endorse participation in the elections reached little agreement in designing a feasible campaign strategy. Some delegates complained that the congress had been called too hastily for them to come prepared for debating such important issues. All in all, it was painfully apparent that the rightist organizations were not ready for the Duma campaign.

Still, the Russian Assembly left the congress pleased that it had provided the initial opportunity for monarchists to meet and achieve at least a basis for further cooperation. With some degree of hope, the Assembly participated in the April Moscow congress, and subsequently in congresses held in Kiev in October 1906 and in Moscow in April 1907. The fourth congress elected as chairman the Assembly's Prince M. L. Shakhovskoi, a tribute to the Assembly's contributions in giving form to the rightist movement. Yet, already by the second congress the Assembly was being overshadowed by other rightist organizations, particularly the Union of the Russian People, which had been growing phenomenally and soon dominated rightist efforts at joint action. The Assembly would remain a secondary political player.[24]

During 1906 and 1907, the Russian Assembly participated in the Duma campaigns, but its reticence toward incisive action meant that it usually followed the lead of other organizations. During both the first and second campaigns the Assembly in St. Petersburg assisted the Union of the Russian People in preparing a joint slate of candidates.[25] In Kiev, the Assembly helped initiate a productive rightist coalition but contributed little practical assistance to the campaigns themselves.[26] Elsewhere, the scattered Assembly branches usually served as auxiliary participants in local rightist blocs. Even when Prince Shakhovskoi replaced Golitsyn as Assembly chairman in 1906, his somewhat more activist inclination had little effect on converting the Assembly into a strong, dynamic political force. Those who wanted greater political involvement generally abandoned the Assembly for more enterprising organizations.

In historical perspective, it becomes evident that the Russian Assembly never completely made the transition to being a political party. Bound by its self-imposed and rather nebulous mission to revitalize a national consciousness among educated Russians, it lacked the temperament, to say nothing of the skill, needed to enter effectively into the political struggle. Although the Assembly amended its restrictive by-laws to permit political activity, most members retained a kind of salon mentality, aware of the need to preserve Russia's traditional institutions but slow to undertake such tasks as political campaigning.

The Russian Assembly also lacked the inclination and resolve to operate as a special-interest group, intent on using its elitist membership in influencing government policies. Unlike such organizations as the Patriotic Union and the United Nobility, the Assembly made little attempt to utilize connections with influential officials in the government and at court, and it neglected even to join other rightist organizations in calling for the dissolution of the first two oppositionist Dumas and a revision of the electoral law.[27] It remained content to send delegations to the tsar, assuring him of its support during "these trying times," and occasionally to encourage key ministers in holding a firm course.

Thus, the Assembly's role remained essentially what its leaders desired: a respectable haven for monarchists who wished to champion Russia's cultural and political traditions without engaging extensively in political action, and a sort of mentor to the rightist movement.

5   The Union of the Russian People

While the Russian Monarchist Party and Union of Russian Men appeared in response to the imperial manifesto of 18 February 1905, it took the tumultuous events of that fall, culminating in the October Manifesto, to arouse the founders of what was to become the most prominent rightist association in Russia: the Union of the Russian People (*Soiuz russkago naroda*). Once created, the Union met with amazing success. From its headquarters in St. Petersburg, it established numerous branches throughout the country, comprising a much greater membership than any other monarchist organization. Apparently, this growth derived largely from the Union's ability to dissociate itself from upper-class interests and present itself as the hub of a national movement, prepared to speak for all "true Russians." Through its intensely antiliberal, antirevolutionary, antisemitic rhetoric, it convinced thousands that only under its banner could they unite effectively against the opposition and heal the widening breach between tsar and people. Intransigent in its demands and aggressive in its program of action, willing even to subdue its enemies by force, the Union gained broad notoriety. Still, supporters and opponents alike viewed the Union as a major political contender, and the tsar himself commended it for its "trustworthy support" of the throne.

First steps

The initiative for founding the Union of the Russian People came from several discontented members of the Russian Assembly, led by Dr. Aleksandr Ivanovich Dubrovin. Born in 1855 into the non-landed nobility, Dubrovin had pursued an active medical career before becoming absorbed in the monarchist cause. After graduating from the St. Petersburg Medical–Surgical Institute in 1879, he served for the next decade and a half as a civilian physician attached to various army units, mainly in and around St. Petersburg. In 1896, he was named adjunct senior medical officer in the Ministry of Internal Affairs' Medical Department. During those years he also reached the prestigious civil rank of State Counselor, the fifth from the top of the state's fourteen-rung Table of Ranks.[1] Staunchly patriotic, Dubrovin met other monarchists in St. Petersburg; and in September 1901, he joined the Russian Assembly, where he remained until the fall of 1905.[2]

Descriptions of Dubrovin's character differ sharply, making a precise appraisal difficult but providing at least some insight into his leadership ability. Sergei Witte referred to him as one of the "heroes of the putrid marketplace."[3] But when Witte once called Dubrovin a scoundrel, the Minister of Internal Affairs, P. N. Durnovo, replied, "You call him that unjustly. The truth is that he is a most fine and honorable man."[4] Boris Nikolskii, who had a falling out with Dubrovin after knowing him in the Russian Assembly and later in the Union of the Russian People, labeled him "a crude brute," to whom no one paid attention.[5] By contrast, M. M. Zelenskii, the Union's secretary, looked to Dubrovin as a cordial individual and the group's natural leader, an assessment shared by many others in the organization.[6] These disparate characterizations no doubt illuminate a salient feature of Dubrovin's personality: his unyielding sense of mission that could both attract and offend potential followers. Whatever his personal qualities, the fact is that Dubrovin proved able to gather around him a coterie of like-minded monarchists as the nucleus of the emerging Union.

Having already watched Russia's growing turmoil during the spring of 1905, Dubrovin found in the events of September and October the impetus he still needed to take resolute action. With strikes sweeping the country, angry demonstrators in the streets, and sporadic outbursts of violence, he was appalled by the government's lack of initiative in handling the crisis. While pondering what course he himself might take in defense of the throne, Dubrovin happened upon an incident that directed his thinking toward the possibility of forming a broad-based monarchist organization, geared to political pursuits far beyond what he had been used to in the Russian Assembly. Early in October, an acquaintance introduced Dubrovin to a delegation from the semi-religious, patriotic Society of Banner Carriers (*Obshchestvo khorugvenostsev*) in Moscow, which had just arrived in the capital for an audience with the tsar. The Banner

Carriers had organized in January 1905 as a "brotherhood" chaired by Bishop Serafim of Moscow, and they included both Orthodox clerics and laymen. Pledging their loyalty to the faith and the autocracy, they marched in colorful processions, carrying icons, flags, and portraits of the tsar. Dubrovin discovered that the Banner Carriers had also organized a People's Defense Corps (*Narodnaia okhrana*) to protect the tsar during his visits to Moscow. To the interested Dubrovin this seemed an excellent idea, one that could be expanded to the national level and given a more universal goal: a genuinely popular organization, militantly disposed to preserving the autocracy.[7]

With this experience fresh in mind, Dubrovin took his first tentative steps toward independent action. With the aid of acquaintances in the Russian Assembly, he arranged and advertised several public meetings. To his satisfaction, tradesmen, shopkeepers, workers, and other common people not usually drawn to the Assembly came to listen to the patriotic speeches. When Assembly leaders criticized these innovations, Dubrovin was even surer that the time had come to launch out on his own.[8]

Dubrovin's friends in the Russian Assembly were eager to help. P. F. Bulatsel', scion of a prosperous landowning family, volunteered his services as a lawyer and publicist. A. A. Maikov, whose father had been the nineteenth-century poet A. N. Maikov, offered his own literary talent to the utilitarian task of writing pamphlets and editorials in support of the autocracy.[9] The most spectacular of Dubrovin's associates was an impetuous young government official, V. M. Purishkevich. A staunch defender of the autocracy, Purishkevich had joined the Russian Assembly, where for a couple of years he contributed to its "cultural evenings" with his poetry and plays in verse. Like Dubrovin, however, he increasingly found the Assembly too tame for his energy and talents. When Dubrovin approached him about forming an independent organization, Purishkevich readily agreed, subsequently becoming second in command of the new venture.[10]

Dubrovin was also making valuable contacts outside the Russian Assembly, particularly among the commercial middle class, a social stratum that the Assembly had hardly touched. Through a mutual friend he met I. I. Baranov, a St. Petersburg fish dealer, who in turn introduced him to several other merchants willing to assist in creating a counterrevolutionary organization. Already, the broad-based character that Dubrovin anticipated for his organization was beginning to appear.

In the midst of these busy days, the tsar issued his October Manifesto. Like a bombshell it brought Dubrovin's proselytizing to a head. On Saturday, 22 October, he called a meeting at his home to discuss the Manifesto and decide a plan of action. Purishkevich, Maikov, Bulatsel', Baranov, and several others who attended concurred with Dubrovin that they should organize. Over the next two weeks, the group worked out a structure and devised a program. On 8 November, it formally announced the founding of the Union of the Russian People, with Dubrovin as chairman.[11]

Building an organization

Carefully selected, the name of the new organization appropriately indicated what its originators conceived as one of their principal objectives: to bind together a divided society. This hope they enunciated in the Union's statutes, which stated that the Union was setting for itself the goal of "firmly unifying Russian people of all estates and statuses (sosloviia i sostoianiia), in order to work together in behalf of our beloved fatherland – Russia, one and indivisible." This restoration of unity seemed imperative because of the current anarchy that was paralyzing national life and inflicting "incalculable losses" on the state and society. The opposition movement must be stopped and the fundamental unity of tsar and people restored.[12]

What Dubrovin and his colleagues envisioned was a popular crusade, an enterprise that contrasted sharply with the government's half-hearted efforts to enlist public support and to the class-oriented activism of other monarchist organizations. Dubrovin also insisted that the Union would not be a political party – it had "broader tasks and higher goals," which transcended the special interests that characterized partisan politics.[13] Although the Union had few precedents on which to draw, its leaders sought to forge an organization that could both stimulate and coordinate patriotic sentiment throughout the country.

Dubrovin moved quickly to attract public attention, probably eliciting a more enthusiastic response than he had expected. On the evening of 21 November 1905, the Union held its first open meeting in the arena of St. Petersburg's Mikhailovskii Riding Hall, a site of frequent public functions. As the crowd of some two thousand assembled, it was greeted by orchestral music and a choir of monks singing "Praise God" and "Tsar Divine." From a rostrum in the center of the arena, the speakers addressed the audience. Boris Nikolskii, who had first introduced Dubrovin to the Society of Banner Carriers, warned that the Russian people must act decisively to thwart those who would destroy institutions that had taken a thousand years to construct. Other speakers echoed Nikolskii's theme. "The speeches themselves were fiery, colorful, and apparently convincing," wrote V. I. Gurko, an Assistant Minister of Internal Affairs, who attended the event. "The atmosphere was charged with electricity. I had the impression that the crowd was prepared to commit any excesses; but, as the speeches did not point out any definite object to be attacked, the crowd dispersed peacefully, singing 'God Save the Tsar!'"[14] Encouraged by this initial success, Dubrovin scheduled other meetings, which continued to draw large audiences.[15]

Equally important, Dubrovin adopted another means of disseminating the Union's message that was fast becoming a mainstay for Russia's political organizations. On 27 November, he launched a newspaper, *Russkoe znamia*, designed to carry a modicum of national news but primarily to feature fervid editorials on political and social issues, and information on Union activities. The Union sold its newspaper on the streets, hoping that it would prove to the public that Russian patriotism was alive and that "true Russians" were flocking to the cause. Union branches, soon to appear in other cities, also distributed *Russkoe znamia*, until the newspaper circulated in most provincial capitals and many smaller towns. As further evidence of the Union's growing strength, some branches began publishing their own newspapers, among them *Russkii bogatyr* (*The Russian Hero*) in Nikolaev; *Nabat* (*The Tocsin*) in Simferopol; *Znamia* (*The Banner*) in Ekaterinburg; *Golos Rybinska* (*The Voice of Rybinsk*) in Iaroslavl province, and *Sychevskaia gazeta* (*The Sychev Gazette*) in Smolensk province.[16] Moreover, the Union issued countless brochures and booklets, selling them for a few kopeks each on the streets and in bookstores or distributing them free of charge to workers, soldiers, and peasants. V. M. Purishkevich stated that from May through November 1906 the Union printed about 13 million brochures.[17] Judging from imprints on individual publications, which show that they were issued by the tens or hundreds of thousands, this figure may be close to correct. In an era of rising literacy in Russia, when the printed word was becoming a significant instrument of persuasion, the Union of the Russian People, more than any other rightist organization, excelled in this form of political propaganda.[18]

The Union also enjoyed phenomenal growth as it labored to build a national organization, a testimony to its leaders' organizational ability and an intimation that indeed many Russians were ready to express their allegiance to tsar and country – and to vent their hostility toward intellectuals, Jews, and other "enemies" of the Russian people. Wasting no time, Dubrovin and his colleagues relied heavily on provincial contacts. Some of their acquaintances frequented monarchist salons while visiting the capital; others attended conferences of the nobility in which Bulatsel' and Purishkevich participated. Father Arsenii, a long-time friend of Dubrovin and abbot of the Voskresenskii Monastery in Iaroslavl province, helped found the Union's first branch there on 26 November. He then traveled around the province, setting up rural subsections and delivering patriotic, and usually antisemitic, speeches.[19]

Other branches soon followed. In the All-Russian Union of Landowners, Bulatsel' knew several members of the prominent Oznobishin family from Saratov province. All became interested in the Union, and N. N. Oznobishin, then living in Moscow, opened a branch there on 22 January 1906. An ardent monarchist, Oznobishin built the branch into a powerhouse, in time overshadowing Moscow's Russian Monarchist Party. On 5 February, another contact, Count A. I. Konovnitsyn, organized a Union branch in Odessa, to which he soon added a network of subsections. Konovnitsyn brought droves of local monarchists under the Union banner, while making Odessa the core of Union activities in southern Russia. Before long, news of the Union's activities was reaching persons unacquainted with its founders. Sometimes, a group of individuals would ask the Union to help them organize a branch; more often a local monarchist association would request affiliation with the Union. By the middle of February 1906, the Union was adding several branches a week.[20]

The size to which the Union eventually grew is difficult to determine, since it apparently did not keep comprehensive membership lists. The Iaroslavl branch reported over 10,000 members in that province alone as early as February 1906. In August 1906, Purishkevich exclaimed that the Union simply could not keep count of the vast numbers of recruits from every corner of Russia. Several years later, N. E. Markov recalled that the membership ran into the millions.[21] These inflated estimates obviously help very little in ascertaining the Union's total membership. It is also difficult to estimate the number of branches. Markov claimed that at its peak in 1907 the Union had 4,000 branches, but this too is probably an exaggeration.[22] However, there are indications that the Union was growing at a remarkable rate. From news items in Union publications and information in government archives, it appears that by the end of 1907 the Union of the Russian People had opened over 1,000 branches, reaching from Arkhangel to the Crimea and from Russia's western border to the middle of Siberia.[23] Based on L. M. Spirin's calculation that in the thirty-two branches for which he had figures the membership per branch ranged from about 100 to 500 persons, one may roughly estimate that the Union had between 200,000 and 300,000 members.[24]

This rapid growth was accompanied by another feature that distinguished the Union from most rightist organizations: the diverse social composition of its adherents. Proposing to act as a unifying agent for the entire population, the Union attracted all levels of society, although by no means equally. According to information that can be gleaned from *Russkoe znamia* and other publications, it appears that the Union drew chiefly from the middle and lower social echelons. Many of the townspeople it enlisted were evidently ordinary citizens, patriotic and conscientious, who welcomed the Union's call for loyalty to crown and country. But others were disgruntled members of the petty bourgeoisie and uprooted peasant-workers, for whom the Union's claims that renegade intellectuals and Jews were causing Russia's economic and political ills could seem quite plausible.

Similarly, in the countryside the Union's ability to attract peasants probably depended more on its appeal to fears and prejudices than on the economic provisions of its program. The Union promised that the government would assist peasants in purchasing land and in enabling resettlement in less crowded regions of the country, but it argued against expropriation of private estates, a solution that the liberal and radical parties advocated and that many peasants approved.[25] More effectively, Union orators reminded the peasants that, as members of the Orthodox faith, they owed devotion both to God and to the tsar. The Union described how Orthodoxy's most treacherous enemies, the Jews, were behind the political opposition's call for agrarian reform, skillfully maneuvering to gain ownership of the land. Aware of this "colossal danger," the Union pledged to fight any legislation that would "enable a single Jew to acquire landed property through which to exploit the local population."[26]

Perhaps because the Union insisted on dissociating itself from the aristocracy and the bureaucracy, it did not draw heavily from the landed nobility, as did the Union of Russian Men, or from the governmental and military elite, as did the Russian Assembly. Those nobles who joined the Union tended to be atypical of their social stratum. Some, disturbed by peasant and worker unrest, pursued a sort of two-pronged defense by participating in the Union and in their own class-oriented institutions as well. Count Konovnitsyn and N. N. Oznobishin, the chairmen of Union branches in Odessa and Moscow, both kept their ties with the Union of Landowners and the United Nobility, and other members of the Oznobishin family held prominent positions in the latter organization.[27] Other nobles who took active roles in the Union were often status-insecure individuals seeking acceptance among their more established social peers. Purishkevich and Bulatsel', for example, as well as G. V. Butmi and P. A. Krushevan, belonged to Moldavian noble families in Bessarabia, who not only embraced the values and traditions of their Russian counterparts but exaggerated their credentials as "true Russians." While the old nobility generally contented itself with defending its social and economic interests, these fringe members seemed impelled to prove themselves as super-patriots. Gravitating toward those organizations where they could express their loyalty most volubly, they found the Union of the Russian People particularly suited to their inclinations.

While the Union's rank-and-file membership comprised a broad range of small shopkeepers, clerks, artisans, industrial workers, and peasants, its leaders came mainly from the professional and commercial middle class. A physician, a lawyer, two engineers, an artist, and several merchants formed the majority of the Union's founding members; others from comparable backgrounds, including journalists and teachers, joined various branches. A merchant in Vladimir and a physician in Iaroslavl helped organize local affiliates. In Elisavetgrad a lawyer became branch chairman, in Vilna a building contractor, and in Kazan a university professor.[28] This is not to imply that the Union abounded in middle-class leaders, like the Kadets and Octobrists, or that its leaders possessed the intellectual capabilities and moral stature of their counterparts in these other parties; it is only to suggest that the Union had at least a moderate supply of competent administrators, available for the task of building and coordinating a sizeable organization.

The Union also benefited from the Russian Orthodox clergy, whose contribution lay not so much in providing leadership as in disseminating the Union's message and enhancing its credibility. Certainly, not all Orthodox clerics were reactionary. Some young priests expressed genuine concern both for administrative reform within the Church and for social and political change. Others contented

themselves with their ecclesiastical duties, ignoring public issues
entirely. But many, especially among the hierarchy, reacted vigorously against the liberal and radical currents extant in Russia.
Preaching counterrevolution, they saw an advantage in aligning
themselves with an organization such as the Union, whose program
they could readily espouse.

Intent on arousing patriotic fervor among the populace, Union
leaders appreciated that some clerics were masters of demagogy.
Abbot Arsenii in Iaroslavl and Bishop Germogen in Saratov recruited
numerous Union members through their fiery counterrevolutionary
sermons.[29] The monk Agafodor toured the environs of his monastery
on the border between Kursk and Chernigov provinces, organizing
Union branches and exhorting audiences to resist the evils of
constitutionalism, socialism, and Jewish rights. His extreme views on
the sanctity of private property may have alienated some peasants,
but his religious passion and appeals to patriotism captivated
others.[30] The most notorious cleric to join the Union was the monk
Iliodor of the Pochaev Monastery in Volynia, a hotbed of reaction in
southwestern Russia. With other monks he edited the monastery's
daily newspaper, *Pochaevskiia izvestiia* (*The Pochaev News*), along with
booklets and brochures in which he vented his counterrevolutionary
and antisemitic spleen. Frequently, he spoke at Union branches in
neighboring villages. Transferred to Tsaritsyn, he organized a branch
of the Union there and continued his inflammatory preaching and
pamphleteering.[31]

One of the more celebrated clerics to uphold the Union was Father
Ioann of Kronstadt, dean of St. Andrew's Cathedral at the naval base
outside St. Petersburg. For years Father Ioann had been the region's
most eloquent preacher. A man of outstanding faith, renowned for his
fervent prayers, he reportedly had great healing powers. Earlier he
had served as private confessor to Alexander III. Now in his late
seventies, still exercising a profound religious influence, he attracted
pilgrims from all over Russia. His ultraconservative political and
social views, together with his religious popularity, induced the
Union to seek his favor. Although he never actually joined, he
delighted Union leaders by accepting an honorary membership and
publicly consecrating the Union's first banner.[32]

Despite the prevailing conservatism in the Orthodox hierarchy,
some clerics refused to support the Union because of its extremism.
When Dubrovin planned a massive public meeting at the Mikhailovskii Riding Hall for 26 November 1906, he invited the three highest

dignitaries in the Orthodox Church: Metropolitans Antonii of St. Petersburg, Vladimir of Moscow, and Flavian of Kiev, as well as Father Ioann of Kronstadt. Father Ioann attended, but to Dubrovin's chagrin neither Vladimir nor Flavian appeared; and Antonii rejected the invitation with the rebuke, "I do not sympathize with your rightist parties, and I consider you to be terrorists. The terrorists on the left throw bombs, while the rightist parties instead hurl stones at all who disagree with them."[33] This accusation infuriated Dubrovin, who retaliated with a scathing attack on Antonii in *Russkoe znamia*, imputing to him a long list of "liberal" sins. These ranged from harboring unreliable bishops in his dioceses and radical teachers in the St. Petersburg Religious Academy to failing to support the war against Japan.[34]

Aside from these occasional setbacks, the Union profited from the presence of clerics, not only the firebrand preachers but others who provided less public services. Some offered prayers at the Union's public meetings or spoke in commendation of its patriotic mission, and a few chaired local branches.[35] Clerical backing proved invaluable in bringing members into the Union and giving it an aura of respectability.

Principles and program

Like other rightist organizations, the Union of the Russian People was not essentially an intellectual movement. Nor did its strength primarily depend on the rationality of its program or on a systematic philosophy. Often it simply used popular slogans – "For tsar, faith, and fatherland" was a favorite – and it interlaced its pronouncements with standard references to autocracy, Orthodoxy, and nationality. Unconcerned with theories, the Union based its program on a few fundamental principles, mainly those drawn from Slavophilic nostalgia for a long defunct political system that posited the people's acceptance of autocratic power and mutual trust vis-à-vis the tsar. The Union maintained that in pre-Petrine times "the tsar and people formed an entity, no barrier existed between them, and the voice of the people reached directly to the tsar." But with the accession of Peter the Great, this relationship was broken: Peter and his successors ruled as absolutists "without adhering to the wishes of the people and in some instances acting against their will." Even worse, this personal absolutism degraded further into a sort of bureaucratic absolutism, in which ministers had almost unlimited power in their own spheres without being held responsible for their actions. Changes since Muscovite times occurred so gradually, the Union said, that neither the tsar nor the people realized fully what had been lost. Therefore, the Union had to impress on both the autocrat and the Russian people the real meaning and function of autocracy. Nicholas must assert his authority, and the Russian people must pledge to him their heartfelt allegiance.[36]

Apparently, the Union believed that because of personal short-comings Nicholas had disastrously compromised his calling. Despite his vow, upon ascending the throne in 1894, that he would reign in the autocratic tradition of his father, he obviously possessed neither his father's decisiveness nor his determination. Count Konovnitsyn, chairman of the Union's Odessa branch, remarked that Nicholas had signed the October Manifesto "in his weakness" – a victim of Witte's coercion.[37] Here the Union labored with a problem that plagued many monarchists: how to halt Nicholas's alarming tendency to make concessions without openly criticizing him. At times, the Union seemed to admit publicly that the concessions were for the best. The announcement of a Duma, it said, was a benevolent act, designed to bring the Russian people into closer harmony with their ruler.[38] In reality, the Union was for months uncertain how Nicholas regarded the proposed Duma, and whether he might be persuaded to grant further concessions.

In order to avert this bleak possibility, the Union decided to encourage Nicholas to exert his will and authority. On 23 December 1905, Dubrovin led a Union delegation to the imperial palace at Tsarskoe Selo for an audience that centered on the nature of the autocracy. As if to remind Nicholas of his heritage, the delegates assured him that any reformist attempts to limit his power contra-vened the earnest desires of the "true Russian people."[39] Over the next several months, as the Union grew, its local branches sent dozens of telegrams urging Nicholas to exercise his prerogatives in dealing with seditionists, Duma oppositionists, and other "internal enemies."[40]

Through its publications and public meetings, the Union strove to revive in Russian society an allegiance to the throne. As a father to his people, the *batiushka-tsar* deserved their respect and obedience. This badly deteriorated relationship must be restored – a genuine union of tsar and people, predicated on affection and trust. Harking back to the Slavophile doctrine that the abiding principle in autocracy was not authority but the fulfillment of mutual obligations, Dubrovin printed in *Russkoe znamia* several excerpts from an address that Ivan Aksakov, the last of the original Slavophiles, had made to the St. Petersburg Slavonic Society in 1881. In old Russia, Aksakov said, no antagonism had divided tsar and people. The autocrat valued the advice of the people, although this in no way limited his power. From time to time he called a zemskii sobor, which "always brought the love and genuine thought of the people." Unfortunately, Peter the Great had opened the way for western ideas that would pervert Russia's traditions and turn its people from their ruler. In consequence of this folly, Russia had suffered greatly. Salvation lay only in a return to once cherished principles. "May there be revived anew," Aksakov concluded, "in life-giving strength and activity, the union of tsar and people, based on love, confidence, unity of spirit, and mutually sincere fellowship."[41] This was the relationship that the Union pledged to revive – a spiritual covenant, unwritten but immanent in the hearts of faithful Russians.

Underscoring the unity of tsar and people, the Union also emphasized the unity of the people themselves. This notion took on a distinctly chauvinistic meaning when applied to Russia's multinational empire. It was one thing to promote greater rapport among the Russians, another to castigate the minority nationalities for failing to accept, even uphold, Russian predominance. Yet the Union, along with many Russian nationalists, argued that for the sake of unity – a Russia "one and indivisible" – Poles, Finns, Armenians, and other non-Russians must recognize that it was the Russians who had created the present state and therefore deserved a superior role in its governance. The slogan "Russia for the Russians" made sense, the Union contended, both for the historical land of Rus' and for the entire Russian Empire.[42]

Why, asked the Union, did minority nationalities, such as the Poles, not appreciate the benefits they had derived from Russian rule? "Russia has done and is doing too much for the Poles," the Union complained, "and they repay in constant ingratitude and hatred of everything Russian ... when they could be united with Russia in one of the most powerful states in the world." Recalling the Polish insurrections of 1830 and 1863, the Union condemned the Poles for taking advantage of Russian leniency. These insurrections were put down and order was restored, but the Poles continued to demand autonomy. Likewise, the Finns wanted to exclude Russian influence without ever acknowledging that only because Russia had expended hundreds of millions of rubles had the Finnish standard of living so vastly improved.[43] Relentlessly deploring ethnic particularism, the Union never conceded that the minority nationalities, like the Russians, might have valid aspirations of their own. It persisted in the illusion, held by the government itself, that Russification could somehow remove the frictions from among the empire's various nationalities.

Enemies within

To those who cherished the ideal union of tsar and people, the current opposition to the throne must have been especially disturbing. Unable to believe that "true Russians" could manifest such disloyalty, the Union sought those alien forces responsible for this subversion. Most obvious were the revolutionaries, whom the Union denounced for their blatant acts of terrorism and plans for insurrection. But to the Union the more insidious enemies – and ultimately the more dangerous – were the liberals, notably the Constitutional Democrats. It was the liberals who had opened the floodgates of subversion by insisting that the tsar's power be constitutionally curtailed, a goal the Union warned would inevitably destroy the monarchy.

Enjoying a newly found freedom of speech as the result of the October Manifesto, the liberals voiced what seemed to be but the beginning of a never-ending list of demands. Today they want a constitution, warned the Union; tomorrow they will try to get rid of the tsar completely.[44] The main difference between the liberals and the radicals was that the liberals pursued their objectives more cleverly. They were more cautious, intelligent, and politically educated, V. M. Purishkevich observed, and they could subvert the political system through legal channels without anyone realizing what was occurring. Before the elections to the Second Duma, Purishkevich extravagantly declared that in those localities where there were no rightist candidates running for election, the voters might better cast their ballots for leftist candidates than for liberals.[46]

The Union was particularly appalled when some Kadet leaders declared they had "no enemies on the left." To the Union this inclination was not simply a matter of political strategy. It proved, said the Union, that a spiritual bond existed between the Kadets and the revolutionaries. By demanding freedom of speech and press, the Kadets were enabling the revolutionaries to disseminate their doctrines openly. By calling for the abolition of the death penalty, the Kadets were encouraging the terrorists. While the Kadets refrained from political violence themselves, their moral principles, the Union asserted, were a sham. How convenient for the Kadets to condemn the execution of terrorists but ignore the assassination of government officials.[46] "Bearers of moral leprosy," Dubrovin called the Kadets, and once he impulsively recommended that the tsar have the Kadet deputies in the Duma committed to a psychiatric hospital.[47]

Aghast at the inroads liberalism was making in society, the Union held that it had crept even into the highest echelons of government. How else to explain the ease with which constitutional demands had obtained official sanction, as evidenced by the creation of a Duma? And who was more to blame than the author of the October Manifesto, Sergei Witte? The Manifesto, charged the Union, had only emboldened the liberal and radical intelligentsia to accelerate their malicious attacks against the tsarist regime. Once, after Dubrovin made an impassioned speech to a crowd of monarchists in St. Petersburg, they streamed onto the street, shouting, "Down with the damned constitution! Death to Count Witte!"[48] Even after his resignation as Chairman of the Council of Ministers in April 1906, Union leaders warned that he would likely attempt a political comeback, a prospect which meant they could not relax their vigilance against the damage he might inflict. Overly concerned about Witte's political future, the Union nonetheless persisted in its attacks.

In its resolve to ferret out Russia's enemies, the Union reserved its greatest antagonism for the Jews, thereby fanning the virulent antisemitism already extant in the country. A dark side of the nationalism pervading Russia since the mid-nineteenth century, this antisemitism disclosed an intuitive willingness to validate one's own identity by denigrating that of others. Undoubtedly, there were many dispirited persons, bewildered by the complexities of modern society and yearning for a more harmonious way of life, who sought comfort by targeting the Jews as the source of their distress. On its part, the Union assiduously denounced the Jews as alien to Russia, scornful of autocracy and Orthodoxy, a clever cabal bent on subverting tradi-tional Russian institutions. In endless speeches, editorials, and brochures, the Union assailed Jewish public figures, such as Vinaver, Herzenstein, Iollos, and other Duma deputies, along with Jewish publicists and lawyers, attributing seditious motives to them all.[49]

Still, it was not these obvious offenders who most vividly stirred Union imaginations. It was instead the "unseen" Jews who aroused the wildest speculations about the hidden perpetrators of the evils besetting Russia. In one of the few publications that Dubrovin wrote personally, *The Secret of Fate*, he described an experience that he regarded as a vision of Russia's past and future. He beheld critical episodes in the country's history that had threatened its very existence, but none had been so perilous as the current danger. As he gazed into the future, he could see nothing but chaos – ruined buildings, deserted streets, desecrated churches. Gradually, he realized that there had been an armed rebellion, which had brought these terrible consequences. No longer was Russia an autocracy, but a democratic republic. In the seat of power, as president, sat a Jew – "the wizard, the black raven of the Russian land." Around him gathered his ministers, all part of the great conspiracy of Jews and their allies. In the background he could hear the moans of prisoners. As he watched spellbound, the vision faded, but he was left with the knowledge that this could be the country's fate, if loyal Russians did not fortify themselves for the task of saving their beloved land.[50]

Aside from Dubrovin's ominous projections, the most striking critique of the Jews occurred in the tirades of G. V. Butmi, a Union member, who frequently spoke at its rallies and wrote for its publications. In one of his most sweeping excursions into the realm of conspiratorial fantasy, published in 1906 and dedicated to the Union under the title *Constitution and Political Freedom*, Butmi portrayed Russia as a vast battlefield in the cosmic struggle between good and evil. Ever since the ancient war in heaven, he contended, the forces of God had been arrayed against those of Satan, and the conflict was in part being acted out on earth. Until the final day, the battle would continue. In Russia's case, those who endeavored to preserve its sacred traditions and the unity of its people composed the army of God; those who strove to destroy, or even tamper with, these traditions and this unity were servants of the devil. More specifically, the Russians had fallen prey to constitutionalism – the "great lie of our times" – little recognizing that behind the entire constitutional movement lurked the Jews. With no attachment to their place of residence, the Jews had placed Russia in the grip of a monstrous conspiracy. Their cry for a constitution was a fraud: they promoted the liberation movement in Russia only in order to gain greater freedom for themselves, so that they could more easily pursue their ultimate objective of enslaving the Russian people and the world.[51]

Obviously, Butmi and others who indulged in these antisemitic tirades believed that the political utility of their accusations far outweighed any question of their authenticity. They understood correctly that by the beginning of the twentieth century, Russian antisemitism had taken on an intensely emotional character, which lent itself to political exploitation. The dichotomy between good and evil offered a simplicity that easily appealed to those who had become distraught over the confused social and political situation in Russia. It also could distort in their minds what may have once been exalted ideals and virtuous motives. Although Butmi's writings, and those of other extremists, abounded with references to the tasks of Christian love, they also expressed an underlying sense of animosity. In the midst of crisis, their essential message was not that of Christian compassion but of Christian combat. The cause was just; let the rancor match the task.

Deeply imbedded in its political rhetoric, the Union's charge of a Jewish conspiracy served as a potent weapon against the constitutional movement, relieving the Union of having to admit that defects in the autocratic system might be contributing to popular discontent. But the Union's demagogic antisemitism had its most damaging consequences by inflaming popular passions to the point of violence against the Jews themselves. Although the Union declared that the anti-Jewish pogroms in Russia were only spontaneous manifestations of the people's wrath, there is little doubt that the Union instigated at least some of them and helped create an incendiary climate conducive to many more. The Union also arranged the assassination of several prominent Jewish political figures.[52] While antisemitism ran throughout the rightist movement, the Union of the Russian People fostered it most blatantly, quite in accord with the Union's extremist stance on most political and social issues.

Perhaps because of its strident call to action, coupled with its promise to restore Russia's hallowed traditions, the Union of the Russian People thrived. Proclaiming the merits of Russian nationality and Orthodoxy, and armed with justifications for autocracy, the Union pursued its mission of reuniting "true Russians" and their tsar. The tsar himself might neglect his autocratic prerogatives, but the Union would instruct him; if he lacked strength of will, the Union would bolster him; should the Russian people lag in their filial affection for the tsar, the Union would rally them. Enlisting members from "all estates and statuses," the Union banked on a commonality of political interests not based on traditional social distinctions, perhaps unintentionally signaling that the estate concept in Russian society was indeed outmoded. As it launched its crusade against the forces of sedition – liberals, radicals, and Jews – the Union on occasion attempted to subdue its enemies by force, its "fighting brotherhoods" indicative of the Union perception of Russia as a country under siege. Yet, for all its militancy, the Union found itself compelled to function within the sphere of practical politics, hoping that, in league with other rightists, it could thwart the opposition parties by gaining control of the Duma.[53] While never as effective in this endeavor as it wished or pretended, the Union took its place at the forefront of the rightist movement, an integral part of Russia's complex political structure.

Plate 2 V. A. Gringmut, editor of *Moskovskiia vedomosti* and founder of the Russian Monarchist Party

Plate 1 A. I. Dubrovin, Chairman of the Union of the Russian People

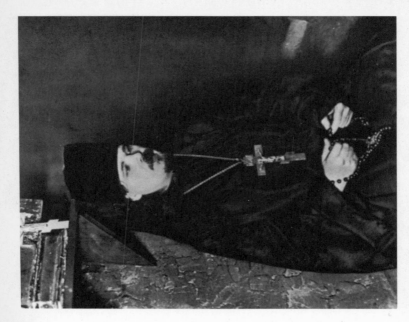

Plate 4 Iliodor, monk and rightist orator at the Pochaev Monastery and elsewhere in Russia

Plate 3 P. A. Krushevan, chairman of the Kishinev branch of the Union of the Russian People and Second Duma deputy

Plate 5 A group of rightist deputies in the Second Duma from Bessarabia province
Seated (l. to r.): V. M. Purishkevich, P. N. Krupinskii, A. K. Demianovich, P. V. Sinadino,
P. A. Krushevan
Standing (l. to r.): E. A. Melenchuk, A. E. Tretiachenko, Iu. G. Herzenberger, Prince D.
N. Sviatopolk-Mirskii

Plate 6 A delegation representing various Moscow monarchist organizations at an
audience with Tsar Nicholas II on 1 December 1905

Plate 7   A monarchist demonstration in Moscow in 1907

Plate 8   Delegates to a national congress of the Union of the Russian People held in Moscow in July 1907

Plate 9   Delegates to the third congress of monarchist organizations held in Kiev in October 1906

Plate 10   Delegates to the fourth congress of monarchist organizations held in Moscow in April 1907

Part II

The formation of regional rightist organizations

6   Rightists in the central provinces

Most political analysts in Russia during the period 1905–1907, who viewed events from the vantage point of either St. Petersburg or Moscow, understandably concentrated their attention on these two centers. Over the years, historians have tended to share that focus, sometimes obscuring the point that in such crucial matters as the Duma elections the provinces played an even more decisive role than the "two capitals." The fact that only ten deputies were allotted to St. Petersburg and Moscow together, while well over four hundred came from the rest of the country, suggests the need to investigate regional politics more thoroughly.

What one finds is that, as rightist parties emerged in St. Petersburg and Moscow during the fall of 1905, loyalists in the provinces also began to organize. Occasionally, they affiliated with national parties; often they operated independently, an indication that the rightist movement was becoming a complex phenomenon. Although these provincial groups all upheld the autocracy, they were also concerned about various regional issues. In the central provinces, where agrarian disorders raged in 1905–1906, rightists stressed the restoration of law and order. In the western borderlands, long marked by ethnic and religious tensions, they emphasized Russian preeminence over the minority nationalities, particularly the Poles and Jews. In both regions, rightists benefited from the presence of natural clienteles – local populaces who welcomed political organizations that promised to resolve these pressing problems.[1]

However, within these general areas, rightists proved stronger in some provinces than in others. In the central agricultural region, they made their biggest impact in Tula, Kursk, and Orel provinces. In the West, they did best in Volynia, Bessarabia, and Minsk provinces, and in the city of Kiev. These variations imply that while regional characteristics were important to the rightist movement, local circumstances had a vital function too. The caliber of leadership appears to have been especially consequential in determining why some rightist organizations outdid others, why moderate or extreme rightists predominated in certain provinces, and why local rightist groups chose either to affiliate with national parties or to remain independent.

In explaining the formation of regional rightist organizations, this chapter will deal with the central agricultural provinces; the following chapter with the western borderlands. Chapter 11 will examine how rightists in these regions fared in the Duma elections.

The agrarian crisis

By all accounts, agrarian problems in the central provinces, which finally triggered peasant violence in 1905, and in turn a conservative reaction, had been building for decades. Victims of chronic economic distress, the peasants suffered especially from the late nineteenth-century population boom. Not only did the peasants, who constituted the bulk of the population, occupy only slightly over half the land, but within that portion family holdings had shrunk appreciably, as shown in Table 3.

In an attempt to distribute land equitably, the communal practice of assigning several small parcels to each household, thus wasting space needed for access to these plots and impeding the use of agricultural machinery, further hampered productivity. Most years, peasants might make a reasonable living; when faced with poor harvests, they could be left in dire circumstances.

Such a crisis occurred in 1905, when the central region was struck by drought. Compared with averages for the previous four years, grain harvests plummeted in Tula, Kursk, Orel, Tambov, Voronezh, and Saratov provinces by 47, 19, 22, 41, 52, and 47 percent respectively, in stark contrast, for instance, to the Ukrainian harvest, which remained close to normal.[2]

Although peasant unrest pervaded Russia in 1905, it erupted most severely in the central provinces. Disorders began in Kursk, then spread swiftly across the entire region. As the Kursk provincial governor, N. N. Gordeev, noted in a report to the Ministry of Internal Affairs, the disturbances focused on "the abnormal relations between private landowners and peasants."[3] This theme was echoed by the Voronezh governor, who attributed the ferment partly to the crippling drought but also to the high rents that peasants had to pay

Table 3 *Central agricultural region*

Province	Peasants in total population	Land held by peasants	Average size of peasant holding (in desiatinas)	
			1877	1905
Tula	90%	55%	9.1	6.3
Kursk	93%	68%	9.5	7.3
Orel	90%	55%	9.8	7.0
Tambov	94%	54%	10.6	7.0
Voronezh	95%	70%	12.7	9.6
Saratov	89%	53%	13.4	9.5

One desiatina equals 2.7 acres.
Sources: *Pervaia vseobshchaia perepis' naseleniia Rossiiskoi imperii 1897 g.* (St. Petersburg, 1904), IX, 2; XX, 2; XXIX, 2; XXXVIII, 2; XLII, 2; XLIV, 2; Tsentral'nyi statisticheskii komitet Ministerstva vnutrennikh del, *Statistika zemlevladeniia 1905 g.* (St. Petersburg, 1906), Vypuski 2, 5, 20, 24, 32, and 37, pp. 10–11 in each.

on estate land.[4] Throughout the central provinces, disaffected peasants demanded lower rents, plus permission to graze their cattle on private meadows and cut wood from private forests.

By mid-summer the situation was growing worse. The Tambov governor reported that crop shortages that year would undoubtedly cause the discontent to spread, and he requested the government to send more troops to the region "just in case they are needed."[5] As the governor anticipated, poor harvests and the approach of winter brought a new surge of peasant disorders. Peasants slaughtered livestock on private estates, burned buildings, and exchanged shots with Cossacks dispatched to quell the disturbances. The authorities soon realized, as did the frightened landowners, that not enough troops were available to stop the violence, which continued to mount.[6] In early December, the procurator of the Tula District Court reported that peasant unrest threatened to develop into a mass phenomenon. He added ominously that "the absence of military force is causing panic among the landowners, whose requests to the administration for assistance appear futile."[7]

Other concerns raised other specters. The central provinces lacked any sizeable worker population, but in the fall of 1905 strikes in Moscow spread rapidly. Early in October, striking railway workers in Kursk and Tula halted all trains and telegraph communication. At first the strikers made the usual economic demands for better wages and working conditions, but before long outside agitators arrived and the rhetoric escalated. Amidst the inflammatory speeches and revolutionary songs, violence frequently broke out. Fights occurred between strikers and skilled workers in the railway shops who refused to join the strikes, and between strikers and soldiers who had been hastily summoned.[8]

This chaotic situation took an even more dramatic turn when the government announced its October Manifesto, proclaiming civil liberties and plans for a popularly elected State Duma. Hardly an incendiary document, the Manifesto nonetheless had a stunning effect, both on oppositionists and on loyalists. In the cities of Tula, Orel, Kursk, Voronezh, and Saratov, anti-government orators claimed a momentary victory but pledged further demands on the autocracy. In response, loyalists paraded through the streets, often clashing with the oppositionists. In Tula, both sides fired shots and a melee ensued, finally broken up by a Cossack detachment but only after a reported nineteen persons had been killed and forty-four wounded. Other cities witnessed similar confrontations.[9]

The mounting turmoil convinced many alarmed conservatives that it was time to act. Unsure what course the government would take, they resolved to marshal their own efforts toward restoring order and producing a loyalist Duma that would challenge the oppositionist forces. Accordingly, several monarchist groups set out to create political parties, the most proficient of which soon appeared in Tula, Kursk, and Orel provinces.

Tula province: the Union for Tsar and Order

Rightist activity in Tula province demonstrates the value of having an existing institutional base upon which to build a party, in this case the provincial zemstvo. Already by October 1905, that body had begun to consider measures for combating disorder and violence. This denoted a marked change in attitude among Tula zemstvists. In August, most had endorsed the government's disclosure that it would convene a consultative assembly, and they had expressed their desire for additional reform. But as peasant and worker unrest grew, some zemstvists retreated to a more defensive position. On 2 October, when Count V. A. Bobrinskii presented a report on the current ferment to the zemstvo assembly, a majority approved his resolution to "unite in upholding order and lawfulness."[10]

Three weeks later, Bobrinskii, A. I. Mosolov, D. D. Levshin, and other conservatives, now a majority in the Tula zemstvo assembly, convened a special session. At it they repudiated the predominantly liberal zemstvo board and agreed to petition the government to bring order to the country. Equally important, they decided to create a political party that could influence the Tula populace to resist revolutionary agitation and elect loyalist deputies to the Duma. This new party they christened the Union for Tsar and Order (*Soiuz za Tsaria i poriadok*).[11]

Bobrinskii became chairman, the most qualified person for the job. Ambitious, energetic, a skilled orator, he exerted a strong imprint on the fledgling organization. After completing his education at Moscow University, he had returned to Tula to manage his wealthy family's estates. Now in his late thirties, he had already served as marshal of the nobility for Bogoroditsk district and as chairman of the Bogoroditsk zemstvo assembly, and for years he had been active in the provincial zemstvo. He also had developed useful connections in St. Petersburg, especially among government officials. Both in Tula and in the capital he enjoyed a solid reputation.

Central to his political objectives, Bobrinskii saw the Duma as the key to reestablishing order and tranquility. He disdained the liberals' enthusiasm for using the Duma to transfer legislative initiative from the throne to the people. Instead, he stated what was fast becoming a standard rightist notion: the Duma should function primarily as a channel of communication between the tsar and his faithful subjects. Through the Duma the restive peasants in particular could convey their concerns to the tsar, confident of a beneficent response.

Given Bobrinskii's personal integrity, there is little reason to doubt his sincerity in championing the peasants' cause, but one can understand that he and his associates also knew that their own economic survival was at stake. They must have a Duma that could help dissuade the peasants from expropriating private property and direct them to government programs for acquiring land through legal means. To achieve both sets of objectives, the Union for Tsar and Order deemed it imperative to convene the Duma quickly.

Early in November, Bobrinskii, Mosolov, and four other Union leaders took their concerns about the Duma to St. Petersburg. There they capitalized on their zemstvo reputations to arrange a meeting with the Chairman of the Council of Ministers, Count Witte, whom they urged to move swiftly in drawing up the election law. Impressed by the delegation's arguments, Witte invited Bobrinskii to attend a

Council of Ministers session, where he repeated his call for speedy action.[12] Shortly afterwards, he made the same plea in an audience with the tsar, painting for Nicholas a poignant vision of peasant ignorance and poverty, compounded by bad harvests. "The peasants in Tula know they cannot expect help from malicious or confused people who tell them lies," Bobrinskii declared, "but only from the tsar. You will learn the truth about the people's needs not by sporadic outcries and complaints but through the State Duma, which you have legally created. We implore you to convene it without delay."[13]

Assured that the government would proceed with sufficient haste in convening the Duma, Bobrinskii and his colleagues returned to Tula, where they set about building their new party. Many conservatives in the provincial zemstvo assembly had already joined; now the Union for Tsar and Order enlisted other landowners. In the city of Tula the Union made converts as well, chiefly among merchants and municipal officials, including the mayor, A. A. Liubomudrov.[14] To broaden its social base, the Union distributed brochures in nearby villages and among employees at the Tula railway depot, where it recruited a number of skilled workers who had opposed the October strike.[15]

The Union's relationship with the Tula railway workers was important because it attested not only to the new organization's reputation but also to cleavages within the labor force. When the Moscow uprising erupted in December 1905, most Tula railway workers walked off the job as a sign of solidarity, closing the Moscow–Kursk line that ran through the city. But on 10 December, the senior telegrapher and his assistants, accompanied by about thirty skilled machinists, met with Union leaders and told them that they wanted to reopen the line but were being prevented by armed revolutionaries. The delegation asked the Union's help to obtain weapons so it could take over the Tula station. In response, Union leaders forwarded the request in person to the Tula vice-governor, A. N. Khvostov, who set up a temporary local railway administration under his own supervision and distributed weapons to loyalist workers. By 15 December, these workers had gotten the trains running again and the Tula shops back into operation. Significantly, Tula was the first location to break the rail stoppage. Moreover, the Union of Tsar and People had secured the allegiance of at least the skilled railway employees.[16]

However, most Union activity did not entail armed resistance to revolutionary agitation but the more routine task of disseminating its message in preparation for the Duma campaigns. In January 1906, it printed 50,000 copies of a speech Bobrinskii had delivered at a Union meeting and a host of brochures. The following month, the Union began publishing a weekly journal, *Truth and Order (Pravda i poriadok)*. In all these materials it called on landowners, peasants, and townspeople alike to uphold the autocracy, asserting that while patriotic Russians were duty-bound to accept the October Manifesto, they should in no way suppose that Russia now had a constitutional monarchy.[17]

Union publications concentrated on agrarian issues. Despite widespread unrest, the Union contended that most peasants recognized that the radical parties were falsely promising free farmland and that far more realistic was the government's guarantee to help obtain additional property through low-interest loans.[18] At a Union meeting in February 1906, a peasant from Bogoroditsk district told his audience that although political agitators had circulated revolutionary proclamations in his village, the peasants there were still "firm in the faith and true to the tsar."[19] This declaration may not have represented peasant attitudes in general, but the Union could well assume that, like the Tula railway workers, the peasants were not of one mind, and that some would heed the Union's patriotic call.

During their first few months, the Union and other Tula parties experienced frequent shifts in membership, evidence that political lines in the provinces had not become as sharply drawn as in the urban centers.[20] Imprecise party labels made it uncertain where a law-and-order association like the Union fitted into the emerging political spectrum. Some Union members defected to the Octobrists, while right-wing Octobrists occasionally went over to the Union.[21] In addition, a few Unionists, who felt the party was not conservative enough, split off and founded the Union for Faith and Order.[22] This group remained only a minor factor in Tula politics, but in August 1906 it collaborated with other ultraconservatives, who either had not yet left the Union for Tsar and Order or had never joined, in opening a branch of the Union of the Russian People. After several leadership disputes, Prince M. A. Cherkasskii, who had published the Union for Tsar and Order's *Pravda i poriadok*, became branch chairman. Less restrained than before his defection, Cherkasskii led the Tula URP in a vehemently antiliberal, antisemitic campaign, making demagogic speeches and distributing thousands of brochures sent from URP headquarters in St. Petersburg.[23]

The contrast between the Union for Tsar and Order and the Union of the Russian People epitomized the distinctions between moderate and extreme rightists. Less reactionary in its program, less combative in its tactics than the URP, the Union for Tsar and Order also appealed to a somewhat different social milieu. As already indicated, the UTO depended primarily on the landed gentry, merchants, nobles residing in the cities, and public officials. Insofar as it attracted workers, these were usually craftsmen and supervisory personnel. The URP, both in Tula and elsewhere, recruited mainly from the *meshchanstvo* – lower middle class townspeople, such as shopkeepers, petty traders, and minor government clerks – and to a lesser extent from the working class. At times, both the moderate and extreme rightists drew peasant support. Although some URP leaders, like Prince Cherkasskii, belonged to the nobility, conservative nobles typically gravitated to the moderately rightist organizations. Still, the differences between moderate and extreme rightists, while discernible, were not profound. In social composition and programs the groups overlapped, and they often cooperated in their political campaigning.[24]

Why the moderate rightist Union for Tsar and Order had greater success in Tula province than the more extreme Union of the Russian People is difficult to explain precisely, but local leadership evidently played a significant part. As Robert Edelman has pointed out in regard to situations elsewhere in the country, locally recognized "men of honor" or eminent families could have a disproportionate influence on provincial politics.[25] In confirming the validity of this observation, one can instructively compare rightist activity in Tula with that in certain other provinces. For example, in Kursk, Count V. F. Dorrer and Prince N. F. Kasatkin-Rostovskii, who headed the province's major rightist organization, the People's Party of Order, relied on their reputations as zemstvists and marshals of the nobility to infuse a highly reactionary temper into their party. In Bessarabia, the powerful Krupinskii family dominated the moderately rightist Center Party, which flourished throughout the province (except in Akkerman district, where the reactionary V. M. Purishkevich, son of an entrenched local family long active in district affairs, built a thriving Union of the Russian People branch). Likewise, in Tula province Bobrinskii and Mosolov, both prominent zemstvists, utilized their zemstvo connections to channel conservative sentiment into their moderately rightist Union for Tsar and Order. As a result, the Union prospered, as can be seen in its remarkable success in the Duma elections, which will be discussed in Chapter 11.

Kursk province: the People's Party of Order

As in Tula province, the major law-and-order party in Kursk originated with local zemstvo leaders, who used this institution as their base of operations. Since 1903, Count V. F. Dorrer, the provincial marshal of the nobility; Prince N. F. Kasatkin-Rostovskii, the Novyi Oskol district marshal; and other ultraconservatives had dominated the Kursk zemstvo. While many zemstvos called for political reform, this one repeatedly voiced its support for the autocracy. Although it briefly endorsed a national assembly in 1904, it declared that it in no way advocated a legislative body.[26]

After the 18 February rescript, which intimated that indeed an assembly would convene, these zemstvists, worried that the assembly's powers might surpass what they could willingly accept, used their influence in an attempt to forestall this possibility. On 20 June 1905, Dorrer, Kasatkin-Rostovskii, and five other Kursk nobles arrived at Peterhof for an audience with the tsar. They encouraged Nicholas to make certain that the assembly would be only a consultative body and that elections would be based on the traditional Russian estates, an apparent effort to prevent the introduction of universal suffrage, which would put the peasantry at a decided advantage over the vastly outnumbered nobility. Nicholas replied that the assembly would be consultative – his first pronouncement on the nature of the proposed body – and he indicated that he favored elections by estates.[27] The next day, Dorrer joined another delegation, led by Count P. S. Sheremetev from the Union of Russian Men and A. A. Bobrinskii from the Patriotic Union. These spokesmen also urged estate representation, and they assured the tsar that this was what both the nobility and the peasantry preferred. This time Nicholas was more equivocal in his reply, leaving the delegation unsure about his intentions.[28]

Perplexed by the monarch's ambivalence and disturbed by the mounting discontent in Russia, Dorrer and his associates concluded that they must take greater initiative themselves.[29] Both Dorrer and Kasatkin-Rostovskii had spent much time in St. Petersburg, where they had already become familiar with monarchist organizations. Dorrer belonged to the Russian Assembly and Kasatkin-Rostovskii to the Patriotic Union.[30] Now they wanted to found a local monarchist party in Kursk. Early that fall – even before the October Manifesto and the ensuing tumult in the city of Kursk – they and their loyalist colleagues announced the creation of the People's Party of Order (*Narodnaia partiia poriadka*).[31]

From the outset, PPO leaders stated that their objective was to unify all strata of Kursk society in restoring order and bolstering the throne. This seemed a difficult task since the landed nobility clearly dominated the new party. Among its founders were six district marshals of the nobility (in addition to Dorrer, the provincial marshal), four land captains, and several other large estate owners, along with a few merchants from the city of Kursk.[32] But PPO leaders reasoned that they could also attract peasants who had not engaged in the agrarian disturbances and who would welcome the Party's emphasis on law and order. Although peasants responded less enthusiastically than anticipated, the PPO claimed in January 1906 to have a membership exceeding 1,500 persons. If even approximately correct, this figure suggests that members came not only from the upper classes. Some were likely peasants, others townspeople, quite possibly including participants in the counter-demonstrations following the October Manifesto.[33]

The PPO initially published a rather conventional rightist program, which emphasized autocratic rule, Orthodoxy, and Russian preeminence. While upholding freedom of speech, press, and assembly – a demand that was rapidly entering Russia's political lexicon – the PPO insisted that the exercise of this freedom must not disrupt the political and social order. On the land question, it took the usual rightist stance of advocating government assistance to peasants who wished to buy additional land or resettle in less densely populated areas. The PPO identified the Kadets as its principal opponents, and it promised to send loyalist deputies to the Duma, who would block the Kadets from turning that body into a full-fledged parliament or a constituent assembly.[34]

In late October 1905, the PPO issued a proclamation having a much harsher tone than its official program. Designed specifically to play on peasant emotions, it painted a dreadful picture of how the Kadets were attempting to subvert the tsar, destroy the holy Orthodox faith, and give equal rights to Jews, who the PPO charged would employ their new-found freedom to enslave the Russian people. So inflammatory was this proclamation that the Kursk provincial governor forbade a PPO meeting scheduled for 5 November, because he feared that it would produce a wave of violence. Still, the proclamation was read in parish churches and distributed in towns and villages. When the correspondent I. P. Belokonskii visited Kursk in early November, he reported that many peasants had already heard this antiliberal, antisemitic message.[35]

Determined to oppose the Kadets in the Duma campaign, the PPO was less sure about what action to take against the revolutionaries. At a PPO meeting on 27 December 1905, most speakers contended that the PPO should limit itself to distributing antirevolutionary literature. But N. E. Markov, a PPO extremist, recommended organizing an armed *druzhina* – a "brotherhood" – to fight the revolutionaries, and over 400 persons reportedly signed up as prospective members.[36] Despite this enthusiastic outburst, there is little evidence that the PPO actually resorted to the use of force. What occurred most frequently was intimidation. In his report on Kursk, Belokonskii noted that rightists were going door to door in the provincial capital, demanding to know whether residents were for or against the tsar and issuing threats against those who declined to pledge their loyalty. Belokonskii did not suggest that these threats resulted in physical injury, but they no doubt had a daunting effect.[37]

Having failed to poll heavily in the First Duma elections in March 1906, the People's Party of Order realized that it must overcome its image as a party dominated by the landed nobility. Consequently, its leaders worked at aligning the PPO with other, more popularly based rightist organizations, such as the newly formed Kursk branch of the Union of Russian Workers. The Union, which had originated in Kiev in September, opened its Kursk branch on 27 November with the goal of uniting loyalist workers and peasants. Besides upholding the autocracy and the Orthodox faith, the Union promised to provide mutual economic support among its members and to raise the moral and educational level of the common people. Count Dorrer made a point of attending the initial meeting of the Union's Kursk branch; and on 6 December, he chaired a session sponsored by PPO and Union leaders, at which the two groups agreed to run joint candidates in the Second Duma campaign.[38]

Dorrer and other PPO leaders then endeavored to expand the Party's popular appeal even further. On 31 December 1906, after extended negotiations, the PPO formally affiliated with the Union of the Russian People. By the Second Duma campaign in early 1907, the PPO had become known as the Kursk Union of the Russian People (Kursk People's Party of Order) – a cumbersome name designed to preserve the PPO's individuality while associating it with the nation-wide URP.[39]

The URP(PPO) also broadened its leadership, at the same time introducing a more demagogic character to its public appeals. Dorrer and Kasatkin-Rostovskii continued to direct the Party, but the reactionary N. E. Markov now became its staunchest spokesman. Markov contributed a remarkably strident tone to the restructured PPO through his vehement antisemitism.[40] The URP(PPO) also utilized the oratorical ability of G. V. Deriugin, a merchant who helped start the PPO and now heralded the monarchist cause among the urban electorate.[41]

Capably led and organized, the People's Party of Order had become a substantial force in Kursk province. Indeed, it suffered from its upper-class origins, but now affiliated with the Union of the Russian People and allied with the Union of Russian Workers, it was drawing wide popular support, presumably sufficient to outbid the oppositionist parties in the Second Duma elections.[42]

Orel province: the Union of Law and Order

The formation of a law-and-order party in Orel province followed the same pattern as in Tula and Kursk, except that the initiative came not from zemstvists but from merchants in the provincial capital. While these merchants lacked the institutional base that the Tula and Kursk zemstvists enjoyed – the Orel provincial zemstvo had never been as effectively organized – they still had a sense of corporate identity, particularly through their representation in the municipal duma. Moreover, they shared a deep concern over the current agrarian turmoil. Merchants in the city of Orel had long maintained close connections with the countryside. Over 60 percent dealt in agricultural trade: grain, livestock, and other rural products.[43] Many owned land, which they rented to peasants, making these merchants almost as distressed about the agrarian unrest as was the landed nobility.

They were disturbed as well by worker ferment in the cities. There was little industry and only a small labor force in the province, but employees in the railway shops in Orel and the iron foundry in Briansk had struck in the fall of 1905. Almost as disquieting was the fact that many workers, fresh from the countryside, expressed their sympathy with the grievances of peasants living in the villages.[44]

The October Manifesto brought these issues to a head. On 18 October, when news of the Manifesto reached Orel, local merchants organized patriotic demonstrations. Loyalists paraded through the streets, frequently clashing with oppositionists, who were celebrating their apparent victory over the autocracy. Passions soared, and soon from the loyalist side a raucous mob was assaulting passers-by and vandalizing Jewish shops. Eventually, Cossacks dispersed both the anti-government and loyalist demonstrators, but the melee left several persons dead or injured.[45]

Although loyalist leaders did not condone the attack on the Jews, they concluded that they must take more systematic action in stopping the opposition. On 22 October, they organized the Union of Law and Order (*Soiuz zakonnosti i poriadka*), choosing Ia. A. Pomerantsev as chairman. Membership grew rapidly and by early December numbered over 400 persons. Many were merchants, but the Union also drew into its ranks priests, artisans, and civil servants, including Orel's mayor. Gradually, nobles, some belonging to the conservative Orel zemstvo, also joined.[46]

In its program, the Union focused on the agrarian problem, towards which it exhibited both the genuine concern about peasant needs and the self-interest that typified law-and-order parties. Promising to help improve the peasants' economic lot, it called for cheaper credit through the Peasant Land Bank for buying private land. It also entreated the tsar to listen to the "true voice of the people" in the forthcoming Duma, which it pictured as a great zemskii sobor, where the peasants could express their needs.[47] The Union left little doubt that it hoped the peasants would simply trust the tsar to act on their behalf, not rely on the Duma to legislate land reform, which the Union knew would encroach on the principle of private property.

Surely, what the Union wanted most was pacification. To this end it publicized statements from peasants themselves that they felt a common purpose with the landed nobility. A letter from an old peasant woman, printed in the Union's newspaper, *Orlovskaia rech'*, read:

> Russian peasants! Something terrible is happening to Rus'. What are you thinking about? Burning farmsteads, slaughtering livestock, stealing grain and dumping it in the river! The landowners are your friends. You need each other ... and Russia needs the estates: nobility, clergy, merchants, peasants – all under God.[48]

The Union also recognized that, like the People's Party of Order in Kursk, it might enhance its popular appeal by joining the "non-estate" Union of the Russian People. However, Union members hesitated to relinquish their independent status and to accede to the URP's extremist orientation. After much debate, they decided in the summer of 1906 to affiliate with the URP but on condition that the Union of Law and Order retain its original name and operate under its own statutes, an arrangement not very satisfactory to the URP.[49] Finally, in June 1907, the Union bowed to URP pressure and became a full-fledged branch, subscribing to the URP's statutes and its ultraconservative image. While losing some members by taking this action, the Union gained others, chiefly local monarchists who would probably have joined the URP if it had simply created a branch in Orel, instead of incorporating the Union of Law and Order.[50]

Because of this organizational maneuvering, rightist activity in Orel province was somewhat complicated. Before affiliating with the URP, the Union of Law and Order had begun to expand its operations: in January 1906, it formed a branch in the town of Sevsk; and it distributed literature in numerous villages. Later in 1906 and in early 1907, this activity continued, but the URP also started its own branches in Briansk, Elets, and several villages. All in all, by the Second Duma elections in March 1907, rightist campaigning had reached throughout the province, making the rightists into serious political contenders.[51]

Other rightist activity

Rightists in the other central agricultural provinces were not as efficiently organized as in Tula, Kursk, and Orel. In Tambov and Voronezh, and in the adjacent middle Volga province of Saratov, peasant disorders in 1905–1906 produced widespread alarm among landowners, urban residents, and even some peasants.[52] But in none of these provinces did major local rightist associations arise. Instead, rightist activity depended primarily on the national rightist organizations' ability to establish branches and enlist popular support.

Occasionally, these branches flourished. In the city of Tambov, a small group calling itself the Party of the Russian People (*Partiia russkikh liudei*) had emerged in the summer of 1905, distributed some patriotic literature, then faded from public view.[53] Apparently, its failure resulted more from lack of proficient leadership than from lack of popular interest, for when the Moscow-based Union of Russian Men formed a branch in Tambov in November 1905, it quickly attracted many townspeople. Archmandrite Feodor served as chairman, and other Orthodox clerics joined. Among its early members were several hundred railway employees, mainly skilled workers, who had not sided with the strike movement during the fall. The Union excelled in disseminating its message, partly through the admonitions of local clerics but also through the thousands of brochures it distributed. With the help of parish priests, the Union soon built branches in about thirty villages, evidence of its ability to identify with the religious and patriotic sensitivities of the peasants.[54]

In addition, the Union of the Russian People opened branches during 1906 and 1907 in the cities of Tambov and Kozlov, and in several villages. Like the Union of Russian Men, it targeted not only the traditionally conservative provincial landowners but also workers and peasants.[55] In this task both the URM and URP evidently succeeded, as indicated by the sizeable rightist vote in the Duma elections (see Chapter 11).

No major local rightist groups and only a few Union of the Russian People branches appeared in Voronezh province, leaving it impossible to know how much popular response might have resulted had there been better rightist leadership.[56]

In Saratov province, the People's Monarchist Party (*Narodno-monarkhicheskaia partiia*), which resembled the law-and-order parties in Tula, Kursk, and Orel, was founded in 1905, but it remained poorly coordinated and exerted little influence.[57] Although the Union of the Russian People and the Union of Russian Men set up several branches in the province, these were little match for those organized by the Peasant Union, Trudoviks, and Socialist Revolutionaries.[58] Clearly, the political dynamism of the rightist parties resided in Tula, Kursk, and Orel.[59]

In assessing rightist activity in the central agricultural provinces, one can hardly exaggerate the impact that the agrarian crisis of 1905–1906 had on regional politics. The law-and-order parties seemed a natural consequence of the landowners' alarm at the current peasant turmoil, a concern shared by many townspeople having ties with the countryside and even by some peasants. Rightist objectives focused on all these social strata. By insisting that the government reestablish order and demonstrating their willingness to campaign against those parties advocating mandatory land redistribution, the rightists were virtually assured of attracting landowners and propertied urban residents. Rightist leaders were less certain of success in persuading peasants to rely on lawful means for acquiring land, but they correctly discerned the value of directing religious and patriotic appeals at their peasant audiences, something that parish clerics had already been doing to considerable avail.

It becomes apparent too that rightist fortunes depended on the adeptness of local leadership in directing this public sentiment to political ends. Enterprising rightist leaders in Tula, Kursk, and Orel provinces capably utilized the zemstvos and municipal dumas as institutional bases for disseminating their message and recruiting members. These leaders also proved instrumental in determining the moderate or extremist orientations of their particular parties and whether or not these would remain independent of national rightist organizations. The significance of regional circumstances and local leadership will become further apparent as we examine rightist activity elsewhere in the country and discuss the Duma elections more thoroughly (in Chapters 7 and 11).

7   Rightists in the western borderlands

Rightist activity in the western borderlands was even more complex than in the central agricultural provinces, mainly because of national and religious issues in the West. It was common knowledge that Russians, Ukrainians, and Belorussians had long experienced friction among themselves, but more crucial to political events in 1905–1907 was the fact that most of them felt a greater antipathy toward Polish Catholics and Jews living in the region. It was hardly an accident that rightist organizations on the western periphery placed these anti-Polish and anti-Jewish concerns at the center of their political agenda, often giving them greater prominence than the standard rightist emphasis on preserving the Russian autocracy.

Rightist fortunes in the West varied from province to province, just as they did in the central region. Rightists were strongest in Volynia, where politically minded monks at the Pochaev Monastery constructed a well-integrated network of branches; in Bessarabia, where the Center Party and Union of the Russian People dominated provincial politics; in Minsk, where the Russian Borderland Union did the same; and in the city of Kiev, where local rightist groups succeeded in assembling a powerful coalition, unmatched anywhere else in the empire. One can safely conclude that in these places, rightist leadership proved invaluable in building efficient party organizations, which were able to channel popular ethnic and religious sentiments to political ends. By the same token, local leaders seem to have been the key in shaping the moderate or extremist character of their organizations and in deciding whether they should affiliate with national parties or remain independent. These features become apparent as one examines rightist operations in the various locations.

Volynia: Rightists at the Pochaev Monastery

The rightists' outstanding success in Volynia province reflected the unusual political role of the Pochaev Monastery. As a base for political activity, the Monastery served in much the same way as the zemstvos did for rightists in Tula and Kursk. Not only did the Pochaev monks enjoy a firm institutional foundation – the Monastery itself – but they engaged clerics throughout the province to disseminate the Monastery's political message and help mold an extensive, highly coordinated political organization.

For decades, the Pochaev Monastery had been a bastion of conservatism. In addition to their typical monastic duties, its four hundred monks published religious tracts and booklets, and since 1887 a weekly religious newspaper, *Pochaevskii listok* (*The Pochaev Leaflet*), which carried the slogan "For the Faith, Tsar, and Fatherland."[1] The monastery's abbot, Archmandrite Vitalii, a dedicated monarchist, abhorred the turmoil erupting across Russia during 1905 and agreed that loyalists must defend the established order. When a close friend, Archmandrite Anastasii, rector of the Moscow Ecclesiastical Seminary, told him about the recently founded Moscow branch of the Union of the Russian People, Vitalii resolved to start a similar body. Following lengthy discussions about whether to create an independent monarchist group or affiliate with the URP, Vitalii and his associates chose to join, albeit with the provision that the Pochaev branch maintain a high degree of autonomy. On 13 August 1906, the branch opened, amidst great ceremony, with Vitalii as its chairman.[2]

Having secured the enthusiastic approval of Archbishop Antonii of Volynia, who urged priests in his diocese to back "the struggle against sedition," the Pochaev branch set to work. In September it began publishing *Pochaevskiia izvestiia* (*The Pochaev News*), a daily news sheet that reported the Monastery's political and religious activities and included frequent patriotic messages. Equally important, Vitalii and the Pochaev monks opened village branches throughout the area. Nominally, these were URP branches, but from their inception they functioned under the Pochaev parent organization. In *Pochaevskiia izvestiia* and through parish priests, the Monastery's leadership encouraged villagers, once they had at least thirty prospective members, to request permission from the local authorities to form their own branch. Soon branches were appearing all over Volynia and even in the adjacent province of Podolia.[3] Although it is difficult to find information on exactly how local monarchists went about affiliating with provincial or national rightist organizations, the following letter, printed in *Pochaevskiia izvestiia*, provides an instructive account of how peasants in the village of Repinets responded to the Monastery's call.[4]

> We will tell you how our union began. On 21 November 1906, fifty householders in Repinets, led by Onufrii Melnik, Savva Kostiuk, and Grigorii Gritsiuk, signed a petition. Then we went to our priest and told him we wanted to open a union. We gave the priest a copy of *Pochaevskiia izvestiia*, which told about the Union of the Russian People being opened in the villages. We requested the father to conduct a service for the well-being of the sovereign and all the tsar's household on 26 November, and we sent news of this to the Pochaev Monastery and to our local police chief. After the regular mass on 26 November, a thanksgiving service was celebrated at noon in our parish church, at which time the police chief arrived. He visited the three of us in our cottage and asked about our intentions for opening a union. We answered that we wanted to join the Union of the Russian People for the sake of the faith, the tsar, and the fatherland. The police chief said, "This is a good thing that the three of you are doing, but you need to take your request to the district police chief." So we went at once with our local police chief to the district police chief in Kamenets, who told us to go to the vice-governor's office. The vice-governor told us in person, "God be with you! This is a good thing to do. Go back home and get your village together with your village elder present, and name your delegate [to the forthcoming electoral assembly for the Second Duma]." We did as he said, and the village elder came to our meeting. On 1 December, we gathered by the parish church's school, went to the church, and had a service to the Lord God. Altogether 129 persons signed up as Union of the Russian People members, and we elected Onufrii Melnik as our delegate.
>
> Signed: Savva Kostiuk, Chairman.

The Pochaev Monastery's efforts to establish URP branches met with great success. On 27 October 1906, URP headquarters in St. Petersburg reported by name 109 village branches in the Volynia area. At about the same time the Pochaev URP informed the tsar that the Union had members in 536 villages in Volynia and Podolia. A week later it raised the figure to "almost 700."[5] This seems an unusually high number, but it may be accurate, since it refers not to the number of branches but of villages having members, meaning that some peasants may have joined branches in neighboring villages. In any case, there is evidence that URP branches stretched entirely across Volynia and well into Podolia.

Given the national and religious animosities that pervaded the western provinces, it is not surprising that the Pochaev Monastery indulged in antisemitic and anti-Polish propaganda. Yet, it is striking how incessantly the Monastery flooded its branches with attacks on the Jews, an unmistakable sign of the depth to which antisemitism was imbedded in Volynia's rightist politics.[6] The Jews, warned *Pochaevskiia izvestiia*, hated the Russian people and intended to subjugate them. In order to avoid the yoke of the "intrusive *zhid*," Christians should not buy goods from Jewish merchants, go to Jewish physicians or lawyers, deal with Jewish bankers, or permit Jewish children to attend school with Orthodox children. Above all, it was imperative to keep Jews out of the Duma and to make sure that the Duma passed no legislation granting equal rights for Jews. Without actually advocating violence against the Jews, the Pochaev URP repeated a common antisemitic charge that "in the pogroms no one is guilty but the Jews themselves."[7]

In its campaign against exploitation by the Jews, the Pochaev URP pledged practical help to the peasants. It argued that what the peasants needed was not mandatory redistribution of private estates, as the radical parties contended, but permission to dissolve the communes and an opportunity to get low-interest government loans for buying private land. Although peasant demands for expropriation abounded in central Russia, the Pochaev URP reasoned, perhaps validly, that Volynian peasants, who were not as economically depressed nor exposed to as much leftist agitation, would accept the option of purchasing land, if indeed they could count on government assistance. To augment its appeal to the peasants, the Pochaev URP and its branches offered direct financial aid. In many villages the URP opened shops where members could purchase sugar, tea, tobacco, and manufactured goods at reasonable prices. Buying at these shops, the URP reminded the peasants, enabled them to avoid being exploited by Jewish shopkeepers.[8]

To its constant anti-Jewish barrage, *Pochaevskiia izvestiia* sometimes added anti-Polish editorials, charging that the Poles had always despised the Russians and Ukrainians, an antipathy instilled in Polish children from infancy.[9] The authors of these anti-Polish diatribes knew that many Volynian peasants resented the fact that Poles comprised over half of the province's landed nobility.[10] *Pochaevskiia izvestiia* also hoped to play on traditional frictions between Orthodox Ukrainian or Russian nobles in Volynia and their Polish Catholic counterparts. Overall, the Pochaev URP anticipated that religious and ethnic bonds between the Volynian peasantry and the Ukrainian and Russian landed nobility would prove stronger than class differences – an assumption adequately borne out by later Duma elections.

The Pochaev URP excelled in disseminating its message. In addition to distributing *Pochaevskiia izvestiia* and numerous brochures, it furnished a ready supply of speakers. Parish priests frequently addressed peasant gatherings and delivered sermons denouncing Jews and liberal intellectuals, and calling for the election of loyalist Duma deputies. Capable orators spoke at the Monastery or toured the province. Undoubtedly, the most renowned – or notorious – speaker was the monk Iliodor, the Russian clergy's *enfant terrible*. Iliodor arrived at the Pochaev Monastery in the fall of 1906, having already achieved a reputation as a persuasive preacher and patriotic orator in Iaroslavl province. Still in his twenties, he spoke with a vehemence that belied his youth, inveighing against the liberal and radical intelligentsia and condemning the Jews for exploiting the Russian people.[11] Years later in his memoirs, Iliodor wrote, "The Jews I hated with every fiber of my soul."[12] He also criticized those landowners who sold land to speculators for cash instead of offering it to Ukrainian and Russian peasants on installments. Combining demagoguery with a basic social and economic logic, Iliodor gave his peasant audiences a potent dose of right-wing populism. His abusive rhetoric may have alienated some listeners, and his assaults on the government prompted Volynia's vice-governor to ask Archbishop Antonii to curb Iliodor's preaching; but he never failed to draw huge crowds.[13] While most Pochaev speakers were less strident than Iliodor, they too contributed to the rightist cause.

Largely because of the Pochaev Monastery, Volynia became a rightist stronghold, as demonstrated by the Volynian rightists' sweeping victory in the Second Duma elections (see Chapter 11). This success testified not only to the Pochaev monks' vitality but to their adeptness in using their ecclesiastical network for political purposes. Particularly significant was the extent to which local clerics reached into rural areas, making the Volynian rightist movement predominantly a peasant phenomenon. While this clergy–peasant connection differentiated Volynia from other provinces, it illustrated the crucial relationship between political leadership, whatever its nature, and the local populace.

Bessarabia: the Bessarabian Center Party and the Union of the Russian People

Rightist strength in Bessarabia, as in Volynia, reflected national and religious issues. However, Bessarabia's rightist leadership came not from the clergy but mainly from Ukrainian, Russian, and Russified Moldavian landowners.[14] This leadership produced two major rightist associations: the moderately rightist Bessarabian Center Party, which functioned independently; and the extremist Union of the Russian People, which was closely affiliated with the central URP organization. Both worked primarily through an already existing zemstvo network to attract landowners and to a lesser degree peasants. As a result, Bessarabia became another rightist bulwark.

The Bessarabian Center Party owed its origins to P. N. Krupinskii and a group of conservative landowners associated as zemstvists. Krupinskii belonged to a prominent and wealthy Bessarabian family, which had for years held posts in the provincial and district zemstvos and served as marshals of the nobility and honorary justices of the peace.[15] During the winter of 1904–1905, Krupinskii cautiously endorsed the Bessarabian provincial zemstvo's call for a national legislative assembly and broad individual liberties. As turmoil intensified in 1905, he and other zemstvists turned more conservative, sensing the growing need to protect their interests as landowners.[16] After the October Manifesto, Krupinskii and his associates concluded that the time had come to organize politically, in preparation for the projected Duma, and to this end they founded the Center Party (*Partiia tsentra*).

Although the Bessarabian Center Party was not as "centrist" as its creators maintained, neither was it extremely rightist. Located on the political spectrum somewhere between the Octobrists and the Union of the Russian People, it can best be described as "moderate rightist." It upheld the principle of autocracy but also endorsed a legislative Duma, a rather ambivalent position, similar to that taken by the Octobrists.[17] Like most rightists in the borderlands, the Center Party emphasized the indivisibility of the Russian empire, and it declared that Russia must be protected against "foreign elements," which intimated both Jews and Poles. In the economic sphere, the Center Party advocated the inviolability of private property. For the peasants, it took the usual rightist stand of urging government assistance in purchasing land and in moving to less populated areas, policies which in no way would interfere with the property rights of the landed nobility.[18]

Within a few months, the Center Party had established itself throughout most of Bessarabia. Because the zemstvos provided a convenient means to communicate with landowners, the Center Party made no attempt to set up branches, operating instead as a single integrated organization. While this approach enabled the Party to build a solid base among major landowners, it hampered efforts to attract peasants. Consequently, the Center Party, as prominent as it became, remained more estate-oriented than did Bessarabia's other premier rightist association – the Union of the Russian People.

The Union of the Russian People developed two power centers in Bessarabia, one in Akkerman district, the other in the provincial capital – Kishinev. In Akkerman district, the URP's principal organizer, V. M. Purishkevich, came from a well-known landowning family. While in his twenties, he had served as chairman of the Akkerman district zemstvo, a body in which his father had been active for years.[19] In 1900, he left Bessarabia to enter government service in St. Petersburg. There he met A. I. Dubrovin, whom he later helped found the Union of the Russian People. Throughout these years, Purishkevich kept close contact with affairs in Bessarabia; and, early in 1906, he opened and chaired the Akkerman URP branch. Already in March he claimed that the branch had over 5,000 members – probably an exaggeration – and was growing daily. Whatever the number, there seem to have been members both in the city of Akkerman and elsewhere in the district. Too late for the First Duma campaign, the branch energetically disseminated patriotic and anti-semitic literature, and urged the tsar to resist any Duma efforts to enact Jewish rights or radical land reform.[20] By the Second Duma campaign, Purishkevich was spending much time in Akkerman district, exhorting the electorate to send reliable deputies to the Duma.

In Kishinev, the preeminent URP leader was P. A. Krushevan, who, until 1905, had been the outspoken antisemitic editor of Kishinev's foremost daily newspaper, *Bessarabets*. In 1903, Krushevan's editorializing had ignited the infamous Kishinev pogrom against the Jews. An unrelenting antisemite and ultramonarchist, Krushevan found his place not in the Bessarabian Center Party but in the URP, a branch of which he opened in Kishinev in June 1906.[21]

From its inception, the branch thrived. It recruited a diverse membership: civil servants, shopkeepers, clerics, military officers, artisans, workers; and it distributed antisemitic and monarchist proclamations.[22] It also planted sub-branches in the city's outskirts and supported the URP in forming branches in nearby towns and villages.[23] Both the parent Kishinev branches and its sub-branches organized *druzhiny* – bands of young activists who reportedly armed themselves, a development that concerned not only local authorities but also the moderately rightist Bessarabian Center Party, which repeatedly criticized Krushevan and his associates for their extremism.

Both the Union of the Russian People and the Center Party grew steadily. Operating independently of each other, they dominated Bessarabian politics, attracting enough voters by the Second Duma elections to produce rightist victories in the province generally and in Kishinev, which had its own Duma deputy (see Chapter 11). Rightist success in Bessarabia, like that in Volynia, thus attested equally to the presence of a natural clientele and to the decisive role of local leadership in capitalizing on popular national and religious concerns.

The city of Kiev and its rightist coalition

The city of Kiev deserves special attention, since it was one of the few large cities where rightists predominated. Kiev provides a striking study of the efficacy of political blocs, for in Kiev a well-integrated rightist coalition proved powerful enough to swing Duma elections and make a lasting political imprint on the local population.

Besides having proficient leadership, several factors contributed to rightist strength in Kiev. Significantly, Kiev was not as industrialized as Moscow and St. Petersburg. Although Kiev was the empire's fourth largest city with a population of about 400,000, only about 2 percent of its residents in 1905 were factory workers. The main railway shops and the Demievka sugar refinery each employed over 1,000 workers, but most Kievan laborers were craftsmen, service personnel, or day workers. Consequently, Kiev experienced less labor agitation than the highly industrialized cities.[24]

The Kievan populace also seemed less politically conscious and more religiously inclined. Kiev had long been a magnet for religious pilgrims, who numbered from 150,000 to 200,000 a year; and many local residents dealt in religious items: candles, incense, and souvenirs. Moreover, professional persons in Kiev tended to be quite conservative, a trait probably related to Kiev's non-industrial and religious nature.[25]

Still, in the fall of 1905, Kiev shared the country's turmoil. Railway workers went on strike in early October; and when the October Manifesto was announced, dissident intellectuals gathered near the

university and marched through the city. In some instances, oppositionists clashed with troops. Patriotic demonstrators staged their own
processions, bearing national flags and portraits of the tsar. Spurred
on by the mounting discord, bands of extremists stormed Jewish
homes and shops over the next several days, often exchanging fire
with Jews attempting to defend themselves. By the time the violence
subsided, the official count of persons killed numbered sixty-eight,
including both Jews and Christians, and property damage and looting
totaled an estimated four million rubles.[26] Perhaps more than
anticipated, these manifestations presaged the intense loyalist sentiment and antisemitism that would pervade rightist politics in Kiev.

Kiev's rightist coalition owed its success to both the harmony and
diversity of its six constituent groups. Not only did they cooperate
remarkably well, with little jealousy over individual prerogatives, but
they attracted different social strata, which gave the coalition an
unusually comprehensive appeal. While the Party of Legal Order,
Russian Monarchist Party, and Union of Russian Workers dominated
the coalition, the Russian Assembly, Union of the Russian People, and
Russian Brotherhood helped project an image of unity and strength.

The first rightist organization to become a substantial political force
in Kiev was a branch of the national Party of Legal Order (*Partiia
pravovago poriadka*). The PLO originated in St. Petersburg in October
1905, fashioned by a splinter group from the zemstvo congress that
had just met in Moscow. Dissatisfied with the liberal participants in
the congress, who went on to form either the Kadets or Octobrists, the
Party of Legal Order nonetheless initially called itself a constitutionalist party. However, this was an ambiguous designation, meaning
only that it advocated individual liberties and reluctantly upheld the
new Duma structure, not that it desired "constitutional" restrictions
on the autocracy. Importantly, the PLO emphasized the preservation
of civil stability through strict adherence to the law and the
indivisibility of the Russian empire through strong state authority.
This blend of Russian nationalism and insistence on law and order,
plus the PLO's explicit objection to Jewish equality, placed it
politically somewhat to the right of the Octobrists.[27]

On 12 November 1905, the Party of Legal Order established a
branch in Kiev, with A. I. Liubinskii, a local noble, as chairman. By its
second meeting on 20 November, the Kiev branch reported over 700
members, and three weeks later it claimed over 1,000. These members
included a preponderance of merchants, nobles, and minor government officials, along with some university professors, physicians,

engineers, active and retired military officers, clerics, and occasionally workers.[28]

Although equipped with a political program mirroring that of the parent body in St. Petersburg, the Kiev PLO lagged in mounting an electoral campaign. For months it concentrated more on administrative details than on popular appeals. In its newspaper, *Pravo i poriadok* (*Law and Order*), begun in November 1905, it devoted most articles to the party's internal mechanism and rather mundane meetings.[29] Not surprisingly, the PLO – as yet Kiev's only major monarchist party – lost the first Duma elections to the Kadets, who had steadily been accumulating influence in Kiev.[30]

In the aftermath of the first elections, both the PLO's Kiev branch and its central leadership in St. Petersburg labored to devise better strategies. They came to two conclusions: first, that they should place greater emphasis on such emotionally laden issues as "the Jewish question"; and, second, that they should form blocs with other loyalist groups.[31] In Kiev these initiatives soon bore fruit.

However, as it turned out, the more influential member of the coalition was not the PLO but the Kiev Russian Monarchist Party (*Kievskaia Russkaia monarkhicheskaia partiia*). Similar in name to V. A. Gringmut's Russian Monarchist Party in Moscow, but not affiliated with it, the Kiev RMP was organized in February 1906, with B. M. Iuzefovich, a government official, as chairman and guiding force. Iuzefovich had previously belonged to the Russian Assembly in St. Petersburg, and since 1904 he had chaired the Assembly's Kiev branch. Impatient with how slowly the Assembly was becoming involved politically, he switched to the RMP, although without formally withdrawing his Assembly membership.[32]

Under Iuzefovich's leadership, the Kiev Russian Monarchist Party vigorously sought popular support. It distributed countless brochures, filled with antisemitic and anti-Polish propaganda. In September 1906, it launched a newspaper, *Zakon i pravda* (*Law and Truth*), whose editorials stressed the need for preserving Russian precedence throughout the empire.[33] At public meetings, RMP orators complained that in the First Duma elections voters had been deceived by liberal candidates, who later used the Duma to defend terrorists, not to bring peace to the country – a situation that must not be repeated.[34] By late 1906, the Russian Monarchist Party had become Kiev's top rightist organization. Its impact would become more apparent as it assumed a leading role in Kiev's rightist coalition.

Without doubt the most spirited group to enter the coalition was the newly formed Union of Russian Workers (*Soiuz russkikh rabochikh*). Founded in September 1906, the Union focused on uniting loyalist workers in Kiev into a single body. For over a year, some workers had belonged to a Union precursor, the Patriotic Concord of Workers (*Patrioticheskoe sodruzhestvo rabochikh*), which had pledged to resist the revolutionary movement. Little had come of the Concord, but the new Union of Russian Workers, led by M. V. Gnevushev, a worker himself, promised an active program. Armed with the slogan "For the faith, tsar, and fatherland," its members protested against strikes in the factories and argued that what the workers needed was moral regeneration – a "liberation from lewdness and drunkenness." The Union formed *druzhiny*, which marched through the city, having enlisted Metropolitan Flavian to bless their banners. Although Union critics – even other monarchists – complained that the *druzhiny* carried weapons and might resort to violence against their political opponents or Jews, little evidence exists that the *druzhiny* actually went to this extreme. Some *druzhina* members may previously have taken part in the pogrom following the October Manifesto, but the Union, despite its counterrevolutionary and antisemitic rhetoric, directed its energies peacefully.[35]

By early 1907, the Union had brought hundreds of Kievan workers into its membership. Drawing support from a social stratum largely missed by the Party of Legal Order, Russian Assembly, and Russian Monarchist Party, the Union contributed substantially to the rightist coalition. The main obstacle facing the Union – and the coalition – was the possibility that the leftist parties would prove even more adept at recruiting workers.[36]

Less influential but still integral participants were the other three members of the coalition. The local branch of the Russian Assembly, which opened in 1904, drew its members primarily from government officials posted in Kiev, military officers, and professional persons. When its first chairman, B. M. Iuzefovich, left to lead the Kiev Russian Monarchist Party, the Assembly's vice-chairman, General Evskii, took over. But since Evskii and the Assembly's council recognized that they had neither the strength nor the ability for intense political campaigning, they welcomed the opportunity to join the rightist coalition. Having done so, they then invited Iuzefovich to resume his chairmanship of the Assembly. To this rather ungainly arrangement Iuzofevich agreed, making him chairman of two monarchist organizations.[37] The overriding significance of these developments, however, was not Iuzefovich's escalating career – he soon would also become head of the new coalition – nor the Russian Assembly's modest political role, but the readiness of the rightists, whatever their capability, to collaborate in future Duma campaigns.

One might have expected the Union of the Russian People to have been more prominent in the coalition. But the URP had been slow establishing itself in Kiev, probably because other rightists had attracted most of the potential leadership; and not until mid-1906 did it open a branch. Like the Union of Russian Workers, the URP assembled a *druzhina* and arranged public processions. In December 1906, it created a second branch in Kiev, followed in May 1907 by a third.[38] Nonetheless, the URP remained sluggish, its branches tending to be overshadowed by other organizations.

Finally, the rightist coalition in Kiev included the Russian Brotherhood (*Russkoe bratstvo*), a semi-political association chaired by the mayor, V. I. Protsenko. This group resembled the Society of Banner Carriers in Moscow and brotherhoods in St. Petersburg, Kharkov, and other cities, which usually operated under the jurisdiction of local Orthodox parishes. Sometimes headed by a layman, sometimes by a cleric, the brotherhoods had a predominantly lay membership. They held meetings and distributed literature designed to instill religious, moral, and patriotic values. The Russian Brotherhood in Kiev was not very active politically, but it publicized the rightist cause and cooperated in the Duma campaigns.[39]

Most important for Kiev's political future, these organizations succeeded in forging a powerful rightist coalition. After the Party of Legal Order's defeat in the First Duma elections, representatives of the PLO, Russian Monarchist Party, Russian Assembly, and Russian Brotherhood met to discuss subsequent strategies. During the summer they worked out plans to construct an electoral bloc for the Second Duma campaign, and they invited the recently formed Union of Russian Workers and the Kiev branch of the Union of the Russian People to participate. In November, the coalition chose Iuzefovich as its chairman.[40]

Calling itself the United Rightist Parties of Kiev, the coalition campaigned jointly in the Second Duma elections. As intended, the Party of Legal Order, Kiev Russian Monarchist Party, and Russian Assembly enlisted the vote of those segments of society they had already been attracting: merchants, nobility, government employees, military officers, professional people, and clerics. In contrast, the Russian Brotherhood, Union of Russian Workers, and Union of the Russian People drew from the lower social strata: tradesmen, laborers, and small shopkeepers. Together these organizations campaigned successfully, proving their ability to marshal conservative sentiments in Kiev into a viable political force. In this endeavor the coalition gained an absolute majority of the vote, making Kiev the only major city in the empire, except for Kishinev, to go rightist in the second elections (as discussed in Chapter 11).

Other rightist activity in the Southwest

Elsewhere in the Southwest, rightists fared less well, often for lack of adequate leadership. Podolia province, for example, shared the national and religious characteristics that contributed to rightist strength in neighboring Volynia. Union of the Russian People branches appeared during 1906 and 1907, mainly as an extension of the Pochaev Monastery's Volynian network; and the Union of Russian Workers opened a few branches. But rightist activity in Podolia never came near matching that in Volynia.[41]

Rightists in Kiev province (outside the city of Kiev itself) encountered somewhat different problems. Presumably, anti-Polish and anti-Jewish sentiments in the province could have aided the rightist cause. Almost 98 percent of the peasants in Kiev province were Orthodox Ukrainians, while 51 percent of the hereditary nobles were Catholic Poles. Moreover, Jews accounted for 12 percent of the population – and in the towns over 53 percent.[42] However, economic grievances evidently had a more pronounced effect on political attitudes than did national and religious concerns. Many peasants in Kiev province worked as hired laborers on large sugar beet plantations, often owned or leased by refining companies. Other peasants provided day labor in grain and potato fields on private estates, which had converted to capitalist agriculture. In either case, peasants frequently became involved in wage disputes with their employers. During 1906, leftist agitators from the cities added to the friction by trying to organize the Kievan workers for "the economic struggle against the landowners." Consequently, peasants went on strike, refusing to proceed with the harvest unless their demands for higher wages were met.[43] Although the Union of the Russian People and the Union of Russian Workers, headquartered in the city of Kiev, founded some branches in towns and villages during late 1906 and early 1907, they could not keep pace with the leftists.[44]

Belorussia: the Russian Borderland Union

Further northward, in Minsk, Mogilev, Vitebsk, and Grodno provinces, rightist activity also reflected the national and religious heterogeneity of the population. While the peasants in these provinces were overwhelmingly Belorussian and Orthodox, many landowners were Polish Catholics, and in the cities over half of the population were Jews – a mix that surely had significant political implications.[45] Before the First Duma elections, loyalist "Russians" in the region – that is, Belorussians, Great Russians, and Ukrainians – foresaw that enough Polish-Catholic landowners and urban Jews might be elected to the provincial assemblies to control the selection of deputies. Prompted by this concern, a delegation met with the tsar on 9 March 1906 to alert him that the Russian population in the West could easily be deprived of Duma representation.[46] As the delegation must have known, the tsar's government, committed to the electoral law it had just issued, could do little to forestall such an eventuality; and the elections proceeded as planned, indeed producing the anticipated result. In the provincial assemblies, Polish Catholic landowners and urban Jews, most of them oriented toward the Kadets, collaborated in sending almost exclusively non-Russian oppositionist deputies to the Duma.[47]

Determined that the failure to elect Russian deputies should not recur in the Second Duma elections, delegates from local Russian associations in the Belorussian provinces of Minsk, Vitebsk, and Grodno; the Lithuanian provinces of Vilna and Kovno; the Baltic provinces of Livonia and Courland; and the Polish provinces met in Vilna on 7–9 October 1906. There they formed the Russian Borderland Union (*Russkii okhrannyi soiuz*), its Organizational Committee to be chaired by G. K. Shmid, a retired army officer and now a Minsk publicist. From the beginning, RBU leaders declared that their goal was forthright and explicit: to unite the Russian population in the West and Northwest in order to secure adequate representation in the Duma and in local administrative bodies.[48]

The Russian Borderland Union's political orientation is difficult to categorize precisely but can probably best be regarded as "moderate rightist." During the Second Duma campaign, Kadet analysts listed Union candidates variously as rightists, moderates, and even progressives, or they simply lumped the Unionists with the Octobrists, which was more misleading yet. The conservative newspaper *Novoe vremia*, in St. Petersburg, labored under the same uncertainty, although it tended to designate RBU candidates as rightists.[49] The RBU itself contributed to the confusion by emphasizing that it was not a political party and that its members were free to join whatever parties they chose (except for those that advocated autonomy for non-Russian nationalities). At one point, the RBU stated that on the whole it would support the Octobrists' political program, while pursuing its primary goal of "upholding the interests of the Russian population in the borderlands in its struggle for equal rights." The RBU accepted the Duma monarchy created by the October Manifesto, but it warned about "the threatening clouds of liberalism and revolution" hanging over the country and the need for Russia's sons to withstand those enemies who wanted to destroy the fatherland. During the Second Duma campaign, the RBU proclaimed: "Stop the Poles! Stop the Zionists!" It reiterated that "Russia above all is for the Russians" – a slogan common to the rightists.[50]

The Russian Borderland Union intended to operate throughout the West and Northwest, but it gained its greatest influence in Belorussia, particularly in Minsk province, where Shmid and the Organizational Committee gave excellent leadership. In lieu of an institutional base, such as the zemstvos used by rightists in some provinces, the RBU leaders relied heavily on Orthodox parish priests and village teachers. Both furnished a convenient means of disseminating the RBU campaign message to the Belorussian peasant electorate. A *Minskoe slovo* editorial pointed out that in a large settlement (*selo*) of a thousand voters, half would probably not bother to vote, and half would be divided in their political inclinations. Therefore, a hundred voters belonging to the Russian Borderland Union could elect whatever candidate they preferred, presumably one endorsed by the Union.[51] In general, this seemed a sound strategy, especially since the RBU pursued a "single-issue" campaign, directed simply at preserving "Russian" interests in the borderlands, without addressing political, economic, and social questions that might cause division among the electorate whose votes it sought.

The other rightist group in this area – the Union of the Russian People – presented a more strident monarchist message but functioned much less capably than the RBU. During 1906, the URP established branches in the cities of Minsk and Bobruisk and in several villages in Minsk province; but a government report that year listed over 12,000 RBU members in the province and only 450 URP members.[52] This disparity suited the RBU, which charged that the URP's tactics served mainly to alienate persons that the RBU had succeeded in attracting.[53] Although the URP organized additional branches in Minsk province during 1907, the RBU remained by far the strongest rightist association.

In Mogilev, Vitebsk, and Grodno provinces, the Russian Borderland Union, lacking the leadership evident in Minsk province, proved less productive; and other rightist organizations functioned erratically. During 1906, the Union of the Russian People opened a few branches in Mogilev province; and the local Union of Patriots operated in the city of Mogilev.[54] Not until late 1906 and 1907 did the URP set up branches in Vitebsk province; and in Grodno province it apparently failed to do so at all.[55] In Belorussia, Minsk province continued as the foremost rightist stronghold, particularly of the Russian Borderland Union.

In examining rightist activity in the western borderlands, one recognizes the significant role that regional concerns and local leadership played in Russian politics. While regarding themselves as part of the overall rightist movement, devoted to upholding the monarchy, rightists in the West focused their programs on indigenous issues, primarily the national and religious conflicts endemic to the region. This is not to say that rightist leaders were simply opportunists, capitalizing on these concerns. No doubt they were convinced that they must protect the integrity of the empire and its Orthodox Russian, Ukrainian, and Belorussian population against the incursions of Jews and Catholic Poles. Unfortunately, the more vehement rightists delivered blistering tirades against these "alien forces," fanning antisemitic fires in particular and exacerbating an already inflammatory situation. While these extremists usually refrained from explicitly calling for pogroms, they openly condoned them as "spontaneous expressions of the people's wrath."

However, most western rightist leaders were more moderate – and more effectual. Adapting rapidly to Russia's new political climate, they concentrated on getting loyalist deputies elected to the Duma, where they could impede legislation granting equal rights to Jews and other minorities, and help strengthen Russian predominance in the empire. During the Duma elections, a striking feature of western political campaigning was how readily local leaders learned the valuable strategy of utilizing political networks. Whether through the zemstvos, as in Bessarabia, or parish priests, as in Volynia and Minsk, these leaders excelled in recruiting members and influencing the electorate. As will be seen later in regard to the Duma elections, the western rightists served as unusually proficient exemplars of partisan politics.

Part III

The role of special-interest groups

8   The Patriotic Union and the United Nobility

Once they had reluctantly accepted the new Duma system as a political fact of life, most rightist associations attempted in the years 1905–1907 to rally popular support for the ailing autocracy and to campaign for loyalist deputies to the Duma. However, it is useful to draw attention to those groups that, because of their unusually elitist social and political backgrounds, adopted different objectives and strategies. Dismayed by the monarchy's temporizing in 1905, these groups chose not to engage in partisan politics but instead to exert direct influence on the tsar and his ministers, in an effort to deter them from altering Russia's traditional autocratic and estate-oriented institutions or from embarking on other "untimely experiments." Admittedly, this approach was also a matter of self-interest, inasmuch as these pressure groups primarily represented the most conservative nobility, which prompted them to focus on policies pertinent to their own favored status.

The two most consequential special interest organizations, whose origins intertwined, were the Patriotic Union and the United Nobility. Both comprised highly talented persons, accustomed to holding positions of authority, but who found themselves amidst a national crisis that severely taxed their abilities. So long had they taken their privileged social status for granted that they were ill equipped to act innovatively or decisively, even in protecting their own interests. Their limited success suggests that it was not these special interest groups but the popular rightist parties that had the greater potential for shaping Russia's future.

The Patriotic Union

The Patriotic Union owed its existence to a circle of high-ranking bureaucrats, former bureaucrats, and prominent public figures, mainly from the landed nobility, who had known one another for years. Most had shared their opinions on governmental policies in the salon of the St. Petersburg writer and publicist K. F. Golovin, one of several gathering places in the capital that encouraged political discussions. Some regarded themselves as moderates, and a few as liberals, such as Prince P. D. Dolgorukov, who joined the Kadets in 1905. Most, however, were conservatives.[1]

This conservatism had led them to take sides on contemporary issues. They had, for example, supported V. K. Pleve's emphasis on agriculture during his tenure as Minister of Internal Affairs from 1902 until his assassination in July 1904, while opposing Sergei Witte's concentration on industrialization, while he was Minister of Finance prior to 1903. Some had engaged in the controversy between the Ministries of Internal Affairs and Finance over which should supervise agrarian economic development. Not surprisingly, the pro-Pleve forces were dedicated to defending the economic interests of the landed nobility. After Pleve's assassination, some of his supporters in the Ministry of Internal Affairs remained; others left or were dismissed. But they maintained close contact and found Golovin's salon a convenient place to exchange views.[2]

Following the 18 February rescript, the most conservative frequenters of the salon – over thirty in all – began additional discussions at the home of B. V. Shtiurmer, a former official in the Ministry of Internal Affairs who also belonged to the State Council. Those attending included A. S. Stishinskii, a member of the State Council and one-time official in the Ministry of Internal Affairs; V. I. Gurko, the energetic head of the Ministry's Land Section; A. P. Strukov, head of the Office for Affairs of the Nobility (and a former marshal of the nobility for Ekaterinoslav province); D. N. Liubimov, a capable bureaucrat whom Pleve had brought from the Imperial Chancellery to direct his own chancellery; N. A. Pavlov, a special duties assistant to Pleve; and A. A. Bashmakov, a functionary in the Land Section, who had broad experience in drafting peasant legislation. There were also several senators: Count A. A. Bobrinskii, a former marshal of the nobility for St. Petersburg province and chairman of the St. Petersburg zemstvo; A. A. Naryshkin, a well-known zemstvo leader from Orel province; and A. A. Shirinskii-Shikhmatov, a former governor of Tver province and at present Assistant Chief Procurator of the Holy Synod.[3] All in all, these were highly qualified members of the bureaucratic and social elite.

Like other loyalists, the participants in these discussions grappled with the question of what course they should take. Aware that individual bureaucrats had not deterred A. G. Bulygin, the new Minister of Internal Affairs, from advocating a representative assembly, they concluded that a corporate voice outside the government might more effectively influence high-level decision-making. This surmise seemed appropriate, since the tsar's ukase of 18 February had in effect welcomed recommendations regarding affairs of state. Consequently, they resolved to organize themselves more formally, and in April they created the Patriotic Union (*Otechestvennyi soiuz*).

Agreed in principle, the Union's founders differed over the question of leadership. V. I. Gurko recalled that when someone suggested electing a presidium consisting of Stishinskii, Liubimov, Pavlov, and himself, he declined with the reply:

> You wish to form a public organization, and yet you propose to head it with officials from the Ministry of the Interior. You choose a former assistant minister, the manager of his chancellery, his special duties clerk, and a director of a department, and yet you hope to be able to attract public forces to this organization! Why, it would seem more like a summons to the police station than an invitation to join a party.[4]

This stinging criticism may have offended Gurko's associates, but eventually the Patriotic Union included some non-bureaucrats among its officers. It selected Bobrinskii as chairman, Naryshkin and Strukov as vice-chairmen, and a council composed of these three along with Golovin; A. A. Kireev, a retired general; Prince V. M. Volkonskii, a district marshal of the nobility from Tambov province; Baron N. A. Wrangel, a landed noble and former government official; and N. A. Khvostov, an Orel zemstvist since the 1860s and currently a member of the Senate. Offended by this modest attempt at diversification, Shtiurmer, Pavlov, and several others withdrew from the Union, a departure which, according to Gurko, did not especially trouble those who remained.[5]

The Patriotic Union's leaders concurred that their immediate goal was to persuade the tsar to curtail the constituency and functions of the projected representative assembly. In May the Union's council drew up a scheme for assembly elections based on the traditional Russian estates – nobility, peasantry, and clergy – plus non-noble landowners and urban residents who met certain property-value qualifications. According to the proposal, elections would be conducted on the principle of proportional representation, which would weight them in favor of Russia's primarily agrarian population. The assembly would consist of two bodies: a 612-member zemskii sobor and a 128-member zemskaia duma selected by the zemskii sobor from its own members. The zemskii sobor would convene whenever the tsar requested counsel; the zemskaia duma would meet separately to suggest legislation relating to questions submitted to the zemskii sobor. The zemskaia duma's projects would go to the tsar and the State Council for final action. Neither the zemskii sobor nor the zemskaia duma would limit the power of the autocrat – their task would be only to assist him.[6]

The Union hoped to present its proposal to the Council of Ministers under the terms of the February rescript. While awaiting an appropriate opportunity, the Union leaders found another occasion to express their views on estate representation. On 21 June 1905, Bobrinskii, Naryshkin, and Kireev were granted an audience with the tsar as part of a delegation that also included Count P. S. Sheremetev, chairman of the Union of Russian Men; Count V. F. Dorrer, marshal of the nobility for Kursk province; and a Moscow merchant, a Novgorod townsman, and three peasants. Quite intentionally, the delegation exemplified Russia's traditional estates. Addressing the tsar, Bobrinskii raised the issue of estate representation – a significant emphasis since he had reason to suspect that the tsar's commitment to the existing social structure was faltering. Bobrinskii noted that two weeks previously Prince S. N. Trubetskoi, speaking for the third zemstvo congress, had asked for an assembly that would represent not the estates but the general public. Responding to Trubetskoi's plea, Bobrinskii assured Nicholas that "as always you are the tsar of the nobility and the tsar of the peasantry and of all the other estates."[7]

Still unsure of Nicholas's position on estate representation, Bobrinskii and other Union leaders continued to bring their argument to his attention, primarily through contacts they had at court.[8] As a result, both the Union's proposal and the draft prepared by the Bulygin commission were placed on the agenda of the high-level conference held at Peterhof, on 19–26 July 1905, to discuss the forthcoming assembly. Nicholas presided over the conference, which included his ministers and department heads, court functionaries, senators, State Council members, grand princes, several high-ranking military officers, and various public figures. Bobrinskii, Stishinskii, Shirinskii-Shikhmatov, Naryshkin, and Strukov attended as Senate or State Council members or as representatives of the bureaucracy, but they also spoke as leaders of the Patriotic Union. Debate at the conference proceeded mainly between two sets of clearly divided opponents: on one side, the reform-minded Bulygin circle; on the other, the "die-hards" – Bobrinskii, his colleagues, and ultraconservative members of the State Council, such as Count A. P. Ignatiev, who opposed any appreciable change in governmental structure.[9]

While both sides acknowledged the need to preserve the autocracy, the "die-hards," particularly Stishinskii, insisted that the assembly be only a zemskii sobor without explicit powers, even as a consultative body, and that the tsar appoint its members from the various estates. Stishinskii knew that the Bulygin commission envisioned an elected assembly, but he argued that the elections should nonetheless be based on the estates, primarily the nobility and peasantry, with each estate naming its own deputies. Throughout the debates, Union leaders opposed the Bulygin proposal that the electorate be divided into curiae – landowners, peasants, and townspeople – which would vote separately for electors, who in turn would select deputies, a system similar to that used in zemstvo and municipal elections. Stishinskii also objected to the Bulygin proposal that legislative projects voted down by the assembly would be returned to the appropriate ministers. In Stishinskii's view this would make the ministers responsible to the assembly, which smacked of western parliamentarianism and would likely lead to an assembly demanding full legislative powers. Undeterred, the Bulyginists replied that at present the State Council often returned draft legislation to ministers without infringing on the principle of autocracy.

Whatever the merits of the Patriotic Union's arguments, Nicholas sided with the Bulyginists, whose recommendations he had already tentatively approved. Under some pressure from his ministers, he added no Unionists to the commission that drafted the law of 6 August 1905. This crucial law stated that the new assembly – to be called the State Duma – would be a periodically convened consultative body for which elections would be indirect and, as Bulygin had recommended, based on curiae, not estates.

During these months of political uncertainty, the Patriotic Union and other staunchly conservative groups could only wait to see if the autocracy's tendency toward concessions would go further. When the tsar issued his October Manifesto that fall, the Union's worst fears seemed confirmed. Clearly, the legislative powers given the Duma went beyond what even the Bulyginists had intended. Bobrinskii lamented that he no longer knew what loyalists like himself should advocate, since Russia was now traveling the road of "limited autocracy" – a contradiction in terms, he noted, but nonetheless a political fact.[10] His Union colleagues agreed. No matter that the Russian Assembly, the Union of Russian Men, and other monarchist associations contended that the October Manifesto did not presage fundamental changes in the state structure and was not a constitution. Monarchical power, Union leaders realized, had been severely curtailed.[11]

Reluctantly, the Union attempted to adjust to the realities of Russian political life. Like many parties, it drew up a program, which, however, was not primarily designed to garner public support for the ailing autocracy, particularly in the Duma elections, but to instruct the government about its duties. First and foremost, the Union stressed that Russia must maintain a strong central authority and not permit the Duma to be transformed into a constituent assembly. Further, it requested the government to set strict limits on the civil rights guaranteed in the October Manifesto. Charging that the newly won freedom of the press had opened the floodgates of sedition and that freedom of assembly was producing meetings that openly advocated armed uprising, the Union admonished the government to deal harshly with those who transgressed these rights. It also warned that any notion of confiscating private land to appease the current agrarian unrest was a totally unacceptable solution to the peasant question. What the government must do was move quickly to reimpose order, both in the countryside and in the cities.[12]

In view of its objectives as a pressure group, one can hardly be surprised that the Union did not use its program as a guide for political campaigning. Never did it seek a popular following. During the Duma campaigns, Union leaders simply studied the electoral lists of other organizations and indicated to Union members which candidates they preferred.[13]

In essence, the Patriotic Union was unprepared to fill either of the two roles open to it in the rapidly changing Russian political structure. Disinclined to become a regular political party, it also failed to exert much influence on the government. Although many Unionists were present or former government officials, none (with the exception of Gurko and Stishinskii) was close to government policy makers. Self-limited in function, the Union began to decline by early 1906, and many members looked for other avenues through which to achieve their initial goal of influencing the government. This opportunity they soon found, as did others, in a conservative organization just emerging – the United Nobility.

The United Nobility

The United Nobility (*Ob"edinennoe dvorianstvo*) became the most prominent right-wing association that, instead of soliciting popular support, tried to influence government policy directly – in this case to the advantage of the landed nobility.[14] Primarily an alliance of provincial landowners and titled St. Petersburg residents who had been active in the Patriotic Union, the United Nobility resulted only after several previous attempts to unite conservative landowners into a national entity. These efforts began when N. A. Pavlov, V. N. Oznobishin, and others in Saratov province formed a local Union of Landowners in September 1905. Soon estate owners in neighboring provinces followed suit. Early in October, A. A. Chemodurov, the Samara provincial marshal of the nobility, sent invitations to about a thousand leading landowners throughout Russia to attend a congress for the purpose of organizing a national union. The congress, meeting in Moscow on 17–20 November 1905, attracted 227 persons from 33 provinces, including several provincial marshals of the nobility. When the congress formally organized a national Union of Landowners, it selected Chemodurov as chairman of its Permanent Council.[15]

In its statement of principles, the congress understandably focused on the most urgent land issues. It overwhelmingly affirmed the inviolability of private ownership. A majority of the delegates also favored dissolution of the peasant commune as a means of creating a class of smallholders, who presumably would be less inclined toward expropriation than the allotment peasants. Others, holding to Slavophile convictions, warned that abandoning the commune would seriously disrupt the traditional peasant way of life, thus causing greater unrest than already existed. Neither side could offer more than speculative arguments, nor could the congress propose a sure way to prevent the forthcoming Duma from addressing the question of expropriation. Rather half-heartedly, the congress agreed to urge the tsar to summon a zemskii sobor for "preparatory work" before the Duma convened, apparently hoping that this would cushion debate in the Duma itself.[16]

When the Second Congress of Landowners met in Moscow on 12–16 February 1906, it reaffirmed the Union's stand on these agrarian issues. Particularly, it condemned the land policy put forth in November by N. N. Kutler, head of the government's Main Administration of Land Organization and Agriculture. Kutler's project called for the expropriation – with compensation – of those portions of private estates currently being rented to peasants or lying unused, a proposal that gained the approval of Count Witte, the Chairman of the Council of Ministers. Although the tsar and most of his advisers rejected Kutler's plan, the Union of Landowners feared that the government's land policy, if influenced by the Duma, might move toward expropriation. The Union reiterated that the only land reforms it could accept would permit peasants to withdraw from communes and assist them to buy private land.[17]

Plagued by uncertainties, the congress deliberated under an aura of pessimism that did not bode well for the Union of Landowners. Chemodurov noted that the December delegation in its audience with the tsar had requested a zemskii sobor in vain. Pavlov alluded to the sparse attendance at the congress and to the Union's difficulty in attracting members.[18] Indeed, few nobles showed much enthusiasm for a broad-based, all-estate organization, nor did non-noble land-owners, who saw the Union as an instrument for protecting the special interests of the nobility.

Given these circumstances, the Second Congress made little progress. Soon the Union of Landowners slipped into oblivion, and most of its leaders – Chemodurov, Pavlov, Oznobishin, and others – shifted their energies toward forming a body designed specifically for the nobility.

Such efforts proceeded haphazardly, but eventually they produced the desired results. On 4 February 1906, a Moscow group formed the Circle of Nobles Loyal to their Oath (*Kruzhok dvorian vernykh prisiage*), that is, their oath to serve the autocratic tsar; and they invited others to join. Seeing in the Moscow Circle the seed of a national organization, the disillusioned leaders of the Union of Landowners called a national congress oriented toward the nobility. This congress met in Moscow on 22–25 April 1906, a few days before the opening of the First Duma. Count V. F. Dorrer, the Kursk provincial marshal of the nobility, who had served on the council of the Union of Landowners, presided. The delegates named Oznobishin to head a permanent national council, which would consist also of Dorrer, Pavlov, Shcherbatov, Kislovskii, Prince V. D. Golitsyn, Count A. A. Saltykov, and Iu. V. Arseniev, all prominent members of the Union of Landowners. Like the Union, the congress pledged to support an unlimited monarchy and the traditional estate structure of Russian society. It would oppose any Duma initiatives to expropriate private property. The congress also petitioned the tsar to appoint a military commander with dictatorial authority to suppress popular disorders. Most congress participants concurred on the need for an effective national nobles' association, evidently convinced that the Circle of Nobles would not be the answer.[19]

In fact, some Circle leaders were already moving in this direction. Seeking a groundwork for a national organization, they looked to an existing institutional structure: the provincial nobles' assemblies. In the past, the assemblies had dealt primarily with routine economic and social problems, but during the crises of 1905–1906 they turned increasingly to political issues. In January 1906, Tambov and Kursk nobles recommended that all the provincial assemblies choose delegates to a national congress. By the end of March, twenty-six of the thirty-five assemblies had endorsed the idea. In response, the Moscow provincial marshal of the nobility, Prince P. N. Trubetskoi, an acknowledged assembly leader, agreed to form a committee to arrange a national congress. However, Trubetskoi moved slowly, probably because, as a political moderate, he believed the Duma should address the land and other important issues without pressure from the nobility.[20]

The delay did little to impede the formation of a national nobles' association. Various provincial assemblies chose representatives to the planning committee, but the rather indiscriminate selection process made it uncertain who would attend and what views they would express. When the committee gathered in Moscow on 20 April, Trubetskoi chaired the session. He quickly found that most of the other thirteen participants, several of whom had belonged to the Circle of Nobles, were far more conservative than he. Unceremoniously, these rightists replaced him with N. F. Kasatkin-Rostovskii, a veteran of the Patriotic Union. In protest, Trubetskoi and three other moderates – V. V. Gudovich, A. N. Brianchaninov, and Prince Aleksandr Golitsyn – walked out. In their place, more and more rightists, mainly from the Circle of Nobles, attended committee sessions over the next three days. With the rightists now firmly in control, the preparatory committee established an organizational bureau to set the agenda for a national congress. Two representatives from each provincial nobles' assembly and other persons who might benefit the congress would make up the bureau. Among those asked to participate on the bureau as "collaborators" were A. A. Bobrinskii, A. A. Naryshkin, and K. F. Golovin, who had helped lead the Patriotic Union.[21]

During the next few weeks, the shift toward the right continued.

Meeting in St. Petersburg on 16–20 May, the bureau voted to include Bobrinskii, Naryshkin, Golovin, and other former Patriotic Union leaders in the congress, along with any Circle of Nobles members who wished to participate. Having placed the land question on the congress agenda, the bureau also invited agrarian experts from the Ministry of Internal Affairs: A. S. Stishinskii, V. I. Gurko, S. S. Bekhteev, and D. I. Pestrzhetskii.[22]

The first Congress of Representatives of the Nobles' Assemblies opened in the capital on 21 May – an exclusive and very conservative body, hardly typical of the entire nobility.[23] Recognizing Bobrinskii's administrative ability and solid reputation, the congress chose him to lead its sessions and then to chair its newly created Permanent Council of the United Nobility, with Kasatkin-Rostovskii and Naryshkin as vice-chairmen. Like the congress itself, the emerging United Nobility consisted primarily of right-wing wealthy nobles from the provinces and former bureaucrats in St. Petersburg, most of whom had been active in the Patriotic Union. Together they determined to uphold the landed interests of the nobility. Instead of a loosely coordinated collection of provincial assemblies, conservative nobles now had a single, permanent national association to act as their advocate.

Despite Trubetskoi's earlier endeavors to defer the land question, the organizational bureau for the first congress, deeply disturbed by the mounting agrarian crisis, had named a committee to draw up policy recommendations.[24] At the congress, D. I. Pestrzhetskii, the guiding force on the committee, presented the committee's "theses." Most of these the congress approved, strongly endorsing the ones that advocated the dissolution of the peasant commune, reassignment of allotment land to private peasant ownership, assistance through the Peasant Bank for peasants wanting to buy additional land, and government aid in resettling peasants. The congress rejected any hint of expropriating private estates.[25]

Troubled by the fact that the Duma, now in session for almost a month, was considering legislation that called for land expropriation, the congress turned to political matters. A. Iu. Oznobishin contended that creating the Duma had been "a massive error," which the government should correct by dismissing it and refusing to convene a new one. Other delegates concurred, but some, such as A. I. Zybin and K. N. Grimm, warned that such action would only further agitate the populace. The moderate A. N. Brianchaninov, an Octobrist, urged that the nobility accept the Duma and admit that it must make a fresh approach to the changing social and political system. On the whole, the mood of the congress seemed to fall somewhere between the positions of Oznobishin and Brianchaninov, but there was no strong consensus on the Duma issue, a sign that not even the congress members, let alone the nobility as a whole, were as united as the name of their new organization implied. Their decision not to attack the Duma probably also reflected their fear that such interference could jeopardize the nobility's influence on the government, whose good will it needed in regard to agrarian policy.[26]

On occasion, the Permanent Council took a firmer stand against the Duma than had the congress. When peasant disorders erupted in the central agricultural provinces in June 1906, and rumors circulated that the government might yield to the Duma's demand for land expropriation, the Council arranged a meeting with P. A. Stolypin, the Minister of Internal Affairs. Besides urging Stolypin to curb peasant excesses, the Council advised dissolution of the Duma. It got no commitment from Stolypin, but a few days later it learned from an official in the Ministry of Internal Affairs that Stolypin had reported the Council's views to the tsar, who indicated that he was aware of the nobility's concerns and "highly valued its activities."[27] Still, there is little evidence that it was the United Nobility that persuaded the government to dissolve the Duma. The efforts of the Permanent Council, like those of other rightist organizations, seem to have served mainly to reinforce the conclusions that Nicholas and his ministers reached on their own.[28]

After the First Duma's dissolution on 9 July 1906, the United Nobility, diverse as ever in its opinions, turned to the problem of Russia's political future. Some members, afraid that the projected Second Duma would revive demands for land redistribution, called for a revision of the electoral law. In a letter to the Permanent Council, P. N. Krupinskii, a district marshal of the nobility in Bessarabia, declared that "the dissolution of the State Duma undoubtedly saved Russia from inevitable ruin, but if the electoral law is not changed the new Duma may again misrepresent the people and, as before, amount to nothing more than a revolutionary meeting." By fall, the Council was debating whether the time was opportune to request a revised electoral law. Some thought it presumptuous to petition the government on this sensitive matter; others argued against delay, since local authorities would soon be preparing voter lists based on the existing law. Finally, the Council agreed to place the question on the agenda for the Second Congress of the United Nobility, slated to convene in St. Petersburg on 14 November 1906.[29]

In the meantime, the Council discussed what changes it wanted in the electoral law. N. A. Pavlov, arguing for estate representation, declared that otherwise "the nobility would be forced to relinquish its dominant position and even the monarchy would be endangered." However, the majority of the Council, while it upheld Russia's traditional estates in principle, voted to recommend to the congress an electoral scheme based on "naturally occurring groups or classes" in society. This meant that the Council accepted the existing curial system of representation. It suggested only two minor amendments to the electoral law: first, that a curia for small landowners be added; and second, that in the provincial assemblies each curia – large landowners, small landowners, peasants, and urban residents – elect a Duma deputy separately, before the assembly jointly chose the remaining deputies.[30] This would at least ensure some landowner representation from each province.

At the second congress, the usual lines of debate emerged. Pavlov again declared that Russia must have an electoral law based on estate representation as the only way for the nobility to maintain its position of leadership in a troubled society. But Bobrinskii and Brianchaninov spoke against elections by estates and argued that the nobility was not a closed caste with special voting privileges. Divided on this issue, the congress finally endorsed the Council's recommendation of a revised law that would create a small landowners' curia and grant each curia the right to elect a deputy of its own. However, despite the fact that the Council publicized this resolution and sent a copy to Stolypin, the congress had little effect. Stolypin was not yet ready to make major electoral changes – nor was the tsar. They preferred to risk a Second Duma based on the original law.[31]

The United Nobility was more encouraged by the imperial ukase released on 9 November, which would allow peasants to withdraw from the communes, consolidate their land allotments, and become individual landowners. The United Nobility assumed that it had inspired this reform, since two of its coopted participants, V. I. Gurko, Assistant Minister of Internal Affairs, and A. S. Stishinskii, head of the Main Administration of Land Organization and Agriculture, had argued during the spring of 1906 for dissolution of the commune. Moreover, in September, Gurko had been placed in charge of a commission to draft reform legislation. The resulting plan, which became the basis of the 9 November ukase, reflected the principles that Gurko and Stishinskii had promoted as an alternative to the limited expropriation that Kutler had unsuccessfully proposed in 1905.[32]

How much the United Nobility actually influenced the government's land reform is difficult to tell. Gurko undoubtedly realized that his plan had support not only from government officials but from the conservative nobility. Still, Gurko was used to forming his own opinions, and the most that can be safely concluded is that he and the United Nobility shared common purposes. Both presumed that as private property owners the peasants would develop more positive attitudes toward the government and the nobility.[33]

However, the United Nobility also had reasons to distrust the government. Stolypin seemed far too ready to accommodate the Duma; and with Gurko and Stishinskii having been replaced by mid-fall 1906, there were rumors that the government might again consider some form of land expropriation. So apprehensive was the Permanent Council that Count Tsertelev exclaimed, "The nobility is facing a struggle not with the left wing of the Duma but with the government."[34] In a speech to the Second Duma on 19 March 1907, Stishinskii's successor, Prince V. A. Vasilchikov, hinted that if peasants needed more land to establish private farmsteads, the government might implement "the moving of boundary lines," that is, expropriate private land. Alarmed, the Council invited Vasilchikov to meet with it on 21 March and clarify his position. Again, he intimated the possibility of at least limited expropriation, leaving the Council even more fearful that the government might side with the Duma on the land issue.[35]

To add to the Permanent Council's concern about its eroding role in rural affairs, Stolypin had also prepared a legislative project for local administrative reform. This he regarded as a corollary to his agrarian policy. He reasoned that if the peasantry was afforded expanded economic opportunities it must also be permitted greater participation in local government. Specifically, Stolypin proposed that the curiae participating in zemstvo elections – private landowners (whatever their estate), urban property owners, and communal peasants – should no longer vote according to the amount of property they owned but to the zemstvo taxes they paid. He calculated, quite correctly, that more peasants would have the vote if it was based on taxation, not on property value. This would, of course, dilute the nobility's predominant position in the landowners' curia – a prospect that worried the Permanent Council. On 27 February, A. A. Naryshkin reported that two days earlier he and Stishinskii had an interview with Stolypin, at which Stishinskii told the prime minister that several State Council members objected to his project, convinced that it would "demolish all significance of the nobility's estate in the countryside." Stolypin replied that estate representation in the zemstvos had already lost its significance and the time had come to extend the curial system even further. Greater peasant participation posed no threat, he said, because "the innate common sense of the peasants discerns admirably who can most effectively guide local life." Taken aback by Naryshkin's report, the Permanent Council reversed its previous decision to send a delegation to discuss local reform with Stolypin. It now believed that the United Nobility had little chance of dissuading him from his intended course.[36]

Disheartened, the Council agreed to defer action on the local reform issue until it could be discussed by the Third Congress of the United Nobility, scheduled to begin on 27 March. After a long debate, the congress somberly conceded that, like the Council, it had little hope of stopping Stolypin from taking his reform plans to the Duma and no means of its own to introduce counter-proposals. It decided only to appoint a committee to examine Stolypin's draft legislation in detail, distribute its conclusions to the provincial marshals of the nobility, and ask them to have their respective nobles' assemblies discuss the reform. If they chose, the assemblies could then convey their opinions to the tsar or to Stolypin, but the congress voted against submitting appeals of its own.[37]

Significantly, the Third Congress did not address the bothersome issue of whether to petition the tsar to dissolve the Second Duma and announce new election procedures. Initially, the Council had placed this question on the congress agenda; but unsure about what position to take, it withheld debate.[38] Consequently, the United Nobility contributed less to determining the Duma's future than did other rightist organizations. During the spring of 1907, Union of the Russian People branches sent thousands of telegrams to the tsar and Stolypin, calling for dissolution and a revised law. Daily the rightist press made the same requests, as did the fourth monarchist congress in April.[39] As discussed more extensively in Chapter 11, Nicholas apparently relied on these messages as justification for his eventual decision to disband the Duma and issue a new electoral law. It was to the Union of the Russian People, not the United Nobility, that he sent a telegram on 3 June, the day of the dissolution, thanking his faithful subjects for their support.[40]

The United Nobility seems also to have played only a peripheral role in prompting Stolypin's eventual retreat on the local reform and land issues. Stolypin may have been influenced by the 1907 zemstvo congress, which opposed his scheme for local representation according to zemstvo taxes and instead strongly endorsed representation based on property.[41] More important, however, was Stolypin's relation with the Third Duma. A conservative body that owed its composition to his new electoral law, the Third Duma nonetheless proved a mixed blessing to him. Stolypin had previously broken with the Second Duma when it insisted on more extensive land expropriation than he was willing to endorse; now the Third Duma rejected whatever intentions he held for even limited expropriation. It also resisted his plans for "democratizing" local government. Forced to shelve his legislative proposals, Stolypin spent the next several years sparring with the Duma on other aspects of local reform.[42] Suffice it to say that in 1907 the United Nobility, stymied in its endeavors to influence government policy and divided on what action to take, served as only one of many forces that contributed to preserving the landed nobility's preeminence in the countryside.

In broad perspective, several observations can be made about the United Nobility. Clearly, it sought to maintain Russia's autocratic system and even more its traditional social order. Just as evident, in pursuing these objectives it did not unite the Russian nobility as much as it had expected. Its congresses drew delegates from only slightly over half of the provincial nobles' assemblies; its membership profile shows that it essentially represented the wealthier and most conservative landed nobles, not the nobility as a whole. Moreover, in championing the inviolability of private property, the United Nobility concentrated almost exclusively on its members' own large estates without giving much thought to non-noble landowners. Neither did it identify with the landowners' curia in Duma and zemstvo elections nor enlist landowners generally in its efforts to influence the government's agrarian policies.

As a pressure group, the United Nobility's elitist membership did have access to high-ranking officials: Stishinskii, Gurko, and others in the Ministry of Internal Affairs, even Goremykin and Stolypin as Chairmen of the Council of Ministers. Yet, despite its ability to convey its wishes to the government, the United Nobility exerted less influence on policy than it had anticipated. The government's decisions to dissolve the First and Second Dumas, revise the electoral law, permit peasants to withdraw from the communes and become private landowners, and abandon its plans for land expropriation and zemstvo reform all accorded with the United Nobility's desires; but little evidence suggests that the government heard and heeded the United Nobility on these issues any more than it did the popularly based rightist organizations.

This lack of leverage testifies to the fact that the government was coming to terms with the changing nature of Russian society more rapidly than was the United Nobility. Stolypin and other ministers recognized that new economic classes were replacing the old estates. While the autocracy was by no means ready to abandon the landed nobility, it sought support for its policies from all strata of society. Furthermore, in trying to modernize Russian agriculture by converting the village communes into small private landholdings, it chose a program that would benefit the peasants more than the landed nobility. Given the widespread peasant discontent in 1905–1907 and the prospect of expropriation, the United Nobility endorsed the government's agrarian program, but it had trouble accepting the likelihood that in the end Russia's agrarian system would be overwhelmingly grounded on peasant farmsteads. The best it could do was encourage the government to preserve private ownership and assume that the old order would somehow survive.

Part IV

Rightist strategies and achievements

9   Rightists and the use of violence

One alarming aspect of rightist activity was the willingness of some right-wing extremists to engage in violence. Most rightists were content to carry on the political struggle through the press and in the Duma, but others insisted that rhetoric was not enough: more aggressive action must be taken. Even if it meant resorting to illegal means, such extremist organizations as the Union of the Russian People claimed they had a moral right to mete out punishment to wrongdoers, a just retribution that would also serve as a deterrent to others. Accordingly, extremist leaders organized "fighting brotherhoods" (*boevye druzhiny*) – armed bands equipped to battle revolutionary workers and on occasion to assassinate allegedly seditious political figures. In addition, the antisemitism pervading the rightist movement found its utmost expression in the URP and other extremist groups, which incited attacks against Jews that often escalated into full-scale pogroms. While the use of violence did not represent the rightists as a whole, it became a visible trademark of at least the movement's ultraradical wing.

The call to arms

Given the intensity with which many monarchists reacted to the specter of insurrection, it is not surprising that the call for armed confrontation came early in the revolutionary period. In June 1905, a monarchist group in Tambov province demanded "death to the revolutionaries" and summoned patriotic Russians to "step forth boldly, weapons in hand."[1] In another of the inflammatory brochures that flooded the country, the Central All-Russian Patriotic Committee in Bessarabia exhorted its readers:

> Russians, defend that which to you is sacred. Strike down the enemy without pity. We did not want this hostility, but we have been forced

to take up arms ... and we have the right to save Russia by dealing with its enemies in our own way. Rise up, Russian people, strike and destroy! Death to the enemy! Long live those who take the law into their own hands against the seditionists![2]

A further sign of this alarmist tendency was the haste with which some Orthodox clerics demanded coercion. In October 1905, Bishop Nikon of Moscow declared that "crowds of workers are on the rampage, demanding the impossible, often those things they do not even understand, not listening to any kind of admonition; they are on the verge of turning into wild animals let out of a cage ... Against such animals there is one measure to be taken: armed force."[3] Probably, Nikon preferred that the government provide this repression through the police or military units, but other clerics called for popular initiative. In November, Bishop Antonii of Volynia wrote to Boris Nikolskii, the prominent rightist orator in St. Petersburg, that in order to stop the revolution, Russia might require "an appeal to the entire population to armed self-defense and the lynching of revolutionaries." Antonii added, "Of course, as a cleric I cannot take part in a civil war."[4] But this did not prevent him from preaching counterrevolutionary sermons, designed to quicken his listeners' impulse to popular action.

In his letter to Nikolskii, Bishop Antonii also anticipated a direction that private justice would take in Russia, when he confided, "I am convinced theoretically that the fight against the revolution should begin with the execution of Count Witte."[5] The demand for the assassination of key political figures was a dramatic leap from the use of force against revolutionary terrorists and riotous workers or peasants, no more vindictive perhaps than a local lynching, but a formidable political weapon. It had already become a choice instrument of some Russian leftists, primarily anarchists and Socialist Revolutionaries; now it was being considered by rightists.

Those loyalists who advocated using popular force against the opposition drew on at least one recent precedent for organizing public defense units. In 1881, a group of court and government officials had formed a secret organization, the Holy Brotherhood (*Sviashchennaia druzhina*), to protect the new tsar, Alexander III, who had just succeeded his assassinated father. Whenever the imperial family traveled about the capital or visited Moscow, the Holy Brotherhood and its volunteer assistants guarded the streets along the route. It also joined the fight against sedition by infiltrating revolutionary organizations, and it led a fascinating, if somewhat ineffective, existence until it was disbanded at the end of 1882.[6]

When a new wave of revolutionary activity erupted in 1905, the idea of a *druzhina* reappeared, this time among those who were not so much concerned about guarding the personal safety of the tsar, which presumably could be handled by his bodyguards and the police, as about preserving the autocratic system and restoring law and order. As early as February 1905, there were reports of a *druzhina* in Saratov province.[7] Later in the spring landowners in southern Russia organized a *druzhina* for protection against peasant arsonists. This group armed itself and on at least one occasion attacked unruly peasants, who in return got guns of their own.[8] During the October strike, the Union of Russian Men in Moscow called for the creation of local parish committees of order, bodies analogous to the *druzhiny* if not bearing the name, to join the "struggle against disturbances." The Union recommended that after divine services on Sunday, 16 October, every parish in the city should organize a committee of at least ten persons, which in turn would choose a central supervisory board. However, when the appointed time arrived, hardly any of the parishes responded, and the Union did not pursue the idea further.[9] Nor did the mild-mannered Russian Assembly or the Russian Monarchist Party, despite their condemnation of the dissidents, favor using force against them. It remained for more militant groups to put the notion of a *druzhina* into practice.

Armed struggle in the streets

As revolutionary tensions mounted in the fall of 1905, it quickly became evident that indeed there were zealous patriots ready to fight fire with fire. In December, two brothers, Sergei and Dmitrii Kuzmin, both engineers in St. Petersburg, along with V. N. Stepanova, the widow of a tax assessor, requested permission from the Ministry of Internal Affairs to organize the Society for Active Struggle against Revolution and Anarchy (*Obshchestvo aktivnoi bor'by s revoliutsiei i anarkhiei*). Their intention, they asserted, was to acquire handguns and bring "the armed struggle into the streets." Members of the Society would use their weapons against strikers, and in the event of an uprising, they would turn the revolutionaries they apprehended over to the authorities. To this end, the St. Petersburg city governor, with the approval of the Ministry of Internal Affairs, granted the Society permits to carry weapons.[10] Soon, Leontii Dezobri, a retired officer who married Stepanova, became a leading figure in the Society, and eventually he helped organize branches in Moscow, Kiev, and other cities. Dezobri also had close ties with the Union of the Russian People, which may have borrowed his techniques in forming its own paramilitary units.[11] While the Society continued to recruit workers during 1906, it seems not to have engaged in much counterrevolutionary activity except sporadic brawls with leftist workers.[12] Lacking accomplished leadership, it was rapidly overshadowed by the URP's newly founded *druzhiny*.

The URP *druzhiny* represented the most dubious aspect of this militant organization, which throughout its existence hovered between the legitimate world of partisan politics and the clandestine realm of armed violence. Already in December 1905, the Union established its first *druzhina*, headed by a retired bureaucrat, N. M. Iuskevich-Kraskovskii, who obviously relished the intrigue of clandestine operations.[13] The Union directed its appeal for *druzhina* members toward loyalist workers who opposed the strike movement and who realized how powerless they were against revolutionaries in the factories. When those factories that had shut down resumed operation in late October, the friction between revolutionary and loyalist workers continued, and to the latter the Union promised organized assistance. As workers registered for membership, the Union formed them into local units by tens and hundreds. In St. Petersburg, the Union recruited enough workers to divide the city into five districts, each containing a *druzhina* of several hundred workers. In Moscow, the Union organized three *druzhiny*, and it soon had units in Odessa, Iaroslavl, Kishinev, Tula, Elisavetgrad, and about a dozen other cities. While those who joined were chiefly unskilled workers, the *druzhiny* also attracted technicians and engineers, who often took charge of local units. All recruits swore an oath of secrecy about *druzhina* activities.[14]

After the Moscow uprising in December 1905, the *druzhiny*, anticipating similar eruptions elsewhere, began to arm. In St. Petersburg, the city governor, who also feared insurrection, issued a hundred used police revolvers to URP *druzhiniki*; and in Odessa, the governor-general permitted *druzhiniki* to carry both revolvers and rifles.[15] When subsequent uprisings failed to materialize, the *druzhiny* used their weapons mainly in spasmodic fighting with revolutionary workers and assaults against political opponents, Jews, and others they regarded as enemies of the Russian people.

At times, the enmity between *druzhiniki* and oppositionists led to serious violence. In January 1906, radical workers hurled a bomb into an eating house near St. Petersburg's Nevskii Gate, where loyalist workers frequently met, killing two and wounding eleven occupants. Nearly all the casualties belonged to the Union of the Russian People, which responded angrily that this challenge would not pass unheeded.[16] Dubrovin himself warned that the Union would follow the motto of "an eye for an eye" in the ensuing struggle.[17] But by and large it was an uneven battle. On one occasion revolutionary workers seized the revolvers of a *druzhina* unit and crushed them under a hydraulic press. During most factory shootouts the outnumbered rightists suffered the greater casualties.[18]

In Odessa, the Union's *druzhiniki*, acting under the direction of the branch chairman, Count Konovnitsyn, were even more conspicuous than those in the capital. Formed into para-military units, they wore uniforms and carried firearms. As they strode along the streets, they accosted pedestrians and skirmished with radical workers – an early version of the fascist militias that appeared in western Europe two decades later. Once during a dispute, when Odessa dock workers threw rocks at a band of *druzhiniki*, the latter opened fire with their revolvers, killing one worker and injuring five others.[19] Frequently, *druzhiniki* also assaulted students and Jews. By the end of 1906, the Odessa city governor had become so disturbed by the "slaughter in the streets" that he insisted that the *druzhina* there be disbanded.[20] One can safely say that generally the URP's *druzhiny* proved less of a help than a hindrance in reestablishing order in Russia. Usually, they acted at cross-purposes with governmental authorities, sometimes causing greater consternation than did the dissidents they claimed to be subduing.

Political assassination

The Union of the Russian People's vigilante mentality prompted it to undertake another, more specific form of violence: the assassination of certain public figures. From their roster of adversaries, Dubrovin and his aides chose forty-three persons who they decreed should speedily be "brought to justice." Among the intended victims were:[21]

S. Iu. Witte	Former Chairman of the Council of Ministers and author of the October Manifesto
P. N. Miliukov	Principal spokesman for the Kadet party and co-editor of the liberal newspaper *Rech'*
I. V. Gessen	The other co-editor of *Rech'* and editor of the law journal *Pravo*

F. I. Rodichev	Veteran zemstvo constitutionalist and Kadet deputy in the Duma
M. M. Vinaver	Kadet parliamentarian in the Duma
M. Ia. Herzenstein	Kadet specialist on agrarian affairs in the Duma
G. B. Iollos	Co-editor of the liberal Moscow newspaper *Russkiia vedomosti* and Kadet deputy in the Duma
A. F. Aladin	Trudovik deputy in the Duma known for his outspoken attacks on the government
S. V. Anikin	Another Trudovik deputy in the Duma
S. M. Propper	Editor of the newspaper *Birzhevyia vedomosti* and other liberal publications
O. O. Gruzenberg	The most prominent Jewish criminal lawyer in St. Petersburg and a liberal
G. B. Sliozberg	Another influential Jewish lawyer

Significantly, the Union singled out not revolutionaries but liberals and moderate socialists, whom it regarded as the more insidious agents of sedition, those who could influence public opinion through the press or the government through the Duma. Included were several Jews or converted Jews: Gessen, Vinaver, Herzenstein, Iollos, Gruzenberg, and Sliozberg. As might be expected, the Union accorded a special place to the unforgivable Witte. Although he had been replaced as Chairman of the Council of Ministers in April 1906, he remained a target for retribution.

The Union failed to implement most of its assassination plans, but it soon made several attempts. Its first victim was M. Ia. Herzenstein. A lecturer in financial law at Moscow University, Herzenstein had achieved considerable prominence as the Kadets' best authority on agrarian affairs, and he served as vice-chairman of the Duma's Agrarian Commission.[22] He had also incurred the rightists' wrath for advocating compulsory land redistribution. In a Duma speech, Herzenstein urged that reform legislation be passed before "illuminations" – meaning fires from peasants burning homesteads on the landed estates, which already were being reported – enveloped Russia.[23] The rightist press straightway accused Herzenstein of instigating these "illuminations," and it quickly noted that he was a Jew, even though he had converted to Orthodoxy and had little contact with Jews in Moscow or in the Duma.[24]

Restrained but resolute, Herzenstein on occasion could act impulsively. When the Kadet deputies met in Vyborg, Finland, after the dissolution of the First Duma, Herzenstein was among the first to sign their hastily conceived manifesto, calling for nationwide passive resistance to government taxation and military conscription, a weapon they hoped would chastise the government for its precipitous action toward the Duma. The manifesto actually had little effect on the Russian populace, but it further antagonized the rightists. A rumor reached the dissident deputies in Vyborg that angry loyalists were waiting to ambush them when they returned to Russia.[25] Although no attack occurred as the deputies made their way back, it was a different matter for Herzenstein, who remained in Finland for a short vacation. On the evening of 18 July 1906, as he walked with his wife and daughter through a woods near Terioki, two revolver shots killed him instantly, while his assailant fled.[26]

The subsequent handling of the case reveals much about the Russian government's inconsistencies in dispensing justice. The investigation moved slowly, but G. F. Weber, an assistant to the St. Petersburg lawyer O. O. Gruzenberg (whose name was also on the Union's assassination list), uncovered sufficient evidence for the Finnish authorities to bring murder charges against several members of the Union of the Russian People.[27] In January 1907, the trial opened in Kivennapa, 20 kilometers north of Terioki. Alarmed, the Union petitioned the tsar to have the trial moved to a Russian court, contending that the Finnish court would be biased against the defendants. However, a transfer apparently would have involved the Russian authorities in the case more deeply than they wished, and the petition was denied.[28]

As evidence continued to unfold, the Finnish court subpoenaed Dubrovin himself to testify.[29] Since the Russian authorities did not comply with the Finnish request to serve the subpoena, the court sent two Finnish police officials to St. Petersburg to present their demand personally to the Minister of Justice, I. G. Shcheglovitov, who had final jurisdiction in the matter. Shcheglovitov turned them away, explaining later that he would have gladly complied had Dubrovin not already fled into hiding in the Crimea, a rather flimsy excuse inasmuch as Shcheglovitov made no attempt to locate Dubrovin or extradite him to the capital.[30]

Delayed by legal maneuvering from the defense, the trial dragged on for almost two years. Finally, the court handed down convictions to four Union functionaries, including Iuskevich-Kraskovskii, head of the Union's *druzhina*, and sentenced them to prison.[31] However, all the effort came to naught, for almost immediately the Union appealed to the tsar; and Nicholas, sympathetic as usual to the Union's patriotic efforts, pardoned those convicted in the case.[32] The most that can be said for the trial is that it exposed the Union's terrorist activities – and the autocracy's misshapen sense of justice.

In the meantime, the Union had become involved in two other assassination attempts, the first of them on Sergei Witte. As early as August 1906, Prince M. M. Andronnikov, who had become acquainted with Dubrovin and attended Union meetings, heard at one of them that Dubrovin was planning to kill Witte upon his return from a trip to western Europe. The prince immediately sent Witte a telegram, warning him that his life was in danger. When Witte arrived in St. Petersburg, Andronnikov told him the details of what he had heard. Witte did not seem especially disturbed, since by this time he had accumulated various enemies and was used to threats.[33]

However, the Union meant to put its intentions into action. With Iuskevich-Kraskovskii overseeing the operation, a subordinate, Aleksandr Kazantsev, recruited two unemployed workers, Vasilii Fedorov and Aleksandr Stepanov, to commit the crime. Since both Fedorov and Stepanov were Socialist Revolutionaries, Kazantsev told them that he too was a party member. As he gained their confidence, he impressed upon them how seriously Witte had harmed the revolutionaries by making concessions to the liberals while ignoring socialist demands. In their naivety Fedorov and Stepanov believed Kazantsev; when he assured them that the time had come to kill Witte, they agreed to help.

Fortunately for Witte, the would-be assassins botched the job. On the night of 29 January 1907, they lowered two time bombs into a chimney of Witte's town house; but, improperly fused, the bombs failed to explode. Perplexed about the clogged chimney, the building's furnace attendant dislodged the strange objects, and Witte called the police. When a URP lookout warned Kazantsev, Fedorov, and Stepanov that an investigation was underway, they hurriedly left for Moscow to await further instructions.[34]

In Moscow, Kazantsev informed his young accomplices that they had been given a new assignment, this time to kill a certain rightist leader there, who was menacing the Socialist Revolutionaries. Far from being a rightist, the victim was actually G. B. Iollos, a leading Kadet deputy in the First Duma and a Jew, who for years had served on the editorial staff of the mildly liberal Moscow newspaper *Russkiia vedomosti* (*The Russian Gazette*).[35]

Kazantsev explained the plan to Fedorov and Stepanov. This time they would use not bombs but guns; and he gave them each a Browning revolver.[36] A few days later, on a quiet street in Moscow, Fedorov approached the person who had been pointed out as his target and shot him, then hurried away, still unaware of the dying man's identity. According to Stepanov, only when they read about the murder in the newspapers did he and Fedorov realize whom they had killed. It was then they began to understand that Kazantsev had deceived them, a fact that Fedorov confirmed when he found rightist literature among Kazantsev's belongings.[37]

Keeping his newly discovered knowledge to himself, Fedorov planned his revenge. Upon returning with Kazantsev to St. Petersburg, ostensibly for a second attempt on Witte, he instead killed Kazantsev. Immediately, Fedorov left the country and eventually made his way to Paris, while back in Russia Stepanov disappeared into the provinces.[38]

Meanwhile, the authorities seemed at a loss to determine who had attacked Witte and Iollos. Although the St. Petersburg police interrogated several Union members about the Witte affair, none divulged the slightest information.[39] In Moscow, court investigators questioned witnesses to the Iollos murder and a number of suspects, mainly local rightists known to have been antagonistic to Iollos. The investigation ultimately focused on Kazantsev, Stepanov, and Fedorov, but without solid evidence to incriminate them.[40] However, in Paris, Fedorov disclosed his involvement in the Iollos murder and the attempt on Witte, and his story made its way back to Russia.[41] Witte insisted that the Ministry of Justice request Fedorov's extradition, but when it did the French government refused to comply, contending that Fedorov had been accused of political crimes and therefore could not be extradited under international law.[42] With Fedorov safe in Paris, Stepanov in hiding, and Kazantsev dead, the authorities had no one to prosecute, unless they wanted to gather evidence that could implicate Iuskevich-Kraskovskii or other high officials of the Union of the Russian People. As in the Herzenstein case, they chose not to probe deeply, but little doubt remained about the Union's involvement.[43]

The Union did not pursue the other persons on its list, possibly because the risk was becoming too great, more likely because it concluded that the need for political assassination had passed. After the government dissolved the Second Duma in June 1907 and revised the electoral law, which contributed to a decided shift to the right in the Third Duma elections, the Union recognized that the threat of liberal constitutionalism had waned; and it reduced its assault against its political enemies. This did not reflect a lack of will, only of incentive, based upon a reassessment of changing circumstances. In 1906 and early 1907, when the battle was at its height, the Union indeed had proved ready to engage in political violence. Never did its assassination attempts remotely approach the scope of those conducted by such radical oppositionists as the Socialist Revolutionaries. But the Union was the one rightist organization willing to adopt these terrorist techniques as part of its own counterrevolutionary arsenal, while at the same time denying that it would ever act in contradiction to the law and order it had pledged itself to defend.

The pogroms

More obscure was the rightists' role in another dramatic manifestation of violence – the pogroms. The tragic reality of these mob assaults on alleged enemies of the Russian people – revolutionaries and liberal intellectuals but above all Jews – has been well documented by contemporary newspaper reports, eye-witness accounts, and police dispatches. Since the 1880s, pogroms had occurred spasmodically in Russia, the most frenzied being the notorious Kishinev massacre in 1903. During 1905–1906, a new wave of pogroms struck dozens of Russian towns and cities, taking hundreds of lives and causing immeasurable damage.[44]

Even more difficult than calculating the casualties is determining how the pogroms originated. Were they strictly spontaneous manifestations of the people's wrath, as many antisemites claimed? Or were they well-organized and planned massacres, as some critics of the pogromists contended? And to what extent were rightist organizations involved?

N. E. Markov, a Union of the Russian People leader, declared that neither the Union nor any other rightist organization planned the pogroms: they were the natural outpouring of popular resentment and required no outside direction. The Union, he admitted years later, did arrange the assassinations of Herzenstein and Iollos, which, in his words, had "a great educational effect on the Jews." He also suggested that it might have been worthwhile "to eliminate a few hundred more of the most obvious instigators of revolution." But he maintained that the Union did not arrange pogroms.[45]

In contrast, a prominent historian of the Jews in Russia and Poland, S. M. Dubnow, asserted that "in hundreds of cities the carefully concealed army of counterrevolutionaries, evidently obeying a pre-arranged signal, crawled out from beneath the ground, to indulge in an orgy of blood..."[46] Dubnow's accounts offer a wealth of information about these calamitous events, but since he did not present specific documentation to support his contention of an orchestrated conspiracy, he left unsettled this troublesome question.

Certainly, it bears emphasizing that in a general sense rightist organizations, at both the national and local levels, contributed to the pogroms through antisemitic propaganda that often explicitly called for violence. Yet, a thorough examination of the evidence suggests that the actual implementation of the pogroms was usually a local matter and took various courses. In some instances, there is little doubt that local rightist organizations arranged pogroms, usually invoking a particular incident as a pretext to attack Jews at random. At other times, rightist groups served chiefly to abet police and soldiers who indulged in antisemitic violence. Finally, some pogroms erupted as the result of bitter antagonisms between Christians and Jews but apparently without premeditation.[47]

The Elisavetgrad pogrom in February 1907 illustrates the role of deliberate planning by local rightists. During 1906, the Union of the Russian People in Elisavetgrad had been proclaiming a flagrant antisemitism. So pronounced was the enmity that the provincial vice-governor observed that many Union members were united not in devotion to the crown or homeland but "almost exclusively by their hatred of the Jews." On 25 February 1907, when an unidentified assailant shot to death the head of the Union's *druzhina*, the Union immediately blamed the Jews, which caused widespread fear that a pogrom was imminent.[48] On the day of the funeral, a crowd of Unionists, led by the branch's vice-chairman, A. A. Bankovskii, left the cemetery, shouting "Down with the Jews!" Part of the crowd evaded police cordons along the city's main thoroughfare and ran through the side streets, plundering Jewish shops and assaulting Jews with sticks and clubs. By the end of the rampage, the Unionists had killed one person and injured over a dozen others. The police arrested several of the culprits and charged Bankovskii with inciting a pogrom, but the damage had already been done.[49] Remarkably, the Union denied any wrong doing, and blamed the Jews for their own misfortunes, not a very convincing argument but one conveniently employed.

Similarly, the pogrom in Gomel, on 13–14 January 1906, appears to have been instigated by a local rightist organization, the Union of

Russian Patriots. Anti-Jewish feelings in Gomel had intensified during 1905, as Jewish extremists joined other revolutionaries to make anti-government speeches, organize strikes, and occasionally attack the local police. On 11 January 1906, an unknown assailant shot and killed a police officer, an act that antisemites at once attributed to the Jews. After the funeral, gangs burned Jewish homes and shops, looted others, and attacked Jewish residents, killing one and wounding ten. The understaffed police force did little to stop the pogrom; and some of the troops stationed near Gomel took part in the looting. Still, an investigation by the Ministry of Internal Affairs was probably correct in concluding that most of the pogromists belonged to or had been recruited by the Union of Russian Patriots.[50]

Local rightist organizations sometimes instigated violence unsuc-cessfully, most likely because they lacked a precipitating incident to give their intended assaults sufficient impetus. In February 1906, A. A. Makarov, an Assistant Minister of Internal Affairs, submitted a report to the Minister, P. N. Durnovo, stating that a pogrom was rumored to be in the making at Aleksandrovsk in Ekaterinoslav province. Makarov said that he had received two dispatches from the Aleksandrovsk police chief Budogovskii, which, in Makarov's opinion, left no doubt that Budogovskii knew that a pogrom was imminent and was even encouraging it. Makarov went on to explain that attached to Budogovskii's dispatches were six lithographed and two printed leaflets prepared by local patriotic organizations. All the leaflets were highly inflammatory in their attacks on revolutionaries, students, and Jews. One of them, issued by a militant organization called the Russian Brotherhood (*Russkaia druzhina*), urged the local citizenry to lay in a supply of weapons. "Whoever is for the tsar, motherland, and Orthodox faith," it proclaimed, "should gather at the first alarm with guns, scythes, and pitchforks on the square by the municipal building and march under the Russian tricolor with the Aleksandrovsk Russian Brotherhood, which will descend with a portrait of the tsar and holy icons on our red-flagged enemies." In his dispatch, Budogovskii argued weakly that he was acquainted with the local patriotic organizations and permitted them to disseminate their literature, because he believed these helped restrain radicals from committing acts of violence against constituted authority. He seemed blithely unconcerned about the prospect of violence by the rightists. At the end of his report, Makarov indicated that rightists in Aleksandrovsk not only were inciting the local populace to action but were planning to trigger a particular outburst, possibly in mid-

February.[51] However, no violence occurred until early May and then proceeded sporadically, as ruffians accosted occasional persons on the streets without inflicting serious harm.[52] Luckily, the rightist organizations had not provided as much specific direction as Makarov anticipated. Nonetheless, it was painfully evident that the antisemitic and counterrevolutionary propaganda disseminated in Aleksandrovsk had been fueling a potentially explosive situation and that local authorities either condoned or added to the hostility.

Sometimes, rightists played an auxiliary role in the assaults. When a special Duma committee investigated the Belostok pogrom of 1–3 June 1906, it determined that police and soldiers were primarily responsible for fomenting and conducting the outrage. The committee noted that before the pogrom relations between most Christians and Jews in Belostok had been amiable, and that the Jews themselves had commended the local police chief for his even-handedness. However, on 21 May, when the chief was called to the site of a minor altercation between soldiers and young Jews, someone shot and killed him. An official inquiry failed to identify the culprit, but some of the police accused the Jews and intimated that there would be retribution, as did a local rightist organization, the Union of True Russians. Soon rumors of a pogrom were circulating through the city. The provincial governor assumed that the Jews were at fault and rashly declared that if a single Jewish shot was fired, the troops stationed in Belostok would use their weapons. Two days later, during an Orthodox religious procession, someone in a nearby building shot at the marchers. Almost immediately, troops arrived and began firing into the building, and a hastily formed mob ran through the streets, plundering Jewish shops and homes. To their credit, a few soldiers tried to restore order, but others enthusiastically joined the mob. Unfortunately, police also took advantage of the mayhem to ransack homes as they hunted for reported revolutionaries. Troops also exchanged shots with Jewish "defense units" that had been organized in Belostok after previous threats against the Jewish population. When the tumult subsided on the third day, at least eighty-three Jews and six Christians had been killed, and seventy Jews and twelve Christians had been injured. While the Duma committee charged that troops and police had arranged this so-called "military pogrom," it also emphasized the assistance given by the Union of True Russians.[53]

On occasion, the pogroms seem to have been spontaneous, as minor clashes between loyalists and oppositionists escalated into major violence. Such pogroms often followed provocative antigovernment demonstrations, in which the participants incensed patriotic onlookers by insulting the tsar or shouting "Down with the autocracy!" Although Jews at times took part in these demonstrations, rarely did they voice their displeasure as a Jewish minority, but rather as individuals joining non-Jews in criticizing the government. However, angry loyalists frequently responded with physical violence toward the Jewish participants and indiscriminate attacks on the rest of the local Jewish population. This occurred in Kursk in the wake of the October Manifesto. On 19 October 1905, antigovernment demonstrators marched through the city, waving red flags and singing revolutionary songs. Suddenly, a band of loyalists emerged and confronted the marchers. When the demonstrators fired some random shots, the loyalists dispersed, only to reassemble and let loose a barrage of rocks. The demonstrators returned a round of small arms fire, but at this point Cossacks and police broke up the procession. The counterdemonstrators then withdrew to a nearby monastery for a celebration of public prayer, after which they began their own procession, complete with martial music and portraits of the tsar. By now both sides had contributed amply to the mounting tension, the antigovernment demonstrators mostly because of using firearms. But the worst violence was yet to come. During the next two nights, mobs roamed the streets of Kursk, shouting that the Jews had started the disturbances and plundering Jewish shops and homes. Information on the extent of the pogrom is sparse, but according to police reports one person was killed and thirty-eight were injured.[54]

In some cities similar confrontations resulted in greater bloodshed. The Odessa pogrom of 18–22 October 1905 dramatically illustrates how popular passions needed only a precipitating incident to turn them into violence. When news of the October Manifesto reached Odessa, antigovernment demonstrators excitedly filled the streets, where they clashed with police, wounding several of them, one so badly that he died. Patriotic counterdemonstrators, who had noted Jews among the protesters, immediately blamed the Jews in general for the turmoil. Fearful that a pogrom might be in the making, Jewish defense units formed, which the counterdemonstrators charged were simply a cover for young Jews involved in revolutionary activities. Soon counterdemonstrators were marching through the streets, shouting "Down with the Jews!" When shots fired from a building along the route killed several marchers, the antisemitic fervor quickly burgeoned into a massive assault on the Jewish population. The police, already under attack, hesitated to reenter the melee. Those who did show up often abetted the pogromists, and some looted Jewish homes and shops. The district military commander, General Kaulbars, sympathetic with the anti-Jewish forces, declined to send in troops, which was clearly the only means of putting an immediate halt to the violence. By the time the tumult subsided, over 500 persons had been killed, about 400 of whom were Jews. Certainly, the authorities' feeble response to this and other pogroms not only failed to stem these terrible outbursts but in the public mind tended to implicate the government, an association that it could ill afford.[55]

One may conclude that the autocracy did not gain much from the rightists' use of violence, whether street fighting, political assassinations, or pogroms. For that matter neither did the rightists. On the contrary, those extremists who engaged in violence brought upon the movement its greatest disrepute. Even moderate rightists criticized these excesses. Perhaps, in resorting to violence, the participants gratified their desire for revenge on those they regarded as enemies, but it was far from certain that political assassinations were curbing the liberationists or that pogroms were helping the rightists' campaign against Jewish equality. Most rightist leaders, even those in the militant Union of the Russian People, came reluctantly to recognize that, as a matter of strategy, they might better leave suppression to the army, police, and courts. They could more profitably devote their own energies to fighting the autocracy's opponents in such fields of combat as the Duma campaigns – an area where indeed they made a stronger imprint.

10   Rightists and the government

The apparent affinity between the rightist movement and the tsarist government prompts one to look closely at that relationship. As emphasized in previous chapters, there is little evidence to suggest that the government created or controlled the rightist organizations. The question, then, concerns the government's attitude toward them and the extent to which it supported – or suppressed – their activities. What becomes evident is that at both the national and local levels, some officials proved extremely sympathetic to the rightist cause, while others remained indifferent, suspicious, or even antagonistic. Most could accept the rightist movement in principle, but they tended to doubt the rightists' reliability. The Ministry of Internal Affairs, in particular, as it monitored various political organizations, approached the rightists cautiously. On occasion, it subsidized rightist publications; early in the revolutionary period, it even supplied weapons to certain militant groups that pledged their help in restoring order. But overall, the Ministry of Internal Affairs distrusted at least the more extreme rightists, who in their zeal frequently added to the current chaos. Moreover, the government, accustomed to its long monopoly on political initiative, looked askance at any independent public organizations, even those dedicated to defending the autocracy. In dealing with its problems, it preferred to act on its own.

Attitudes within the government

Divergent attitudes toward the rightists existed at the highest levels of government. Tsar Nicholas himself showed great sympathy for the rightist movement. While he may not have comprehended the full significance of Russia's troubles in 1905–1906, he recognized that the autocracy had come seriously under attack. In his 18 February 1905 manifesto, he intuitively turned to "persons of good will" for support.[1] He welcomed their expressions of loyalty, usually without questioning whether those who proclaimed their allegiance represented the general population. It was easier to believe that the oppositionists were an aberration on an otherwise tranquil political landscape. Nicholas seemed to find solace in the traditional myth of the Russian people's love for their tsar. Even when his supporters quite frankly admonished him to stand firm amidst Russia's turmoil, they reinforced his abiding, if somewhat errant, sense of duty.

Repeatedly, Nicholas received rightist delegations, which assured him that true Russians everywhere upheld his autocratic power. On 23 December 1905, he accepted a Union of the Russian People badge from its chairman, Dr. Dubrovin, and wished the Union "total success" in its efforts to unify loyal Russians.[2] After the dissolution of the unruly Second Duma, Nicholas sent Dubrovin a telegram, in which he expressed to all the Union's members "his heartfelt gratitude for their devotion and readiness to serve the throne and the welfare of our dear homeland."[3]

Not all of Nicholas's ministers shared his sympathetic sentiments. Count Sergei Witte, as Chairman of the Council of Ministers in late 1905 and early 1906, openly expressed his hostility. Offended by the attacks on his conciliatory policies that appeared in the URP's *Russkoe znamia*, V. A. Gringmut's *Moskovskiia vedomosti*, and other rightist publications, he condemned the rightist leaders and their parties. To Witte the URP was "a gang of mercenary hooligans" and Dubrovin "a petty swindler" – a judgment that Witte held even more adamantly after the URP's attempt on his life in early 1907. Elaborating on the URP, Witte wrote: "This party is fundamentally patriotic and, given our cosmopolitanism, should be well received. But its patriotism is elemental, based not on reason and a sense of nobility, but on passion. Most of its leaders are unscrupulous politicians of sordid intellect and feeling, without one viable or upright political idea. Their efforts are directed at arousing the basest instincts of the ignorant crowd."[4] It may be that Witte's antagonism toward the extremist URP unduly biased him against the rightist movement as a whole, but there is little to suggest that he accepted rightists of any kind. He saw scant value in their endeavors to rally support for the autocracy, and he flatly discounted whatever influence they might exert on the government.

Witte's Minister of Internal Affairs, P. N. Durnovo, was more amiably disposed toward the rightists, an attitude in keeping with his determination to employ severe measures in quashing opposition to the throne. When Witte criticized Dubrovin and the Union of the Russian People, Durnovo replied that he had met Dubrovin and found him to be "a most honorable and excellent person."[5] While never officially endorsing the URP, Durnovo enabled it more easily to find favor with the tsar. In December 1905, when Dubrovin requested the Minister of the Imperial Court, Baron Frederiks, to arrange a URP audience with Nicholas, Frederiks asked Durnovo's opinion of this organization, thus far unknown to him. Durnovo showed no hesitation in recommending Dubrovin and the Union to Frederiks, who proceeded to arrange the audience. During the rest of his tenure as Minister of Internal Affairs, until April 1906, Durnovo continued to act sympathetically toward the URP, the Union of Russian Men, and other rightist organizations, even though Witte disapproved.[6]

Peter Stolypin, when he became Minister of Internal Affairs in April 1906 and Chairman of the Council of Ministers in July of that year, expressed none of Witte's rancor toward the rightists, but neither did he indulge them. Intent on suppressing the opposition movement, Stolypin fully understood the benefit of conservative backing for the autocracy, especially in the Duma. What he disliked was having the government share with the rightists its initiative in restoring order. He was even more concerned that extremist groups like the Union of the Russian People often added more to the country's ferment than to its tranquility. Stolypin best expressed his basic policy toward the rightists in a circular addressed to provincial governors in September 1906, in which he wrote: "One must recognize the service rendered by patriotic and monarchist societies throughout the empire. Nonetheless, in this sphere, government officials should be very discriminating, and, when coming into contact with leaders of these organizations, should impress upon them that the government expects *absolutely loyal support* and rejects any pursuits that involve internecine conflict, terroristic undertakings, or the like."[7]

Within the Ministry of Internal Affairs, most officials shared Stolypin's wariness. Some openly expressed their distaste for at least the extreme rightists, while still admitting that in certain cases it might be politically expedient to assist them. V. I. Gurko, an assistant minister in 1906, remarked in his memoirs: "Personally, I have never sympathized with organizations like the Union of the Russian People ... but during times of revolutionary unrest, when the people are in the grip of mass psychosis, the government must support individual organizations that spring up to support it."[8]

Government subsidies

But what support to give? And what benefits to get in return? Aware that the rightist organizations operated independently, the government wished to ascertain that any aid it offered would be used to further its own objectives. Some officials felt that the government would be best advised to limit its assistance to helping finance monarchist publications. The government itself was printing anti-oppositionist pamphlets having such titles as "The Truth about the Kadets" and "Our Socialists," usually in quantities of at least 100,000 copies each.[9] It knew that rightist organizations were publishing similar materials but were often having trouble meeting expenses. Indeed, publication costs were among the rightists' most burdensome expenditures. At one point the Union of the Russian People considered discontinuing its widely circulated newspaper, *Russkoe znamia*, for lack of funds.[10] In Bessarabia, the URP's Akkerman branch distributed thousands of brochures paid for with money that it admitted "had been collected kopek by kopek."[11] Therefore, government subsidies expressly earmarked to meet publication costs seemed a worthwhile investment.

How much money the government allotted for rightist publications is difficult to estimate, since it disbursed such funds secretly. In his memoirs, S. E. Kryzhanovskii, an Assistant Minister of Internal Affairs in 1906, stated that the government subsidized about thirty loyalist newspapers and channeled funds to various monarchist groups to help print patriotic brochures. Kryzhanovskii specifically mentions money given to Dubrovin, as editor of *Russkoe znamia*, and to I. I. Vostorgov, a leading figure in the Russian Monarchist Party, who published a series of loyalist pamphlets.[12] V. N. Kokovtsov, Minister of Finance from 1902 to 1914, estimated that the government spent about three million rubles through his office to help rightist parties during the years 1910–1912, intimating that earlier it had also provided subsidies, although smaller ones.[13]

While most rightist leaders remained silent on the question of government subsidies, some corroborated Kryzhanovskii's statement. Elena Poloboiarinova, who became the Union of the Russian People's treasurer near the end of 1907, affirmed that by then the Union was already receiving regular government payments for *Russkoe znamia* and other publications.[14] However, I. I. Baranov, who served as URP treasurer before Poloboiarinova, contended that the Union got no money from the government in 1905–1907 but was financed solely from private donations and membership dues. Actually, this discrepancy may not bear so much on the question of whether or not the government offered financial assistance as on the more technical matter of how aid was dispensed. According to V. I. Gurko, the government seldom gave money to organizations, channeling funds instead to individuals.[15] Thus, it made payments not to the Union itself but to Dubrovin as editor of *Russkoe znamia*. Similarly, Count A. I. Konovnitsyn, chairman of the Odessa URP branch, said that he personally received several payments of 500 rubles each in late 1907 and 1,000 rubles in 1908 from the head of the Main Administration for Affairs of the Press to assist in publishing a URP newspaper, *Za tsaria i rodinu*.[16]

On occasion, the government furnished money for other expenses related to the dissemination of monarchist literature. In July 1906, the Ministry of Internal Affairs allotted 5,000 rubles to the St. Petersburg city governor, V. F. von der Launits, to help the Union of the Russian People open tearooms. These modest dining facilities, located in working-class neighborhoods and stocked with patriotic literature, served as an appropriate means to divert workers from the radical propaganda that abounded in the factories and engage them in the monarchist cause. Willing to provide assistance, the Ministry of Internal Affairs nonetheless acted covertly, transmitting the money through von der Launits and marking its memorandum to him "secret."[17] These precautions may have been taken partly because some government officials objected to such disbursements, but probably more because the government wished to avoid the adverse publicity that surely would have resulted had the oppositionist parties learned that the government was subsidizing the URP.

The question of arms

The Ministry of Internal Affairs also grappled with the troublesome question of whether or not to accommodate those militant rightists who were eager to join the armed struggle against the revolutionary movement. Afraid that paramilitary action could easily get out of hand, the authorities generally preferred that independent organizations, even those that staunchly upheld the autocracy, would leave the use of force to the police and army. However, exceptions to this policy occurred already during the tumultuous fall and winter of 1905–1906. The Department of Police had recently placed Colonel A. V. Gerasimov, a gendarme officer, in charge of its Section for Maintaining Public Safety and Order in the Capital (*Otdelenie po okhraneniiu obshchestvennoi bezopasnosti i poriadka v stolitse*) – commonly known as the Okhrana. Gerasimov assembled some 250 men to run surveillance on members of revolutionary parties, conduct searches, and confiscate weapons and illegal presses. In the course of ferreting out revolutionary activity, Gerasimov was approached by the newly formed Union of the Russian People and the smaller Society for Active Struggle against Revolution and Anarchy.[18] On the basis of Gerasimov's reports, the Ministry of Internal Affairs conceded that these two organizations might be useful in helping protect the city from revolutionary violence. The Ministry particularly feared that the December uprising in Moscow would spark a similar outburst in the capital – rumor had it that this action might come on 9 January, the first anniversary of Bloody Sunday. Consequently, the Ministry authorized the St. Petersburg city governor, Major General V. A. Dediulin, to issue permits for the URP and the Society for Active Struggle to arm their *druzhiny* with handguns. The Ministry even told Dediulin that he could distribute a hundred used police revolvers and ammunition to *druzhiniki*, so they could protect public buildings, government presses, and state liquor stores. However, the winter passed without an insurrection; and in March 1906, the Department of Police requested the St. Petersburg city governor – by then V. F. von der Launits – to retrieve the revolvers.[19] Relieved that order was being restored in the capital, the government evidently felt that it could now rely on the police to handle isolated acts of revolutionary violence, and it resumed its reluctance to entrust weapons to private hands.[20]

The question of distributing weapons to rightist groups sometimes produced dissension among the authorities. In January 1907, the URP's Elisavetgrad branch told Baron Kaulbars, the Commander of the Odessa Military District, that it wanted to buy twenty army rifles and ammunition to defend the branch's printing office and treasury from local revolutionaries. Kaulbars directed that the acting governor-general of Odessa, Major General Boufal, dispense the rifles, although to individuals, not to the URP branch. Boufal soon reported that the rifles and ammunition had been procured from the district arsenal to be sold as directed; but since martial law had just been lifted from the area, he sent the rifles to Kherson province's civilian administrator, Governor Malaev, for distribution at his discretion. When the director of the Department of Police in St. Petersburg received complaints that Kaulbars's decision to sell weapons to URP *druzhiniki* was causing panic among the local populace, he asked Kaulbars and Malaev for an explanation. Both played down the situation, and Malaev noted that some months before, while the area was still under martial law, Kaulbars had disbursed ten rifles to the Elisavetgrad URP without telling the police and that these weapons had not created any serious disorders. In any event, Malaev assured the Department of Police that he had not actually released the twenty rifles in question but had transferred them to the Elisavetgrad chief of police for storage. There the matter remained, although it had become obvious that Kaulbars had transgressed the government's general policy on distributing arms.[21]

The issue of supplying weapons became even more acute a few weeks later, when Kaulbars ordered that twenty revolvers be issued to URP members in Odessa, ostensibly to help guard merchant ships in Odessa harbor. Immediately, the Odessa city governor, Major General Grigoriev, demanded that the order be rescinded, charging that Kaulbars was ruining his own efforts to keep the URP's *druzhiniki* from intimidating the local population.[22] In blaming Kaulbars for contributing to the volatile political situation in Odessa, Grigoriev reflected the concern of many officials, who felt that by arming the militant rightists the government undermined its own efforts at reestablishing law and order. By and large, both the Ministry of Internal Affairs and local authorities pursued a reasonably consistent policy toward the rightist organizations, regarding them as perhaps useful in rallying public support for the autocracy but not in acting as paramilitary units.

Precautions and restrictions

Not only was the government careful about aiding rightist organizations, but the prospect of right-wing extremists adding to Russia's turmoil prompted the Ministry of Internal Affairs to monitor, and even curtail, rightist activities.[23] In Bessarabia, for example, it gave special attention to those operations directed by P. A. Krushevan, the notorious antisemitic publicist, who had been largely responsible for the 1903 Kishinev pogrom. In June 1906, Krushevan established a URP branch in Kishinev and subsequently opened several nearby sub-branches, each with its own *druzhina*. What these *druzhiny* intended to do was not clear, whether simply to organize patriotic demonstrations or to engage in armed violence, which might lead to new pogroms. When the Ministry of Internal Affairs learned of these *druzhiny*, it immediately asked Governor Kharuzin of Bessarabia if they constituted a danger to the tranquility of the province, reminding him that any possession of weapons must not be tolerated. Kharuzin replied that some URP sub-branches were attracting quite despicable members, and he circulated a directive to all district police officers, stating that while he appreciated the URP's patriotism, he was troubled by its "inexperienced, unskilled, and often depraved leaders." Kharuzin ordered local authorities to watch the *druzhiny* and report any activity that violated public safety.[24] Although violence did not occur, tensions ran high because of the *druzhiny*, and the government maintained its vigilant stance.[25]

Elsewhere the authorities also tried to curb the Union of the Russian People. Along with attacking General Kaulbars for authorizing the distribution of weapons to the Odessa URP, General Grigoriev repeatedly criticized the URP branch chairman, Count A. I. Konovnitsyn. In a letter to the Minister of Internal Affairs, Grigoriev complained about Konovnitsyn's "premeditated disrespect for the law and for directives from local authorities." Later, he charged that under Konovnitsyn the Odessa URP branch attracted the lowest strata of society and led them into all kinds of disreputable activity.[26] Grigoriev particularly feared that the URP would instigate a new pogrom in Odessa, possibly worse than the one that occurred in October 1905. "Every day," he told the Minister of Internal Affairs in May 1907, "one may anticipate a terrible catastrophe."[27] Grigoriev's successor as Odessa city governor, General G. L. Novitskii, also distrusted Konovnitsyn and the URP. In September 1907, he submitted to Stolypin, as Chairman of the Council of Ministers, information he had obtained from military authorities that Konovnitsyn had been forced into retirement from military service for embezzling public funds. This corruption, Novitskii declared, still characterized Konovnitsyn's behavior as leader of the Odessa URP. Major General I. N. Tolmachev, who succeeded Novitskii in December 1907, looked more favorably on the URP, but complaints continued to reach St. Petersburg about Konovnitsyn's conduct, including his drunkenness and lewdness.[28] For its part, the central government pursued a somewhat inconsistent policy toward the Odessa URP. On one hand, the Main Administration for Affairs of the Press gave Konovnitsyn money to help finance his newspaper; on the other, the Ministry of Internal Affairs backed Odessa authorities in their attempts to prevent URP functionaries from making a show of force. Whether because of faulty internal communication or ambiguity of purpose, the government could condone, even encourage, inflammatory rightist rhetoric, while suppressing the pernicious behavior to which this rhetoric might lead. Department of Police records indicate other instances when provincial officials restricted URP activities because they felt that public safety was at risk. In February 1906, the Ekaterinoslav governor cancelled a URP demonstration in the provincial capital, because he anticipated that Union activists would provoke a clash with radical workers. The governor also warned URP leaders not to exacerbate the volatile tensions already existing between Russians and Jews in the city, which could easily lead to a pogrom.[29] Similarly, in March 1907, Governor Bolotov of Perm province refused the URP permission to conduct a patriotic procession, because he feared it would inflame counterrevolutionary passions and lead to violence. Bolotov reported to the Department of Police that URP leaders in Perm had already shown themselves to be "unrestrained and intolerant, without tact, and absolutely untrustworthy," sufficient reason for turning down their request.[30]

Even when local rightist organizations did not threaten public tranquility, the Ministry of Internal Affairs had the task of enforcing imperial regulations that prohibited governmental and military personnel from participating in political organizations.[31] This constraint presumably applied not only to oppositionist but also to loyalist groups, although the Ministry did not regard all rightist organizations as being sufficiently "political" to warrant its attention. It largely ignored the Russian Assembly, which had existed since 1901 as a "cultural association" and only in late 1905 began to assume a political character. Not until early 1907 did government agents attend Assembly meetings to ascertain that it was a reliable organization.[32] But the Ministry of Internal Affairs did object to officials being involved with such explicitly political organizations as the Union of the Russian People, even in localities where the URP conducted itself peaceably. When the governor of Orel province was invited to attend the opening of the Elets URP branch in January 1907, he dutifully replied that he was not permitted to participate in party gatherings.[33] Likewise, when informed that a minor police official in Kharkov province was serving as secretary of the Kupiansk URP branch, the Department of Police replied that such activity should be terminated.[34]

Sometimes, the question of participation was difficult to resolve. In Yalta the ranking military officer, Colonel Dumbadze, members of his staff, and the local gendarme chief, Popov, attended a gala URP meeting, at which Dumbadze made a speech and accepted a Union badge as an honorary member. When the director of the Department of Police, M. I. Trusevich, learned of the incident, he questioned Popov about the meeting. Popov contended that the gathering was simply patriotic, not political, and therefore he and the others were not at fault. Nonetheless, Trusevich warned Popov to refrain from such activities, and he asked the provincial governor to explain personally to Dumbadze that, as a representative of the government, his appearance at the URP meeting ran counter to imperial policy.[35] In general, the Ministry of Internal Affairs took seriously the ban on political participation. Local authorities were at times less diligent, especially when their sympathies lay with the rightist organizations and they could argue, like Popov, that they were simply fulfilling their patriotic obligations.

Overall, the relationship between the rightist organizations and the government was at best ambivalent. Indeed, the two shared fundamental impulses, which would seem the basis of a natural linkage. Both wanted to preserve Russia's political and social structure, its religious and cultural traditions. Both directed themselves to crushing the revolutionaries and containing the liberals. The rightists constantly proclaimed their allegiance to the tsar, who in return gratefully acknowledged their support.

Yet, despite a commonality of purpose, the government and the rightists never felt convinced that they could rely on one another. Most rightists wished that the tsar and his ministers would act more resolutely in confronting the opposition. Nicholas they perceived as too vacillating, Witte as too conciliatory. Stolypin, while more decisive, seemed distressingly indifferent to loyalist support. By choice and by necessity, the rightists concluded that it was they who must take the initiative in rescuing the autocracy from its enemies and from itself. But this initiative was exactly what disturbed the government. By intuition the tsar and his ministers prized their monopoly on political action. Not only did they find it difficult to accept the role of the moderate oppositionists in Russia's emerging political structure, but they had trouble accommodating even the loyalists. To be sure, government officials had reason to distrust some of the rightists, particularly those extremists who, in their attempts to suppress revolutionary violence, contributed their own brand of lawlessness. As a result of these concerns, the government and the rightists remained uneasy allies, their tenuous relationship reflecting the ambiguities generally inherent in Russia's emerging political structure.

11   Rightists and the Duma

Earlier chapters have dealt with the formation and programs of the leading national and provincial rightist organizations. This chapter will examine more closely the relationship between the rightists and the Duma: their attitudes toward this institution, their participation in the Duma campaigns, and the effect they had on the Duma's future.

It should be emphasized that for many rightists the Duma posed a singularly difficult problem. Extreme rightists in particular faced the dilemma of upholding in practice an institution they opposed in principle. They were doubly disturbed by the nature of the new Duma: first, because the tsar himself had granted it legislative power, which implied a limitation on his sovereignty; and, second, because many constitutionalists, especially the Kadets, seemed eager to use the Duma to gain further political concessions. The extreme rightists decided that their best hope was to get enough loyalists elected to the Duma for it not to attempt to exercise its legislative power, but to function, in effect, only as a consultative assembly. As Father Vostorgov of the Russian Monarchist Party advised, "The Duma deputies, honorably and conscientiously, should express the people's needs, but this should be counsel, not decision-making, for decision-making belongs to the tsar."[1]

Moderate rightists seemed more willing to accept the Duma as the legislative body it was intended to be. They wanted no additional change in Russia's political system, but they foresaw rightist deputies participating in the give and take of partisan politics on the Duma floor, promoting legislation that accorded with their own conservative views. Consequently, both moderate and extreme rightists campaigned for Duma seats, even if for somewhat different reasons.

Much can be learned about rightist influences among the Russian electorate by analyzing the first three Duma elections, held successively in March 1906, February 1907, and October 1907; but the

Second Duma elections provide the most discriminating profile of voter preferences. This is true in part because the second elections reflected a keener political consciousness than had existed in the first elections, when most voters and even many Duma deputies had designated themselves simply as non-party. By the second elections the voters had become better acquainted with the various parties and had a greater range of candidates from which to choose. Besides the already active Kadets and Octobrists, the leftist parties, most of which had boycotted the first elections, now campaigned. The rightists, who by this time had established themselves throughout the country, completed the political spectrum.

The Second Duma elections also enable a more accurate political appraisal to be made than those to the Third Duma. Although the rightists fared remarkably well in the third elections, which finally produced a loyalist Duma majority, it took the government's revised electoral law, favoring the conservative voters, to ensure this outcome. Less disproportionate, the Second Duma elections distinguish better the relative strengths of the political parties.

In the second elections, the rightists polled much more heavily than in the first. They found their greatest support in the troubled central agricultural provinces and the ethnically diverse western borderlands. There they drew not only from landowners, as might be anticipated, but also from peasants and townspeople, who responded to the rightists' major themes: the restoration of law and order, Russian superiority over non-Russian minorities, and loyalty to the autocratic tsar. The rightists almost certainly would never match the oppositionists' appeal to the Russian populace as a whole; but in the second elections they obtained a large enough following to carry several provinces and prove themselves viable contenders in others.

The First Duma

Getting deputies elected to the Duma was itself a cumbersome process. Elections were indirect, involving successive steps from the local level to the provincial assemblies, where the final selection of deputies occurred.[2] Moreover, the electorate was divided into four curiae – peasants, landowners, townspeople, and workers – each of which had its own electoral procedures.

a) In the villages, *peasants* who held communal land chose representatives to local (*volost*) assemblies, which in turn sent delegates to district (*uezd*) assemblies, from which peasant electors went on to the provincial (*guberniia*) assemblies.

b) *Small landowners* (including those few peasants who owned private land, either solely or in addition to their communal holdings) met in local assemblies to select delegates to district assemblies. These delegates were joined there by *large landowners*, each having a direct vote. The combined participants in the district assemblies then chose electors to the provincial assemblies.

c) *Townspeople* voted for representatives to municipal assemblies, which chose electors to the provincial assemblies.

d) *Workers* sent delegates from their factories to preliminary assemblies, which chose electors to the provincial assemblies.

In the 51 provincial assemblies of European Russia, the electors selected 384 of the Duma's 524 deputies. The peasants in each assembly met separately to elect one deputy from their own number; the combined electors chose the rest. In the 20 largest cities, which had separate representation, the electoral process was simpler: voters chose representatives from each municipal district, who then met to select the city's deputy or deputies. Most cities having separate representation were allotted one deputy, but St. Petersburg was large enough to have six, while Moscow had four, making a total of 28.[3] The remaining deputies came from Poland, the Caucasus, Siberia, and Central Asia, which had special electoral laws.

Since the rightists had not organized widely before the First Duma elections, their campaigning occurred mostly in the major cities. Even there, rightist groups usually constructed alliances, since they lacked independent strength. In St. Petersburg, the Russian Assembly and the Union of the Russian People announced that they would campaign together, and they published a joint list of candidates from the city's 12 electoral districts – 160 names in all. Both Prince Dmitrii Golitsyn, chairman of the Russian Assembly, and A. I. Dubrovin, head of the Union of the Russian People, were candidates. Approximately 30 others were middle-echelon government bureaucrats (typical Russian Assembly members); about 95 were merchants, physicians, lawyers, publicists, writers, clerics, and retired military and naval officers; and the remaining 35 were workers recruited by the Union of the Russian People from the city's Vyborg and Petersburg districts, where the workers' vote was considered critical. In affluent areas, such as the Liteiny and Moscow districts, candidates from the commercial, professional, and bureaucratic social strata predominated, as did those with titles, which included five princes, three counts, and two barons.[4]

In Moscow, the Russian Monarchist Party, Union of Russian Men, and Union of the Russian People formed a loose coalition, which some smaller associations also joined. V. A. Gringmut, founder of the Monarchist Party, spearheaded the campaign. In his newspaper, *Moskovskiia vedomosti*, he warned his readers to resist the clever manipulations of the liberals, who, like wolves in sheep's clothing, called themselves "representatives of the people." Make sure, Gringmut cautioned, to vote for electors who would truly represent the Russian people – those who were Christian and loyal to the tsar.[5]

Rightist organizations had not yet built enough strength in the provinces to campaign effectively. By mid-March the Union of the Russian People had 25 branches, the Russian Monarchist Party four, the Russian Assembly seven, and the Union of Russian Men about a dozen.[6] Some local rightist organizations had also appeared. As discussed in Chapters 6 and 7, these included the Tula Union for Tsar and Order, Kursk People's Party of Order, Orel Union of Law and Order, and Bessarabian Center Party. Less active were the Nizhnii Novgorod Union of the White Banner, Kazan People's Tsarist Society, Arkhangel Faithful Sons of Russia, Kaluga Party for Tsar and Order, Gomel Union of Russian Patriots, and Ivanovo-Voznesensk Autocratic–Monarchist Party. Still, a few dozen branches of the national rightist associations and some local organizations, even if they had acquired strength in their immediate areas, did not constitute a decisive political movement.

The first stage of the elections – the choosing of electors to the provincial assemblies – confirmed whatever apprehensions the rightists may have had. Tables 4–9 show the small number and percentage of rightist electors by curia, along with those of other political affiliations, in each provincial assembly.[7]

Although political lines often were not firmly drawn, the categories used in these tables correspond to those adopted by political observers at the time. The "rightists" included electors affiliated with established national or local monarchist associations or, if unaffiliated, expressing ultraloyalist attitudes. The Trade and Industry Party, similar to the Octobrists but organizationally distinct, is listed because in Moscow and a few other industrial areas it ran its own campaign. More widely located, the "Octobrist bloc" consisted of Octobrists themselves and candidates inclined toward them, sometimes running on a joint slate. "Progressives" were usually non-party electors

Table 4 First Duma: Peasant electors in provincial assemblies

Province	Total allotted	Total reported	Rightists	Trade and Industry Party	Octobrist bloc	Progressives	Kadet bloc	Non-party
Arkhangel	19	19	5 26%	–	–	–	1 5%	13 68%
Astrakhan	24	24	3 13%	–	–	–	–	21 88%
Bessarabia	43	43	– –	–	3 7%	3 7%	–	37 86%
Vilna	40	40	1 3%	–	–	12 30%	–	27 68%
Vitebsk	31	31	– –	–	–	2 6%	–	29 94%
Vladimir	26	26	– –	–	–	6 23%	–	20 77%
Vologda	46	46	– –	–	–	9 20%	–	37 80%
Volynia	69	69	5 7%	–	1 1%	–	1 1%	62 90%
Voronezh	101	101	6 6%	–	–	2 2%	–	93 92%
Viatka	148	148	13 9%	–	–	29 20%	10 7%	96 65%
Grodno	43	43	– –	–	–	1 2%	–	42 98%
Don Oblast	93	93	4 4%	–	–	1 1%	–	88 95%
Ekaterinoslav	34	34	– –	–	–	–	1 3%	33 97%
Kazan	98	98	– –	–	–	5 5%	–	93 95%
Kaluga	30	26	3 12%	–	–	3 12%	1 4%	19 73%
Kiev	80	69	7 10%	–	–	5 7%	1 1%	56 81%
Kovno	39	39	– –	–	–	12 31%	–	27 69%
Kostroma	29	29	4 14%	–	–	1 3%	5 17%	19 66%
Courland	13	8	1 *	*	*	2 *	3 *	2 *
Kursk	78	74	4 5%	–	–	26 35%	7 9%	37 50%
Livonia	21	5	– *	*	*	–	5 *	– *
Minsk	41	15	– *	–	–	–	1 *	15 90%
Mogilev	40	40	3 8%	–	–	–	1 3%	36 90%
Moscow	16	16	4 25%	–	–	–	1 6%	11 69%

Nizhnii Novgorod	42	38	3	8%	–	–	–	–	4	11%	4	11%	27	71%
Novgorod	31	31	–	–	–	–	–	–	5	16%	–	–	26	84%
Olonets	27	27	2	7%	–	*	–	*	–	–	–	–	25	93%
Orenburg	63	2	–	–	–	–	–	–	–	*	–	*	2	*
Orel	59	59	2	3%	–	–	–	–	8	14%	1	1%	48	81%
Penza	47	47	3	6%	–	–	–	–	7	15%	–	–	37	79%
Perm	86	86	2	2%	–	–	–	–	2	2%	–	–	82	95%
Podolia	82	82	–	–	–	*	–	*	–	–	–	–	82	100%
Poltava	23	3	1	*	–	–	–	–	–	*	–	*	2	*
Pskov	24	24	–	–	–	–	–	–	11	46%	2	8%	11	46%
Riazan	54	52	10	19%	–	–	2	4%	8	15%	1	2%	31	60%
Samara	97	97	–	–	–	–	–	–	–	–	–	–	97	100%
St. Petersburg	14	14	–	–	–	*	–	–	13	93%	–	*	1	7%
Saratov	64	26	–	*	–	–	–	*	12	*	14	–	–	*
Simbirsk	44	44	4	14%	–	–	–	–	12	27%	–	–	32	73%
Smolensk	31	29	–	–	–	–	–	–	4	14%	1	3%	20	69%
Stavropol	33	33	–	–	–	–	–	–	–	–	–	–	33	100%
Tauride	42	42	21	24%	–	–	–	–	3	7%	3	7%	36	86%
Tambov	92	86	–	–	–	–	–	–	4	5%	–	–	61	71%
Tver	49	49	1	3%	–	–	5	10%	9	18%	2	4%	33	67%
Tula	32	32	–	–	–	–	1	3%	1	3%	1	3%	28	88%
Ufa	88	88	–	–	–	–	–	–	–	–	–	–	88	100%
Kharkov	64	60	5	8%	–	–	4	7%	–	–	6	10%	45	75%
Kherson	50	50	1	2%	–	–	2	4%	4	8%	10	20%	33	66%
Chernigov	63	12	–	*	–	*	–	*	6	*	–	*	6	*
Estonia	10	–	–	–	–	–	–	–	–	*	–	*	–	*
Iaroslavl	17	16	–	–	–	–	–	–	5	31%	1	6%	10	63%

* Insufficient data.

Table 5 First Duma: Landowner electors in provincial assemblies

Province	Total allotted	Total reported	Rightists	Trade and Industry Party	Octobrist bloc	Progressives	Kadet bloc	Non-party
Arkhangel[a]	—	—	— —	—	—	— —	— —	— —
Astrakhan	5	5	— —	—	—	— —	— —	5 100%
Bessarabia	56	56	12 21%	—	—	14 25%	9 16%	21 38%
Vilna	44	44	— —	—	3 7%	14 32%	7 16%	20 45%
Vitebsk	39	39	5 13%	—	—	11 28%	5 13%	18 46%
Vladimir	18	18	7 39%	—	1 6%	3 17%	2 11%	5 28%
Vologda	21	21	8 38%	—	1 5%	2 10%	2 10%	8 38%
Volynia	86	86	7 8%	—	7 8%	6 7%	7 8%	59 69%
Voronezh	42	38	12 32%	—	4 11%	3 8%	1 3%	18 47%
Viatka	18	18	4 22%	—	—	4 22%	1 6%	9 50%
Grodno	36	36	7 19%	—	—	2 6%	3 8%	24 67%
Don Oblast	47	47	— —	—	16 34%	— —	4 9%	27 57%
Ekaterinoslav	38	38	4 11%	—	7 18%	4 11%	2 5%	21 55%
Kazan	23	23	7 30%	—	2 9%	3 13%	2 9%	9 39%
Kaluga	25	24	12 50%	1 4%	2 8%	3 13%	4 17%	2 8%
Kiev	74	43	4 9%	—	1 2%	8 19%	6 14%	24 56%
Kovno	35	35	5 14%	—	—	5 14%	— —	25 71%
Kostroma	35	35	3 9%	2 6%	—	2 6%	7 20%	21 60%
Courland	14	2	— *	1 *	— *	1 *	— *	1 *
Kursk	44	44	10 23%	—	—	10 23%	— —	24 55%
Livonia	25	1	— *	— *	— *	— *	1 *	— *
Minsk	74	44	2 5%	—	—	5 11%	16 36%	21 48%
Mogilev	53	53	1 2%	—	—	8 15%	10 19%	34 64%
Moscow	13	13	5 38%	1 8%	3 23%	1 8%	2 15%	1 8%

Province														
Nizhnii Novgorod	30	27	9	33%	—	—	3	11%	4	15%	4	15%	7	26%
Novgorod	45	45	8	18%	—	—	4	9%	5	11%	1	2%	27	60%
Olonets	9	9	—	—	—	—	—	—	—	—	—	—	9	100%
Orenburg	19	—	—	*	—	*	—	*	—	*	—	*	—	*
Orel	45	43	12	28%	—	—	4	9%	3	7%	3	7%	21	49%
Penza	28	28	—	—	—	—	—	—	3	11%	—	—	25	89%
Perm	58	56	9	16%	4	7%[a]	2	4%	16	29%	4	7%	21	38%
Podolia	76	76	15	20%	—	—	—	—	6	8%	5	7%	50	66%
Poltava	109	76	9	12%	—	—	—	—	33	43%	15	20%	19	25%
Pskov	27	27	4	15%	—	—	—	—	4	15%	3	11%	16	59%
Riazan	40	40	2	5%	—	—	11	28%	5	13%	2	5%	20	50%
Samara	52	43	5	12%	—	—	4	9%	—	—	—	—	34	79%
St. Petersburg	18	18	1	6%	—	—	5	28%	5	28%	5	28%	2	11%
Saratov	51	31	14	45%	—	—	1	3%	7	23%	7	23%	2	6%
Simbirsk	29	29	—	—	—	—	—	—	6	21%	4	14%	19	66%
Smolensk	40	33	5	15%	—	—	10	30%	4	12%	9	27%	5	15%
Stavropol	6	6	—	—	—	—	—	—	1	17%	—	—	5	83%
Tauride	31	31	10	32%	—	—	7	23%	6	19%	8	26%	—	—
Tambov	62	60	24	40%	4	7%[a]	10	17%	6	10%	5	8%	11	18%
Tver	41	41	—	—	—	—	6	15%	1	2%	15	37%	19	46%
Tula	29	29	7	24%	—	—	2	7%	—	—	—	—	20	69%
Ufa	36	36	5	14%	—	—	—	—	—	—	—	—	31	86%
Kharkov	43	43	1	2%	—	—	19	44%	4	9%	8	19%	11	26%
Kherson	69	65	34	52%	—	—	11	17%	8	12%	4	6%	8	12%
Chernigov	50	50	6	12%	—	—	—	—	7	14%	—	—	37	74%
Estonia	21	—	—	*	—	*	—	*	—	*	—	*	—	*
Iaroslavl	20	20	—	—	—	—	2	10%	3	15%	5	25%	10	50%

* Insufficient data.   [a] Combined with urban curia.

Table 6 *First Duma: Urban electors in provincial assemblies*

Province	Total allotted	Total reported	Rightists	Trade and Industry Party	Octobrist bloc	Progressives	Kadet bloc	Non-party
Arkhangel[a]	13	13	–	–	–	–	6 46%	7 54%
Astrakhan	16	16	1 6%	–	–	–	– –	15 94%
Bessarabia	21	21	3 14%	–	–	3 14%	6 29%	9 43%
Vilna	7	7	–	–	–	3 43%	2 29%	2 29%
Vitebsk	20	20	1 5%	–	–	5 25%	8 40%	6 30%
Vladimir	48	47	3 6%	1 2%	7 15%	3 6%	25 53%	8 17%
Vologda	13	13	4 31%	–	1 8%	1 8%	5 38%	2 15%
Volynia	40	40	1 3%	–	–	13 33%	5 13%	21 53%
Voronezh	22	22	– –	1 5%	–	4 18%	6 27%	11 50%
Viatka	34	34	3 9%	–	–	2 6%	19 56%	10 29%
Grodno	26	26	1 4%	–	–	6 23%	7 27%	12 46%
Don Oblast	37	37	–	–	1 3%	3 8%	10 27%	23 62%
Ekaterinoslav	63	63	–	–	1 2%	1 2%	23 37%	38 60%
Kazan	18	18	–	–	–	1 6%	5 28%	12 67%
Kaluga	21	21	4 19%	1 5%	–	4 19%	11 52%	1 5%
Kiev	71	22	1 *	–	– *	7 *	6 *	8 *
Kovno	16	16	–	–	–	8 50%	2 13%	6 38%
Kostroma	28	26	–	4 15%	3 12%	–	16 62%	3 12%
Courland	19	–	*	*	*	*	– *	– *
Kursk	28	27	2 7%	–	–	6 22%	13 48%	6 22%
Livonia	15	9	– *	– * *	– *	– * *	9 *	– *
Minsk	20	9	– *	–	– *	– *	9 *	– *
Mogilev	16	16	–	–	–	–	14 88%	2 13%
Moscow	63	63	2 3%	24 38%	4 6%	1 2%	21 33%	11 17%

Province														
Nizhnii Novgorod	18	18	2	11%	–	–	–	–	5	28%	8	44%	3	17%
Novgorod	16	16	–	–	–	–	5	31%	3	19%	2	13%	6	38%
Olonets	14	14	–	–	–	–	–	–	–	–	–	–	14	100%
Orenburg	23	–	–	*	–	*	–	*	–	*	–	*	–	*
Orel	18	18	4	22%	3	17%	1	6%	2	11%	6	33%	2	11%
Penza	15	11	8	15%	4	8%	–	–	2	18%	–	–	9	82%
Perm	52	52	–	–	–	–	–	–	5	10%	23	44%	12	23%
Podolia	37	31	–	*	–	–	–	–	12	39%	6	19%	13	42%
Poltava	49	9	–	*	–	*	*	*	–	*	9	*	–	*
Pskov	10	10	5	–	4	–	2	20%	–	–	6	60%	2	20%
Riazan	27	27	7	19%	–	15%	4	15%	2	7%	6	22%	6	22%
Samara	31	31	2	23%	–	–	–	–	–	–	11	35%	13	42%
St. Petersburg	19	17	1	12%	–	–	1	6%	1	6%	13	76%	–	–
Saratov	35	29	–	–	–	–	–	–	4	14%	24	83%	1	3%
Simbirsk	17	17	1	6%	–	–	–	–	7	41%	6	35%	3	18%
Smolensk	19	7	–	*	–	*	*	*	1	*	5	*	1	*
Stavropol	8	8	–	–	–	–	2	25%	2	25%	1	13%	3	38%
Tauride	23	22	2	9%	–	–	3	14%	2	9%	15	68%	–	–
Tambov	26	22	1	5%	–	–	1	5%	2	9%	7	32%	11	50%
Tver	30	30	–	–	–	–	13	43%	6	20%	11	37%	9	60%
Tula	15	15	3	20%	–	–	1	7%	1	7%	6	7%	10	38%
Ufa	26	26	2	8%	–	–	–	–	8	31%	6	23%	12	28%
Kharkov	43	43	5	12%	–	–	7	16%	5	12%	14	33%	9	36%
Kherson	31	25	–	–	–	–	–	–	1	4%	15	60%	1	6%
Chernigov	37	18	–	*	–	*	–	–	12	67%	5	28%	–	*
Estonia	14	1	–	*	–	*	–	*	–	*	1	*	1	*
Iaroslavl	23	23	–	–	–	–	1	4%	4	17%	14	61%	4	17%

* Insufficient data.   a Includes landowners.

Table 7 *First Duma: Worker electors in provincial assemblies*

Province	Total allotted	Total reported
Arkhangel	1	—
Astrakhan	1	—
Bessarabia	—	—
Vilna	1	—
Vitebsk	—	—
Vladimir	16	2 rightists, 2 moderates, 9 progressives, 1 leftist, 2 unknown
Vologda	—	—
Volynia	2	—
Voronezh	1	—
Viatka	4	—
Grodno	2	—
Don Oblast	5	—
Ekaterinoslav	6	6 leftists
Kazan	2	—
Kaluga	2	—
Kiev	7	5 progressives, 2 leftists
Kovno	—	—
Kostroma	7	3 Kadets, 2 leftists, 2 non-party
Courland	2	—
Kursk	2	—
Livonia	1	—
Minsk	2	—
Mogilev	1	—
Moscow	17	1 Trade and Industry Party, 6 Kadets, 8 leftists, 2 non-party
Nizhnii Novgorod	2	—
Novgorod	2	—
Olonets	—	—
Orenburg	1	—
Orel	3	—
Penza	2	—
Perm	10	—
Podolia	4	—
Poltava	1	—
Pskov	—	—
Riazan	2	—
Samara	1	—
St. Petersburg	10	—
Saratov	4	—
Simbirsk	2	—

Smolensk	1	—
Stavropol	—	—
Taurida	1	—
Tambov	3	—
Tver	4	—
Tula	1	1 progressive
Ufa	4	—
Kharkov	4	—
Kherson	4	4 moderates
Chernigov	3	—
Estonia	2	—
Iaroslavl	2	—

somewhat opposed to the autocracy. (By the Second Duma elections, a new designation – "moderates" – identified non-party electors who regarded themselves as loyalists.) Like the Octobrist bloc, the "Kadet bloc" comprised party members and those inclined toward it. Since the radical parties generally boycotted the elections, perceiving the Duma as falling far short of the sweeping changes they advocated, few electors identified themselves as "leftists." The "non-party" electors consisted of persons not affiliated with any party or whose political inclinations were unclear.

As shown in Tables 4–9, no party or political persuasion polled heavily. The Kadets did best, but in most provinces even they received no more than 25 percent of the vote. The rightists usually accounted for only from about 5 to 15 percent, and the Octobrists, on average, got even less. Most striking was the high percentage of "non-party" electors in all curiae, especially among the peasants. Obviously, the notion of partisan politics had not yet taken root except in a few cities where the parties had been particularly active. In the countryside, many peasants, regarding the Duma as an intermediary for petitioning the tsar on the land issue, apparently felt no need to elect representatives affiliated with a specific party, although it soon became evident that many non-party peasant electors were inclined toward the left. Equally crucial, the numerous "progressive" electors, while not associated with any party, held at least modestly oppositionist views. Overall, the preliminary elections indicated that many provincial assemblies would be oppositionist; and, in the absence of leftist parties, the Kadets stood an excellent chance of taking the lead in forming successful voting blocs once the assemblies met.

In cities having separate representation, the Kadets did exceptionally well, generally sweeping the elections. Only in Tula and Orel did

Table 8 *First Duma: Combined peasant, landowner, urban, and worker electors in provincial assemblies*

Province	Total allotted	Total reported	Rightists		Trade and Industry Party		Octobrist bloc		Progressives		Kadet bloc		Leftists		Non-party	
Arkhangel	33	32	5	16%	—	—	—	—	—	—	7	22%	—	—	20	63%
Astrakhan	46	45	4	9%	—	—	—	—	—	—	—	—	—	—	41	91%
Bessarabia	120	120	15	13%	—	—	3	3%	20	17%	15	13%	—	—	67	56%
Vilna	92	91	1	1%	—	—	3	3%	29	32%	9	10%	—	—	49	54%
Vitebsk	90	90	6	7%	—	—	—	—	18	20%	13	14%	—	—	53	59%
Vladimir	108	107	12	11%	1	1%	8	7%	21	20%	27	25%	1	1%	37ᵃ	35%
Vologda	80	80	12	15%	—	—	2	3%	12	15%	7	9%	—	—	47	59%
Volynia	197	195	13	7%	—	—	8	4%	19	10%	13	7%	—	—	142	73%
Voronezh	166	161	18	11%	1	1%	4	2%	9	6%	7	4%	—	—	122	76%
Viatka	204	200	20	10%	—	—	—	—	35	18%	30	15%	—	—	115	58%
Grodno	107	105	8	8%	—	—	—	—	9	9%	10	10%	—	—	78	74%
Don Oblast	182	177	4	2%	—	—	17	10%	4	2%	14	8%	—	—	138	78%
Ekaterinoslav	141	141	4	3%	—	—	8	6%	5	4%	26	18%	6	4%	92	65%
Kazan	141	139	7	5%	—	—	2	1%	9	6%	7	5%	—	—	114	82%
Kaluga	78	71	19	27%	2	3%	2	3%	10	14%	16	23%	—	—	22	31%
Kiev	232	141	12	9%	—	—	1	1%	25	18%	13	9%	2	1%	88	62%
Kovno	90	90	5	6%	—	—	—	—	25	28%	2	2%	—	—	58	64%
Kostroma	99	90	7	8%	6	7%	3	3%	3	3%	28	31%	—	—	43	48%
Courland	48	10	1	*	—	*	—	*	3	*	3	*	—	*	3	*
Kursk	152	145	16	11%	—	—	—	—	42	29%	20	14%	—	—	67	46%
Livonia	62	15	—	*	—	*	—	*	—	*	15	*	—	*	—	*
Minsk	137	68	2	*	—	*	—	*	5	*	25	*	—	*	36	*
Mogilev	110	109	4	4%	—	—	—	—	8	7%	25	23%	—	—	72	66%
Moscow	109	109	11	10%	26	24%	7	6%	2	2%	30	28%	8	7%	25	23%

Nizhnii Novgorod	92	83	14	17%	—	—	3	4%	13	16%	16	19%	—	37	45%
Novgorod	94	92	8	9%	—	—	9	10%	13	14%	3	3%	—	59	64%
Olonets	50	50	2	4%	—	—	—	—	—	—	—	—	—	48	96%
Orenburg	106	2	—	*	—	—	—	*	—	*	—	*	*	2	*
Orel	125	120	18	15%	3	3%	5	4%	13	11%	10	8%	—	71	59%
Penza	92	86	3	3%	—	—	—	—	12	14%	—	—	—	71	83%
Perm	206	194	19	10%	8	4%	2	1%	23	12%	27	14%	—	115	59%
Podolia	199	189	15	8%	—	—	—	—	18	10%	11	6%	—	145	77%
Poltava	181	88	10	*	—	*	—	*	33	*	24	*	*	21	*
Pskov	61	61	4	7%	—	—	2	3%	15	25%	11	18%	—	29	48%
Riazan	123	119	17	14%	4	3%	17	14%	15	13%	9	8%	—	57	48%
Samara	181	171	12	7%	—	—	4	2%	—	—	11	6%	—	144	84%
St. Petersburg	61	49	3	6%	—	—	6	12%	19	39%	18	37%	—	3	6%
Saratov	154	86	14	16%	—	—	1	1%	23	27%	45	52%	—	3	3%
Simbirsk	92	90	1	1%	—	—	—	—	25	28%	10	11%	—	54	60%
Smolensk	91	69	9	13%	—	—	10	14%	9	13%	15	22%	—	26	38%
Stavropol	47	47	—	—	—	—	2	4%	3	6%	1	2%	—	41	87%
Tauride	97	95	12	13%	—	—	10	11%	11	12%	26	27%	—	36	38%
Tambov	183	168	46	27%	4	2%	11	7%	12	7%	12	7%	—	83	49%
Tver	124	120	—	—	—	—	24	20%	16	13%	28	23%	—	52	43%
Tula	77	76	11	14%	—	—	4	5%	2	3%	2	3%	—	57	75%
Ufa	154	150	7	5%	—	—	—	—	8	5%	6	4%	—	129	86%
Kharkov	154	146	11	8%	—	—	30	21%	9	6%	28	19%	—	68	47%
Kherson	154	140	35	25%	—	—	13	9%	13	9%	29	21%	—	50	36%
Chernigov	153	80	6	8%	—	—	—	—	25	31%	5	6%	—	44	55%
Estonia	47	1	—	*	—	—	—	*	—	*	1	*	*	—	*
Iaroslavl	62	59	—	—	—	—	3	5%	12	20%	20	34%	—	24	41%

* Insufficient data. a Includes 2 moderates and 2 unknown

Table 9 *First Duma: General electors in cities having separate representation (European Russia)*

City	Total allotted	Total reported	Rightists	Trade and Industry Party	Octobrist bloc	Progressives	Kadet bloc	Worker electors in these cities Total allotted	Total reported
Astrakhan	80	80	—	27 34%	—	—	53 66%	1	—
Vilna	80	80	—	—	—	21 26%	59 74%	—	—
Voronezh	80	80	—	—	—	—	80 100%	1	—
Ekaterinoslav	80	80	(←	54 ——— 68%	——→)	—	26 33%	1	1 leftist
Kazan	80	80	—	—	14 18%	—	66 83%	—	—
Kiev	80	80	7 9%	—	3 4%	2 3%	68 85%	2	2 progressives
Kishinev	80	80	—	—	36 45%	6 8%	38 48%	—	—
Kursk	80	80	—	—	—	—	80 100%	1	—
Moscow	160	160	—	—	—	—	160 100%	18	5 Kadets, 11 leftists, 2 non-party
Nizhnii Novgorod	80	80	—	—	—	—	80 100%	2	—
Odessa	80	80	—	—	—	—	80 100%	2	—
Orel	80	80	20 25%	—	—	2 3%	58 73%	—	—
Riga	80	80	—	—	10[a] 13%	—	70 88%	4	—
Rostov-on-Don	80	80	—	—	23 29%	1 1%	56 70%	1	—
Samara	80	80	—	—	—	—	80 100%	—	—
St. Petersburg	160	160	—	—	—	—	160 100%	15	—
Saratov	80	80	—	—	—	—	80 100%	—	—
Tula	80	80	25 31%	—	35 44%	—	20 25%	1	—
Kharkov	80	80	—	—	—	—	80 100%	3	—
Iaroslavl	80	80	—	—	7 9%	—	73 91%	2	—

No moderate or non-party general electors were reported

[a] Includes Baltic Constitutional Monarchists.

the rightists, who were well organized there, get a substantial portion of the vote. In Tula, the local Union for Tsar and Order might have been even more effective had its hopes for forming an electoral bloc with the Octobrists materialized. However, because some right-wing Octobrists had already defected to the Union, those remaining opposed the Union's initiatives. Instead, the Tula Octobrists, acting independently of directives from the national Octobrist leadership, chose to ally with the local Kadets, and they pledged their support for the moderate Kadet candidate, Prince G. E. Lvov. As the city's 80 electors, the Tula voters chose 25 Unionists, 35 Octobrists, and 20 Kadets. Although no party had a majority, the Kadets and Octobrists selected Prince Lvov as the city's deputy.[8]

In the city of Orel, the Union of Law and Order gained a sizeable portion of the vote, although not enough to overcome the Kadets. Friction between the two parties flared throughout the campaign. The Kadets complained that in the city's first district the election committee, which consisted exclusively of Union members, illegally prevented the Kadets from distributing their candidate lists. Perhaps this was a valid allegation, since an unusually high number of electors chosen in the city's first district – 20 out of 24 – were Union candidates, whereas in the second district the Kadets got 35 of the 37 electors and all 19 in the third district. When the electors met, the Kadet majority of 58 out of 80 electors chose its candidate, F. V. Tatarinov, as Orel's deputy.[9]

As anticipated, the rightists did little better in the provincial assemblies. Only six deputies selected there were rightists, and four of these were but slightly more conservative than the Octobrists.[10] As many as 22 non-party deputies in the First Duma may have leaned toward the right, but this was usually a tenuous association, inasmuch as several later collaborated with dissident Octobrists in founding the centrist Party of Peaceful Renewal.[11]

Even though some deputies did not clearly designate their political orientation and others shifted during the Duma session, the political distribution of deputies in the First Duma, when it convened in late April 1906, was approximately that shown in Table 10.[12]

The elections were a bitter loss for the rightists, who immediately tried to rationalize their defeat. "It is a sad and difficult time," *Russkoe znamia* lamented, "a time of celebration for the dark forces. Lord, Lord, these are elections to the State Duma, and for a glass of tea the voters are ready to elect anybody." Thousands of voters in St. Petersburg, the Union of the Russian People claimed, had been unable to obtain

Table 10 *Deputies in the First Duma*

Rightists	6	1%
Octobrists	26	6%
Progressives	36	8%
Kadet bloc	182	41%
Left of Kadets	47	10%
Nationalists	60	13%
Non-party	83	19%
Other	8	2%
	448	100%

Source: See Note 12.

candidate lists, preventing them from learning which parties the candidates represented. As a result, the Kadets had misled many unwary voters. Moreover, said the Union, it was no secret that the Jews had financed the Kadets. True Russians had every right to be indignant that in St. Petersburg and Moscow two Jews – Vinaver and Herzenstein – had emerged victorious, especially since they must have won by subterfuge.[13] These unsubstantiated charges obviously shed little light on the monarchists' failure at the polls.

A frequent speaker at rightist rallies, Boris Nikolskii, offered a more elaborate explanation. Nikolskii insinuated that the government itself was to blame, because it held the elections at precisely the worst time. A year earlier, Nikolskii said, the government could have gathered solid backing from the electorate; it could even have gotten by with a consultative assembly. But in the interim public opinion had shifted decidedly to the left. Peasants, workers, merchants, and nobles had all become infected with a mounting discontent. At that moment the government scheduled the elections. It was as if a bank called a stockholders' meeting just when its capital had sunk to an all-time low. Whichever party most sharply voiced its dissatisfaction could be assured of winning. If the Social Democrats, Socialist Revolutionaries, or anarchists had campaigned, they would now control the Duma. As it was, the Kadets had pursued an open road to victory.[14]

Nikolskii no doubt overestimated the radical opposition, although when the Social Democrats and Socialist Revolutionaries campaigned in the Second Duma elections the following year, they polled well (see Tables 11 through 16). More than he probably intended, Nikolskii correctly interpreted the election returns as reflecting a pervasive discontent in Russia; he was right in conceding that many voters regarded the Kadets as best equipped to bring about political and social change.

When the First Duma convened in April 1906, the rightists refused to admit that it was a truly legitimate body. They objected to the casual manner in which the Duma members greeted the tsar's appearance at the opening session; a few days later they read in horror the Duma's "address to the tsar." In it the Kadet-led deputies requested a complete amnesty for political offenders and a ministry responsible to the Duma, not to the monarch. Dubrovin himself declared that from the beginning the Duma had engaged in a seditious struggle against the government and that its members had forfeited any right to call themselves representatives of the people.[15]

The government, headed now by I. L. Goremykin, who had succeeded Witte in April 1906, knew that many loyalists shared these sentiments. Beginning in May, the government newspaper *Pravitel'stvennyi vestnik* (*The Government Messenger*) printed almost daily messages from rightist organizations condemning the Duma as a traitorous body.[16] By mid-June, Goremykin had received hundreds of telegrams, mainly from Union of the Russian People branches, imploring him to ask the tsar to sign a dissolution order.[17]

Although Nicholas intimated that he favored dissolution, the final decision came slowly. In fact, during June, Nicholas and some of his advisers considered making conciliatory moves toward the Duma by inviting party leaders, particularly Kadets, to accept ministerial posts. From fragmentary and sometimes contradictory accounts by participants in the various discussions and negotiations, there seem to have been two proposals. Apparently, the tsar himself authorized his Minister of Foreign Affairs, A. P. Izvolskii, and his Minister of Internal Affairs, P. A. Stolypin, to work out a tentative plan for forming a coalition cabinet. Izvolskii and Stolypin suggested that most current ministers retain their posts but that a few Duma leaders and other public figures be brought into the government. At the same time, General D. F. Trepov, commandant of the imperial court, approached the Kadet leader, P. N. Miliukov, who accepted his overtures and outlined a scheme whereby Kadets (and possibly a non-Kadet moderate, such as D. N. Shipov) would occupy the key posts of Chairman of the Council of Ministers and Ministers of Internal Affairs, Foreign Affairs, Justice, Finance, and Agriculture. This arrangement Trepov recommended to the tsar.

V. N. Kokovtsov, then Minister of Finance, relates that some time between 15 and 20 June, Nicholas asked him his opinion on a Kadet ministry along the line of Trepov's proposal. Kokovtsov replied that it would be unwise to take such a step or to embark on any "new experiments," which would only lead further toward parliamentary government. Kokovtsov may have realized that a Kadet cabinet would cost him his ministerial post, but the tsar had reason to heed his advice, since Kokovtsov was widely regarded as a man of high intelligence and forceful logic.

Unwilling to accept Trepov's proposal of a Kadet ministry, Nicholas pondered Izvolskii's suggestion to bring at least a few public figures into the cabinet. Cautiously, he summoned one of the rare political leaders he trusted, D. N. Shipov, to discuss the matter. Before his audience with the tsar, Shipov hurriedly called on Stolypin, whom he found willing to support a coalition ministry. However, upon approaching the Kadet leaders, Shipov discovered that they would agree only to a ministry in which they predominated. On 28 June, when Shipov met with the tsar, he told Nicholas of the Kadets' position. Shipov argued that if the Kadets were permitted this ministerial responsibility, they might be willing to support the government against the even greater threat to the autocracy – the radical socialists.

Nicholas listened to Shipov's argument, but in the end he decided against any kind of coalition cabinet and in favor of dissolving the Duma. When Goremykin met with the tsar on 8 July, he reiterated Kokovtsov's advice and told Nicholas that both he and his fellow ministers recommended dissolving the Duma. Nicholas then signed the dissolution order.[18]

How best, then, to interpret the tsar's decision to dismiss the First Duma? Surely, Nicholas had been aware of the many telegrams criticizing the Duma and requesting dissolution. It seems likely, however, that he depended most on trustworthy advisers like Kokovtsov and Goremykin, and that they themselves were not unduly influenced by rightist groups – or anyone else. There is no evidence that rightists directed their requests at Kokovtsov as Minister of Finance. And in his memoirs, V. I. Gurko, the Assistant Minister of Internal Affairs, says that although he and several colleagues urged Goremykin to argue for dissolution, they probably had little effect, since Goremykin was a person who "arrived at decisions quite independently."[19] Rightist organizations that called for dissolution seem mainly to have served in assuring the tsar that he had sufficient public approval to justify such action. Somewhat inaccurately, Nicholas could believe that he had responded to the genuine desires of his people.

The Second Duma

The rightists now turned to the Second Duma. They had seven months before the February elections, long enough to prepare a stronger campaign than the one they had conducted for the First Duma. Prospects seemed better too, since some rightist organizations were growing rapidly. Between the First and Second Duma elections, the Union of the Russian People increased its branches from 25 to several hundred, located in 36 provinces.[20] Other national rightist organizations moved more slowly: the Union of Russian Men added only six branches, the Russian Monarchist Party three or four, and the Russian Assembly two.[21] More important than many contemporary analysts recognized were the provincial rightist associations, which had been gaining strength, notably the Tula Union for Tsar and Order, Kursk People's Party of Order, Orel Union of Law and Order, Bessarabian Center Party, Minsk Russian Borderland Union, and several rightist groups in the city of Kiev (see Chapters 6 and 7).

Still, the rightists knew they were facing formidable opposition, mainly from the Kadets but also from the Socialist Revolutionaries and Social Democrats, who concluded they had erred in boycotting the First Duma and now joined the campaign. The rightists remained undecided on how to regard the Octobrists, who had extended their organizational structure in the provinces and were gaining influence among the landowners. Because of the Octobrists' ambiguous position on Jewish rights and on the principle of autocracy, many rightists declined to consider them as potential allies.

Recognizing their need to campaign more effectively, some rightists sought, rather ineffectually, to create a unified front. The third monarchist congress, which met in Kiev from 1 to 7 October 1906, asked V. A. Gringmut, chairman of the Russian Monarchist Party, to develop a joint political program for the various organizations, and A. I. Dubrovin, chairman of the Union of the Russian People, to coordinate rightist campaign activities. However, the participating organizations, unwilling to surrender their individual prerogatives, stipulated that each group should retain full administrative autonomy.[22] This arrangement may have been appealing in principle, but in practice it meant that the Second Duma campaign would likely proceed much the same as its predecessor, with electoral blocs forming on an *ad hoc* basis at the local level.

All political parties realized that the Second Duma elections would better indicate the country's political mood than had the previous elections. The broader range of parties participating in the campaign and a more knowledgeable electorate portended fewer non-party electors and greater representation at both ends of the political spectrum.

Tables 11–16 show that this forecast proved true.[23] The Kadets again polled heavily in the cities, including St. Petersburg and Moscow, where they easily overcame rightist blocs, and leftist parties attracted many worker and peasant votes.[24] But in some parts of the country the rightists made remarkable gains. Significantly, these advances occurred mainly in those areas where local rightist organizations had become most active – in the restive central agricultural provinces, where rightists called for law and order, and in the western borderlands, where they addressed urgent national and religious concerns. Because of strong rightist showings in these regions, the elections there bear close scrutiny.

The central agricultural provinces

As shown in the tables, rightists in Tula, Kursk, and Orel provinces, where they were especially well organized, received over 40 percent of the vote. This gave them a plurality in each provincial assembly and in Tula province enough strength to capture most of the Duma seats.

In *Tula province*, rightist politics had become more complex than during the First Duma campaign. The Union for Tsar and Order continued as the principal rightist organization, concentrating on the law-and-order theme; but a group of dissatisfied members, along with some unaffiliated ultramonarchists, had gone their own way and opened a branch of the Union of the Russian People. Immediately, they launched a virulently antiliberal, antisemitic barrage, designed to reach voters who might not have been attracted by the more moderate Union for Tsar and Order. Yet, despite their differences, these divergent rightists appreciated the expediency of collaborating during the campaign. In the city of Tula, they also negotiated with local Octobrists, who, having recognized that their cooperation with the Kadets in the first elections had contributed to an oppositionist Duma, now decided to ally with the rightists.[25]

The alliance proved effective. After a spirited campaign, voting in the city yielded a rightist–Octobrist majority of 46 out of 80 electors. The Kadets got only 23, and the leftists 11. After wrangling over who should be their nominee as Tula's deputy, the rightists and Octobrists eventually settled on I. A. Vorontsov-Veliaminov, a right-wing Octobrist, who easily defeated the Kadets' candidate, Prince Lvov, in the electoral assembly.[26]

In the rest of Tula province, where the Octobrists were not well established, the rightists campaigned on their own. The Union for Tsar and Order utilized the provincial zemstvo structure adeptly in disseminating its message among the landowners; however, it did not launch a campaign blitz among the peasantry, as did, for example, the more demagogic People's Party of Order in neighboring Kursk province. The Union of the Russian People attempted to reach the peasants from some newly formed village branches, but it faced tough competition from the Trudoviks and Socialist Revolutionaries.[27]

Although the rightists failed to gain much peasant support, their strength among the landowners, together with the backing of many urban voters, enabled them to get 30 of the 73 provincial electors. Needing only a few non-party and moderate peasant votes to achieve a majority in the provincial assembly, V. A. Bobrinskii and M. A. Cherkasskii, the UTO and URP chairmen, reportedly treated the peasant electors to meals and vodka just before the assembly convened.[28] Whether this in itself persuaded these peasants is uncertain, but some agreed to vote for two rightist landowner candidates in exchange for which the rightist electors promised to back two peasant candidates, as long as these candidates were loyalists.

When the assembly met, the rightists prevailed. The peasant electors, voting first by themselves for a peasant deputy, as specified in the electoral law, chose a non-party candidate with oppositionist leanings. But then the combined curiae selected two rightist-oriented peasants and two rightist landowners – Count Bobrinskii and Prince A. P. Urusov, both of whom belonged to the Union for Tsar and Order.[29] With four of the five deputies in the rightist camp, the Second Duma elections in Tula province emerged historically as one of the country's major rightist victories.

In *Kursk province*, the People's Party of Order had by this time affiliated with the Union of the Russian People (while maintaining considerable local autonomy) and had cemented an alliance with the smaller Union of Russian Workers – all for the sake of building a

Table 11 *Second Duma: Peasant electors in provincial assemblies*

Province	Total allotted	Total reported	Rightists		Octobrist bloc		Moderates		Progressives		Kadet bloc		Leftists		Non-party	
Arkhangel	19	18	1	6%	–	–	2	11%	7	39%	2	11%	2	11%	4	22%
Astrakhan	24	24	2	8%	2	8%	–	–	12	50%	2	8%	6	25%	–	–
Bessarabia	43	40	6	15%	–	–	18[a]	45%	9	23%	–	–	2	5%	5	13%
Vilna	40	24	5	21%	–	–	9	38%	9[c]	38%	–	–	1	4%	–	–
Vitebsk	31	21	3	14%	–	–	–	–	9	43%	–	–	3	14%	6	29%
Vladimir	26	26	5	19%	–	–	6	23%	4	15%	7	27%	4	15%	–	–
Vologda	46	43	4	9%	–	–	1	2%	23	53%	–	–	8	19%	7	16%
Volynia	69	69	57	83%	–	–	–	–	6	9%	–	–	–	–	6	9%
Voronezh	101	87	6	7%	1	1%	7	8%	38	44%	3	3%	17	20%	15	17%
Viatka	148	143	27	19%	–	–	1	1%	98	69%	1	1%	1	1%	15	10%
Grodno	43	23	12	52%	–	–	4	17%	–	–	–	–	6	26%	1	4%
Don Oblast	93	87	28	32%	2	2%	4	5%	26	30%	20	23%	7	8%	–	–
Ekaterinoslav	34	34	1	3%	3	9%	1	3%	12	35%	2	6%	11	32%	4	12%
Kazan	98	91	3	3%	6	7%	3	3%	50	55%	1[d]	1%	23	25%	5	5%
Kaluga	30	30	9	30%	–	–	4	13%	11	37%	–	–	–	–	6	20%
Kiev	80	80	1	1%	–	–	13	16%	19	24%	1	1%	22	28%	25	31%
Kovno	39	22	–	–	–	–	–	–	8	36%	1	5%	13	59%	–	–
Kostroma	29	27	2	7%	–	–	4	15%	3	11%	9	33%	6	22%	3	11%
Courland	13	1	–	*	–	*	–	*	1	*	–	*	–	*	–	*
Kursk	78	78	31	40%	–	–	–	–	6	8%	6	8%	29	37%	6	8%
Livonia	21	21	–	–	–	–	–	–	9	43%	–	–	12	57%	–	–
Minsk	41	41	9	22%	–	–	11[b]	27%	12	29%	–	–	9	22%	–	–
Mogilev	40	32	18	56%	2	6%	–	–	2	6%	–	–	4	13%	6	19%
Moscow	16	15	7	47%	–	–	1	7%	–	–	–	–	7	47%	–	–
Nizhnii Novgorod	42	35	11	31%	–	–	–	–	5	14%	1	3%	18	51%	–	–
Novgorod	31	27	1	4%	–	–	–	–	15	56%	2	7%	9	33%	–	–
Olonets	27	3	3	*	–	*	–	*	–	*	–	*	–	*	–	*
Orenburg	63	60	16	27%	2	–	3	5%	13	22%	5[d]	8%	12	20%	11	18%
Orel	59	56	31	55%	2	4%	6	11%	1	2%	1	2%	11	20%	4	7%

Penza	47	47	3	6%	—	—	5	11%	3	6%	2	4%	12	26%	22	47%
Perm	86	72	33	46%	—	—	17	24%	4	6%	5	7%	9	13%	4	6%
Podolia	82	64	21	33%	1	8%	6	9%	16	25%	—	—	16	25%	5	8%
Poltava	23	12	—	—	—	—	—	—	—	—	2	17%	9	75%	—	—
Pskov	24	23	—	—	5	10%	2	4%	—	—	—	—	11	48%	12	52%
Riazan	54	51	10	20%	9	9%	2	4%	12	24%	3	6%	9	18%	10	20%
Samara	97	97	20	21%	—	—	—	—	2	2%	3	3%	37	38%	26	27%
St. Petersburg	14	13	2	15%	6	14%	—	—	1	8%	3	23%	7	54%	—	—
Saratov	64	62	6	10%	—	—	1	2%	6	10%	6	10%	44	71%	—	—
Simbirsk	44	44	2	5%	—	—	1	2%	4	9%	—	—	31	70%	—	—
Smolensk	31	26	12	46%	—	—	7	21%	—	—	—	—	14	54%	—	—
Stavropol	33	33	9	27%	—	—	1	2%	—	—	—	—	17	52%	—	—
Tauride	42	42	6	14%	—	—	2	2%	23	55%	1	2%	11	26%	—	—
Tambov	92	87	28	32%	—	—	—	—	24	28%	—	—	17	20%	16	18%
Tver	49	46	5	11%	—	—	4	14%	8	17%	9	20%	24	52%	—	—
Tula	32	28	1	4%	—	—	5	13%	3	11%	3	11%	8	29%	9	32%
Ufa	88	38	25	66%	—	—	7	16%	—	—	—	—	8	21%	—	—
Kharkov	64	45	11	24%	3	7%	—	—	6	13%	3	7%	12	27%	3	7%
Kherson	50	46	3	7%	—	—	—	—	25	54%	—	—	13	28%	5	11%
Chernigov	63	57	22	39%	1	2%	2	4%	3	5%	2	4%	21	37%	6	11%
Estonia	10	10	—	—	—	—	—	—	5	50%	—	—	2	20%	3	30%
Iaroslavl	17	15	2	13%	—	—	1	7%	9	60%	—	—	3	20%	—	—

* Insufficient data.

a Includes candidates of the Bessarabian Center Party, who belong under "rightists" (see Chapter 7).

b Includes candidates of the Russian Borderland Union, who belong under "rightists" (see Chapter 7).

c Probably Polish–Lithuanian Nationalists.   d Includes Muslim "progressives".

Table 12 *Second Duma: Landowner electors in provincial assemblies*

Province	Total allotted	Total reported	Rightists	Octobrist bloc	Moderates	Progressives	Kadet bloc	Leftists	Non-party
Arkhangel[a]	–	–	–	–	–	–	–	–	–
Astrakhan	5	3	–	–	–	–	–	3 100%	–
Bessarabia	56	56	24 43%	17 30%	5 9%	9 16%	–	5 11%	1 2%
Vilna	44	44	2 5%	1 2%	1 2%	34[c] 77%	–	5 13%	1 2%
Vitebsk	39	39	13 33%	3 8%	5 13%	4 10%	–	–	9 23%
Vladimir	18	18	10 56%	3 17%	–	4 22%	–	1 6%	–
Vologda	21	21	10 48%	1 5%	2 10%	4 19%	1 5%	–	3 14%
Volynia	86	86	49 57%	25 29%	–	7 8%	3 3%	2 2%	–
Voronezh	42	32	11 34%	11 34%	4 13%	2 6%	–	–	4 13%
Viatka	18	13	5 38%	2 15%	–	4 31%	1 8%	–	1 8%
Grodno	36	23	7 30%	6 26%	6 26%	–	–	3 13%	1 4%
Don Oblast	47	33	1 3%	8 24%	–	9 27%	12 36%	–	3 9%
Ekaterinoslav	38	38	28 74%	8 21%	–	2 5%	–	–	–
Kazan	23	22	7 32%	3 14%	–	5 23%	4[d] 18%	1 5%	2 9%
Kaluga	25	25	13 52%	5 20%	2 8%	4 16%	1 4%	–	–
Kiev	74	74	56 76%	2 3%	3 4%	5 7%	–	–	8 11%
Kovno	35	21	1 5%	4 19%	4 19%	6 29%	2 10%	–	4 19%
Kostroma	35	29	9 31%	1 3%	–	2 7%	17 59%	–	–
Courland	14	4	–	4[b] *	–	–	–	–	–
Kursk	44	36	28 78%	4 11%	–	–	1 3%	2 6%	1 3%
Livonia	25	25	–	23[b] 92%	2 8%	–	–	–	–
Minsk	74	73	43 59%	2 3%	22 30%	–	6 8%	–	–
Mogilev	53	53	18 34%	12 23%	4 8%	8 15%	1 2%	4 8%	6 11%
Moscow	13	12	5 42%	2 17%	–	2 17%	2 17%	–	1 8%
Nizhnii Novgorod	30	30	18 60%	–	–	–	12 40%	–	–
Novgorod	45	43	15 35%	19 44%	1 2%	7 16%	–	1 2%	–
Olonets	9	2	–	2 *	–	–	–	–	–
Orenburg	19	18	6 33%	6 33%	–	–	6 33%	–	–
Orel	45	38	19 50%	8 21%	–	7 18%	2 5%	–	2 5%

Penza	28	14	7 50%	5 36%	1 7%	—	—	—	1 7%
Perm	58	51	10 20%	—	13 25%	13 25%	1 2%	2 4%	12 24%
Podolia	76	62	43 69%	7 11%	—	6 10%	10 19%	5 8%	1 2%
Poltava	109	54	23 43%	10 19%	1 2%	8 15%	2 8%	2 4%	—
Pskov	27	26	20 77%	2 8%	—	1 4%	2 5%	1 4%	1 3%
Riazan	40	40	15 38%	17 43%	—	5 13%	9 17%	—	—
Samara	52	52	25 48%	13 25%	—	3 6%	9 19%	2 4%	1 6%
St. Petersburg	18	16	2 13%	2 13%	1 2%	5 31%	2 4%	3 19%	2 4%
Saratov	51	51	35 69%	6 12%	6 21%	5 10%	5 18%	—	4 14%
Simbirsk	29	28	9 32%	1 4%	1 3%	2 7%	5 13%	1 4%	3 8%
Smolensk	40	38	8 21%	18 47%	1 20%	2 5%	—	1 3%	—
Stavropol	6	5	2 40%	—	—	—	2 13%	2 40%	—
Tauride	31	31	12 39%	10 32%	—	2 6%	3 13%	3 10%	—
Tambov	62	61	35 57%	14 23%	—	3 5%	7 11%	7 11%	—
Tver	41	38	8 21%	4 11%	—	11 29%	10 26%	5 13%	—
Tula	29	29	25 86%	2 7%	—	2 7%	16d 53%	—	—
Ufa	36	30	10 33%	—	—	—	1 2%	4 13%	7 17%
Kharkov	43	42	11 26%	18 43%	9 17%	3 7%	1 2%	2 5%	—
Kherson	69	53	30 57%	—	2 4%	12 23%	2 4%	—	—
Chernigov	50	46	27 59%	5 11%	—	—	2 4%	10 22%	—
Estonia	21	21	—	21b 100%	—	—	—	—	—
Iaroslavl	20	20	1 5%	—	—	7 35%	5 25%	4 20%	3 15%

* Insufficient data.   a Combined with urban curia.   c Includes Polish–Lithuanian nationalists.
b Baltic Constitutional Monarchists.
d Includes Muslim "progressives".

Table 13 *Second Duma: Urban electors in provincial assemblies*

Province	Total allotted	Total reported	Rightists	Octobrist bloc	Moderates	Progressives	Kadet bloc	Leftists	Non-party
Arkhangel[a]	13	10	4 40%	1 10%	—	2 20%	1 10%	2 20%	—
Astrakhan	16	16	—	—	—	—	4 25%	8 50%	4 25%
Bessarabia	21	21	1 5%	—	—	15 71%	2 10%	3 14%	—
Vilna	7	7	—	—	—	2 29%	3 43%	2 29%	—
Vitebsk	20	20	1 5%	—	—	7 35%	8 40%	4 20%	—
Vladimir	48	48	2 4%	5 10%	—	13 27%	27 56%	1 2%	—
Vologda	13	12	6 50%	—	—	1 8%	3 25%	2 17%	—
Volynia	40	34	—	—	—	12 35%	10 29%	11 32%	1 3%
Voronezh	22	22	3 14%	1 5%	—	5 23%	13 59%	—	—
Viatka	34	34	4 12%	1 3%	—	10 29%	7 21%	12 35%	—
Grodno	26	15	—	—	—	5[b] 33%	8 53%	2 13%	—
Don Oblast	37	37	—	—	1 3%	2 5%	27 73%	7 19%	—
Ekaterinoslav	63	63	2 3%	4 6%	—	20 32%	9 14%	28 44%	—
Kazan	18	17	1 6%	—	3 18%	3 18%	7[c] 41%	3 18%	1 6%
Kaluga	21	18	2 11%	2 11%	—	6 33%	7 39%	—	—
Kiev	71	71	10 14%	—	1 1%	26 37%	21 30%	11 15%	2 3%
Kovno	16	16	—	—	1 6%	9 56%	2 13%	4 25%	—
Kostroma	28	28	2 7%	2 7%	—	2 7%	18 64%	4 14%	—
Courland	19	19	—	1 5%	—	11 58%	2 11%	5 26%	—
Kursk	28	27	2 7%	—	—	5 19%	7 26%	13 48%	—
Livonia	15	15	2 13%	—	—	7 47%	—	6 40%	—
Minsk	20	20	1 5%	—	1 5%	6 30%	6 30%	5 25%	1 5%
Mogilev	16	16	2 13%	—	—	4 25%	7 44%	3 19%	—
Moscow	63	55	21 38%	8 15%	2 4%	2 4%	21 38%	—	1 2%
Nizhnii Novgorod	18	18	4 22%	1 6%	—	2 11%	5 28%	5 28%	1 6%
Novgorod	16	16	2 13%	1 6%	—	6 38%	4 25%	3 19%	—
Olonets	14	3	1 *	— *	— *	— *	— *	2 *	—
Orenburg	23	22	—	—	—	—	15[c] 68%	7 32%	—
Orel	18	18	2 11%	—	—	7 39%	9 50%	—	—

Province																		
Penza	15	14	4	29%	—	—	—	—	2	14%	1	7%	6	43%	1	7%		
Perm	52	47	1	2%	—	—	1	2%	2	4%	15	32%	28	60%	—	—		
Podolia	37	37	3	5%	—	—	1	3%	19	51%	14	38%	1	3%	—	—		
Poltava	49	41	2	7%	—	—	—	—	7	17%	23	56%	8	20%	—	—		
Pskov	10	10	2	20%	3	11%	—	—	1	10%	6	60%	1	10%	—	—		
Riazan	27	27	2	7%	1	3%	—	—	5	19%	13	48%	2	7%	2	7%		
Samara	31	29	1	3%	1	6%	—	—	2	7%	9	31%	15	52%	1	3%		
St. Petersburg	19	18	—	—	—	—	—	—	2	11%	12	67%	3	17%	—	—		
Saratov	35	34	—	—	—	—	—	—	6	18%	6	18%	22	65%	—	—		
Simbirsk	17	17	—	—	—	—	—	—	4	24%	1	6%	12	71%	—	—		
Smolensk	19	19	4	21%	1	5%	2	25%	—	—	11	58%	—	—	3	16%		
Stavropol	8	8	1	13%	—	—	—	—	—	—	—	—	5	63%	—	—		
Tauride	23	22	—	—	4	15%	—	—	2	9%	9	41%	11	50%	—	—		
Tambov	26	26	3	12%	9	30%	1	4%	1	4%	8	31%	7	27%	2	8%		
Tver	30	30	—	—	—	—	—	—	—	—	17	57%	4	13%	—	—		
Tula	15	15	4	27%	—	—	—	—	3	20%	7	47%	1	7%	—	—		
Ufa	26	26	—	—	—	—	—	—	5	19%	14[c]	54%	7	27%	—	—		
Kharkov	43	37	2	5%	3	8%	—	—	3	8%	15	41%	10	27%	4	11%		
Kherson	31	30	—	—	6	20%	—	—	6	20%	15	50%	—	—	3	10%		
Chernigov	37	37	8	22%	—	—	—	—	4	11%	20	54%	5	14%	—	—		
Estonia	14	14	—	—	—	—	—	—	4	29%	—	—	10	71%	—	—		
Iaroslavl	23	21	—	—	—	—	—	—	—	—	16	76%	4	19%	1	5%		

* Insufficient data.   ^b Includes Polish–Lithuanian nationalists.
^a Includes landowners.   ^c Includes Muslim "progressives".

Table 14 *Second Duma: Worker electors in provincial assemblies*

Province	Total allotted	Total reported
Arkhangel	1	1 lefitst
Astrakhan	1	1 leftist
Bessarabia	—	—
Vilna	1	1 leftist
Vitebsk	—	—
Vladimir	16	16 leftists
Vologda	—	—
Volynia	2	2 leftists
Voronezh	1	1 leftist
Viatka	4	4 leftists
Grodno	2	—
Don Oblast	5	5 leftists
Ekaterinoslav	6	6 leftists
Kazan	2	2 leftists
Kaluga	2	2 leftists
Kiev	7	7 leftists
Kovno	—	—
Kostroma	7	7 leftists
Courland	2	—
Kursk	2	2 leftists
Livonia	1	1 leftist
Minsk	2	2 leftists
Mogilev	1	—
Moscow	17	16 leftists
Nizhnii Novgorod	2	2 leftists
Novgorod	2	2 leftists
Olonets	—	—
Orenburg	1	1 leftist
Orel	3	3 leftists
Penza	2	2 leftists
Perm	10	10 leftists
Podolia	4	4 leftists
Poltava	1	1 leftist
Pskov	—	—
Riazan	2	1 progressive
Samara	1	1 leftist
St. Petersburg	10	10 leftists
Saratov	4	4 leftists
Simbirsk	2	1 leftist, 1 non-party
Smolensk	1	1 leftist
Stavropol	—	—

Table 14 (*cont.*)

Province	Total allotted	Total reported
Taurida	1	1 leftist
Tambov	3	2 leftists, 1 non-party
Tver	4	4 leftists
Tula	1	1 leftist
Ufa	4	4 leftists
Kharkov	4	4 leftists
Kherson	4	4 leftists
Chernigov	3	—
Estonia	2	2 leftists
Iaroslavl	2	2 progressives

broader social base. The Party had also increased its supply of demagogic orators, who proclaimed the Union's message throughout the province.[30]

During the second elections, the PPO dominated its relationship with the Union of Russian Workers, which ran advertisements urging the electorate to vote for PPO candidates.[31] In the cities, the PPO–URW coalition encountered its greatest competition from the Kadets, who had allied with some leftists, and in the countryside from the Trudoviks, along with some Peasant Unionists, Socialist Revolutionaries, and Social Democrats.[32] In early 1907, the Union of the Russian People opened several village branches, but rightist strength in Kursk province stayed mainly with the PPO–URW coalition.[33]

The election results for Kursk showed significant changes from those for the First Duma. While the Kadets again got all 80 electors in the city of Kursk,[34] rightists gained substantially in the rest of the province. As shown in Tables 11–12, they polled not only an impressive 78 percent among the landowners but 40 percent among the peasants.

This substantial peasant support suggests that one should look carefully at peasant attitudes during this period, both in Kursk and in the central agricultural region generally. A study conducted by the St. Petersburg-based Free Economic Society in 1907 disclosed that peasants in the central provinces were far from united during the disorders. Older peasants tended to be more passive than younger peasants; poverty-stricken villagers joined the "peasant movement" far

Table 15 *Second Duma: Combined peasant, landowner, urban, and worker electors in provincial assemblies*

Province	Total allotted	Total reported	Rightists		Octobrist bloc		Moderates		Progressives		Kadet bloc		Leftists		Non-party	
Arkhangel	33	29	5	17%	1	3%	2	7%	9	31%	3	10%	5	17%	4	14%
Astrakhan	46	44	2	5%	2	5%	–	–	12	27%	6	14%	18	41%	4	9%
Bessarabia	120	117	31	26%	17	15%	23[b]	20%	33	28%	3	3%	5	4%	5	4%
Vilna	92	76	7	9%	1	1%	10	13%	45[d]	59%	3	4%	9	12%	1	1%
Vitebsk	90	80	17	21%	3	4%	5	6%	20	25%	8	10%	12	15%	15	19%
Vladimir	108	108	17	16%	8	7%	6	6%	21	19%	34	31%	22	20%	–	–
Vologda	80	76	20	26%	1	1%	3	4%	28	37%	4	5%	10	13%	10	13%
Volynia	197	191	106	55%	25	13%	–	–	25	13%	13	7%	15	8%	7	4%
Voronezh	166	142	20	14%	13	9%	11	8%	45	32%	16	11%	18	13%	19	13%
Viatka	204	194	36	19%	3	2%	1	1%	112	58%	9	5%	17	9%	16	8%
Grodno	107	61	19	31%	6	10%	10	16%	5[d]	8%	8	13%	11	18%	2	3%
Don Oblast	182	162	29	18%	10	6%	5	3%	37	23%	59	36%	19	12%	3	2%
Ekaterinoslav	141	141	31	22%	15	11%	1	1%	34	24%	11	8%	45	32%	4	3%
Kazan	141	132	11	8%	9	7%	6	5%	58	44%	12[e]	9%	29	22%	7	5%
Kaluga	78	75	24	32%	7	9%	6	8%	21	28%	8	11%	2	3%	7	9%
Kiev	232	232	67	29%	2	1%	17	7%	50	22%	21	9%	40	17%	35	15%
Kovno	90	59	1	2%	4	7%	5	8%	23	39%	5	8%	17	29%	4	7%
Kostroma	99	91	13	14%	3	3%	4	4%	7	8%	44	48%	17	19%	3	3%
Courland	48	24	–	–	5[a]	21%	–	–	12	50%	2	8%	5	21%	–	–
Kursk	152	143	61	43%	4	3%	–	–	11	8%	14	10%	46	32%	7	5%
Livonia	62	62	–	–	25[a]	40%	2	3%	16	26%	–	–	19	31%	–	–
Minsk	137	136	53	39%	2	1%	34[c]	25%	18	13%	12	9%	16	12%	1	1%
Mogilev	110	101	38	38%	14	14%	4	4%	14	14%	8	8%	11	11%	12	12%
Moscow	109	98	33	34%	10	10%	3	3%	4	4%	23	23%	23	23%	2	2%
Nizhnii Novgorod	92	85	33	39%	1	1%	–	–	7	8%	18	21%	25	29%	1	1%
Novgorod	94	88	18	20%	20	23%	1	1%	28	32%	6	7%	14	16%	1	1%
Olonets	50	8	4	*	2	*	–	*	–	*	–	*	2	*	–	*
Orenburg	106	101	22	22%	6	6%	3	3%	13	13%	26[c]	26%	20	20%	11	11%
Orel	125	115	52	45%	10	9%	6	5%	15	13%	12	10%	14	12%	6	5%

Penza	92	72	10	14%	5	7%	6	8%	5	7%	3	4%	20	28%	23	32%
Perm	206	171	44	26%	—	—	31	18%	19	11%	21	12%	40	23%	16	9%
Podolia	199	167	66	40%	7	4%	7	4%	41	25%	14	8%	26	16%	6	4%
Poltava	181	108	26	24%	11	10%	1	1%	15	14%	35	32%	20	19%	—	—
Pskov	61	59	22	37%	2	3%	—	—	2	3%	8	14%	13	22%	12	20%
Riazan	123	119	27	23%	25	21%	2	2%	23	19%	18	15%	11	9%	13	11%
Samara	181	179	46	26%	23	13%	—	—	7	4%	21	12%	55	31%	27	15%
St. Petersburg	61	57	4	7%	3	5%	—	—	8	14%	18	32%	23	40%	1	2%
Saratov	154	151	41	27%	6	4%	1	1%	17	11%	14	9%	70	46%	2	1%
Simbirsk	92	91	11	12%	7	8%	7	8%	10	11%	6	7%	45	49%	5	5%
Smolensk	91	84	24	29%	19	23%	1	1%	2	3%	16	19%	16	19%	6	7%
Stavropol	47	46	12	26%	—	—	10	22%	—	—	—	—	24	52%	—	—
Tauride	97	96	18	19%	10	10%	1	1%	27	28%	14	15%	26	27%	—	—
Tambov	183	177	66	37%	18	10%	3	2%	28	16%	10	6%	33	19%	19	11%
Tver	124	118	13	11%	13	11%	—	—	19	16%	36	31%	37	31%	—	—
Tula	77	73	30	41%	2	3%	4	5%	8	11%	10	14%	10	14%	9	12%
Ufa	154	98	35	36%	—	—	5	5%	5	5%	30[e]	31%	23	23%	—	—
Kharkov	154	128	24	19%	24	19%	7	5%	12	9%	19	15%	28	22%	14	11%
Kherson	154	133	33	25%	6	5%	9	7%	43	32%	17	13%	17	13%	8	6%
Chernigov	153	140	57	41%	6	4%	4	3%	7	5%	24	17%	36	26%	6	4%
Estonia	47	47	—	—	21[a]	45%	1	—	9	19%	—	—	14	30%	3	6%
Iaroslavl	62	58	3	5%	—	—	1	2%	18	31%	21	36%	11	19%	4	7%

* Insufficient data.

[a] Baltic Constitutional Monarchists.

[b] Includes candidates of the Bessarabian Center Party, who belong under "rightists" (see Chapter 7).

[c] Includes candidates of the Russian Borderland Union, who belong under "rightists" (see Chapter 7).

[d] Includes Polish–Lithuanian nationalists.

[e] Includes Muslim "progressives."

Table 16 *Second Duma: General electors in cities having separate representation (European Russia)*

City	Total allotted	Total reported	Rightists	Octobrist bloc	Progressives	Kadet bloc	Leftists	Worker electors in these cities Total allotted	Total reported
Astrakhan	80	80	10 13%	—	—	48[a] 60%	22 28%	1	—
Vilna	80	80	—	—	47[b] 59%	33 41%	—	—	—
Voronezh	80	80	—	—	—	55 69%	25 31%	1	—
Ekaterinoslav	80	80	—	—	—	15 19%	65 81%	1	1 leftist
Kazan	80	80	—	46 58%	—	33 41%	1 1%	—	—
Kiev	80	80	41 51%	1 1%	—	38 48%	—	2	—
Kishinev	80	80	47 59%	—	—	33 41%	—	—	—
Kursk	80	80	—	—	—	80 100%	—	1	—
Moscow	160	160	—	—	—	160 100%	—	18	—
Nizhnii Novgorod	80	80	—	3 4%	—	38 48%	39 49%	2	2 leftists
Odessa	80	80	4 5%	—	30 38%	23 29%	23 29%	2	—
Orel	80	80	34 43%	—	—	46 58%	—	—	—
Riga	80	80	22 28%	—	—	(←— 58 73% —→)		4	—
Rostov-on-Don	80	80	5 6%	—	—	(←— 75 94% —→)		1	1 leftist
Samara	80	80	5 6%	40 50%	—	35 44%	—	—	—
St. Petersburg	160	160	—	—	—	151 94%	9 6%	15	—
Saratov	80	80	—	—	—	6 8%	74 93%	—	—
Tula	80	81 [sic]	(←— 46 57% —→)		—	23 28%	12 15%	1	1 moderate
Kharkov	80	80	15 19%	—	—	(←— 65 81% —→)		3	—
Iaroslavl	80	80	2 3%	—	—	78 98%	—	2	2 leftists

No moderate or non-party general electors were reported.
[a] Includes Muslim "progressives."   [b] Includes Polish–Lithuanian nationalists.

more readily than those less economically distressed. While many peasants insisted that private estates be distributed free of charge, others relied on buying land with assistance from the Peasant Bank – a conventional procedure endorsed by most rightist organizations, including the People's Party of Order.[35] When the journalist I. P. Belokonskii visited Kursk late in 1905, he noted that the PPO had already given the peasants thousands of brochures and was sending speakers throughout the province. Besides addressing the land issue, the PPO appealed to the peasants' religious and ethnic sentiments. A Kursk peasant confided to Belokonskii, "They say that the Jews are trying to do away with the tsar and destroy the Orthodox faith." When Belokonskii inquired who "they" were, he found that the peasant had been listening to rightist propaganda, and he subsequently discovered that emotionally laden attitudes oriented many peasants toward the right.[36]

With both landowner and peasant support, the Kursk rightists had a 43 percent plurality in the provincial assembly, better than the leftists" 32 percent and the Kadets" 10 percent, but not sufficient to stop an oppositionist bloc of leftists, Kadets, progressives, and a couple of non-party peasants from controlling the selection of deputies. Leftist peasants were the key element in the bloc. The Kadets, recognizing that they had no chance of winning on their own, agreed to a division of candidates heavily in favor of the peasants. This arrangement, reportedly worked out before the assembly met, enabled the leftist peasants to get eight Duma seats, while the Kadets picked up the other two. Although Count Dorrer persuaded five of the seven non-party peasant electors to vote for rightist candidates, this combination still did not match the strength of the oppositionist bloc.[37] Ironically, the Kursk rightists polled better than any other political persuasion but sent no deputies to the Duma.

After its poor showing in the first elections, the Union of Law and Order in *Orel province* followed the strategy of the People's Party of Order in Kursk and affiliated with the Union of the Russian People. This move, designed to expand the Union's social base, helped get 34 rightist electors chosen in the city of Orel, considerably more than the 20 in the first elections, yet short of the 41 required for a majority. As before, the Kadet candidate, F. V. Tatarinov, was chosen to represent Orel in the Duma.[38]

Elsewhere in the province, the combined forces of the Union of Law and Order and Union of the Russian People had set up branches and opened tearooms stocked with rightist literature at stations along the

Table 17 Deputies in the Second Duma

Province	Total	Rightists	Octobrist bloc	Moderates	Progressives	Kadet bloc	Leftists	Non-party	Nationalists and others
Arkhangel	2	—	—	—	—	—	2	—	—
Astrakhan	3	1	—	—	—	—	2	—	—
Bessarabia	8	7	1	—	—	—	—	—	—
Vilna	6	—	—	—	—	—	—	—	6 Polish
Vitebsk	6	2	1	1	—	—	—	—	2 Polish
Vladimir	6	—	—	—	1	3	2	—	—
Vologda	5	—	—	—	—	1	4	—	—
Volynia	13	11	1	—	—	1	—	—	—
Voronezh	11	—	—	3	1	2	5	—	—
Viatka	13	—	—	—	—	—	13	—	—
Grodno	7	2	—	2	2	—	—	—	1 Polish
Don Oblast	11	—	—	—	1	—	—	—	10 Cossack
Ekaterinoslav	9	—	—	—	—	3	6	—	—
Kazan	9	4	—	—	—	1	—	—	4 Muslim[a]
Kaluga	5	—	1	—	—	—	4	—	—
Kiev	15	1	—	—	—	—	14	—	—
Kovno	6	—	—	—	—	1	5	—	—
Kostroma	6	—	—	—	1	3	2	—	—
Courland	3	—	—	—	—	3	—	—	—
Kursk	10	—	—	—	—	2	8	—	—
Livonia	4	—	—	—	—	4[b]	—	—	—
Minsk	9	6	3	—	—	—	—	—	—
Mogilev	7	3	1	—	3	—	—	—	1 Polish
Moscow	6	—	—	—	—	2	4	—	—
Nizhnii Novgorod	6	—	1	1[c]	1	3	—	—	—
Novgorod	6	3	1	2	—	—	—	—	—
Olonets	3	—	—	—	—	3	—	—	—

Province	Total													Notes
Orenburg	7	—	—	—	2	2	2	2	—	—	—	—	—	2 Muslim / 2 Muslim 1 Cossack 1 Cossack
Orel	8	—	1	1	2	2	2	1	2	3	1	1ᶜ	2	—
Penza	6	1	1	1	2	2	1	1	1	1	1	1	2	—
Perm	13	—	—	—	6	11	5	2	—	—	—	—	—	—
Podolia	13	—	—	—	11	11	11	2	—	2	—	—	—	1 Polish
Poltava	12	8	3	6	12	11	2	1	—	2	—	5	3	6
Pskov	4	—	—	—	1	1	1	1	—	—	—	—	—	—
Riazan	8	—	—	—	3	2	3	3	2	2	—	—	—	—
Samara	12	—	—	—	10	3	5	2	—	—	—	—	—	—
St. Petersburg	3	—	—	—	2	3	2	1	—	—	—	—	—	—
Saratov	10	—	—	—	10	10	1	—	—	—	—	—	—	—
Simbirsk	6	—	—	—	6	2	—	—	—	2	—	—	—	—
Smolensk	6	1	4	—	6	6	—	—	—	—	—	3	4	—
Stavropol	3	—	—	—	3	—	—	—	—	—	3	—	—	1 Muslim / 1 Muslim
Tauride	6	—	—	—	3	3	3	1	1	—	—	—	—	—
Tambov	12	2	—	—	4	4	3	1	—	1	—	—	—	—
Tver	8	4	—	—	9	8	2	2	—	—	—	—	—	—
Tula	5	—	3	3	5	5	2	1	1	1	—	1ᶜ	—	—
Ufa	10	—	1	1	—	—	—	—	—	—	—	—	—	Muslim⁴ 6 Muslim
Kharkov	10	1	—	—	4	3	1	1	—	2	—	—	—	—
Kherson	10	10	7	3	8	6	3	—	—	—	1	3	6	—
Chernigov	10	—	—	—	6	6	1	3	—	—	—	—	—	—
Estonia	3	—	—	—	2	1	—	2ᵇ	—	—	—	—	—	—
Iaroslavl	4	—	—	—	—	1	1	2	—	—	—	—	—	—

Table 17 (*cont.*)

City	Total	Rightists	Octobrist bloc	Moderates	Progressives	Kadet bloc	Leftists	Non-party	Nationalists and others
Astrakhan	1	–	–	–	–	1	1	–	–
Vilna	1	–	–	–	–	1	1	–	1 Polish 1 Polish
Voronezh	1	–	–	–	–	1 1	–	–	–
Ekaterinoslav	1	–	1 1	–	–	–	1	–	–
Kazan	1	1 1	–	–	–	–	–	–	–
Kishinev	1	1 1	–	–	–	–	–	–	–
Kiev	1	1	1	–	–	–	–	–	–
Kursk	1	–	–	–	–	1 1	–	–	–
Moscow	4	–	–	–	–	4 4	–	–	–
Nizhnii Novgorod	1	–	–	–	–	1	1	–	–
Odessa	1	–	–	–	–	1 1	–	–	–
Orel	1	–	–	–	–	1 1	1	–	–
Riga	1	–	–	–	–	1	1	–	–
Rostov	1	–	1	–	–	1 1	–	–	–
Samara	1	–	1	–	–	–	1	–	–
St. Petersburg	6	–	–	–	–	5 5	1 1	–	–
Saratov	1	–	–	–	–	5	1	–	–
Tula	1	–	1	–	–	–	1	–	–
Kharkov	1	–	1	–	–	1	–	–	–
Iaroslavl	1	–	–	–	–	1	1	–	–

Left column: Affiliation reported at time of elections.   Right column: Affiliation according to official Duma register.

[a] These Muslim deputies were inclined toward the Kadets.   [b] Estonian Progressive Party.   [c] Party of Peaceful Renewal.

railways. Rightist leaders also solicited help from the Orthodox clergy. Bishop Serafim publicly endorsed the rightists, preached patriotic sermons, and urged priests throughout the province to do the same.[39]

As in Kursk province, the Orel rightists' ability to disseminate their message in the countryside bore results. In the elections, they received an impressive 55 percent of the peasant vote, better even than the 50 percent support they got from the landowners. Only a disappointing 11 percent of the urban vote prevented the rightists from having a majority in the provincial assembly, although they still achieved a 45 percent plurality overall.

The political diversity among electors in the assembly complicated the selection of deputies. In order to achieve a voting majority, the rightists needed complete unity among their electors and assistance from the Octobrists, who constituted 9 percent of the assembly, in which event they would divide the deputies. In the chaotic atmosphere of the assembly, neither of these contingencies occurred. Often, class interests prevailed over party discipline, a significant feature in Orel province, where most parties were not yet firmly established and tightly controlled. In some instances, rightist peasants, intent on getting deputies elected from their curia, actually sided with oppositionists. Similarly, the Octobrist electors, unsure that an alliance with the rightists would bear fruit, sometimes agreed with the oppositionists to support compromise candidates, provided these candidates were landowners. As the voting began, the peasant curia chose as its deputy a non-party Russo-Japanese War hero by a single vote. Next, the general body selected M. A. Stakhovich, the popular provincial marshal of the nobility, who since the First Duma had left the Octobrists and helped found the Party of Peaceful Renewal. Then the assembly reached an impasse: no curia or party could enlist sufficient support to get its candidates elected. Finally, after several dozen candidates failed to obtain a majority, a few peasants (including rightists) relented, which gave enough votes to elect some middle-of-the-road landowner and urban candidates: two Octobrist district marshals of the nobility, a non-party socialist, and a moderate Kadet. At this point the oppositionist urban electors decided they might better endorse progressive peasant candidates for the two remaining seats than chance the election of more Octobrist landowners. Consequently, the assembly chose two non-party progressive peasant deputies.[40] Like their counterparts in Kursk, the Orel rightists, despite their plurality in the provincial assembly, got none of their candidates elected.

In the *other central provinces*, where rightists lacked proficient leadership and faced intensive leftist agitation, their fortunes varied. Rightists in *Tambov province* failed to create a local political organization, although, during 1906, the Union of the Russian People and the Union of Russian Men each established a number of branches. Despite rather haphazard campaigning, rightists secured 37 percent of the vote, not enough, however, to keep the provincial assembly from choosing only oppositionist deputies.[41]

No major local rightist organizations operated in *Voronezh province* either, and very few Union of the Russian People branches appeared. The rightists got only 14 percent in the vote, while the Octobrists, moderates, progressives, Kadets, leftists, and non-party candidates divided the rest almost equally. The resulting melange of electors sent a mixture of oppositionist and moderate deputies to the Duma.[42]

In *Saratov province*, the People's Monarchist Party, a struggling law-and-order organization, ran into strong leftist competition, as did the scattered Union of the Russian People and Union of Russian Men branches. During the campaign, the Trudoviks, Socialist Revolutionaries, Social Democrats, and Popular Socialists formed a bloc, which drew heavily from the urban electorate and peasants. While the rightists won 69 percent of the landowner vote, they controlled only 27 percent of the total electors in the provincial assembly, where the radical opposition chose leftists as all ten of Saratov's deputies.[43]

The Second Duma elections in the central agricultural region thus reflected the electorate's growing political consciousness. Few electors still designated themselves as non-party, and while Kadets and progressives benefited from the politicizing that had occurred, the two ends of the political spectrum clearly made the greatest gains. As could be expected, leftists attracted many aggrieved peasants by advocating the expropriation of private estates, but worth noting is the fact that rightists, in provinces where they propagandized widely, got more peasant votes than did the leftists. Among the landowners, the leftists understandably drew hardly at all, while the rightists obtained an even higher vote than in the first elections. This support may have indicated landowner alarm over the First Duma's attention to compulsory land redistribution, but it is significant that rightists polled most heavily among landowners in Kursk and Tula provinces, where rightist parties were best organized and adeptly used existing zemstvo structures to mobilize the vote. Although rightist pluralities lost out to oppositionist blocs in some provincial assemblies, the

Second Duma elections demonstrated that indigenous rightist organizations in the central agricultural provinces had indeed become a viable political force.

The western borderlands

Rightists in the western borderlands also met with success. Capitalizing on regional ethnic and religious issues, they drew substantial support from both peasants and landowners, and in a few cases from townspeople, especially in those provinces where they had established efficient political organizations. Generally, the key was the countryside, a critical factor in an area that was predominantly rural.

The rightists' most striking victory came in *Volynia*, where the Pochaev Monastery had built a thriving network of village branches. Operating under the auspices of the Union of the Russian People, Pochaev orators and parish priests appealed to their listeners' ethnic and religious sentiments, and they assured the peasants that the government would help them acquire land. The monk Iliodor warned his audiences "not to repeat the error committed in the last elections, when the peasants sent deputies to the Duma who drew their ten rubles a day, sat in their quarters, and failed to speak up in defense of the tsar, the church, and the Russian people."[44]

No other political parties in Volynia matched the URP campaign. The Kadets and leftists were active in the provincial capital of Zhitomir and a few towns, but in the countryside the Pochaev rightists swept the peasant vote and polled strongly enough among the landowners to achieve an absolute majority in the provincial assembly. With rightist peasant and landowner electors cooperating, the assembly selected 11 rightist deputies, (eight peasants, two landowners, and a Czech settler), along with a right Octobrist, who sided with the rightists in the Duma, and a moderate.[45] Volynia thus contributed the largest rightist delegation in the Second Duma.

In *Bessarabia*, both the Center Party and the Union of the Russian People were primed for the Second Duma campaign. P. N. Krupinskii's Center Party continued to attract landowners through the zemstvos, and it sent more speakers than ever among the peasants. From his URP stronghold in Kishinev, P. A. Krushevan disseminated an intensely patriotic and antisemitic message, as did V. M. Purishkevich in Akkerman district, where he exhorted local landowners that the Jews were promoting a movement to expropriate landed estates and that a Kadet Duma would carry out these insidious designs.[46]

In Kishinev, the URP and a Kadet bloc of "progressives" ran a close race, but the rightists' slight edge in three of the city's five districts let them emerge with a total of 47 electors to the Kadets' 33 – a decisive rightist victory. The electoral assembly then chose Krushevan as the city's deputy.[47] Stung by their disheartening loss, the Kadets could only bemoan "this black day in Kishinev," while the rightists celebrated their triumph.[48]

In the rest of the province, rightists fared better than in the first elections too. The statistics in Tables 11–15, compiled by Kadet analysts, may be misleading, since most electors listed as "moderates" probably were Center Party members, whom the compilers hesitated to combine with more extreme candidates under the rubric of "rightists."[49] Even after the appropriate corrections, the data show that the rightists did not quite hold a majority in the provincial assembly, having at most 54 of the 117 electors. However, they added to their plurality by gaining the support of some uncommitted peasants, along with a few German landowners, who agreed to cast their ballots for rightist candidates if the rightists would vote for at least one German candidate.[50] The arrangement worked. Besides a non-party rightist deputy selected by the peasant curia, all the other deputies, except for a German Octobrist, were rightist landowners: four Centrists, including Krupinskii, and two extreme rightists, one of whom was Purishkevich. Later, in the Duma, even the German Octobrist gravitated toward the rightist camp.[51] Clearly, in Bessarabia the rightists had prevailed.

In *Minsk province*, the newly organized, moderately rightist Russian Borderland Union entered the Second Duma campaign with reasonable prospects of success. The RBU felt it had little to fear from the Kadets and leftists, who had established themselves in the city of Minsk but not extensively throughout the province. It took a neutral stand toward the Octobrists, who had acquired some influence among Belorussian and Russian landowners. Counting on anti-Polish and anti-Jewish sentiment as its greatest resource, the RBU made its watchword: "Stop the Poles! Stop the Zionists!"[52]

In the elections, RBU campaigning accounted for much of the 39 percent rightist vote, but it still took skillful RBU maneuvering to prevail in the provincial assembly. As in the previous assembly, some Polish and Belorussian landowners, intent on protecting their class interests, formed a coalition with the urban electors. However, other Belorussian landowners, mostly Octobrists, chose to cooperate with rightist peasants.[53] As a result, the rightist–Octobrist bloc controlled the assembly, which selected entirely loyalist deputies: six RBU members (five peasants and an Orthodox priest) and three Octobrists (two landowners and a village clerk).[54] Impressively, the elections demonstrated that in a short time the Russian Borderland Union had become the dominant political force in Minsk province.

In *Mogilev province*, rightists did well in the preliminary elections, only to falter in the provincial assembly. There was no major indigenous rightist party in the province, but the Union of the Russian People had set up branches in the capital city of Mogilev and in Gomel, Orsha, Chausy, and several villages. By the middle of 1906, the URP claimed it had over 8,000 members in Gomel and its environs alone, perhaps an exaggeration but indicative of URP strength. In January 1906, Gomel had witnessed a serious pogrom, and the URP continued to inflame anti-Jewish passions, both there and elsewhere. Smaller groups, like the Union of Russian Patriots, added to the rightist fervor.[55] One can assume that this antisemitism, along with the antipathy that many Mogilev peasants felt toward Polish land-owners, contributed greatly to the rightist cause. At the same time, nationalist sentiments were not as pronounced among Belorussian landowners, who sometimes sided with Polish landowners to protect mutual class interests, even if at the expense of the Belorussian peasants. Drawing 56 percent from the peasants but only 34 percent from the landowners, the rightists still had a 38 percent plurality in the provincial assembly.

When the assembly met, the peasant curia first elected from its own ranks a non-party deputy inclined toward the right. Then, in the general sessions, the voting became more complicated, as a group of rightist Belorussian landowners formed a bloc with the Polish landowners, promising them two or three seats if together they elected only landowner deputies. In separate negotiations the Belorussian landowners also enlisted the support of some Belorussian peasant electors by playing on their national sentiments. The assembly proceeded to elect two rightist Russian landowners and a Polish nationalist landowner, but by that time some Poles were having second thoughts about helping elect rightist Russians, and the peasants were becoming disturbed because no one from their curia had been chosen. Therefore, both the Poles and the peasants quit the bloc. The peasants then turned to the urban electors, who agreed to vote for peasant candidates, if they were not loyalists. The assembly finally elected a progressive peasant, a non-party peasant, and a progressive priest. Thus, only three of Mogilev's seven deputies were rightists. National and class interests had prevented what otherwise might have been a rightist landslide.[56]

The western rightists also scored a victory in the city of *Kiev*, a notable feat, since rightists elsewhere generally fared poorly among the urban electorate. Rightist success in Kiev stemmed mainly from the political coalition that developed between the first and second elections (see Chapter 7). Calling itself the United Rightist Parties of Kiev and comprising all the local rightist groups – the Party of Legal Order, Russian Monarchist Party, Russian Assembly, Union of Russian Workers, Union of the Russian People, and Russian Brotherhood – this coalition campaigned methodically for its list of candidates. Committees in each of the city's eight electoral districts distributed literature, arranged public meetings, and provided speakers, concentrating on antiliberal and antisemitic themes. The coalition's main opponents were the ever-active Kadets, who had negotiated an alliance with the leftists. Since the Octobrists were weak in Kiev, they ran candidates in only a couple of districts.[57]

When the returns came in they showed that the rightists had won a narrow majority of 41 out of 80 electors, while the Kadets had got 38 and the Octobrists one. The Octobrist elector and even one Kadet elector voted with the rightists in selecting Bishop Platon, a staunch loyalist, as Kiev's deputy.[58] Through adept campaigning, the rightist coalition had successfully tapped the conservative vein long evident among Kiev's population.

Like the central agricultural provinces, the western borderlands exhibited significant changes in the Second Duma elections. Political parties had become more active, and the electorate more politicized, which contributed to a marked polarization in voting patterns. In this altered political climate, it took the second elections to demonstrate how politically viable the western rightists had become. Throughout the region they posted striking gains, polling far more heavily than either liberals or leftists. Focusing on ethnic and religious issues, and encountering less peasant discontent than existed in the central region, rightists in the West obtained a plurality of the vote in nine provinces. In three of these – Volynia, Bessarabia, and Minsk – where rightists were most capably organized, they had sufficient strength to send almost entirely rightist delegations to the Duma. As in the central provinces, regional characteristics, combined with competent local leadership, played a decisive role in rightist politics.

Election results in the West also confirmed that rightists there tended toward a moderate rather than an extremist orientation. Despite their often demagogic anti-Jewish, anti-Polish rhetoric and their support of the autocracy, they generally accepted the reality of the Duma and the need for at least modest reform. The moderately rightist stance taken by the Center Party in Bessarabia and the Russian Borderland Union in Minsk manifested itself in the deputies from these provinces. The Pochaev organization in Volynia, while affiliated with the Union of the Russian People, even chose mainly moderate rightist deputies. After minor shifts once the Duma convened, the deputies from these three provinces fell into the following categories: from Bessarabia, six moderate rightists and two extreme rightists; from Minsk, six moderate rightists, no extreme rightists, and three Octobrists; and from Volynia, eleven moderate rightists, one extreme rightist, and one Kadet.[59] In other western provinces moderate rightists also predominated, even if they were not strong enough to control the provincial assemblies. This orientation became even clearer a few months later, when moderate rightists in Podolia, Mogilev, Poltava, and Kiev provinces emerged victorious in the Third Duma elections.

Other provinces

Elsewhere in the country, rightist victories were scattered and at times erratic. *Kherson province*, for example, presented an unusual situation. On the basis of slightly incomplete election returns, Kadet analysts specified only 33 of 133 electors as rightists. By the time of the provincial assembly, 143 electors were on hand, which may have increased the number of rightists but still left them in a decided minority. However, 63 oppositionist electors walked out in protest over the nullification of elections in the cities of Kherson and Nikolaev. The rightist electors and a few supporters, now finding themselves in a slim majority, proceeded to select ten rightist deputies (three of whom may actually have been right Octobrists) – an unexpected victory in Kherson.[60]

A similar situation occurred in *Poltava province*. There the rightists in the provincial assembly comprised only about a quarter of those present, but when most oppositionist electors left in a dispute over irregularities in election procedures, the rightists and Octobrists, now a majority, chose eight rightist and three Octobrist deputies. Only the peasant curia, voting separately, sent an oppositionist candidate to the Duma.[61]

The elections in *Novgorod province* also need explanation. In the provincial assembly, the peasant electors, meeting separately, chose a leftist deputy. Then, in the general sessions, no political group had a majority, and it appeared that bargaining would be required to elect the remaining deputies. To this end the rightists and Octobrists formed a bloc, as did most Kadets, leftists, and progressives; but neither side quite achieved a majority (which the oppositionists would have had if eight of their electors had not been disqualified). Finally, a rightist priest persuaded eight peasant electors, who previously had sat among the progressives, to vote for loyalist candidates. This enabled the election of three rightists, an Octobrist, and a member of the Party of Peaceful Renewal.[62]

In *Moscow province*, where the Russian Monarchist Party, the Union of the Russian People, and the Union of Russian Men all campaigned, rightists obtained a plurality in the provincial assembly, but Kadets and leftists combined to block them, which enabled the assembly to elect only opposition deputies.[63] Similarly, in *Nizhnii Novgorod province*, where the local Union of the White Banner gained a large following, the rightists achieved a plurality in the provincial assembly, but a Kadet–leftist alliance succeeded in getting only its candidates elected.[64]

Rightists in the Second Duma

Although the rightists did much better in the second elections than in the first, they constituted only a minority in the Second Duma, which remained strongly oppositionist, as shown in Table 18.[65]

As indicated in Table 18, rightist deputies in the Second Duma separated into three categories, the ten most reactionary being labelled simply as "rightists," 23 as "moderate rightists," and 24 as "non-party rightists." Their differences focused mainly on attitudes toward the new Duma monarchy. The extreme rightists, who from the start had opposed the creation of a Duma, frequently used their presence in that body to act as obstructionists. They fostered tensions in the Duma and repeatedly assailed the oppositionist majority as seditionists. The moderate rightists were more conciliatory. While considering themselves as loyal to the autocracy as the extreme rightists, they endorsed a legislative Duma, popular representation, and partisan politics. Usually, they dissociated themselves from the disruptive tactics of extremist deputies, such as V. M. Purishkevich and N. E. Markov, who excelled in interrupting debate on the Duma

222

Table 18 *Representation in the Second Duma*

Rightists	10	2%
Moderate rightists	23	4%
Non-party rightists	24	4%
Octobrists and supporters	22	4%
Moderates	14	3%
Progressives	5	1%
Kadets and supporters	100	19%
Popular Socialists	16	3%
Trudoviks and Peasant Union	104	20%
Social Democrats	65	13%
Socialist Revolutionaries	37	7%
Non-party leftists	2	1%
Non-party (inclination unknown)	3	1%
Polish group	46	9%
Muslim group	30	6%
Cossack group	17	3%
	518	100%

Source: Gosudarstvennaia Duma, *Ukazatel' k stenograficheskim otchetam: vtoroi sozyv, 1907 g.*

floor. The non-party rightists differed little from the moderate rightists except in social composition. Most moderate rightists were landowners, professional persons, or Orthodox clergy; all 24 of the non-party rightists were peasants. Like many peasant deputies in the First Duma, these non-party rightists declined to state a political affiliation, but they identified themselves as firm, if not radical, monarchists.[66]

Almost immediately, the ultrarightists attacked the Second Duma. On 28 February 1907, eight days after the Duma convened, Purishkevich notified local Union of the Russian People branches that, when they saw a black cross printed in *Russkoe znamia*, they should deluge the tsar and Stolypin with telegrams requesting dissolution.[67] On 14 March, the black cross appeared, and at once the telegram campaign began. From 18 March until late May, *Russkoe znamia* published copies of messages from URP branches across the country, imploring the tsar and Stolypin to dismiss the Duma. In May 1907, Archmandrite Vitalii led a delegation from the Pochaev Monastery to assure Nicholas that the widespread monarchist support in Volynia represented the Russian people generally and that the Second Duma was essentially a false body.[68] In Moscow, the Russian Monarchist Party's

V. A. Gringmut launched his own attack in *Moskovskiia vedomosti*. On 2 March, he wrote a feature article condemning the Duma's "revolutionary activities"; and, beginning on 24 March, he ran daily headlines proclaiming: "First of all the Duma must be dissolved!" When the fourth monarchist congress met in Moscow on 25 April, it too asked for dissolution, along with a revised electoral law that would exclude "politically unreliable persons" from voting or being elected to the Duma.[69]

The extent to which this flood of messages influenced the tsar is difficult to determine, but probably it encouraged him to make his final decision. On 29 March, he wrote to his mother, "I am getting telegrams from everywhere petitioning me to order a dissolution; but it is too early for that. One must let them [the Duma deputies] do something manifestly stupid or mean, and then – slap! And they are gone."[70] Apparently, Nicholas regarded the messages as a popular endorsement of what he and his ministers had already been contemplating. V. N. Kokovtsov, Nicholas's Minister of Finance, testified in 1917 that by the end of 1906, even before the Second Duma elections, the tsar and some of his cabinet had discussed dissolving the Duma once it met and revising the electoral law, so as to ensure submissive future Dumas. Kokovtsov stated that P. Kh. Shvanebakh, the State Comptroller, presented the most insistent arguments for dissolution, while A. P. Izvolskii, the Foreign Minister, contended that such action would place Russia in an unfavorable light abroad. Stolypin tentatively agreed with Shvanebakh but preferred to wait until the Duma met before making a final recommendation. When the Duma convened on 20 February, Kokovtsov said, the ministers recognized that it would be as intractable as its predecessor. In March, even Izvolskii changed his mind upon learning from the Russian ambassador in Lisbon about how easily the Portuguese Cortes had just been dissolved. By April, Stolypin and the others agreed to ask Nicholas to dissolve the Duma at the earliest opportunity and simultaneously revise the electoral law. The ministers realized that changing the existing law without Duma approval could be construed as contradicting the Fundamental Laws of the Empire, but they believed they could justify revision by claiming that unusual circumstances forced the tsar to take these measures.[71]

Early in May, S. E. Kryzhanovskii, the Assistant Minister of Internal Affairs, began writing the new electoral law. While it still extended the franchise to all segments of the population, it greatly favored the presumably conservative landed nobility at the expense of the peasants, who by and large had sided with the opposition parties in the first two Dumas. The law lowered the number of peasant electors from 2,535 to 1,147, while raising the number of landowner electors from 1,965 to 2,644. This meant that peasant electors dropped from 43 percent to 22 percent, and landholder electors increased from 34 percent to 51 percent. Whereas peasant electors previously had an absolute majority in 13 of the 51 provincial assemblies in European Russia, they now had a majority in none. In contrast, the landholders earlier had an absolute majority in only two provincial assemblies, but now they had a majority in 27 and an even half of the votes in four others. In addition, the new electoral law divided the urban electorate into two categories, the first having higher property qualifications than the second. Each category would vote for its own electors. The revised law also reduced the number of cities having separate representation from 20 to six, and provided for residents in these cities to vote directly for Duma candidates instead of for electors. Finally, the law increased the residence requirements for the peasant curia, and specified that in the provincial assemblies the peasant curia would no longer select a peasant deputy before meeting with the entire assembly. Each provincial assembly would select at least one peasant deputy – and at least one landowner and one urban deputy – but these would all be chosen by the entire assembly.[72]

Having prepared for dissolution, the tsar and his ministers needed only a specific reason – an incident or emergency – in order to act. This occurred in May, when the government announced that it had uncovered an alleged plot to assassinate the tsar, which implicated several Social Democrats in the Duma. When the Duma refused to waive the immunity of these deputies, Stolypin announced the Imperial Manifesto of 3 June 1907, dissolving the Second Duma; and he published the new electoral law.[73]

That same day, Nicholas sent A. I. Dubrovin a telegram, which implied that he had taken into account the rightists' call for dissolution. The telegram read:

> Convey to all branch chairmen and members of the Union of the Russian People who have sent me spirited expressions of their feelings my heartfelt gratitude for their devotion and readiness to serve the throne and the welfare of our dear homeland. I am confident that now all truly faithful and affectionate sons of the Russian homeland will unite still more closely, and as they continually increase their numbers they will assist me in bringing about a peaceful renewal of our great and holy Russia and in

improving her people's goodly way of life. Certainly, the Union of
the Russian People will be for me a trustworthy support, serving
everyone as a constant example of legality and order.[74]

Count Witte remarked that this telegram revealed "all the poverty
of political thought and morbidity of soul of the autocratic
emperor."[75] But Dubrovin regarded it as a great honor. Along with
reprinting the imperial manifesto that dissolved the Duma, he
published Nicholas's telegram in *Russkoe znamia*. He also included his
own message to "the true Russian people," in which he referred
ecstatically to the tsar's acknowledgement of their efforts and urged
them to "stand fast in filial unity with the autocratic monarch."[76]

During the next several days, Nicholas received telegrams from
many organizations – URP branches, local monarchist associations,
nobles' assemblies, and conservative zemstvos – all conveying their
gratitude for dissolving the Duma. In response, the imperial chancellery conveyed the tsar's appreciation for these loyal responses.[77] But
Nicholas's most important message had been his telegram to
Dubrovin, which intimated that the tsar had been heeding rightist
anti-Duma sentiment even before the order for dissolution.

The Third Duma

In revising the electoral law, the autocracy employed a
strategy almost certain to create a compliant Third Duma. Tables 19–
27 show that the third elections indeed produced loyalist majorities
(rightists, Octobrists, and moderates) in 35 provinces. Nine provinces
– Tula, Kursk, Orel, Volynia, Bessarabia, Podolia, Mogilev, Poltava,
and Kherson – had exclusively rightist majorities (51–77 percent), and
three others – Tambov, Kiev, and Minsk – fell barely short (48–50
percent).[78] Most of these provinces lay in the central agricultural
region or the western borderlands, confirmation of the role that
regional characteristics played in determining political fortunes.[79]

An examination of the Third Duma elections also helps verify the
observations made in Chapters 6 and 7, and previously in this
chapter, that the caliber of rightist leadership in various provinces
largely determined whether moderate or extremist organizations
would predominate. In *Tula province*, V. A. Bobrinskii's well-
grounded Union for Tsar and Order, already strong by the second
elections, retained its edge over the more radical Union of the Russian
People. The URP opened a number of branches in Tula during 1907,

and some Union for Tsar and Order supporters switched to the URP, but Bobrinskii and other Union for Tsar and Order leaders continued to wield substantial influence, especially among Tula landowners. In the provincial assembly, moderate rightists outnumbered extremists. Although the two groups cooperated in forming a majority coalition, which had no difficulty in getting rightists chosen as Tula's five deputies, four of these, including Bobrinskii, belonged to the Union for Tsar and Order.[80]

In contrast to Bobrinskii's moderate rightists, the ultraconservative People's Party of Order, led by Count Dorrer and Prince Kasatkin-Rostovskii, prevailed in nearby *Kursk province*. Loosely affiliated with the Union of the Russian People since December 1906, the PPO had subsequently labored to set up URP branches throughout the province.[81] These efforts paid off: not only did a sizeable rightist majority in the provincial assembly choose rightists as Kursk's 11 deputies, but most of these were candidates of the PPO.[82]

Rightists in *Orel province* had greater difficulty. The Union of Law and Order, now a full-fledged branch of the Union of the Russian People, contributed to the 53 percent rightist majority in the provincial assembly, as did other URP branches. But this majority was lost, when rightist peasant and urban electors could not agree with rightist landowners on which candidates to support. Consequently, the rightist landowners formed a voting bloc with the Octobrists and the moderate Party of Peaceful Renewal. This bloc succeeded in controlling the voting, but the rightists had to settle for only three deputies, while the Octobrists got five and the Party of Peaceful Renewal one – a clean sweep for the loyalists if not for the rightists.[83]

In *Volynia*, the Pochaev Monastery's URP network again swept the elections, enabling the provincial assembly to choose 13 rightist deputies. Unlike most of Volynia's deputies in the Second Duma, who called themselves "non-party rightists," the deputies this time identified themselves more precisely: nine affiliated with the extreme rightist faction in the Third Duma, while one designated himself as a moderate rightist, and three eventually joined the newly formed National group.[84]

The Center Party in *Bessarabia*, ably led by P. N. Krupinskii, continued to overshadow the more extremely rightist Union of the Russian People. The Center Party enjoyed a landslide in the voting, getting 68 of the 85 rightist electors. Eight of Bessarabia's nine deputies, including Krupinskii, belonged to the Center Party; only V.

Table 19 *Third Duma: Peasant electors in provincial assemblies*

Province	Total allotted	Total reported	Rightists		Octobrist bloc		Moderates		Progressives		Kadet bloc		Leftists		Non-party	
Arkhangel	9	9	3	33%	—		—		1	11%	1	11%	1	11%	3	33%
Astrakhan	10	10	2	20%	1	10%	4	40%	2	20%	—		1	10%	—	
Bessarabia	23	19	13	68%	—		—		—		—		1	5%	5	26%
Vilna	19	18	2	11%	—		—		2[d]	11%	—		10	56%	4	22%
Vitebsk	31	30	16	53%	—		2	7%	—		—		—		12	40%
Vladimir	13	13	6	46%	—		1	8%	2	15%	2	15%	2	15%	—	
Vologda	19	19	4	21%	—		—		5	26%	—		4	21%	6	32%
Volynia	42	42	36	86%	—		—		—		—		—		6	14%
Voronezh	35	35	3	9%	—		7	20%	8	23%	6	17%	11	31%	—	
Viatka	23	23	3	13%	—		—		8	35%	2	9%	7	30%	3	13%
Grodno	38	38	6	16%	—		—		1[d]	3%	—		—		31[c]	82%
Don Oblast	31	25	17	68%	2	11%	2	8%	—		1	4%	4	16%	1	4%
Ekaterinoslav	18	18	—		2	6%	5	28%	6	33%	1	6%	4	22%	—	
Kazan	33	33	17[a]	52%	—		—		10	30%	1[e]	3%	1	3%	2	6%
Kaluga	14	14	8	57%	—		—		3	21%	1	7%	—		2	14%
Kiev	36	36	6	17%	—		—		22	61%	—		8	22%	—	
Kovno	23	22	8	36%	—		2	9%	3	14%	—		2	9%	7	32%
Kostroma	17	15	5	33%	1	7%	—		3	20%	1	7%	4	27%	1	7%
Courland	11	7	1	14%	—		1	14%	2	29%	1	14%	—		2	29%
Kursk	31	25	15	60%	—		3	12%	—		—		2	8%	5	20%
Livonia	12	12	—		5[b]	42%	—		3	25%	1	8%	1	8%	2	17%
Minsk	41	41	20	49%	—		17[e]	41%	—		—		4	10%	—	
Mogilev	35	35	28	80%	1	7%	4	29%	—		—		—		7	20%
Moscow	15	14	6	43%	—		1	5%	1	7%	1	7%	1	7%	—	
Nizhnii Novgorod	21	21	5	24%	1	5%	—		—		1	5%	6	29%	8	38%
Novgorod	16	16	—		—		—		—		—		7	44%	9	56%
Olonets	17	17	—		—		—		—		1	6%	1	6%	15	88%
Orenburg	20	13	2	15%	1	8%	1	18%	—		3[e]	23%	—		6	46%
Orel	23	22[f]	8	36%	—		—		—		—		4	18%	10	45%

Province									
Penza	22	22	5 23%	—	—	2 9%	2 9%	3 14%	10 45%
Perm	26	26	10 38%	1 4%	1 4%	3 12%	2 8%	3 12%	6 23%
Podolia	42	42	23 55%	—	17 40%	—	—	2 5%	—
Poltava	21	21	5 24%	—	2 10%	2 10%	—	8 38%	4 19%
Pskov	14	13	1 8%	—	—	—	—	2 15%	10 77%
Riazan	24	24	4 17%	—	1 4%	—	3 12%	6 25%	10 42%
Samara	33	32	2 6%	—	—	9 28%	5 16%	13 41%	3 9%
St. Petersburg	8	2	—	—	—	1 50%	1 50%	—	—
Saratov	27	27	7 26%	—	—	—	—	19 70%	1 4%
Simbirsk	17	17	1 6%	—	—	5 29%	1 6%	10 59%	—
Smolensk	16	16	8 50%	—	—	—	—	4 25%	4 25%
Stavropol	15	15	3 20%	—	6 40%	3 20%	—	3 20%	—
Tauride	18	18	3 17%	—	2 11%	2 11%	—	11 61%	—
Tambov	26	26	17 65%	—	2 8%	—	—	3 12%	4 15%
Tver	22	22	3 14%	—	5 23%	2 9%	1 5%	10 45%	1 5%
Tula	16	14	8 57%	—	—	4 29%	—	—	2 14%
Ufa	30	30	7 23%	—	—	—	9[e] 30%	6 20%	8 27%
Kharkov	28	28	9 32%	—	3 11%	11 39%	—	1 4%	4 14%
Kherson	20	20	2 10%	—	3 15%	10 50%	—	3 15%	2 10%
Chernigov	24	24	7 29%	—	—	—	—	5 21%	12 50%
Estonia	6	6	—	—	1 18%	2 33%	—	3 50%	—
Iaroslavl	12	12	4 33%	2 17%	—	5 42%	—	—	1 8%

[a] Includes electors who voted for Octobrist and Kadet nominees in the provincial assembly.
[b] Baltic Constitutional Monarchists.
[c] Apparently mainly members of the moderately rightist Russian Borderland Union.
[d] Possibly Polish–Lithuanian nationalists.   [e] Includes Muslim "progressives."   [f] See elsewhere in Chapter 11 for Orel electors.

Table 20 *Third Duma: Landowner electors in provincial assemblies*

Province	Total allotted	Total reported	Rightists	Octobrist bloc	Moderates	Progressives	Kadet bloc	Leftists	Non-party
Arkhangel[a]	—	—	—	—	—	—	—	—	—
Astrakhan	12	8	2 25%	—	6 75%	—	—	—	—
Bessarabia	66	65	62 95%	1 2%	—	1 2%	—	—	—
Vilna	38	38	8 21%	—	10 26%	20[c] 53%	1 2%	—	—
Vitebsk	48	47	26 55%	7 15%	—	5 11%	1 2%	—	8 17%
Vladimir	38	38	16 42%	12 32%	—	3 8%	7 18%	—	—
Vologda	32	30	14 47%	1 3%	1 3%	1 3%	—	—	13 43%
Volynia	83	79	50 63%	1 1%	1 1%	10 13%	1 1%	2 3%	15 19%
Voronezh	75	70	26 37%	26 37%	7 10%	8 11%	—	—	2 3%
Viatka	53	49	12 24%	—	—	20 41%	7 14%	5 10%	5 10%
Grodno	44	39	14 36%	2 5%	2 5%	5 13%	2 3%	1 1%	16[e] 41%
Don Oblast	79	78	24 31%	30 38%	—	16 21%	—	—	5 6%
Ekaterinoslav	62	62	15 24%	44 71%	—	2 3%	1 2%	—	—
Kazan	50	48	34 71%	5 10%	—	—	4[d] 8%	5 10%	—
Kaluga	35	35	11 31%	19 54%	—	—	1 3%	—	4 11%
Kiev	78	78	62 79%	2 3%	—	3 4%	1 1%	—	10 13%
Kovno	35	35	4 11%	2 6%	—	9 26%	—	—	20 57%
Kostroma	42	42	11 26%	2 5%	3 7%	9 21%	7 17%	3 7%	7 17%
Courland	24	24	—	24[b] 100%	—	—	—	—	—
Kursk	71	71	67 94%	2 3%	—	—	2 3%	—	—
Livonia	43	43	—	43[b] 100%	—	—	—	—	—
Minsk	71	71	43 61%	4 6%	—	18[e] 25%	—	—	6 8%
Mogilev	64	43	35 81%	—	7 16%	—	1 2%	—	—
Moscow	42	42	21 50%	10 24%	—	—	11 26%	—	—
Nizhnii Novgorod	50	50	24 48%	5 10%	1 2%	3 6%	8 16%	1 2%	8 16%
Novgorod	55	54	28 52%	13 24%	4 7%	3 6%	3 6%	—	3 6%
Olonets	26	13	3 23%	3 23%	7 54%	—	—	—	—
Orenburg	32	29	26 90%	—	—	—	—	—	3 10%
Orel	58	58	40 69%	14 24%	1 1%	3 5%	—	—	—

Province																
Penza	47	47	33	70%	2	4%	4	9%	6	13%	–	–	–	–	2	4%
Perm	59	47	12	26%	1	2%	8	17%	5	11%	5	11%	–	–	16	34%
Podolia	76	76	57	75%	2	3%	5	7%	6	8%	3	4%	3	4%	–	–
Poltava	100	100	72	72%	14	14%	12	12%	–	–	–	–	–	–	2	2%
Pskov	38	37	21	57%	5	14%	9	24%	–	–	2	5%	–	–	7	13%
Riazan	52	52	23	44%	18	35%	–	–	4	8%	–	–	–	–	–	–
Samara	76	70	10	14%	44	63%	–	–	8	11%	6	9%	2	3%	–	–
St. Petersburg	31	30	4	13%	18	60%	5	17%	–	–	2	7%	1	3%	–	–
Saratov	68	68	45	66%	7	10%	2	3%	6	9%	4	6%	–	–	4	6%
Simbirsk	43	42	36	86%	4	10%	–	–	2	5%	–	–	–	–	–	–
Smolensk	51	51	23	45%	23	45%	–	–	2	4%	3	6%	–	–	–	–
Stavropol[a]	–	–	–	–	–	–	–	–	–	–	–	–	–	–	–	–
Tauride	45	45	26	58%	2	4%	7	16%	1	2%	5	11%	–	–	4	9%
Tambov	70	70	37	53%	27	39%	2	3%	–	–	4	6%	–	–	–	–
Tver	54	54	32	59%	6	11%	2	4%	5	9%	7	13%	–	–	2	4%
Tula	46	46	28	61%	16	35%	–	–	–	–	2	4%	–	–	–	–
Ufa	58	57	13	23%	2	4%	1	2%	18	32%	15[d]	26%	8	14%	–	–
Kharkov	71	71	48	68%	22	31%	–	–	1	1%	1	1%	–	–	–	–
Kherson	76	75	49	65%	24	32%	–	–	1	1%	1	1%	–	–	–	–
Chernigov	65	65	29	45%	–	–	16	25%	12	18%	6	9%	2	3%	–	–
Estonia	26	26	–	–	26[b]	100%	–	–	–	–	–	–	–	–	–	–
Iaroslavl	36	36	13	36%	10	28%	–	–	5	14%	4	11%	–	–	4	11%

[a] Combined with (Category I) urban curia.

[b] Baltic Constitutional Monarchists.

[c] Includes Polish–Lithuanian nationalists.

[d] Includes Muslim "progressives."

[e] Apparently includes members of the moderately rightist Russian Borderland Union.

Table 21 *Third Duma: Urban electors (Category 1)* in provincial assemblies*

* For an explanation of this category, see p. 199.

Province	Total allotted	Total reported	Rightists		Octobrist bloc		Moderates		Progressives		Kadet bloc		Leftists		Non-party	
Arkhangel[a]	26	22	8	36%	–	–	4	18%	3	14%	2	9%	2	9%	3	14%
Astrakhan	16	16	4	25%	2	13%	5	31%	1	6%	3	19%	1	6%	–	–
Bessarabia	16	16	6	38%	–	–	–	–	3	19%	4	25%	–	–	3	19%
Vilna	10	10	6	60%	1	10%	–	–	2	20%	1	10%	–	–	–	–
Vitebsk	14	14	1	7%	1	7%	–	–	6	43%	5	36%	1	7%	–	–
Vladimir	18	18	5	28%	4	22%	–	–	7	39%	2	11%	–	–	–	–
Vologda	13	13	4	31%	1	8%	1	8%	3	23%	–	–	–	–	4	31%
Volynia	17	17	2	12%	–	–	1	6%	5	29%	2	12%	5	29%	2	12%
Voronezh	15	15	2	13%	3	20%	1	7%	3	20%	4	27%	1	7%	1	7%
Viatka	17	17	3	18%	2	12%	–	–	7	41%	5	29%	–	–	–	–
Grodno	12	12	2	17%	1	8%	–	–	6[c]	50%	3	25%	–	–	–	–
Don Oblast	18	18	7	39%	–	–	1	6%	–	–	10	56%	–	–	–	–
Ekaterinoslav	15	15	1	7%	6	40%	1	7%	5	33%	2	13%	–	–	–	–
Kazan	18	15	2	13%	9	60%	–	–	–	–	1[d]	7%	3	20%	–	–
Kaluga	14	14	2	14%	7	50%	–	–	2	14%	3	21%	–	–	1	6%
Kiev	16	16	5	31%	–	–	–	–	7	43%	2	13%	1	6%	2	22%
Kovno	9	9	–	–	–	–	–	–	1	11%	6	67%	–	–	1	8%
Kostroma	13	12	3	25%	2[b]	17%	1	8%	3	25%	2	17%	–	–	1	8%
Courland	14	13	–	–	3[b]	23%	–	–	1	8%	9	69%	–	–	–	–
Kursk	17	17	8	47%	–	–	–	–	2	12%	6	35%	1	6%	–	–
Livonia	10	10	–	–	8[b]	80%	–	–	1	10%	–	–	–	–	1	10%
Minsk	12	12	1	8%	1	8%	–	–	4	33%	5	42%	–	–	1	8%
Mogilev	13	13	–	–	1	8%	–	–	1	8%	11	85%	–	–	–	–
Moscow	15	15	7	47%	2	13%	–	–	2	13%	4	27%	–	–	–	–
Nizhnii Novgorod	15	15	5	33%	–	–	–	–	1	7%	6	40%	–	–	3	20%
Novgorod	13	13	–	–	4	31%	2	15%	7	54%	–	–	–	–	–	–
Olonets	9	9	2	22%	–	–	2	22%	3	33%	2	22%	–	–	–	–
Orenburg	7	6	–	–	1	17%	–	–	1	17%	2[d]	33%	1	17%	1	17%

Province									
Orel	17	17	8 47%	4 24%	—	2 12%	3 18%	—	—
Penza	11	11	5 45%	1 9%	1 9%	2 18%	—	1 9%	1 9%
Perm	17	17	7 41%	—	—	2 12%	6 35%	—	2 12%
Podolia	16	15	1 7%	1 6%	—	2 13%	7 47%	5 33%	—
Poltava	17	17	1 6%	—	—	3 18%	11 65%	1 6%	—
Pskov	10	10	3 30%	3 30%	3 30%	1 10%	3 30%	—	—
Riazan	14	14	3 21%	2 14%	2 14%	—	4 29%	—	2 14%
Samara	13	13	—	8 62%	—	1 8%	2 15%	—	2 15%
St. Petersburg	15	15	2 13%	3 20%	1 7%	4 27%	5 33%	2 11%	—
Saratov	18	18	4 22%	1 6%	—	5 28%	6 33%	4 40%	—
Simbirsk	10	10	—	2 20%	—	—	4 40%	3 21%	—
Smolensk	14	14	3 21%	1 7%	—	2 14%	5 36%	—	—
Stavropol[a]	24	15	7 47%	—	2 13%	1 7%	5 33%	—	—
Tauride	13	13	1 8%	—	—	2 15%	10 77%	—	—
Tambov	14	14	3 21%	5 36%	—	4 29%	2 14%	—	—
Tver	15	15	—	5 33%	1 7%	1 7%	8 53%	—	—
Tula	15	15	8 53%	2 13%	1 7%	2 13%	1 7%	1 8%	1 7%
Ufa	12	12	4 33%	—	1 8%	—	6[d] 50%	2 12%	—
Kharkov	17	17	9 47%	3 18%	—	2 12%	2 12%	—	—
Kherson	14	14	9 64%	—	—	3 21%	2 14%	—	—
Chernigov	17	16	3 19%	1 6%	1 6%	—	5 31%	3 19%	3 19%
Estonia	7	6	—	6[b] 100%	—	—	—	—	—
Iaroslavl	16	16	1 6%	6 38%	2 13%	5 31%	2 13%	—	—

[a] Includes landowners.

[b] Baltic Constitutional Monarchists.

[c] Includes Polish–Lithuanian nationalists.

[d] Includes Muslim "progressives."

Table 22 *Third Duma: Urban electors (Category II)* in provincial assemblies*
* For an explanation of this category, see p. 199.

Province	Total allotted	Total reported	Rightists	Octobrist bloc	Moderates	Progressives	Kadet bloc	Leftists	Non-party
Arkhangel	10	10	3 30%	— —	— —	2 20%	3 30%	2 20%	— —
Astrakhan	7	7	— —	— —	1 14%	1 14%	5 71%	— —	— —
Bessarabia	10	10	4 40%	— —	— —	3 30%	2 20%	1 10%	— —
Vilna	8	8	1 12%	— —	— —	3[b] 38%	2 25%	2 25%	— —
Vitebsk	13	8	— —	— —	— —	2 25%	3 38%	2 25%	1 13%
Vladimir	14	14	— —	— —	— —	1 7%	11 79%	2 14%	— —
Vologda	11	10	3 30%	— —	— —	— —	3 30%	2 20%	2 20%
Volynia	14	14	1 7%	— —	— —	8 57%	— —	4 29%	1 7%
Voronezh	13	12	— —	— —	— —	4 33%	6 50%	1 8%	1 8%
Viatka	12	12	— —	— —	— —	2 17%	5 42%	5 42%	— —
Grodno	11	10	— —	— —	— —	7[b] 70%	3 30%	— —	— —
Don Oblast	14	14	1 7%	1 7%	1 7%	3 21%	6 43%	1 7%	1 7%
Ekaterinoslav	9	9	2 22%	1 11%	1 11%	— —	3 33%	2 22%	— —
Kazan	14	14	3 21%	4 29%	— —	— —	2 14%	5 36%	— —
Kaluga	12	11	1 9%	1 9%	— —	— —	9 82%	— —	— —
Kiev	15	15	2 13%	— —	— —	6 40%	4 27%	— —	3 30%
Kovno	8	8	— —	— —	— —	4 50%	1 13%	1 13%	2 25%
Kostroma	13	13	1 8%	1[a] 8%	— —	— —	4 31%	5 38%	2 15%
Courland	11	10	— —	1[a] 10%	1 10%	1 10%	7 70%	2 15%	— —
Kursk	16	16	2 13%	1 6%	— —	1 6%	7 44%	4 25%	1 6%
Livonia	10	10	— —	4[a] 40%	1 10%	5 50%	— —	— —	— —
Minsk	11	10	1 10%	— —	2 20%	6 60%	— —	1 10%	— —
Mogilev	12	12	3 25%	— —	1 8%	2 17%	6 50%	— —	— —
Moscow	13	13	3 23%	2 15%	— —	— —	8 62%	— —	— —
Nizhnii Novgorod	12	12	2 17%	— —	— —	2 17%	8 67%	— —	— —
Novgorod	12	10	— —	— —	2 20%	— —	8 80%	— —	— —
Olonets	8	8	— —	— —	2 25%	4 50%	1 13%	1 13%	— —
Orenburg	6	5	— —	1 20%	— —	— —	1[c] 20%	3 60%	— —

Orel	13	12	3 25%	—	—	4 33%	4 33%	1 8%	—
Penza	10	10	1 10%	—	3 30%	3 30%	2 20%	1 10%	—
Perm	13	13	1 8%	—	2 15%	—	5 38%	4 31%	1 8%
Podolia	14	14	3 21%	—	—	4 29%	4 29%	3 21%	—
Poltava	16	14	1 7%	—	—	3 21%	5 36%	5 36%	—
Pskov	8	8	1 13%	1 8%	—	—	1 13%	6 75%	4 31%
Riazan	13	13	—	2 25%	1 13%	—	6 46%	2 15%	—
Samara	8	8	1 13%	1 11%	—	1 13%	1 13%	2 25%	—
St. Petersburg	10	9	—	—	—	3 33%	4 44%	1 11%	—
Saratov	12	12	—	1 11%	—	—	4 33%	8 67%	—
Simbirsk	9	9	—	—	—	2 22%	1 11%	5 56%	—
Smolensk	13	12	3 25%	—	—	—	6 50%	3 25%	—
Stavropol	6	5	1 20%	—	—	—	4 80%	—	—
Tauride	9	8	—	—	—	—	7 88%	1 13%	—
Tambov	13	13	2 15%	1 8%	—	1 8%	7 54%	2 15%	1 8%
Tver	13	13	1 8%	1 8%	—	1 8%	9 69%	1 8%	—
Tula	13	12	2 17%	1 8%	—	3 25%	4 33%	1 8%	1 8%
Ufa	7	7	—	—	—	2 14%	4[c] 57%	2 29%	—
Kharkov	12	10	3 30%	—	2 25%	2 20%	3 30%	2 20%	—
Kherson	9	8	2 25%	—	1 8%	2 25%	2 25%	—	—
Chernigov	17	12	4 33%	—	—	—	4 33%	1 8%	2 17%
Estonia	5	5	—	—	—	—	2 40%	2 40%	1 20%
Iaroslavl	11	11	2 18%	—	—	3 27%	6 55%	—	—

[a] Baltic Constitutional Monarchists.   [c] Includes Muslim "progressives."

[b] Includes Polish–Lithuanian nationalists.

Table 23 *Third Duma: Worker electors in provincial assemblies*

Province	Total allotted	Total reported
Arkhangel	1	1 leftist
Astrakhan	1	1 leftist
Bessarabia	—	—
Vilna	1	1 leftist
Vitebsk	—	—
Vladimir	6	6 leftists
Vologda	—	—
Volynia	2	2 leftists
Voronezh	2	2 leftists
Viatka	4	4 leftists
Grodno	2	1 leftist
Don Oblast	3	3 leftists
Ekaterinoslav	4	4 leftists
Kazan	2	2 leftists
Kaluga	2	1 leftist, 1 non-party
Kiev	5	5 leftists
Kovno	—	—
Kostroma	5	5 leftists
Courland	2	2 leftists
Kursk	2	2 leftists
Livonia	3	—
Minsk	2	2 leftists
Mogilev	1	1 leftist
Moscow	9	9 leftists
Nizhnii Novgorod	2	2 leftists
Novgorod	2	2 leftists
Olonets	—	—
Orenburg	1	1 leftist
Orel	2	2 leftists
Penza	2	2 leftists
Perm	5	5 leftists
Podolia	2	1 leftist, 1 non-party
Poltava	1	1 leftist
Pskov	—	—
Riazan	1	1 non-party
Samara	1	1 leftist
St. Petersburg	6	6 leftists
Saratov	2	2 leftists
Simbirsk	1	1 progressive
Smolensk	1	1 Kadet
Stavropol	—	—

Table 23 (*cont.*)

Province	Total allotted	Total reported
Taurida	1	1 leftist
Tambov	2	2 leftists
Tver	2	2 leftists
Tula	2	2 leftists
Ufa	3	3 leftists
Kharkov	4	3 leftists
Kherson	4	4 leftists
Chernigov	2	2 leftists
Estonia	2	2 leftists
Iaroslavl	2	2 leftists

I. Purishkevich came from the Union of the Russian People.[85]

In *Minsk province*, the moderately rightist Russian Borderland Union, already thriving by the second elections, remained the dominant political group, stronger than the Union of the Russian People, which established only a few branches in 1907. As in the second elections, some electors whom analysts listed as moderates probably belonged to the RBU, which meant that the rightists had a substantial majority in the provincial assembly. After considerable contention among the curiae, the assembly chose three peasants, two priests, two landowners, a teacher, and a retired army officer as deputies – a socially diverse delegation but all rightists. In the Duma, six deputies called themselves moderate rightists and one an extreme rightist, while another gravitated to the Octobrists and one – the RBU leader, G. K. Schmid – was excluded from Duma membership on a technicality.[86]

Provinces that had rightist majorities or pluralities but where neither extreme nor moderate leadership predominated usually yielded a mixture of rightist deputies. In *Podolia*, for example, the rightist victory drew on several sources. During 1907, the Pochaev Monastery in Volynia extended its network of URP branches further into Podolia. The patriotic Union of Russian Workers, based in Kiev, also opened several Podolian branches. And some non-party, moderately rightist local leaders, such as P. N. Balashov, A. S. Gizhitskii, A. A. Pototskii, and D. N. Chikhachev, all current or recent district marshals of the nobility, utilized their contacts among provincial landowners to solicit rightist support.[87] In the provincial

Table 24 *Third Duma: Combined peasant, landowner, urban, and worker electors in provincial assemblies*

Province	Total allotted	Total reported	Rightists		Octobrist bloc		Moderates		Progressives		Kadet bloc		Leftists		Non-party	
Arkhangel	46	42	14	33%	—	—	4	10%	6	14%	6	14%	6	14%	6	14%
Astrakhan	46	42	8	19%	3	7%	16	38%	4	10%	8	19%	3	7%	—	—
Bessarabia	115	110	85	77%	1	1%	—	—	7	6%	7	6%	2	2%	8	7%
Vilna	76	75	17	23%	1	1%	10	13%	27[d]	36%	3	4%	13	17%	4	5%
Vitebsk	106	99	43	43%	8	8%	2	2%	13	13%	9	9%	3	3%	21	21%
Vladimir	89	89	27	30%	16	18%	1	1%	13	15%	22	25%	10	11%	—	—
Vologda	75	72	25	35%	2	3%	2	3%	9	12%	3	4%	6	8%	25	35%
Volynia	158	154	89	58%	1	1%	2	1%	23	15%	3	1%	13	8%	24	16%
Voronezh	140	134	31	23%	29	22%	15	11%	23	17%	17	13%	15	11%	4	3%
Viatka	109	105	18	17%	2	2%	—	—	37	35%	19	18%	21	20%	8	8%
Grodno	107	100	22	22%	3	3%	2	2%	19[d]	19%	6	6%	1	1%	47[c]	47%
Don Oblast	142	138	49	36%	31	22%	4	3%	19	14%	19	14%	9	7%	7	5%
Ekaterinoslav	108	108	18	17%	53	49%	7	6%	13	12%	7	6%	10	9%	—	—
Kazan	117	112	56[a]	50%	20	18%	—	—	10	9%	8[e]	7%	16	14%	2	2%
Kaluga	77	76	22	29%	27	36%	—	—	5	7%	14	18%	1	1%	2	9%
Kiev	150	150	75	50%	2	1%	—	—	38	25%	7	5%	14	9%	14	9%
Kovno	75	74	12	16%	2	3%	2	3%	17	23%	7	9%	3	4%	31	42%
Kostroma	90	87	20	23%	6	7%	4	5%	15	17%	14	16%	17	20%	11	13%
Courland	62	56	1	2%	28[b]	50%	2	4%	4	7%	17	30%	2	4%	2	4%
Kursk	137	131	92	70%	3	2%	3	2%	3	2%	15	11%	9	7%	6	5%
Livonia	78	75	—	—	60[b]	80%	1	1%	9	12%	1	1%	1	1%	3	4%
Minsk	137	136	65	48%	5	4%	19[c]	14%	28	21%	5	4%	7	5%	3	5%
Mogilev	125	104	66	63%	1	1%	8	8%	3	3%	18	17%	1	1%	7	7%
Moscow	94	93	37	40%	15	16%	4	4%	3	3%	24	26%	10	11%	—	—
Nizhnii Novgorod	100	100	36	36%	5	5%	2	2%	6	6%	23	23%	9	9%	19	19%
Novgorod	98	95	28	29%	17	18%	8	8%	10	11%	11	12%	9	9%	12	13%
Olonets	60	47	5	11%	3	6%	11	23%	7	15%	4	9%	2	4%	15	32%
Orenburg	66	54	28	52%	3	6%	1	2%	1	2%	6[e]	11%	5	9%	10	19%
Orel	113	111[f]	59	53%	18	16%	1	1%	9	8%	7	6%	7	6%	10	9%

Penza	92	92	44 48%	3 3%	8 9%	13 14%	4 4%	7 8%	13 14%
Perm	120	108	30 28%	2 2%	11 10%	10 9%	18 17%	12 11%	25 23%
Podolia	150	149	84 56%	2 1%	22 15%	12 8%	14 9%	14 9%	1 1%
Poltava	155	154	79 51%	15 10%	14 9%	8 5%	17 11%	15 10%	6 4%
Pskov	70	68	26 38%	5 7%	12 18%	1 1%	6 9%	8 12%	10 15%
Riazan	104	104	30 29%	22 21%	3 3%	4 4%	13 12%	8 8%	24 23%
Samara	131	124	13 10%	54 44%	1 1%	19 15%	14 11%	18 15%	5 4%
St. Petersburg	70	62	6 10%	22 35%	6 10%	8 13%	12 19%	8 13%	– –
Saratov	127	127	56 44%	8 6%	2 2%	11 9%	14 11%	31 24%	5 4%
Simbirsk	80	79	37 47%	7 9%	– –	10 13%	6 8%	19 24%	– –
Smolensk	95	94	37 39%	24 26%	– –	4 4%	15 16%	10 11%	4 4%
Stavropol	45	35	11 31%	– –	8 2%	4 1%	9 3%	3 1%	– –
Tauride	86	85	30 35%	2 2%	9 11%	5 6%	22 26%	13 15%	4 5%
Tambov	125	125	61 49%	33 26%	4 3%	5 4%	13 10%	5 4%	4 3%
Tver	106	106	36 34%	12 11%	8 8%	9 8%	25 24%	13 12%	3 3%
Tula	92	89	46 52%	19 21%	1 1%	9 10%	7 8%	3 3%	4 4%
Ufa	110	109	24 22%	2 2%	2 2%	19 17%	34ᵉ 31%	20 18%	8 7%
Kharkov	134	129	68 53%	25 19%	3 2%	15 12%	6 5%	8 6%	4 3%
Kherson	123	121	62 51%	24 20%	5 4%	16 13%	5 4%	7 6%	2 2%
Chernigov	127	119	43 36%	1 1%	18 15%	12 10%	15 13%	13 11%	17 14%
Estonia	46	45	– –	32ᵇ 71%	1 2%	2 4%	2 4%	7 16%	1 2%
Iaroslavl	77	77	20 26%	18 23%	– 3%	18 23%	12 16%	2 3%	5 6%

ᵃ Includes electors who voted for Octobrist and Kadet nominees in the provincial assembly.

ᵇ Baltic Constitutional Monarchists.

ᶜ Apparently mainly members of the moderately rightist Russian Borderland Union.

ᵈ Includes Polish–Lithuanian nationalists.

ᵉ Includes Muslim "progressives."

ᶠ See elsewhere in Chapter 11 for Orel electors.

Table 25 Third Duma: Elections in cities having separate representation (Electoral Category I)*
* For an explanation of this category, see p. 199.

City	Deputies allotted	Rightists		Octobrist bloc		Kadet bloc		Leftists		Non-party and others	
Kiev	1	757	50%[a]	—	—	(←———	756	50%———→)		—	—
Moscow	2	399	10%	2,091	49%	1,812	42%	—	—	—	—
		408	10%	2,034	47%	1,792	42%	—	—	—	—
Run-off:		148	3%	2,561	56%	1,875	41%				
		147	3%	2,522	55%	1,860	41%				
Odessa	1	464	c. 30%	—		843	c. 55%	—		c. 220	c. 14%
Riga	1			≥50%[b]		≤50%		—		—	
St. Petersburg	3	175	8%	1,204	54%	871	39%	—		413	19%
		178	8%	990	45%	829	37%	—		151	7%
		186	8%	745	34%	810	37%	—		—	
Run-off:		25	1%	1,212	60%	782	39%			248	12%
		11	<1%	960	48%	746	37%			6	1%
		20	<1%			14	<1%				

All candidates in a given city were listed on a single ballot for that city. In Moscow each voter could vote for two candidates on the ballot, in St. Petersburg for three. To be elected, a candidate had to be voted for on over half of the total ballots cast. Each percentage given in the table indicates the percentage of the total ballots.
[a] One-vote majority.
[b] Baltic Constitutional Party.

Table 26 *Third Duma: Elections in cities having separate representation (Electoral Category II)**
* For an explanation of this category, see p. 199.

City	Deputies allotted	Rightists	Octobrist bloc	Kadet bloc	Social Democrats	Popular Socialists	Other Leftists	Non-part- and other
Kiev	1	5,406 44.5%	—	6,070 49.9%	—	—	—	685 5.6%
Run-off:		6,073 49.7%		6,153 50.3%				
Moscow	2	2,047 8%	5,872 22%	16,361 61%	2,270 8%	394 1%	236[d] 1%	—
		1,944 7%	5,752 21%	16,407 61%	2,221 8%	393 1%	234[d] 1%	—
Odessa	1	?	—	?	plurality[g]	—	?[e]	—
Run-off:		2,982 29%	—	7,354 71%				
Riga	1	5,482[a] 41%	—	1,376[b] 10%	4,862 36%	—	720 5%	—
				1,051[c] 8%				
Run-off:		5,992 48%			6,363 52%			
St. Petersburg	3	4,393 10%	9,150 21%	22,714 51%	5,213 12%	—	5,654[f] 13%	679 2%
		4,273 10%	8,609 19%	20,995 47%	3,729 8%	—	3,446[f] 8%	313 1%
		4,096 9%	8,379 19%	17,219 39%	3,562 8%	—	2,968[f] 7%	66 —
Run-off:		570 2%	7,235 21%	20,432 60%	4,834 14%		5,287 15%	
		1,215 4%	6,291 18%	19,350 57%				
		748 2%	840 2%					

All candidates in a given city were listed on a single ballot for that city. In Moscow each voter could vote for two candidates on the ballot, in St. Petersburg for three. To be elected, a candidate had to be voted for on over half of the total ballots cast. Each percentage given in the table indicates the percentage of the total ballots.
[a] Lettish–German bloc. [b] Lettish Kadet group. [c] Russian–Jewish Kadet group. [d] Peasant Union. [e] Zionist group. [f] Trudoviks. [g] The SD candidate was disqualified before the run-off; most of his supporters shifted to the Kadet candidate.

Table 27 Deputies in the Third Duma

Province	Total	Rightists	Octobrist bloc	Moderates	Progressives	Kadet bloc	Leftists	Non-party	Nationalists and others
Arkhangel	2	—	—	—	—	2	—	—	—
Astrakhan	4	1	1	—	1	1	—	—	—
Bessarabia	9	9	—	—	—	—	—	—	—
Vilna	7[a]	2[b]	—	—	—	—	—	—	5 Polish–Lithuanian
Vitebsk	6	4	2	—	—	—	—	—	—
Vladimir[e]	6	1	1	1	—	1	1	—	—
Vologda	5	5	—	—	—	—	—	—	—
Volynia	13	13	—	—	2	1	—	—	—
Voronezh[e]	12	3	5	—	1	1	—	1	—
Viatka	8	—	—	—	1	3	5	—	—
Grodno	7	6	—	—	1	—	—	—	1 Polish–Lithuanian
Don Oblast	12	5	1	—	2	5	1	—	—
Ekaterinoslav	10	2	6	1	1	—	1	—	—
Kazan[e]	10	—	4	—	1	3	—	—	2 Muslim
Kaluga	5	1	4	—	—	—	—	—	—
Kiev	13	13	—	—	—	—	—	—	—
Kovno[c]	6	1[d]	—	—	—	1	2	—	2 Polish–Lithuanian
Kostroma	6	2	1	—	1	1	1	—	—
Courland	3	—	1[h]	—	1	1	—	1	—
Kursk	11	11	—	—	—	—	—	—	—
Livonia	4	—	3[h]	—	—	1	—	—	—
Minsk[e]	9	9	—	—	—	1	—	—	—
Mogilev	7	7	—	—	—	1	1	—	—
Moscow	6	2	4	—	—	1	1	—	—

Province														
Nizhnii Novgorod	7	2	—	3	3	—	1	1	—	—	3	—	1	—
Novgorod	6	1	—	6	—	—	1	—	3	1	3	1	—	—
Olonets	3	3	1	3	—	—	—	—	—	—	—	—	—	—
Orenburg[e]	6	3	3	—	1	2	—	1	1	1	1	—	—	1 Muslim[g] 1 Muslim
Orel[e]	9	4	2	5	—	1	—	—	—	—	—	—	—	—
Penza	6	3	—	4	—	—	—	—	—	—	—	—	—	—
Perm	9	—	13	—	—	3	—	3	3	4	3	—	—	—
Podolia	13	13	2	8	—	—	—	—	—	—	—	—	—	—
Poltava[ef]	12	11	5	—	—	—	—	—	—	—	—	—	—	—
Pskov	5	3	1	5	—	2	—	—	—	—	—	—	—	—
Riazan	8	3	1	—	—	—	—	—	2	2	—	—	—	—
Samara	13	—	—	12	—	2	2	1	1	1	1	—	—	—
St. Petersburg	4	—	—	3	—	1	1	—	—	1	1	—	—	—
Saratov	11	6	6	3	—	—	—	—	1	1	1	—	—	—
Simbirsk	6	3	3	2	—	—	1	—	—	1	1	—	—	—
Smolensk	6	1	—	4	1	—	—	2	—	—	—	—	—	—
Stavropol	3	—	—	—	—	—	—	—	2	1	1	2	—	—
Tauride	6	2	—	2	—	—	—	—	—	—	—	—	—	—
Tambov[f]	12	4	3	8	—	2	—	—	2	2	2	—	—	—
Tver	8	5	3	5	—	—	—	—	—	—	—	—	—	—
Tula	6	6	5	1	—	—	—	—	—	—	—	—	—	—
Ufa	8	—	—	—	—	1	1	1	1	2	2	1	—	4 Muslim[g] 4 Muslim
Kharkov	11	8	2	8	—	1	—	—	—	1	2	—	—	—
Kherson	10	9	7	2	—	1	—	—	—	1	—	—	—	—
Chernigov[f]	10	5	—	9	—	—	—	—	—	—	—	—	—	—
Estonia	3	—	—	2[h]	1	—	—	—	—	1	1	—	—	—
Iaroslavl	5	—	1	3	—	—	—	3	—	1	1	—	3	—

Table 27 (cont.)

City	Total	Rightists		Octobrist bloc		Moderates		Progressives		Kadet bloc		Leftists		Non-party		Nationalists and others	
Kiev	2	1	1	1	—	—	—	—	—	1	1	—	—	—	—	—	—
Moscow	4	—	—	2	2	—	—	—	—	2	2	—	—	—	—	—	—
Odessa	2	—	—	—	—	—	—	—	—	2	2	—	—	—	—	—	—
Riga	2	—	—	1	1	—	—	—	—	—	—	1	1	—	—	—	—
St. Petersburg	6	—	—	3	3	—	—	—	—	3	3	—	—	—	—	—	—

Left column: Affiliation reported at time of elections. Right column: Affiliation according to official Duma register.

[a] The electoral law specified that two deputies were to be Russian.

[b] Russian deputies.

[c] The electoral law specified that one deputy was to be Russian.

[d] Russian deputy.

[e] One deputy was disqualified.

[f] One deputy died soon after the elections.

[g] These Muslim deputies were inclined toward the Kadets.

[h] Baltic Constitutional Monarchists.

assembly, a rightist coalition controlled the selection of all 13 deputies: four extreme rightists and nine moderate rightists, including the four leaders named above.[88]

In *Mogilev province*, the URP branches and local rightist groups that had mobilized anti-Jewish and anti-Polish sentiment in the second elections proved proficient again in the third, particularly among the peasantry. But, as before, many Belorussian landowners, while conservative, seemed more concerned with upholding their class interests than with championing ethnic and religious causes. Moderate rightist landowners, who held a plurality if not a majority in the provincial assembly, managed to control most of the voting, possibly by soliciting some extreme rightist support in exchange for backing Bishop Mitrofan, the URP's prime candidate. Besides Mitrofan and an extreme rightist teacher, the assembly chose five moderate rightists: three landowners, a priest (probably a small landowner), and a peasant, whom the landowners endorsed only because the electoral law required the combined assembly to choose at least one peasant deputy.[89]

In *Poltava province*, the almost two dozen URP branches established in 1907, coupled with strong influence from the Orthodox clergy, contributed to the 51 percent rightist vote. But apparently, many URP members were essentially moderate rightists who chose the URP by default, since there was no other rightist organization with which to affiliate.[90] In the provincial assembly, where rightist electors cooperated with Octobrists to form a firmer majority, the compromises involved made it difficult to distinguish candidates. *Rech'* and *Novoe vremia* both reported the Poltava deputies as 11 rightists and one Octobrist; *Golos Moskvy* listed them as five non-party rightists, one extreme rightist, four Octobrists, and two moderates; and the Duma register classified them as two moderate rightists and eight Octobrists (besides a deputy who had died and one who had been disqualified).[91] Evidently, "rightist" electors felt unbound by party labels and moved even into the Octobrist camp. In any event, the Poltava elections indicated that rightists there were a diverse lot.

Vitebsk province presents an unusual situation. Between the second and third campaigns, the province experienced an increase in rightist activity, primarily by the Union of the Russian people, less so by the Russian Borderland Union.[92] Rightists achieved slim majorities among the peasant and landowner electors, but because of oppositionist strength in the urban curia, they fell just short of a majority in the provincial assembly. However, when some 30 Polish landowner and Jewish urban electors withdrew in protest over a procedural question, the remaining electors, now dominated by rightists and Octobrists, chose four rightists and two Octobrists as deputies. One rightist deputy belonged to the URP, another identified himself as a non-party but extreme rightist, a third was a moderate rightist, and the fourth shifted to the Octobrists in the Duma.[93]

In *Tambov province*, the Union of the Russian People had opened a number of branches in 1907, but it is difficult to determine how decided an advantage they held over moderate rightists. In the provincial assembly the rightist electors, who had a 49 percent plurality, dissipated their strength. Rightist landowner and peasant electors could not agree on which candidates to support, making it impossible for either group to carrying the voting on their own. Finally, the rightist landowners collaborated with Octobrists, who held the balance of power. As a result, the assembly selected as deputies eight Octobrists but only four rightists, three of whom belonged to the URP, while the other was a non-party moderate.[94]

The partial rightist victory in the city of *Kiev* calls for special explanation. Although the revised electoral law removed most cities from separate representation, Kiev was large enough to retain its status. In fact, since the revised law divided the urban electorate into two categories, the first having higher income qualifications for voting than the second, Kiev was entitled to elect one deputy from each category. As before, the voting was close. In the first category, the rightist candidate, V. N. Protsenko, won by a single vote – 757 to 756 – over his Kadet opponent. In the second category, where the Kadet bloc was stronger, its candidate, I. V. Luchitskii, got 6,070 votes to 5,406 votes for the rightist candidate, A. I. Savenko. However, since several lesser candidates together received 685 votes, Luchitskii did not have a majority, and it took a run-off election a week later for him to defeat Savenko, 6,153 to 6,073.[95] Although the rightists in Kiev succeeded in sending only one deputy to the Duma, instead of the two they anticipated, they did better than rightists in other cities that retained separate representation (St. Petersburg, Moscow, Odessa, Riga, and Warsaw), all of which elected Kadets, Octobrists, or in one instance a leftist. Kiev remained the exception.

Finally, Kherson and Kiev provinces, which required the revised electoral law for their rightist victories, produced both extreme and moderate rightist deputies. In *Kherson province*, rightists in the second elections polled only 7 percent among the peasants, and in the

Table 28 *Representation in the Third Duma*

Rightists	49	11%
Moderate rightists	69	16%
National Group (rightists)	26	6%
Octobrists and supporters	151	35%
Progressives	24	6%
Kadets and supporters	51	12%
Trudoviks	14	3%
Social Democrats	19	4%
Polish group	11	3%
Polish–Lithuanian–Belorussian group	7	2%
Muslim group	8	2%
Unspecified	1	—
Total	430	100%

Source: *Ukazatel' ... tretii sozyv*, 3-18.

third elections only 10 percent. Among the landowners the rightist vote grew slightly from 57 percent to 65 percent. But with increased representation, the landowners held the key to the 51 percent rightist majority in the provincial assembly. Even then they solicited Octobrist help in electing deputies, which resulted in four extreme and five moderate rightists and one Octobrist.[96]

In *Kiev province* the expanded landowner curia accounted for most of the 50 percent rightist plurality. The rightist vote among the peasants remained low (up from 1 percent in the second elections to 17 percent in the third); and the already high 76 percent rightist landowner vote in the second elections stayed about the same at 79 percent.[97] In the assembly, rightist fortunes rose as some non-party landowners (including priests having small holdings) and uncommitted peasants supported rightist candidates after a spirited admonition by Archpriest Innokentii. The assembly proceeded to select six priests, five landowners, and two peasants – all rightists – as deputies. In the Third Duma, three of these sat as extreme rightists and seven as moderate rightists, while the other three went over to the Octobrists.[98]

Table 28 shows that the third elections resulted in a comfortable loyalist majority in the Third Duma. The table includes deputies from the 51 provinces and six cities having separate representation in European Russia, plus those from Poland, the Caucasus, Siberia, and Central Asia. The rightists, with 33 percent of the deputies, were exceeded only by the Octobrists with 35 percent.

Table 29 *Rightist deputies in the Third Duma: social status*

	Landowners	Peasants	Clergy	Other
Extreme rightists	20	6	16	7
Moderate rightists	23	24	13	9
National Group	19	3	2	2
Total	62	33	31	18

Source: G. Iurekii, *Pravye v Tret'ei Gosudarstvennoi Dume* (Kharkov, 1912); Edelman, "The Elections to the Third Duma: The Roots of the Nationalist Party." The social, occupational, and professional status of the deputies appears in *Novoe vremia*, 15–24 October 1907.

As in the Second Duma, the rightist deputies separated into three categories (see Table 29). The most reactionary again were labeled simply as "rightists," while the others composed the "moderate rightists" and the "National Group." Although both of the latter upheld the autocracy and opposed autonomy for non-Russian nationalities and equal rights for Jews, they accepted the Duma system with its principle of participatory government. Willing to accommodate limited political change, they seemed more fitted than the extreme right to participate in Russia's new governmental system. The "moderate rightists" and "National Group" differed from each other in that the former regarded themselves as an amalgamation of non-party monarchists, while the latter anticipated becoming a bonafide political party. This divergence in self-perception most likely reflected the fact that the moderate rightists drew primarily from less highly politicized peasants and village priests, while the National Group consisted mainly of politically educated landowners. However, the distinctions between the two groups were not great, and in 1909 they joined in creating the Nationalist Party.[99]

As shown in Table 30, all three rightist categories in the Duma had polled strongly in the western borderlands and fairly well in the central agricultural provinces – areas of rightist strength already by the Second Duma elections.

For the rightists the new electoral law and the Third Duma elections seemed a triumph in stemming the tide of liberal constitutionalism. Although the victory may have resulted more from the government's initiative than from the influence of rightist organizations, it satisfied them both. Many rightists now anticipated the kind of Duma they had been advocating, whose main function would be to facilitate a closer

Table 30 *Rightist deputies in the Third Duma: location*

	Central agricultural provinces	Western borderlands	Elsewhere
Extreme rightists	24	10	15
Moderate rightists	36	11	22
National Group	12	6	8
Total	72	27	45

Source: Gosudarstvennaia Duma, *Ukazatel' ... tretii sozyv*, 3–18.

bond between the "true Russian people" and their tsar. A few days after the Third Duma convened in early November, most rightist deputies – 115 in all – sent a telegram to Nicholas saying: "Our hearts are filled with deepest gratitude for this great act of restoring the long-desired unity of tsar and people, which is now fulfilled in the State Duma." Pledging their faithfulness, they affirmed Russia's traditional principle of autocracy.[100]

Actually, the Third Duma only partially fulfilled this ideal. Gone was the intense antagonism that had divided the throne and the First and Second Dumas, but the rightist–Octobrist majority in the Third Duma still often found itself at odds with the government. It opposed, for example, Stolypin's plan for local administrative reform, which would diminish the predominant role of the landed nobility – the loyalists' foremost social base. Both the rightists and the Octobrists gradually came to realize that the government intended to pursue its own political agenda without necessarily relying on Russia's traditional estates or on the rightists' cherished myth of the unity of tsar and people. But the rightists had no choice: they accepted what they knew to be an imperfect system, hoping they could maintain a reasonably workable relationship with the autocracy.[101]

In assessing the rightists' historical significance in connection with the Duma, one learns a great deal about the evolving political climate in Russia. The First Duma elections, in early 1906, indeed demonstrated a marked opposition to the autocracy, as evidenced by the large number of Kadet deputies. Still, the first elections left several questions unanswered: How many voters who called themselves "non-party" were actually inclined either toward the left or toward the right? What would have been the results had the leftist parties not boycotted the elections? What would have happened had the rightist parties been better organized?

The Second Duma elections, a year later, helped answer these questions. While the Kadets again emerged as the dominant party in the Duma, both the left and right made major gains. Campaigning vigorously, they contributed to a growing political consciousness among the Russian voters and provided a wider range of political alternatives.

While rightist gains by no means sufficed to produce a Second Duma majority, or even a plurality, they confirmed that rightists enjoyed substantial support in certain parts of the country. The rightists' emphasis on law and order in the central provinces and on national and religious issues in the West played a paramount role in attracting both landowners and peasants. Important too were the rightists' campaign procedures, most notably their proficiency at building political networks. Zemstvo structures in Kursk and Tula, parish clergy in Volynia and Minsk, the city duma in Orel, all assisted the rightists in reaching a broad political clientele. Clearly, rightist organizations were gaining significant political expertise.

The Duma elections also helped differentiate between moderate and extreme rightists. This distinction was evident already in the second elections; it became even clearer as the third elections yielded more rightist deputies among which to make comparisons. No doubt such extremist deputies as V. M. Purishkevich and V. F. Dorrer gave the impression that rightists in the Duma intended mainly to act as obstructionists. However, the fact is that most rightist deputies were moderates, who chose to use the Duma, as did other partisans, in promoting legislation favorable to their own political persuasions. Willing to cooperate with Octobrist deputies in forming a Duma majority, these moderate rightists, more than the extremists, helped determine the Duma's place in Russia's new political system.

Conclusion and epilogue

The rightist movement that arose in Russia during 1905–1907 reveals much about the defects and dilemmas of the old regime. It is clear that by the early twentieth century the autocracy was no longer the tutor of society that it once had been, providing leadership and direction to the Russian people. Although it was taking considerable initiative in such matters as economic development, it had increasingly become a bastion for protecting its own interests. Deficient even in this ability and facing unprecedented opposition from reformers and revolutionaries, it finally resorted to two measures, both of which transgressed against its very essence. Not only did the tsar yield, in February 1905, to demands for a popularly elected consultative assembly (later extended into a legislative assembly by the October Manifesto), but he also issued a formal call to his faithful subjects for support. Even in the latter case, he was acting almost as if political power resided in the people, instead of simply ruling by virtue of his own self-proclaimed authority. Surely, many loyalists, as they entered the political arena, sensed the paradox of taking independent public action in order to place – or replace – autocratic power in the ruler's hands. It seemed that the only way to reclaim Russia's apolitical tradition was for the emerging monarchist organizations to succeed politically.

Undeterred, these new "rightists," as they soon became known, pledged to uphold the autocracy, which many of them believed was incapable of surviving the liberal and radical opposition if left to its own devices. Alarmed that Russia was moving toward constitutionalism, the rightists correctly understood that autocracy and constitutionalism were incompatible. However, they faced the formidable question of how to break the impasse that the tsar had reached in granting a legislative Duma while asserting that he retained his autocratic prerogatives. Could they undo the damage that had already occurred and return Russia to its old traditions? Or should they accept the new Duma monarchy, even participate in it along with other political parties, but guard against further encroachment on monarchical power?

These questions are worth considering, because they differentiated two major persuasions within the rightist movement, one intent on restoring a vanished past, the other resigned to preserving what could still be saved. Those, such as the Union of Russian Men, who favored the Slavophile doctrine of popular autocracy, wished to revive the intimate relationship between the tsar and his people that they imagined had once existed in old Muscovy, as expressed in the zemskii sobor. They thought that by persuading the tsar to convene a modern-day "assembly of the land" as a consultative body, they might make superfluous the new State Duma with its legislative powers, nipping in the bud the drift toward western European parliamentary forms. Others, like the Russian Monarchist Party, ignored the old Muscovite ideal of popular autocracy, concentrating instead on restoring the autocratic principles that had marked the recent reign of Alexander III but had been eroded under Nicholas II. Emphasizing the need for an authoritarian rule that could bolster Russia's international prestige and impose internal discipline, these rightists hoped to induce Nicholas to assert his autocratic prerogatives and ignore the Duma. Yet, most rightists recognized that it was impossible to recreate the long-discarded zemskii sobor or, for that matter, to transform Nicholas II into another Alexander III. The Union of the Russian People and others who cherished the ideal unity of tsar and people wanted at least to convert the Duma into a virtual consultative assembly. If the Union and other rightist organizations could get enough loyalist deputies elected, they could ensure a body that would leave legislative initiative to the autocrat and serve only to convey to him the people's needs. Theoretically, this objective seemed plausible; practically, it was an enormous task, given the prevailing political mood of the Russian electorate, which did not seem conducive to a loyalist victory.

The chore of getting loyalist deputies elected also faced those rightists who accepted the Duma for what it was – a legislative body in which their candidates would function as a partisan group to secure legislation for keeping the political and social order as intact as possible. This moderate preservationist approach could be found especially among provincial rightists, who had a greater chance of realizing their goals than did those extremists who tried to obstruct the new Duma system.

The role of these provincial parties is invaluable in discerning the range of rightist concerns. While unfailingly dedicated to the autocracy, provincial rightists nonetheless focused their attention on immediate regional issues. Notably in the central agricultural provinces, the Tula Union for Tsar and Order, the Kursk People's Party of Order and the Orel Union of Law and Order, demanded that law and order be reestablished in a countryside beset by peasant violence. In the ethnically diverse western borderlands, the Bessarabian Center Party, the Minsk Russian Borderland Union, and the numerous branches formed by the Pochaev Monastery in Volynia called for the preservation of Russian predominance among the minority nationalities, particularly the Jews and Poles.

In pursuing their objectives, rightists of all persuasions engaged in a remarkably high level of political activism. They published countless pamphlets, held demonstrations, and made speeches extolling the official trilogy of "autocracy, Orthodoxy, and nationality," which by the twentieth century had become an article of faith for "true Russians." They lamented the cosmopolitanism that had crept into Russian intellectual life and the faithlessness of those Russians who had succumbed to western-style constitutionalism. Searching further for culprits, they bemoaned the perfidy of the Jews and other non-Russians within the empire, who allegedly felt no allegiance to the tsar or the Russian people.

Incessant in their criticism of the Jews, the rightists offered little that was original, drawing mainly on a current of antisemitism that had been growing along with the surge of Russian nationalism in the late nineteenth century. What the rightist organizations did was to politicize this antisemitism and use it in countering those liberals who advocated Jewish rights. Most rightists claimed that the Jews deserved whatever disfavor they encountered because of their own animosity toward the Christians.

Still, the rightists varied in the intensity with which they pursued these issues, differentiating them into what came to be known as the "moderate right" and the "extreme right." Both persuasions existed in most rightist organizations, although extremists usually gravitated to such groups as the Union of the Russian People and the Russian Monarchist Party, while moderate rightists were apt to be found in the regional parties. Generally, extreme rightists were more militant in denouncing the liberal and radical opposition, more virulent in expressing their Russian chauvinism (including their antisemitism), and more intransigent in rejecting the new political system. Most subscribed to the restorationist persuasion and wanted nothing less than a revival of traditional autocracy. In contrast, the moderate rightists, themselves far from championing the Duma system, affirmed their willingness to work within its confines. On some issues they formed alliances with the extreme rightists, but they insisted on maintaining their own identity. Just as diligently, they kept from straying too far in the other direction, which left them slightly to the right of the Octobrists.

The extreme rightists also intimated that the autocracy, to which they pledged their fervent devotion, was incapable of retaining authority on its own. Impugning government officials as compromisers and hinting that the tsar himself was the victim of false counsel, they were convinced that it was their mission to rescue the autocracy, both from its enemies and from itself. While urging the government to find and punish terrorists, seditionists, and other political offenders, some rightist organizations decided that they must take matters into their own hands. Like vigilantes, the Union of the Russian People and several smaller extremist groups issued weapons to its "fighting brotherhoods" for use against revolutionaries and on occasion for assassinating political figures they regarded as seditious. Most disturbingly, Union leaders and other extremists also incited pogroms against the Jews, usually through inflammatory rhetoric, but sometimes by actually orchestrating the attacks. These activities obviously struck a responsive chord with many Russians, but they also brought the rightist movement into disrepute.

Rightists generally contended, however, that the more insidious and dangerous enemies were the liberals. They found it appalling that the tsar had bent to liberal pressure in October 1905 by granting a legislative Duma. Even if neither the autocrat nor the rightists would publicly admit it, they knew that this change in the political structure meant limiting the autocracy's traditional power. As the rightists correctly perceived, many liberals regarded the Duma as the first step toward a popularly elected constituent assembly.

Consequently, most rightist organizations placed the Duma campaigns at the center of their political agenda. Indeed, the Duma campaigns gave the rightists their biggest opportunity for political influence. Slow in getting started, the rightists had little impact on the First Duma elections in the spring of 1906; but in the Second Duma campaign a year later rightists throughout the country ran slates of candidates. Especially effective were law-and-order parties in the central agricultural region, which addressed the current peasant turmoil there, and rightist organizations in the western borderlands, which concentrated on endemic ethnic and religious issues. In several provinces, skillfully led rightist parties succeeded in gaining majorities or strong pluralities – Tula, Kursk, Orel, Tambov, Volynia, Podolia, Bessarabia, Minsk, Mogilev, Chernigov – still short of producing a loyalist Duma, yet indicative that in certain areas the rightist parties had a politically significant constituency. With the revised electoral law of 3 June 1907 supplementing their efforts in the Third Duma campaign, the rightists won majorities in a dozen provinces, contributed to rightist–Octobrist majorities in a dozen more, and had a large representation in several other provincial assemblies. The resultant loyalist Third Duma that met in November 1907 undoubtedly gave the rightist organizations their greatest sense of victory.

Many rightists also believed they had been instrumental in persuading the tsar to take resolute action during this time of crisis. They recognized that Nicholas had yielded to advisers in making what he knew were weak-willed concessions and that he needed bolstering from "the true Russian people." No firmer affirmations of loyalty reached him than those proclaimed by the rightist organizations, which attempted to convey the impression that an overwhelming majority of the Russian populace favored a return to unqualified autocracy. To the rightists' satisfaction, Nicholas and his ministers eventually instituted measures that curtailed previously granted concessions. Above all, the rightists welcomed the dissolution of the first two Dumas and the revision of the electoral law – measures that they had insistently advocated. Although the government had already been considering these measures, Nicholas apparently implemented them only after the major rightist organizations assured him that he had wide-ranging popular support. It must have gratified the rightists when Nicholas publicly thanked them for their devotion, implying that he had heeded their calls. They could rest satisfied that they had helped save the autocracy and shatter the prospects of liberal constitutionalism.

Some observers have suggested that the Russian rightists exceeded their self-appointed task of sustaining the old regime and actually served as an early version of what later became a full-fledged European fascism.[1] To be sure, similarities existed between the extreme Russian rightist organizations, particularly the Union of the Russian People, and fascist movements in the 1920s and 1930s. Both made a populist appeal for authoritarian rule, rejected political and economic liberalism, resorted to blatant antisemitism, and used radical tactics against their opponents. Moreover, some Russian rightist émigrés later joined fascist parties in western Europe or established their own in the Far East and the United States.[2] However, as Hans Rogger has pointed out, Russia lacked the objective conditions that elsewhere gave rise to fascist movements: the malaise of modern civilization, a sense of alienation from existing institutions, and a willingness to reject the past in favor of a new order that promised to give direction and meaning to life. As Rogger argues, Russia was experiencing not a crisis of civilization but a specific assault on the autocracy and privileged social classes.[3] While a few extreme rightist leaders, such as V. M. Purishkevich and N. E. Markov, might be regarded as "proto-fascists," the Russian rightists as a whole adhered to the old regime.

After the crucial years of 1905–1907, the rightists no longer felt as much need to contend against liberal constitutionalism or revolutionary violence, both of which had seemingly been contained. Relieved that the Duma now had a loyalist majority, most rightists made peace with the new political system. Many rightist deputies participated freely in the Duma, especially those moderates who in 1909 formed the Nationalist Party. Drawing mainly from the western borderlands, the Nationalist Party upheld those principles that rightists in their region had already emphasized in 1906 and 1907: the unity of the empire, Russian precedence among the various nationalities, opposition to Jewish equality, the inviolability of private property, and government economic aid to peasants in acquiring additional land. When appropriate, the Nationalists took a stand on specific legislation. In 1910, for instance, they successfully voted as a bloc with extreme rightists and Octobrists to limit Polish representation in the zemstvos which were being introduced into the western provinces.[4] Through their participation in the Duma, these moderate rightists became an integral part of Russia's political fabric during the relatively quiescent years between 1907 and the outbreak of World War I.

The extreme rightists assumed a less functional role, perhaps because they were not as disposed to work within the new political system, even if the autocracy had regained most of its challenged authority. In the Duma, they tended to be more outspoken and less cooperative than the moderate rightists. Deputies like Purishkevich and Markov never fully reconciled themselves to the Duma's existence as a legislative assembly. They would have preferred a purely consultative Duma, although they conceded that it was at least better to have a loyalist majority there than an oppositionist one.

After 1907, the major national and provincial rightist organizations faded from prominence. The Russian Assembly resumed its place as a cultural association, its foray into politics having been only a temporary expedient. The Russian Monarchist Party declined after the death of its founder, V. A. Gringmut, in September 1907; and the Union of Russian Men, whose leaders continued to express their Slavophile views, no longer seemed to have an organizational purpose. The Union of the Russian People, the most dynamic rightist association in 1905–1907, fell victim to internal dissension. By 1910, it had split into three factions. N. E. Markov took over the largest of these, which kept the URP name; V. M. Purishkevich started his own Union of the Archangel Michael; and A. I. Dubrovin, the Union's original chairman, was left with a small band of followers, who called themselves the True Union of the Russian People.

During World War I, rightists patriotically supported the war effort, but these were individual contributions. Efforts to revive and reunite the rightist associations proved unsuccessful. When the autocracy fell in February 1917, organized rightist activity disappeared almost completely. Later that year, a few isolated rightist groups tried feebly to mount an opposition to the Bolsheviks; and during the civil war, some rightists joined the White Armies, while others emigrated, often to congregate in rightist cliques abroad. But clearly, the rightists' day in Russia had passed. In order to judge their historical significance, one must go back to the political turmoil of 1905–1907.[5]

In that period, the rightists, as a vocal and persistent minority, played a distinctive role, impressing upon the tsar that a host of "true Russians" stood solidly behind the autocracy. Reluctantly at first, then vigorously, they entered the political arena, where they mobilized a substantial segment of the Russian population, particularly during the Duma campaigns. It may be true that the rightists overestimated their achievements, both in influencing the tsar and in conducting Duma campaigns. Perhaps they did not understand that, like themselves, those who rallied to their side frequently mistook the symptoms of Russia's turmoil for its causes, without realizing that muting the opposition and restoring order did not necessarily remove those underlying grievances that had long been building. Few rightists recognized how profound were the cleavages between society and the throne – and within society. Nor did they perceive that the bond between the tsar and his faithful, if restive, subjects was largely an illusion, based at best on myth and hardly adequate as the foundation for Russia's political future. Yet, at the time, the preservation of autocracy and the established social order seemed a real possibility. Not as prophets, but as protectors, the Russian rightists made their greatest contribution.

Notes

Abbreviations

ch.	chast' (part)
d.	delo (file unit)
f.	fond (archival group)
op.	opis' (archival subgroup)
t.	tom (volume)
TsGAOR SSSR	Tsentral'nyi gosudarstvennyi arkhiv Oktiabr'skoi revoliutsii SSSR (now Gosudarstvennyi arkhiv Rossiiskoi Federatsii)
TsGIA Leningrada	Tsentral'nyi gosudarstvennyi istoricheskii arkhiv Leningrada (now Tsentral'nyi gosudarstvennyi istoricheskii arkhiv S.-Peterburga)
TsGIA SSSR	Tsentral'nyi gosudarstvennyi istoricheskii arkhiv SSSR (now Rossiiskii gosudarstvennyi istoricheskii arkhiv)

Introduction

1. As far as I know, those historical studies dealing specifically with the Russian right consist of the following works. Among western scholars, Hans Rogger examined the major national rightist organizations in three excellent articles: "The Formation of the Russian Right, 1900–1906," *California Slavic Studies*, 3 (1964), 66–94; "Was There a Russian Fascism? The Union of the Russian People," *Journal of Modern History*, 36 (December 1964), 398–415; and "Russia" in Hans Rogger and Eugen Weber, eds., *The European Right* (Berkeley and Los Angeles, 1965), 443–500. The first two articles have been reprinted in Rogger's *Jewish Policies and Right-Wing Politics in Imperial Russia* (London, 1986), 118–211 and 212–232. Robert Edelman published his study of the formation and role of the Nationalist Party in "The Elections to the Third Duma: The Roots of the Nationalist Party," in Leopold H. Haimson, ed., *The Politics of Rural Russia, 1905–1914* (Bloomington, 1979); and in Edelman's book, *Gentry Politics on the Eve of the Russian Revolution: The Nationalist Party, 1907–1917* (New Brunswick, 1980). Rex Rexheuser has contributed to our understanding of the social

background of rightist Duma deputies and of rightist activity in Kursk province in his *Dumawahlen und lokale Gesellschaft: Studien zur Sozial- geschichte der russischen Rechten vor 1917* (Cologne and Vienna, 1980). Two related analyses of the rightist United Nobility are found in Geoffrey A. Hosking and Roberta Thompson Manning's article "What Was the United Nobility?" in Haimson, *The Politics of Rural Russia, 1905–1914,* 142–183; and in parts of Manning's book *The Crisis of the Old Order in Russia* (Princeton, 1982). The latest material on rightist organizations in 1905–1907 appears in a background chapter of Walter Laqueur's book on the current rightist revival, *Black Hundred: The Rise of the Extreme Right in Russia* (New York, 1993), 16–28.

For years, Soviet historians writing on the early twentieth century understandably focused on the revolutionary movement, particularly the Bolsheviks. Occasionally, some scholars investigated the liberals, such as E. D. Chermenskii in his *Burzhuaziia i tsarizm v pervoi russkoi revoliutsii* (1st edn., Moscow, 1939; 2nd edn., Moscow, 1970). With fewer constraints on their research during the late Soviet and post-Soviet period, Russian historians have undertaken a more comprehensive inquiry into the development of political parties and into the status of the old regime during its final phase, as evidenced most notably in V. V. Shelokhaev, *Partiia Oktiabristov v period pervoi rossiiskoi revoliutsii* (Moscow, 1987); D. A. Kolesnichenko, *Trudoviki v period pervoi rossiiskoi revoliutsii* (Moscow, 1985); B. V. Anan'ich and others, *Krizis samoderzhaviia v Rossii, 1895–1917* (Leningrad, 1984); R. Sh. Ganelin, *Rossiiskoie samoderzhavie v 1905 gody: reformy i revoliutsiia* (St. Petersburg, 1991); and Iu. B. Solov'ev, *Samoder- zhavie i dvorianstvo v 1902–1907 gg.* (Leningrad, 1981) and *Samoderzhavie i dvorianstvo v 1907–1914 gg.* (Leningrad, 1990). As yet, only a few works have addressed the rightists. In both of his books, Solov'ev presented valuable information on the United Nobility; L. M. Spirin devoted a section of his *Krushenie pomeshchich'ikh i burzhuaznykh partii v Rossii (nachalo XX v.–1920 g.)* (Moscow, 1977) to the monarchist parties; and E. K. Beliaeva reported her investigation of Moscow rightists in "Chernoso- tennye organizatsii i ikh bor'ba s revoliutsionnym dvizheniem v 1905 g.," *Vestnik Moskovskogo Universiteta: Seriia istoriia,* No. 2 (1978), 32–44. Recently, S. A. Stepanov expanded his 1982 dissertation into *Chernaia sotnia v Rossii (1905–1914 gg.)* (Moscow, 1992), in which he examined the extreme rightists, concentrating on the ideology and structure of the major national organizations and their use of violence, attempts to solicit worker and peasant support, and activity in the Dumas. He gave little attention to provincial organizations or the moderate rightists. Other studies of the rightist parties have been slow in emerging, except for V. M. Ostretsov's sympathetic summary in his rather popularized *Chernaia sotnia i krasnaia sotnia* (Moscow, 1991).

In western scholarship, several unpublished doctoral dissertations are also available: Ernest R. Zimmermann, "The Right Radical Movement in Russia, 1905–1917" (London University, 1967); John W. Bohon, "Reactionary Politics in Russia, 1905–1907" (University of North Carolina, 1967); John J. Brock, "The Theory and Practice of the Union of the Russian People, 1905–1907: A Case Study of 'Black-Hundred' Politics" (University of Michigan, 1972); and Don C. Rawson, "The Union of the Russian People, 1905–1907: A Study of the Radical Right" (University of Washington, 1971). In addition, Sherman D. Spector has provided a useful study of the Union of the Russian People based on its newspaper, *Russkoe znamia*, in his "The Doctrine and Program of the Union of the Russian People in 1906" (Essay for the certificate of the Russian Institute of Columbia University, 1952).

The most substantial contemporary account of the rightist organizations is V. Levitskii's "Pravyia partii," in L. Martov and others, eds., *Obshchestvennoe dvizhenie v Rossii v nachale XX-go veka* (4 vols.: St. Petersburg, 1909–1914), III, 347–469. Less reliable but also useful are V. Mech, *Sily reaktsii* (Moscow, 1907); and L-g, "Momenty kontr-revoliutsii," in *Itogy i perspektivy: sbornik statei* (Moscow, 1906).

For the most recent and finest overall history of the 1905 Revolution, see Abraham Ascher's *The Revolution of 1905: Russia in Disarray* (Stanford, 1988) and *The Revolution of 1905: Authority Restored* (Stanford, 1992). For a critical analysis of revolutionary events, also consult Teodor Shanin, *Russia, 1905–07: Revolution as a Moment of Truth* (Houndmills and London, 1986).

1: The advent of the rightist movement

1. See D. Kol'tsov, "Rabochie v 1890–1904 gg." in L. Martov and others, *Obshchestvennoe dvizhenie v Rossii v nachale XX-go veka*, II, 224–225.
2. *Ibid.*, 213–214.
3. See more detailed discussion in Chapter 6.
4. S. S. Ol'denburg, *Tsarstvovanie Imperatora Nikolaia II* (2 vols.: Belgrade, 1939–49), I, 180–181.
5. D. N. Shipov, *Vospominaniia i dumy o perezhitom* (Moscow, 1918), 233–234. For an interpretation of Pleve's relationship with the zemstvos, see Edward H. Judge, *Plehve: Repression and Reform in Imperial Russia, 1902–1906* (Syracuse, 1983), 38–62, 88–92.
6. Shipov, *Vospominaniia*, 261–265.
7. *Ibid.*, 278–280.
8. S. E. Kryzhanovskii, *Vospominaniia* (Berlin, 1938), 22–27.
9. S. Iu. Witte, *Vospominaniia* (2 vols.: Berlin, 1922), I, 300.
10. *Pravo*, 19 December 1904, cols. 3512–3514.
11. *Ibid.*, cols. 3515–3516.
12. For public reaction to Bloody Sunday, see Sidney Harcave, *First Blood: The Russian Revolution of 1905* (New York, 1964), 98–117.
13. The draft of a manifesto and detailed notes of the meeting appear in *Krasnyi arkhiv*, 11–12 (1925), 26–38.
14. A. S. Ermolov, "Zapiski A. S. Ermolova," *Krasnyi arkhiv*, 8 (1925), 49–58.
15. *Ibid.*, 58–69.

16. For a discussion of the meeting and other relevant events, see R. Sh. Ganelin, "Tsarizm posle nachala pervoi russkoi revoliutsii (Akty 18 fevralia 1905 g.)," in *Voprosy istorii Rossii XIX–nachala XX veka* (Leningrad, 1983), 96–112. Ganelin elaborates somewhat on the acts of 18 February in a chapter in his *Rossiiskoe samoderzhavie v 1905 gody: reformy i revoliutsiia* (St. Petersburg, 1991), 85–121. See also "Dnevnik A. A. Bobrinskago," *Krasnyi arkhiv*, 26 (1928), 131, on the meeting; and V. N. Kokovtsov, *Iz moego proshlago* (2 vols.: Paris, 1933), I, 55–62, on the French loan.

17. Witte, *Vospominaniia*, II, 338; Nicholas II, *Dnevnik Imperatora Nikolaia II* (Berlin, 1923), 197.

18. Ganelin, "Tsarizm posle nachale pervoi russkoi revoliutsii," 101; *Dnevnik Imperatora Nikolaia II*, 199; *Krasnyi arkhiv*, 26 (1928), 131.

19. Witte, *Vospominaniia*, II, 339–341. Witte's account is substantiated by an incident related by Princess Olga Trubetskaia. She recalls that S. A. Lopukhin, the public procurator in Kiev, told the Trubetskoi family that he had been with Minister of Justice Manukhin on 17 February, when Manukhin received drafts of the manifesto and ukase for publication. Manukhin expressed surprise at the manifesto and telephoned Bulygin, who replied that, although he was aware that the tsar was contemplating some kind of declaration, he had been neither consulted nor informed about the present document. Bulygin arrived at the meeting in Tsarskoe Selo on 18 February with only a draft of the intended rescript. Olga Trubetskaia, *Kniaz' S. N. Trubetskoi: vospominaniia sestry* (New York, 1953), 113–114.

20. The texts of the three documents appear in *Novoe vremia*, 19 February 1905, 1; and other newspapers.

21. For Trepov's role, see Chermenskii, *Burzhuaziia i tsarizm*, 57–58.

22. Witte, *Vospominaniia*, II, 339–340.

23. V. A. Maklakov, *Vlast' i obshchestvennost' na zakate staroi Rossii* (Paris, 1936), 355–362. The veteran zemstvo constitutionalist I. I. Petrunkevich and I. V. Gessen, soon to be one of the founders of the Constitutional Democratic Party, agreed that the acts were contradictory but that some use could be made of the ukase. "Iz zapisok obshchestvennago deiatelia: vospominaniia," *Arkhiv russkoi revoliutsii*, 20 (1934), 370; and "V dvukh vekakh," *ibid.*, 22 (1937), 195–196.

24. For immediate responses of zemstvo assemblies and city dumas, see *Pravo*, 26 February 1905, cols. 601–604.

25. For a discussion of this congress, see Manning, *The Crisis of the Old Order in Russia*, 96–101.

26. Shipov, *Vospominaniia*, 292–294.

27. Manning, *The Crisis of the Old Order in Russia*, 97, 102; Terence Emmons, *The Formation of Political Parties and the First National Elections in Russia* (Cambridge, 1983), 36–41, 97–112.

28. *Novoe vremia*, 19 February 1905, 3.

29. *Moskovskiia vedomosti*, 22 February 1905, 1–2.

30. *Russkoe delo*, 31 March 1905, 2–3.

2: The Russian Monarchist Party

1. Most of this biographical material on Gringmut's pedagogical and journalistic career is drawn from *Vladimir Andreevich Gringmut: Ocherk ego zhizni i deiatel'nosti* (Moscow, 1913), 5–71.
2. *Ibid.*, 63. For the Russian Assembly, see Chapter 4.
3. *Moskovskiia vedomosti*, 22 February 1905, 1–2; 24 February 1905, 1–2. Many of Gringmut's editorials were subsequently published in V. A. Gringmut, *Sobranie statei V. A. Gringmuta, 1896–1907* (4 parts: Moscow, 1908–1910).
4. *Moskovskiia vedomosti*, 19 December 1896, 2.
5. *Ibid.*, 3 March 1905, 1–2; 5 May 1905, 1–2.
6. *Grazhdanin*, 12 May 1905, 18–19.
7. *Moskovskiia vedomosti*, 28 March 1905, 1.
8. *Ibid.*, 18 May 1905, 1. See also 1 February 1905, 2; 12 July 1905, 1–2.
9. L. A. Tikhomirov, "25 let nazad; iz dnevnika L. Tikhomirova," *Krasnyi arkhiv*, 40 (1930), 73.
10. *Moskovskiia vedomosti*, 5 October 1905, 1.
11. *Ibid.*, 15 October 1905, 1–2. The program is also included in V. Ivanovich, ed., *Rossiiskiia partii, soiuzy i ligi* (St. Petersburg, 1906), 110–117.
12. *Moskovskiia vedomosti*, 21 October 1905, 1–2; 19 December 1905, 2; 20 December 1905, 2; 30 January 1906, 1.
13. *Ibid.*, 15 October 1905, 1–2.
14. *Ibid.*
15. *Ibid.*, 4 June 1906, 1–2; 8 October 1905, 1.
16. *Ibid.*, 15 October 1905, 1–2.
17. *Vladimir Andreevich Gringmut: Ocherk ego zhizni i deiatel'nosti*, 76; Gringmut, *Sobranie statei V. A. Gringmuta*, III, 281–282.
18. *Moskovskiia vedomosti*, 6 February 1906, 3.
19. I. I. Vostorgov, *Polnoe sobranie sochinenii* (3 vols.: Moscow, 1914–1915), II, 516–519. In addition to his sermons, Vostorgov proclaimed his religious and patriotic message in a variety of booklets and brochures. For example, see his *Pravoslavnomu russkomu narodu dobroe slovo* (Moscow, 1906).
20. *Moskovskiia vedomosti*, 17 April 1906, 2; 2 July 1906, 3; 14 November 1906, 4; 15 November 1906, 4; 17 November 1906, 3–4; Levitskii, "Pravyia partii," 405–406; *Vladimir Andreevich Gringmut: Ocherk ego zhizni i deiatel'nosti*, 114.
21. *Moskovskiia vedomosti*, 5 December 1905, 1.
22. *Krasnyi arkhiv*, 40 (1930), 108; *Vladimir Andreevich Gringmut: Ocherk ego zhizni i deiatel'nosti*, 97–98. Relations between the Russian Monarchist Party and the Moscow branch of the Union of the Russian People remained close. At a joint meeting on 18 February 1907, Gringmut and Oznobishin announced that they hoped to merge the two groups. Apparently, this unification never came to fruition, possibly because of Gringmut's death a few months later. *Vestnik Russkago sobraniia*, 2 March 1907, 7.

23. Levitskii, "Pravyia partii," 445; *Moskovskiia vedomosti*, 4 January 1906, 1; 25–29 January 1907, various pages.
24. *Ibid.*, 14 February 1906, 2.

3: The Union of Russian Men

1. Terence Emmons, "The Beseda Circle, 1899–1905," *Slavic Review*, 32 (September 1973), 461–490.
2. *Russkoe delo*, 31 March 1905, 2–3. Also in Pavel Sheremet'ev, *Zametki, 1900–1905* (Moscow, 1905), 108–113.
3. *Pravo*, 8 June 1905, cols. 1820–1821; *Russkiia vedomosti*, 24 May 1905, 3; 1 June 1905, 3; TsGAOR SSSR, f. 102, op. 1905, d. 999, ch. 39, t. 1, pp. 13–17.
4. *Pravo*, 8 June 1905, cols. 1820–1821. The Union of Russian Men tended to project its non-partisan image on to the rightist movement as a whole. At the second monarchist congress in April 1906, Prince Shcherbatov declared, "We are not parties, we are spokesmen for the spirit of the people" – an ethereal notion, which did not translate well into precisely stated goals or practical procedures. *Moskovskiia vedomosti*, 8 April 1906, 2.
5. *Vestnik Russkago sobraniia*, 16 February 1907, 3, lists twenty titles of Union brochures, several of which are still available, such as *Voice from the Provinces* (*Golos iz provintsii*), *The Struggle for the Orthodox Faith* (*Bor'ba za veru pravoslavuiu*), and *The Agrarian Question* (*Zemel'nyi vopros*), all published in Moscow in 1906.
6. *Vestnik Russkago sobraniia*, 16 February 1907, 3; 3 March 1906, 3; *Russkoe znamia*, 20 February 1906, 3; 4 March 1906, 2; 29 August 1906, 1; TsGAOR SSSR, f. 102, op. 1905, d. 999, ch. 39, t. 1, pp. 32, 149. In March 1906, the Union claimed that its membership numbered in the tens of thousands. However, like other rightist organizations, the Union probably based its figures on rough estimates of attendance at public speeches more than on actual membership.
7. A. Gratieux, *Le Mouvement Slavophile à la veille de la révolution: Dmitri A. Khomiakov* (Paris, 1953), 127–131, 150–172, quoting brochures written by Khomiakov.
8. *Ibid.*, 147.
9. *Russkoe delo*, 29 October 1905, 6; 12 November 1905, 2.
10. *Ibid*, 29 October 1905, 4.
11. *Ibid.*, 26 February 1905, 1–3.
12. Trubetskaia, *Kniaz' S. N. Trubetskoi; vospominaniia sestry*, 138–141. The text of the speech also appears in *Novoe vremia*, 8 June 1905, 2.
13. *Novoe vremia*, 26 June 1905, 1. Shortly after this rebuttal to his brother's speech, P. N. Trubetskoi quit the Union of Russian Men, with which he had already developed some dissatisfaction.
14. *Russkoe delo*, 13 August 1905, 1–2.
15. *Ibid.*, 29 October 1905, 4–5.
16. *Moskovskiia vedomosti*, 25 November 1905, 2; 5 December 1905, 2; 6 December 1905, 2.

17. *Pakhar'* (January 1906), cols. 3–13.
18. For Sharapov's proposed program, see *Russkoe delo*, 12 November 1905, supplement.
19. *Pakhar'* (August–September 1905), cols. 23–25; (September 1906), cols. 16–20.
20. *Moskovskiia vedomosti*, 12 November 1905, 2.
21. Aleksandr Shcherbatov, *Zemel'nyi vopros* (Moscow, 1906), 3–50.
22. *Ibid.*
23. *Moskovskiia vedomosti*, 11 January 1906, 3.
24. *Pakhar'* (November–December 1906), cols. 11–14.

4: The Russian Assembly

1. A. S. Viazigin, *V tumane smutnykh dnei: sbornik statei, dokladov i rechei* (Kharkov, 1908), 130–132.
2. *Izvestiia Russkago sobraniia* (1903), 6–10.
3. *Ibid.*
4. The figures for government and court personnel include thirty-nine persons for 1901 and sixty-seven for 1903, who are listed simply as having civil rank according to the Table of Ranks. I have assumed that they held government or court posts, or were retired from them. Retired military officers are designated as such on the Assembly's membership rosters.
5. *Letopis' Russkago sobraniia* (January 1903), i–xlii.
6. *Novoe vremia*, 15 February 1901, 3; *Letopis' Russkago sobraniia* (May 1901), 5.
7. *Ibid.* (May 1901), 32–44.
8. TsGAOR SSSR, f. 588, op. 1, d. 1243, pp. 1–3.
9. *Izvestiia Russkago sobraniia* (1903), 39–44; *Russkii vestnik* (December 1903), 831–834.
10. TsGAOR SSSR, f. 102, op. 236 (II), d. 186, p. 15; f. 588, op. 1, d. 1243, pp. 4–13; *Vestnik Russkago sobraniia*, 3 March 1906, 3, 4; 16 February 1907, 3; 2 October 1908, 2–3.
11. *Letopis' Russkago sobraniia* (May 1901), 45; *Izvestiia Russkago sobraniia* (1903), 13–33; *Russkii vestnik* (December 1903), 841–843.
12. *Izvestiia Russkago sobraniia* (1903), 15–19.
13. *Russkii vestnik* (December 1903), 835–840.
14. *Ibid.* (February 1905), 835–838.
15. *Moskovskiia vedomosti*, 4 February 1905, 2.
16. P. Strel'skii, *Partii i revoliutsiia 1905 goda* (St. Petersburg, 1906), 58. The "spring" to which Nikolskii referred had a particular connotation. When Pleve was succeeded as Minister of Internal Affairs in August 1904 by Sviatopolk-Mirskii, hopeful liberals proclaimed the advent of a "political spring."
17. TsGAOR SSSR, f. 102, op. 236 (II), d. 186, pp. 43–80.
18. Ivanovich, *Rossiiskiia partii, soiuzy i ligi*, 129–130.
19. *Ibid.*

20. *Vestnik Russkiia sobraniia*, 26 January 1907, 3–4; 9 March 1907, 1–2.
21. Ivanovich, *Rossiiskiia partii, soiuzy i ligi*, 129–130.
22. For information on the delegates, debates, and resolutions of the congress, see *Novoe vremia*, 14 February 1906, 4; 18 February 1906, 4; *Russkoe znamia*, 23 February 1906, 3; *Moskovskiia vedomosti*, 14 February 1906, 2; TsGAOR SSSR, f. 102, op. 236 (II), d. 186, p. 38.
23. *Moskovskiia vedomosti*, 8 April 1906, 2.
24. TsGAOR SSSR, f. 116, op. 1, d. 23, pp. 2–3; f. 588, op. 1, d. 1263, pp. 1–10, 32–33; *Moskovskiia vedomosti*, 3 October 1906, 2; 5 October 1906, 2; 8 October 1906, 2; *Vestnik Russkago sobraniia*, 11 May 1907, 1.
25. *Vestnik Russkago sobraniia*, 19 January 1907, 4; 2 February 1907, 2. In 1906, the Russian Assembly considered collaborating with the Party of Legal Order to create a Russian Legalist Party (*Russkaia pravovaia partiia*), but the majority of Assembly members rejected the proposal because of the PLO's unclear position on the constitutional question. *Vestnik narodnoi svobody*, 17 August 1906, cols. 1380–1381.
26. For the results of these electoral coalitions, see Chapter 11.
27. For the Patriotic Union and the United Nobility, see Chapter 8.

5: The Union of the Russian People

1. TsGAOR SSSR, f. 116, op. 1, d. 797, pp. 25–26.
2. *Ibid.*, p. 1.
3. Witte, *Vospominaniia*, II, 36.
4. *Ibid.*, II, 80.
5. Boris Nikol'skii, "Dnevnik," *Krasnyi arkhiv*, 63 (1934), 88.
6. A. Chernovskii, ed., *Soiuz russkogo naroda; po materialam chrezvychainoi sledstvennoi komissii Vremennogo Pravitel'stva* (Moscow and Leningrad, 1929), 32.
7. Nikol'skii, "Dnevnik," 85–88. Dubrovin's interest in creating a popular defense corps may have been enforced by an acquaintance, P. I. Rachkovskii, Assistant Director of the Department of Police, who had long dreamed of a counterrevolutionary organization that would respond in kind to revolutionary violence. Chernovskii, *Soiuz russkogo naroda*, 84.
8. Nikol'skii, "Dnevnik," 85–88.
9. Having already written articles for *Svet*, *Rossiia*, and other reactionary periodicals, Bulatsel' was soon aiding Dubrovin in editing a newspaper, *Russkoe znamia*, for the new organization. He also served as defense counsel for Union associates who ran afoul of the law. Maikov became the Union's vice-chairman.
10. Nikol'skii, "Dnevnik," 59, 65, 80. Purishkevich later became notorious as one of the more flamboyant rightist deputies in the Duma and finally for his participation in the 1916 murder of Gregorii Rasputin.
11. Other founders included A. I. Trishatnyi, an engineer; P. A. Aleksandrov, an examining magistrate in the St. Petersburg district court; N. M. Iazykov, a land captain from Kazan; V. A. Andreev, the operator of a cold

storage plant; S. D. Chekalov, a tea salesman; D. L. Surin, a fur merchant; E. D. Golubev, a cattle dealer; V. P. Sokolov, a young member of the nobility and recently an engineer; G. V. Butmi, a former army officer and member of the nobility, who soon became widely known as an antisemitic publicist; and a few others. Boris Nikolskii was not present. Although he criticized the Russian Assembly, he had recently been chosen to help write a new program for the Assembly, and at this time he was busy at this project. See Sh. Levin, "Materialy dlia kharakteristiki kontr-revoliutsii 1905 g.," *Byloe*, No. 21 (1923), 169. Eventually, Nikolskii joined the Union.

12. Ivanovich, *Rossiiskiia partii, soiuzy i ligi*, 117–118.
13. Soiuz russkago naroda, *K svedeniiu sluzhashchikh russkikh liudei* (St. Petersburg, 1906), 1.
14. V. I. Gurko, *Features and Figures of the Past: Government and Opinion in the Reign of Nicholas II* (Stanford, 1939), 436–437. See also *Pravo*, 27 November 1905, col. 3826.
15. The St. Petersburg city governor reported to the Minister of Internal Affairs that an "enthusiastic crowd" of three to four thousand persons attended a Union extravaganza in February 1906. TsGAOR SSSR, f. 102, op. 1905, d. 999, ch. 39, t. 1, p. 91.
16. L. N. Beliaeva, ed., *Bibliografiia periodicheskikh izdanii Rossii, 1901–1916* (4 vols.: Leningrad, 1958–1961), I, 408, 653; II, 373, 509; III, 65.
17. Levitskii, "Pravyia partii," 403.
18. Some of these Union publications still extant include Pavel Bulatsel', *Bor'ba za pravdu* (St. Petersburg, 1908); A. A. Maikov, *Revoliutsionery i chernosotentsy* (St. Petersburg, 1907); and V. F. Zaleskii, *Chto takoe Soiuz russkago naroda i dlia chego on nuzhen?* (Kazan, 1907). In addition to its public rallies and publications, the Union also sought to establish grass-roots contact with the common people by opening special "tearooms" in St. Petersburg and several other cities. Patrons could eat and drink tea, leaf through patriotic brochures, and listen to Union speakers. For a description of the tearooms, see P. Timofeev, "V chainoi Soiuza russkago naroda," *Russkoe bogatstvo* (February 1907), 57–81. Other references appear in *Russkoe znamia*, 30 April 1906, 3; 6 June 1906, 4; 27 June 1906, 1.
19. *Russkii narod*, 10 September 1906, 1. *Russkii narod* was the newspaper of the Iaroslavl URP.
20. *Russkoe znamia*, various issues during January–March, 1906.
21. TsGAOR SSSR, f. 102, op. 1905, d. 999, ch. 39, t. 2, p. 111; *Russkoe znamia*, 24 August 1906, 2; Chrezvychainaia sledstvennaia komissiia, *Padenie tsarskago rezhima* (7 vols.: Leningrad, 1924–1927), VI, 176, 197.
22. N. E. Markov, *Istoriia evreiskago shturma Rossii* (Harbin, 1937), 23.
23. I have found 604 branches mentioned by name in *Russkoe znamia* during 1906 and 1907, including 143 established in Volynia and Podolia by the Pochaev Monastery, a Union affiliate (see Chapter 7). *Pochaevskiia izvestiia* for November 1906 through February 1907 — the only issues available to me — listed an additional 116 branches in Volynia and Podolia. Archival

sources from 1907 specified another 70 branches (TsGIA Leningrada, f. 569, op. 13, d. 35, p. 11; op. 24, d. 10, pp. 27–46; TsGAOR SSSR, f. 102, op. 1905, d. 999, ch. 39, tt. 1–2, various pages). Thus, 790 branches can be identified by name. But there were surely more. Since 47 percent of the 1907 issues of *Russkoe znamia* are missing from the collection I used, the number of branches reported that year in *Russkoe znamia* could easily have been at least 250 higher than the 299 I found. (This estimate allows for the possibility that some of the 70 branches cited in archival reports for 1907, which I counted above, also appeared in the missing issues of *Russkoe znamia*. However, probably very few branches listed in *Pochaev-skiia izvestiia* were also reported in the missing issues of *Russkoe znamia*, since I found none in those issues that I did examine.) On the basis of these data and projections, one can reasonably conclude that the total number of Union branches exceeded 1,000.

24. Spirin, *Krushenie pomeschchich'ikh i burzhuaznykh partii v Rossii (nachalo XX v.–1920 g.)*, 167. S. A. Stepanov thinks there may have been over 400,000 Union members. Stepanov, *Chernaia sotnia v Rossii (1905–1914 gg.)* (Moscow, 1992), 107–108.

25. Ivanovich, *Rossiiskiia partii, soiuzy i ligi*, 121; Mech, *Sily reaktsii*, 85.

26. *Russkoe znamia*, 7 December 1906, 1.

27. For studies of nobles' organizations, see George W. Simmonds, "The Congress of Representatives of the Nobles' Associations, 1906–1916: A Case Study of Russian Conservatism," (Columbia University, Ph.D. dissertation, 1964); and Manning, *The Crisis of the Old Order in Russia*. Some nobles also participated in local rightist organizations, such as those in the central agricultural provinces, as explained in Chapter 6.

28. *Vestnik narodnoi svobody*, 21 December 1906, col. 2294; *Rech'*, 12 January 1907, 5; Levitskii, "Pravyia partii," 391.

29. *Russkii narod*, 10 September 1906, 1; P. N. Zyrianov, *Pravoslavnaia tserkov' v bor'be s revoliutsiei 1905–1907 gg.* (Moscow, 1984), 87, 141.

30. S. Lisenko, "Chernaia sotnia v provintsii," *Russkaia mysl'*, No. 2 (1908), 20–28.

31. *Vestnik narodnoi svobody*, 23 November 1906, col. 2051. Extremely volatile, Iliodor eventually turned his venom on the Union, which he felt was not sufficiently dedicated to its mission. Attacking almost everyone and under fire from all sides, he was defrocked in 1912. Four years later he emigrated to the United States, where he published his memoirs under the title *The Mad Monk of Russia, Iliodor* (New York, 1918). For a fuller account of Iliodor's activities in Volynia, see Chapter 7.

32. Chernovskii, *Soiuz russkogo naroda*, 36.

33. *Vestnik narodnoi svobody*, 23 November 1906, col. 2049; *Tovarishch*, 28 November 1906, 5; 30 November 1906, 5; *Russkoe znamia*, 29 November 1906, 1; 5 December 1906, supplement.

34. *Ibid.*

35. TsGAOR SSSR, f. 102, op. 1905, d. 999, ch. 39, t. 2, p. 471; f. 1467, op. 1, d. 848, pp. 30–31, 111.

36. From a 1906 Union leaflet. TsGIA Leningrada, f. 253, op. 10, d. 197, p. 447.
37. Chernovskii, *Soiuz russkogo naroda*, 274.
38. *Russkoe znamia*, 22 January 1906, 2; 26 January 1906, 1–2.
39. TsGAOR SSSR, f. 102, op. 1905, d. 999, ch. 39, t. 1, pp. 38–47; a transcript of the delegation's speeches at the audience appears in *Russkoe znamia*, 9 January 1906, 2–3.
40. *Russkoe znamia* regularly printed copies of these telegrams. Apparently, Nicholas personally read many of them. On one from Dubrovin, urging that revolutionary agitators be dealt with severely, he wrote: "Quite so!" TsGAOR SSSR, f. 102, op. 1905, d. 999, ch. 39, t. l, p. 40.
41. *Russkoe znamia*, 9 February 1906, 1–2. The entire speech can be found in I. S. Aksakov, *Sochineniia* (7 vols.: Moscow, 1886–1891), V, 27–35.
42. *Russkoe znamia*, 28 January 1906, 1–2.
43. *Ibid.*, 21 October 1906, 1.
44. Soiuz russkago naroda, *Rukovodstvo chernosotentsa-monarkhista* (Kremenchug, 1906), 6.
45. P. N. Miliukov, *Vospominaniia, 1859–1907* (2 vols.: New York, 1955), I, 422; II, 18.
46. *Russkoe znamia*, 7 April 1906, 1; 1 July 1906, 3.
47. *Ibid.*, 19 May 1906, 2. While the Union readily assailed the Kadets, it had difficulty in appraising the Octobrists – those moderate reformers who had split with the Kadets after the October Manifesto. The Union recognized that the Octobrists had made their peace with the autocracy, but also that they regarded the October Manifesto as a sort of constitution and at times spoke of favoring a "limited autocracy," which seemed to the Union as but a confusing contradiction in terms. It was not so much that the Octobrists were consciously subversive but that they were incredibly naive. While the Kadets were causing damage by design, the Octobrists were doing so inadvertently. For Union criticism of the Octobrists, see *ibid.*, 7 November 1906, 1–2.
48. *Ibid.*, 5 February 1906, 2; 9 March 1906, 3–4; Witte, *Vospominaniia*, II, 81.
49. See, for example, *Russkoe znamia*, 23 March 1906, 2; 8 May 1906, 1; 20 June 1906, 3; 20 July 1906, 2; 18 March 1907, 2.
50. A. I. Dubrovin, *Taina sud'by* (St. Petersburg, 1907), 1–27.
51. G. V. Butmi, *Konstitutsiia i politicheskaia svoboda* (5th edn.: St. Petersburg, 1906). Butmi also published a Russian version of the notorious *Protocols of the Wise Men of Zion*, a spurious "document," presented as evidence of how a Jewish conspiracy was planning to subdue the entire world. The *Protocols* became mainstays of antisemitic propaganda throughout Europe and America; the Russian editions were disseminated widely by the Union of the Russian People. Butmi's version can be found in his *Vragi roda chelovecheskago* (2nd edn.: St. Petersburg, 1906). The most authoritative analyses of the *Protocols* are in Herman Bernstein, *The History of a Lie* (New York, 1921); John Shelton Curtiss, *An Appraisal of the Protocols of Zion* (New York, 1942); and Norman Cohn, *Warrant for Genocide* (New York, 1966).

52. For the pogroms and other uses of violence, see Chapter 9.
53. For the Union's role in the Duma elections, see Chapter 11.

6: Rightists in the central provinces

1. For observations on the high level of rightist activity in the central and western regions, see Rexheuser, *Dumawahlen und lokale Gesellschaft*, 10–65.
2. Kiev province dropped by 8 percent, Chernigov by 9 percent, and Podolia by less than 1 percent, while Poltava increased by 6 percent. Tsentral'nyi statisticheskii komitet Ministerstva vnutrennikh del, *Ezhegodnik Rossii 1904 g.* (St. Petersburg, 1905), 192–205; *ibid. 1905 g.* (St. Petersburg, 1906), 204–218; *ibid. 1906 g.* (St. Petersburg, 1907), 216–217.
3. S. M. Dubrovskii, *Krest'ianskoe dvizhenie v revoliutsii 1905–1907 gg.* (Moscow, 1956), 46–49; *Revoliutsiia 1905–1907 gg. v Rossii: Dokumenty i materialy. Revoliutsionnoe dvizhenie v Rossii vesnoi i letom 1905 goda, aprel'–sentiabr'. Chast' pervaia* (Moscow, 1957), 685–690; *Krasnyi arkhiv*, 9 (1925), 70.
4. *Revoliutsiia 1905–1907 gg. Revoliutsionnoe dvizhenie v Rossii vesnoi i letom 1905 goda. Chast' pervaia*, 675–676.
5. *Ibid.*, 725–726.
6. *Revoliutsiia 1905–1907 gg. Vysshii pod"em revoliutsii 1905–1907 gg. Vooruzhennye vosstaniia, noiabr'–dekabr' 1905 goda. Chast' vtoraia.* (Moscow, 1955), 213–217, 338–343, 353–375; *Orlovskaia rech'*, 6 December 1905, 1–2; *Novoe vremia*, 16 November 1905, 2.
7. *Revoliutsiia 1905–1907 gg. Vserossiiskaia politicheskaia stachka v oktiabre 1905 goda. Chast' vtoraia*, 404–407. *Vysshii pod"em revoliutsii 1905–1907 gg., Chast' vtoraia*, 212–217. The disorders continued, almost out of control, throughout the winter. An official zemstvo report in March 1906 stated that in the past year there had been 1,598 known cases of arson in Kursk province and that 6,312 homesteads, involving a total of 15,245 buildings, had been burned. *Kurskii listok*, 10 March 1906, 1. Peasants attacked 130 estates in Tambov province and 272 in Saratov province. Voronezh province sustained somewhat less damage. B. B. Veselovskii, *Krest'ianskii vopros i krest'ianskoe dvizhenie v Rossii, 1902–1906 gg.* (St. Petersburg, 1907), 86–87. See also Petr Maslov, *Agrarnyi vopros v Rossii* (2 vols.: St. Petersburg, 1908).
8. *Revoliutsiia 1905–1907 gg. Vserossiiskaia politicheskaia stachka v oktiabre 1905 goda. Chast' pervaia*, 557–560, 576–585.
9. *Ibid.*, 553–555, 585–586; *Novoe vremia*, 22 October 1905, 4; 23 October 1905, 4–5; 24 October 1905, 3; I. P. Belokonskii, "Chernosotennoe dvizhenie ili tainy rossiiskoi kontr-revoliutsii," *Obrazovanie* (January 1906), 59–62.
10. *Pravda i poriadok*, 22 February 1906, 2; *Novoe vremia*, 17 November 1905, 6. See also Manning, *The Crisis of the Old Order in Russia*, 181–183. The Union for Tsar and Order published *Pravda i poriadok* from 22 February through 30 March 1906.
11. *Pravda i poriadok*, 22 February 1906, 3.
12. *Novoe vremia*, 22 November 1905, 2.

13. *Ibid.*, 26 November 1905, 1. Significantly, the Duma that Bobrinskii envisioned was not the legislative body authorized by the October Manifesto but a consultative assembly, such as the government had proposed the previous August.
14. TsGIA SSSR, f. 1276, op. 2, d. 8, pp. 112–117.
15. *Pravda i poriadok*, 22 February 1906, 4–5.
16. *Ibid.*, 3–4; TsGAOR SSSR, f. 102, op. 1905, d. 999, ch. 39, pp. 39–41.
17. *Pravda i poriadok*, 22 February 1906, 4.
18. *Ibid.*, 4, 10–11, 13–15. On 2 February 1906, Bobrinskii and several associates visited Tsarskoe Selo with a petition to the tsar asking that the Peasant Land Bank give greater assistance to peasants in purchasing land in their home communities and in resettling on new land elsewhere. The petition also urged the abolition of the peasant communes, so that peasants generally could become private proprietors. *Novoe vremia*, 3 February 1906, 4.
19. *Pravda i poriadok*, 1 March 1906, 27.
20. Recent studies have shown that in these early stages of partisan politics in Russia, Octobrist and even Kadet leaders at the national level had difficulty maintaining discipline in their branches and affiliates, especially those that had originated locally and adopted programs that did not mesh precisely with those of the national parties. See Emmons, *The Formation of Political Parties*, 153, 206–207.
21. TsGIA SSSR, f. 1276, op. 2, d. 8, pp. 112–117.
22. *Novoe vremia*, 3 February 1906, 5.
23. TsGAOR SSSR, f. 102, op. 1905, d. 999, ch. 39, t. 1, p. 400; f. 116, op. 1, d. 541, pp. 1–6; *Russkoe znamia*, 4 August 1906, 1; *Tul'skaia rech'*, 27 October 1906, 2; 16 November 1906, 3; 8 December 1906, 3; 17 January 1907, 3.
24. For URP membership, program, and activities, see Chapter 5.
25. Edelman, *Gentry Politics on the Eve of the Russian Revolution*, 43–46.
26. See Rexheuser, *Dumawahlen und lokale Gesellschaft*, 87–125, for a discussion of the tensions between different factions in the Kursk provincial zemstvo prior to 1905.
27. *Novoe vremia*, 24 June 1905, 1.
28. *Ibid.*, 26 June 1905, 1; *Pravo*, 3 July 1905, cols. 2132–2135. See also Manning, *The Crisis of the Old Order in Russia*, 113–114; and Solov'ev, *Samoderzhavie i dvorianstvo v 1902–1907 gg.*, 171.
29. Initially, the Dorrer group hoped to mobilize the Kursk provincial and district zemstvos as a base of political operations; but when the zemstvo congress that met in Moscow on 6–9 July tentatively endorsed a constitutional monarchy, they abandoned this idea. See Gurko, *Features and Figures of the Past*, 387.
30. For Dorrer, see *Letopis' Russkago sobraniia* (January 1903), xii; for Kasatkin-Rostovskii's membership in the Patriotic Union, see Hosking and Manning, "What Was the United Nobility?" 174.
31. *Kurskii listok*, 6 January 1906, 2. Kasatkin-Rostovskii became the Party's first chairman, but in December he turned this post over to Dorrer, apparently because of illness.

32. Belokonskii, "Chernosotennoe dvizhenie," 50–51; *Pravo*, 20 November 1905, cols. 3738–3741.
33. *Kurskii listok*, 11 January 1906, 2.
34. *Ibid.*, 1.
35. *Pravo*, 20 November 1905, cols. 3738–3740; Belokonskii, "Chernosotennoe dvizhenie," 55–56.
36. *Kurskii listok*, 6 January 1906, 2. Occasionally, PPO leaders advised using force as a means of self-protection though not necessarily under PPO auspices. In January 1906, Count Dorrer chaired a special assembly of the Kursk nobility, which appropriated 5,000 rubles per district to subsidize local self-defense units in guarding private property against attack from peasant marauders. *Novoe vremia*, 25 January 1906, 2. Guards were often posted, paid for either from these designated funds or by individual estate owners. However, official reports from Kursk province during 1905–1906, which describe peasant disorders in detail, mention armed confrontation only between unruly peasants and soldiers or police, which suggests that private guards seldom clashed with peasants. See various reports in *Revoliutsiia 1905–1907 gg. v Rossii: Dokumenty i materialy*.
37. Belokonskii, "Chernosotennoe dvizhenie," 69.
38. *Kurskaia byl'*, various issues in November and December 1906. N. E. Markov began publishing *Kurskaia byl'* in October 1906. Although the paper was not an organ of the Union of the Russian People, it bore Markov's rightist stamp and carried much news of the URP and other rightist organizations.
39. *Ibid.*, 4 January 1907, 2–3; 23 January 1907, 3; 25 January 1907, 1.
40. See Chapter 5 on the Union of the Russian People for more information on Markov. In 1907, he became a member of the URP's central council, and later took over the chairmanship of the URP from Dr. Dubrovin, continuing in that capacity until 1917.
41. *Kurskaia byl'*, 23 January 1907, 3; 25 January 1907, 1.
42. During 1907, URP headquarters in St. Petersburg established a few additional branches in Kursk province. *Ibid.*, 24 January 1907, 3; 30 January 1907, 3; 6 February 1907, 3. However, rightist strength remained principally in the URP(PPO)–URW coalition operating out of the provincial capital.
43. *Pervaia vseobshchaia perepis'*, XXIX, vii, 156–157.
44. *Revoliutsiia 1905–1907 gg. Revoliutsionnoe dvizhenie v Rossii vesnoi i letom 1905 goda*. Chast' pervaia, 708; *Vserossiiskaia politicheskaia stachka v oktiabre 1905 goda*. Chast' pervaia, 563–564.
45. *Novoe vremia*, 24 October 1905, 3.
46. *Orlovskaia rech'*, 9 December 1905, 4.
47. *Ibid.*, 5 December 1905, 1.
48. *Ibid.*, 6 December 1905, 1–2.
49. *Ibid.*, 15 December 1906, 3; 9 January 1907, 2; 30 January 1907, 1. Sometimes the name Union of Law and Order was followed by Union of the Russian People in parentheses.

50. *Ibid.*, 6 June 1907, 1; 26 June 1907, 3. Throughout the transition, Ia. A. Pomerantsev continued as chairman.

51. TsGAOR SSSR, f. 102, op. 1905, d. 999, ch. 39, t. 2, pp. 4, 448; f. 116, op. 1, d. 329, pp. 4–5; *Russkoe znamia*, 10 August 1906, 1; 12 November 1906, 1; *Orlovskaia rech'*, 24 January 1906, 4; 9 December 1906, 3; *Eletskii krai*, 1 April 1907, 3.

52. See especially Veselovskii, *Krest'ianskii vopros i krest'ianskoe dvizhenie v Rossii*, 86–108; and Imperatorskoe vol'noe ekonomicheskoe obshchestvo, *Agrarnoe dvizhenie v Rossii v 1905–1906 gg.* (2 vols.: St. Petersburg, 1908), I, 72–89, 130–152.

53. TsGAOR SSSR, f. 102, op. 1905, d. 999, ch. 39, t. 1, pp. 32, 156–157; TsGIA SSSR, f. 1276, op. 2, d. 8, pp. 88–93; *Russkoe znamia*, 24 January 1906, 4; 14 March 1906, 2; *Vestnik Russkago sobraniia*, 16 February 1907, 3; 3 March 1906, 3; *Tambovskii krai*, 15 March 1907, 2; 9 May 1907, 2; 4 June 1907, 3; 6 September 1907, 2.

54. *Vestnik Russkago sobraniia*, 16 February 1907, 3; *Russkoe znamia*, 14 March 1906, 2.

55. *Russkoe znamia*, 1 December 1906, 1; 15 December 1906, 2; 27 March 1907, 1.

56. TsGAOR SSSR, f. 102, op. 1905, d. 999, ch. 39, t. 2, p. 482; f. 1467, op. 1, d. 848, p. 21; *Russkoe znamia*, 24 October 1906, 1.

57. TsGIA SSSR, f. 1276, op. 2, d. 8, pp. 291–302; *Moskovskiia vedomosti*, 7 April 1906, 3. A report in *Vestnik Partii narodnoi svobody*, 28 March 1906, col. 302, referred to the People's Monarchist Party as lacking "good agitators" and a sufficiently appealing program for the general populace, an evaluation that may have indicated a Kadet bias but probably identified correctly some major rightist problems in Saratov.

58. *Russkoe znamia*, various issues from May 1906 through September 1907; *Vestnik narodnoi svobody*, 25 January 1907, col. 272; Kolesnichenko, *Trudoviki v period pervoi rossiiskoi revoliutsii*, 151–152. The Peasant Union in particular seems to have been more active in Saratov and Voronezh provinces than elsewhere in the central agricultural region and middle Volga. See L. T. Senchakova, *Krest'ianskoe dvizhenie v revoliutsii 1905–1907 gg.* (Moscow, 1989), 157–161. For a valuable discussion of Peasant Union activity, including its relationship to the Trudoviks, see Scott J. Seregny, "A Different Type of Peasant Movement: The Peasant Unions in the Russian Revolution of 1905," *Slavic Review* (Spring 1988), 51–67.

59. One may note that several minor rightist organizations appeared in provinces adjacent to the central agricultural region. In the fall of 1905, a group of landowners and merchants in Kaluga province formed the Party for Tsar and Order (*Partiiia za tsaria i poriadok*). From its headquarters in the city of Kaluga, the party recruited provincial landowners, using the zemstvos as a means of making contacts. Although the Party for Tsar and Order achieved some success in attracting landowners, along with townspeople, it was generally outshone by the Octobrists. *Moskovskiia vedomosti*, 24 October 1905, 2; Emmons, *The Formation of Political Parties*,

163, 231; Shelokhaev, *Partiia Oktiabristov v period pervoi rossiiskoi revoliutsii*, 141. The Union of the White Banner (*Soiuz "Beloe znamia"*) in Nizhnii Novgorod was a patriotic organization that concentrated its efforts on the provincial capital. In late 1906, it affiliated with the Union of the Russian People, but even then it did not develop enough strength to get more than a small fraction of the vote in the Second Duma elections. *Minin*, 3 November 1906, 3; 5 December 1906, 1; *Volgar'*, 23 October 1906, 3; 3 February 1907, 3. The Ivanovo-Voznesensk Autocratic–Monarchist Party in Vladimir province drew primarily from industrial workers, although not as heavily as did the leftist parties. Extremely patriotic and antisemitic, it too formed a loose association with the Union of the Russian People. *Ivanovskii listok*, 13 February 1907, 1; 3 April 1907, 2–3; 14 June 1907, 2.

7: Rightists in the western borderlands

1. If used with caution, useful information on the Pochaev Monastery and its URP branches can be found in the anti-religious publication by Boris Kandidov, *Krestom i nagaikoi: Pochaevskaia lavra i chernosotennoe dvizhenie* (Moscow, 1928), 5–38.
2. *Russkoe znamia*, 14 August 1906, 2; 19 August 1906, 2.
3. *Pochaevskiia izvestiia*, 2 September 1906, 1; 15 September 1906, 2; 30 October 1906, 1.
4. *Ibid.*, 8 January 1907, 3.
5. *Russkoe znamia*, 27 October 1906, 1; *Pochaevskiia izvestiia*, 24 October 1906, 1–2; 30 October 1906, 2. By March 1907, the Pochaev URP had announced an additional 116 new branches. See various issues of *Pochaevskiia izvestiia*. Some URP branches in Volynia developed independently of the Pochaev Monastery's network, most notably the Zhitomir branch. TsGAOR SSSR, f. 116, op. 1, d. 104, pp. 1–5.
6. Jews comprised 10 percent of Volynia's rural population and in the towns 51 percent. In the countryside, Ukrainian peasants accounted for 69 percent, while Polish and German peasants made up another 4 percent each, the remainder of the rural population being mainly members of the nobility and peasants of other nationalities. *Pervaia vseobshchaia perepis'*, VIII, xi, 248–251.
7. *Pochaevskiia izvestiia*, various issues in September and October 1906.
8. *Ibid.*, various issues from September 1906 through June 1907; TsGAOR SSSR, f. 116, op. 1, d. 541, p. 1.
9. *Pochaevskiia izvestiia*, 3 October 1906, 1.
10. The 1897 census showed that 52 percent of the landed nobility in Volynia were Polish, while only 36 percent Ukrainian and 12 percent were Russian. *Pervaia vseobshchaia perepis'*, VIII, 248.
11. On Iliodor's speeches just before coming to Volynia, see the Iaroslavl newspaper *Russkii narod*, 26 March 1906, 1–3; 14 May 1906, 4; 30 July 1906, 1. On his speeches and activities in Volynia, see *Pochaevskiia izvestiia*,

11 January 1907, 1; 17 April 1907, 1–4; 20 June 1907, 1–4. Accounts of Iliodor are often unreliable, but useful information appears in René Fülöp-Miller, *Rasputin: The Holy Devil* (New York, 1929), 59–62; and Alex de Jonge, *The Life and Times of Grigorii Rasputin* (New York, 1982), 178–181.

12. S. M. Trufanoff (Iliodor), *The Mad Monk of Russia, Iliodor*, 41.

13. TsGAOR SSSR, f. 102, op. 1905, d. 999, ch. 39, t. 2, p. 518. The governor-general of Kiev, Podolia, and Volynia also complained to Stolypin about Iliodor's "extreme intolerance and fanaticism." *Ibid.*, p. 528. Generally, Iliodor received the support of Archmandrite Vitalii, but he was often at odds with Archbishop Antonii. After leaving the Pochaev Monastery in 1908, he spent several years in Tsaritsyn, where he established a loyal following and built a large monastery. But he continued to antagonize both the government and the church hierarchy, until finally the Holy Synod unfrocked him in 1912. In 1916, he emigrated to the United States.

14. The 1897 census listed the rural nobility in Bessarabia as 40 percent Russians, 38 percent Moldavians, 11 percent Poles, 10 percent Ukrainians, and 1 percent Germans. While landowners included persons other than members of the nobility, the composition of the nobility indicates the national diversity of the province. It might also be noted that the peasantry in Bessarabia consisted of about 60 percent Moldavians, 21 percent Ukrainians, 7 percent Bulgarians, 4 percent Russians, and 8 percent other nationalities. Approximately 7 percent of the rural population were Jews living in small settlements of their own. *Pervaia vseobshchaia perepis'*, III, 226–229.

15. S. D. Urusov, *Zapiski gubernatora: Kishinev, 1903–1904 gg.* (Moscow, 1907), 138–140.

16. Manning, *The Crisis of the Old Order in Russia*, 82, 86; *Bessarabskaia zhizn'*, 13 October 1907, 1; *Bessarabets*, 16 March 1906, 1–2.

17. The Center Party's willingness to embrace the new Duma monarchy gave it a constitutional appearance, as some political observers noted at the time. See *Bessarabskaia zhizn'*, 13 October 1907, 1. This orientation was one of the main reasons why analysts often referred to the party as "moderate," rather than "rightist" or "moderate rightist" – a designation that the Center Party members themselves frequently perpetuated.

18. *Bessarabets*, 16 March 1906, 1–2.

19. Urusov, *Zapiski gubernatora*, 144–145.

20. *Russkoe znamia*, 13 March 1906, 1; 17 March 1906, 3; 10 November 1906, 1.

21. *Ibid.*, 6 July 1906, 3.

22. *Ibid.* Since Krushevan was editor of *Bessarabets* only until 1905, he no longer had the use of this newspaper for disseminating his inflammatory views. Under the editorship of P. V. Dicheskul in 1906, *Bessarabets* became decidedly more moderate.

23. TsGAOR SSSR, f. 102, op. 1905, d. 999, ch. 39, pp. 17–19, 25–26; *Russkoe znamia*, various issues from March through December 1906.

24. The city of Kiev had experienced a tremendous growth during the late nineteenth and early twentieth centuries. In 1856, the population was

about 62,000; in 1874, 127,000; in 1897, 248,000; and in 1910, 527,000. In 1910, St. Petersburg had a population of about 1.5 million; Moscow, 1.4 million; and Odessa, 600,000. See Michael F. Hamm, ed., *The City in Late Imperial Russia* (Bloomington, 1986), 3, 83; and *Pervaia vseobshchaia perepis'*, XVI, 260–263. One may also note that the 1897 census listed 54 percent of Kiev's residents as Russians and only 22 percent as Ukrainians. Although the census takers probably counted as Russians many Ukrainians who spoke the Russian language, still a high proportion of the city's population was Russian. Hamm, *The City in Late Imperial Russia*, 2, 88–91.

25. *Ibid.*, 84–87.
26. *Novoe vremia* and *Moskovskiia vedomosti*, various issues in October 1905; Konstantin Paustovsky, *The Story of a Life* (New York, 1964), 105–108, 111–113.
27. V. V. Vodovozov, ed., *Sbornik programm politicheskikh partii v Rossii* (St. Petersburg, 1905), 57–64. Throughout its existence the Party of Legal Order experienced internal dissension between those who regarded it as not liberal enough and others who thought it was too liberal. Some PLO members left to join the Octobrists, some to enter the Union of the Russian People. As early as February 1906, a faction of the St. Petersburg PLO organized its own Constitutional Monarchist Union of Legality (*Konstitutsionno-Monarkhicheskii pravovoi soiuz*), which stressed the indivisibility of Russia, a principle it said was not being sufficiently upheld by the PLO. Emmons, *The Formation of Political Parties*, 443; *Vestnik Russkago sobraniia*, 26 January 1907, 2–3; Ivanovich, *Rossiiskiia partii, soiuzy i ligi*, 130–133.
28. *Pravo i poriadok*, 27 November 1905, 3–11; 18 December 1905, 9; 19 March 1906, 7–8.
29. See, for example, *ibid.*, 12 February 1906, 1–4.
30. *Ibid.*, 9 April 1906, 3–4. See Chapter 11 for details.
31. The PLO's national organization began calling for legislation that would prevent Jews from acquiring land and other property, bar them from state service and Russian schools, and impel them to emigrate from Russia. In Kiev, the PLO branch was soon lacing its message with accusations that the Jews were undermining every facet of Russian life. *Ibid.*, 3 September 1906, 6–8; 22 September 1906, 2–3.
32. TsGIA SSSR, f. 1276, op. 2, d. 8, pp. 271–282; *Russkoe znamia*, 14 February 1906, 4; *Zakon i pravda*, 11 November 1906, 3–4; *Letopis' Russkago sobraniia* (January 1903), xli; *Vestnik Russkago sobraniia*, 6 April 1907, 4; 2 October 1908, 2–3.
33. *Zakon i pravda*, 22 September 1906, 1; 23 September 1906, 2–3. The Russian Monarchist Party upheld the principle of private property and called for government aid in helping peasants buy land.
34. *Ibid.*, 24 October 1906, 1; 6 December 1906, 3.
35. *Ibid.*, various issues from September 1906 through June 1907; *Kievlianin*, 21 May 1907, 2. The Union of Russian Workers enhanced its appeal by promoting mutual aid projects. It set up shops that sold Union members

merchandise at reasonable prices, an enterprise the Union touted as an alternative to buying goods in Jewish shops.

36. The Union of Russian Workers also opened several branches elsewhere in Kiev province, aimed at reaching both workers and peasants; a branch in Kamenets, the capital of nearby Podolia province; and even one in the distant city of Kursk. *Zakon i pravda*, various issues from November 1906 through February 1907; *Kievlianin*, 23 November 1906, 2; 24 January 1907, 4; *Kurskaia byl'*, 29 November 1906, 3.

37. *Vestnik Russkago sobraniia*, 24 May 1907, 3–4; 2 October 1908, 2.

38. *Russkoe znamia*, 10 August 1906, 1; 15 December 1906, 1; 6 January 1907, 3; 15 May 1907, 1; 26 May 1907, 2.

39. TsGIA SSSR, f. 1276, op. 2, d. 8, pp. 271–282; Zyrianov, *Pravoslavnaia tserkov' v bor'be s revoliutsiei 1905–1907 gg.*, 74–75, 127–128; Levitskii, "Pravyia partii," 374; *Russkii vestnik* (May 1906) 331.

40. *Pravda i poriadok*, 30 April 1906, 1; *Zakon i pravda*, 26 September 1906, 2; 18 February 1907, 3.

41. Podolia's peasantry was 96 percent Ukrainian, while its hereditary nobility living in the countryside was 48 percent Polish. Its Jewish residents comprised 12 percent of the total population and in the cities 46 percent. *Pervaia vseobshchaia perepis'*, XXXII, 111, 256–259. For URP and URW branches, see *Russkoe znamia*, various issues in 1906–1907; *Podoliia*, various issues in 1907.

42. *Pervaia vseobshchaia perepis'*, XVI, 1–2, 88–91, 258–259. The hereditary nobility did not include all landowners, particularly small landowners; and some members of the nobility did not own land. However, these data provide an approximation of the nationalities represented among large landowners. They do not include those persons accorded the non-hereditary status of "personal" nobility for state service, who lived mainly in the cities.

43. *Revoliutsiia 1905–1907 gg. Vtoroi period revoliutsii, 1906–1907 gody.* Chast' vtoraia, 91–117.

44. *Russkoe znamia*, 15 December 1906, 1; 18 February 1907, 1; *Kievlianin*, 25 November 1906, 2; 24 January 1907, 4; *Zakon i pravda*, 11 February 1907, 3.

45. *Pervaia vseobshchaia perepis'*, XXII, ix, 3, 84–87, 222–223; XXIII, vii, 3, 250–251; V, 76–79, 254–255; XI, vi, 3, 288–289.

46. *Minskoe slovo*, 5 November 1906, 2.

47. See Chapter 11 for details of the elections.

48. *Minskoe slovo*, 5 November 1906, 2.

49. *Vestnik narodnoi svobody*, 8 February 1907, supplement; *Rech'*, 21 February 1907, 3; *Novoe vremia*, 6 February 1907, 3.

50. *Minskoe slovo*, various issues from November 1906 through February 1907.

51. *Ibid.*, 17 November 1906, 1–2; 25 November 1906, 1; 24 December 1906, 6.

52. *Russkoe znamia*, 12 November 1906, 1; 15 December 1906, 1; 20 March 1907, 6; Edelman, "The Elections to the Third Duma," 98.

53. *Minskoe slovo*, 6 December 1906, 1.

54. *Mogilevskii vestnik*, 23 January 1907, 3; 25 January 1907, 3; TsGAOR SSSR,

f. 102, op. 1905, d. 999, ch. 39, t. 1, pp. 131–132; f. 588, op. 1, d. 1263, p. 37.

55. *Russkoe znamia,* various issues from August 1906 through September 1907; TsGIA SSSR, f. 1276, op. 2, d. 8, pp. 138–140. The Russian Borderland Union, which attracted many Orthodox peasants in Minsk province, had little success in Kovno and Vilna provinces. In Kovno, 85 percent of the peasants were Lithuanian Catholic; in Vilna, only 23 percent were Lithuanian Catholic, but the 71 percent that were Belorussian were also predominantly Catholic. *Pervaia vseobshchaia perepis',* IV, 60–61, 162–163; XVII, 84–87, 208–209. Similarly, the Union of the Russian People established only a few small branches in Kovno and Vilna provinces. *Russkoe znamia,* 12 November 1906, 1; 14 December 1906, 1–2; 15 December 1906, 2; 16 October 1907, 2.

8: The Patriotic Union and the United Nobility

1. Gurko, *Features and Figures of the Past,* 229–230.
2. On the friction between Pleve and Witte, see *ibid.,* 200–226; and Judge, *Plehve,* 62–77.
3. Gurko, *Features and Figures of the Past,* 383–384.
4. *Ibid.*
5. *Ibid.*
6. *Zhurnal Soveta Otechestvennago soiuza,* 29 May 1905, iii–vii. See also the Union's *Zemskii sobor i zemskaia duma* (St. Petersburg, 1905).
7. *Novoe vremia,* 26 June 1905, 1; *Pravo,* 3 July 1905, cols. 2132–2135.
8. Gurko, *Features and Figures of the Past,* 385.
9. For information on and analyses of the Peterhof Conference, see George E. Snow, "The Peterhof Conference of 1905 and the Creation of the Bulygin Duma," *Russian History,* 2 (1975), 149–162; Ann Erickson Healy, *The Russian Autocracy in Crisis, 1905–1907* (Hamden, 1976), 75–88; and Anan'ich, *Krizis samoderzhaviia v Rossii, 1895–1917,* 205–213.
10. *Otchizna,* 24 January 1906, 2–3. *Otchizna* was the newspaper published by the Patriotic Union from January to June 1906.
11. *Ibid.,* 12 March 1906, 4.
12. *Ibid.,* 24 January 1906, 2–3; Ivanovich, *Rossiiskiia partii, soiuzy i ligi,* 126–128.
13. Bobrinskii recomended that the Union support candidates of the Party of Legal Order, contending that the Union should shun the extreme rightist parties, an apparent reference to such demagogic groups as the Union of the Russian People. Naryshkin suggested that the Union endorse Octobrist candidates, noting that the Party of Legal Order tentatively favored limited expropriation of private land. Some Union leaders claimed that the Union was closer to the extreme right than either the Octobrists or the PLO, since both of these parties equivocated on the questions of autocratic power and equal rights for Jews. On these issues, see *Otchizna,* 19 March 1906, 4.

14. The most detailed examination of the United Nobility is Hosking and Manning, "What Was the United Nobility?," 142–183. See also Chapter 11, "The United Nobility and the Crisis of the First Duma," and subsequent portions of Manning's *The Crisis of the Old Order in Russia.* In addition, Solov'ev, *Samoderzhavie i dvorianstvo v 1902–1907 gg.,* contains much useful information about the United Nobility and its antecedent organizations.

15. Solov'ev, *Samoderzhavie i dvorianstvo,* 199–200; *Moskovskiia vedomosti,* 18 November 1905, 2; 19 November 1905, 3; *Novoe vremia,* 19 November 1905, 2; Levitskii, "Pravyia partii," 386–387.

16. *Novoe vremia,* 18 November 1905, 2; 22 November 1905, 1.

17. Solov'ev, *Samoderzhavie i dvorianstvo,* 203–212. Again only a few Slavophile delegates spoke in favor of preserving the commune.

18. *Moskovskiia vedomosti,* 14 February 1906, 3.

19. Solov'ev, *Samoderzhavie i dvorianstvo,* 212; *Moskovskiia vedomosti,* 23 April 1906, 2–3; 25 April 1906, 3; 26 April 1906, 2.

20. This supposition is elaborated in Hosking and Manning, "What Was the United Nobility?," 153.

21. *Moskovskiia vedomosti,* 19 April 1906, 3; 21 April 1906, 3; TsGAOR SSSR, f. 434, op. 1, d. 4, pp. 1–2.

22. *Ibid.,* pp. 2–17.

23. Only twenty-nine provincial assemblies sent delegates. Six assemblies declined the invitation to attend, while fourteen simply did not reply. *Moskovskiia vedomosti,* 25 April 1906, 3. The second and third congresses fared but slightly better, representing thirty-one and thirty-two provincial assemblies respectively.

24. TsGAOR SSSR, f. 434, op. 1, d. 4, p. 2. In addition to Pestrzhetskii, the Agrarian Committee was composed of A. R. Chemodurov, V. I. Denisov, Kh. N. Sergeev, V. M. Volkonskii, A. A. Shults, A. I. Zybin, and Iu. V. Trubnikov – all representing provincial nobles' assemblies – as well as S. S. Bekhteev, who, like Pestrzhetskii, was a government agrarian expert invited to participate in the congress. *Trudy pervago S"ezda upolnomochennykh dvorianskikh obshchestv 29 gubernii* (2nd edn.: St. Petersburg, 1910), 181–182.

25. For the "theses" presented by the Agrarian Committee and debate on the land question, see *Trudy pervago S"ezda,* 36–41, 75, 89–93, and 154–156; and accounts in *Novoe vremia,* 25 May 1906, 4; 26 May 1906, 3; and 27 May 1906, 13. Pestrzhetskii had hinted at limited expropriation, in which private owners would be required to offer small portions of their land to peasant purchasers, but even this modest suggestion went further than his superior in the Ministry of Internal Affairs, V. I. Gurko, proposed in his own land program – or that the First Congress was willing to accept.

26. *Trudy pervago S"ezda,* 102–117.

27. TsGAOR SSSR, f. 434, op. 1, d. 75, pp. 9–13.

28. See Chapter 11 for a more thorough discussion of the dissolution of the First Duma.

29. TsGAOR SSSR, f. 434, op. 1, d. 9, pp. 4–5; d. 76, pp. 6–8, 11–14.
30. *Ibid.*, pp. 20–23.
31. *Novoe vremia*, 17 November 1906, 3; Solov'ev, *Samoderzhavie i dvorianstvo*, 212; TsGAOR SSSR, f. 434, op. 1, d. 8, pp. 2–3; d. 76, p. 48.
32. For a sound overview of proposed land programs by the government and the Duma in 1906, see Dorothy Atkinson, *The End of the Russian Land Commune, 1905–1930* (Stanford, 1983), 47–60; for a thorough examination of the government's reforms, see David A. J. Macey, *Government and Peasant in Russia, 1861–1906: The Prehistory of the Stolypin Reforms* (DeKalb, 1987), 150–249.
33. While noting that the government's land reform and revised electoral law came shortly after the political intervention of the United Nobility, Geoffrey Hosking and Roberta Thompson Manning conclude that "it is exceptionally difficult to prove beyond any doubt that these acts resulted from the interventions of the United Nobility..." Hosking and Manning, "What Was the United Nobility?," 159. David Macey argues that most of the initiative for the government's land reforms came from within the government itself, which was embarking on a comprehensive modernization program, designed to satisfy a discontented peasantry and increase Russia's agricultural productivity. Macey suggests that the United Nobility's support did give the government and the tsar some added confidence to move ahead with its intended agrarian reform. Macey, *Government and Peasant in Russia*, 194, 219–220, 239.
34. TsGAOR SSSR, f. 434, op. 1, d. 76, p. 95.
35. *Ibid.*, pp. 109–112.
36. *Ibid.*, pp. 90–91. The Council also voted not to join the rightist members of the State Council in sending notes to Stolypin on the local reform issue, which suggests that one should be cautious in crediting the United Nobility with exerting its influence through high-placed members or allies in the State Council and other government organs.
37. *Ibid.*, p. 104; *Novoe vremia*, 29 March 1907, 4; 30 March 1907, 5; 31 March 1907, 13; Solov'ev, *Samoderzhavie i dvorianstvo v 1907–1914 gg.*, 47–55.
38. TsGAOR SSSR, f. 434, op. 1, d. 76, p. 92.
39. See various issues of *Russkoe znamia* and *Moskovskiia vedomosti*; and *Vestnik Russkago sobraniia*, 11 May 1907, 1–2.
40. *Russkoe znamia*, 4 June 1907, 1–2.
41. *Novoe vremia*, 12–15 June and 26–30 August 1907, pp. 1–2 in each issue.
42. For a discussion of the United Nobility's attempts to influence government policies in the post-1907 period, see Solov'ev, *Samoderzhavie i dvorianstvo v 1907–1914 gg.*; and Hosking and Manning, "What Was the United Nobility?," 163–169.

9: Rightists and the use of violence

1. TsGAOR SSSR, f. 102, op. 1905, d. 999, ch. 39, t. 1, p. 19.
2. *Ibid.*, d. 13, ch. 7, p. 113.

3. Strel'skii, *Partii i revoliutsiia 1905 goda*, 58.
4. Levin, "Materialy dlia kharakteristiki kontr-revoliutsii 1905 g.," 167–168.
5. *Ibid.*, 171.
6. Stephen Lukashevich, "The Holy Brotherhood, 1881–1883," *American Slavic and East European Review*, 18 (December 1959), 491–509.
7. Levitskii, "Pravyia partii," 371.
8. *Pravo*, 12 June 1905, col. 1920.
9. *Moskovskiia vedomosti*, 14 October 1905, 1; Levitskii, "Pravyia partii," 377.
10. TsGAOR SSSR, f. 102, op. 1906, d. 8, ch. 66, t. 2, pp. 131–132.
11. *Ibid.*, d. 999, ch. 39, pp. 74–75, 83; Chernovskii, *Soiuz russkogo naroda*, 53–54.
12. TsGAOR SSSR, f. 102, op. 1906, d. 999, ch. 39, p. 10.
13. Chernovskii, *Soiuz russkogo naroda*, 41–45; *Vestnik narodnoi svobody*, 7 December 1906, col. 2198.
14. TsGAOR SSSR, f. 102, op. 1905, d. 999, ch. 39, pp. 24–26, 32, 59; Chernovskii, *Soiuz russkogo naroda*, 29, 41, 44, 62. In Kursk, the local People's Party of Order formed a *druzhina*, as did the Union of Russian Workers in Kiev. *Kurskii listok*, 6 January 1906, 2; *Zakon i pravda*, 22 May 1907, 1–2. While there was no secret about the existence of the *druzhiny*, they were not legal organizations. At the fourth monarchist congress, held in Moscow in April 1907, the Union of the Russian People introduced a resolution requesting the government to legalize its *druzhiny* and similar sub-bodies of other monarchist organizations. *Vestnik narodnoi svobody*, 27 May 1907, col. 1224.
15. TsGAOR SSSR, f. 102, op. 1906, d. 8, ch. 66, t. 2, pp. 131–135; op. 1905, d. 999, ch. 39, t. 1, p. 9.
16. *Ibid.*, pp. 1–2; *Russkoe znamia*, 31 January 1906, 1; 4 February 1906, 2.
17. *Ibid.*, 10 March 1906, 2. In addition to the revolvers obtained from the St. Petersburg police, Kraskovskii bought a supply of Browning automatics through a dealer in Terioki, Finland. These he distributed in St. Petersburg or sent to *druzhina* units in the provinces, usually in boxes of Union pamphlets. Chernovskii, *Soiuz russkogo naroda*, 30, 41, 44, 63, 66, 68, 69, 71–72.
18. TsGAOR SSSR, f. 102, op. 1905, d. 999, ch. 39, pp. 10, 114. In April and May 1906, revolutionary workers shot to death at least two Union *druzhniki*. *Ibid.*, ch. 39, t. 1, p. 101. During this same period, the URP *druzhina* murdered two former members who they suspected were divulging *druzhina* secrets to the revolutionaries. *Ibid.*, ch. 39, pp. 11, 114.
19. Chernovskii, *Soiuz russkogo naroda*, 216–218.
20. TsGAOR SSSR, f. 102, op. 1906, d. 8, ch. 66, t. 2, pp. 133–135. Even then, the Odessa *druzhiniki* continued their aggressive activities, still wearing uniforms and carrying weapons, much to the concern of local authorities and the Ministry of Internal Affairs in St. Petersburg. *Ibid.*, f. 1467, op. 1, d. 848, pp. 39–40; d. 855, pp. 36–37.
21. Chernovskii, *Soiuz russkogo naroda*, 85–86. When questioned by the special commission established by the Provisional Government in 1917 to

investigate the Union of the Russian People, Aleksandr Polovnev, a former member of the *druzhina*, said that he and other *druzhina* participants knew of this assassination list and took a special oath not to reveal its existence. In 1907, the St. Petersburg lawyer, G. F. Weber, obtained a copy of the list from a disaffected member of the Union. The names shown here are those that Weber remembered from the list. *Ibid.*, 53, 85–86.

22. Gessen, "V dvukh vekakh," 228; A. A. Kizevetter, *Na rubezhe dvukh stoletii: vospominaniia, 1881–1914* (Prague, 1929), 437.

23. Gosudarstvennaia Duma, *Stenograficheskie otchety: Pervyi sozyv* (2 vols.: St. Petersburg, 1906), I, 524. "Illumination" in this sense was a term that originated during the French Revolution.

24. The Union of the Russian People pictured Herzenstein, in promoting his land program, as an agent for a general Jewish conspiracy. *Russkoe znamia*, 27 June 1906, 3.

25. Miliukov, *Vospominaniia*, I, 406–407.

26. *Novoe vremia*, 20 July 1906, 1; *Rech'*, 19 July 1906, 3; 20 July 1906, 2; TsGAOR SSSR, f. 102, op. 1905, d. 999, ch. 39, p. 111.

27. O. O. Gruzenberg, *Vchera: vospominaniia* (Paris: By the author, 1938), 135–141. An assistant procurator of the St. Petersburg district court, V. Ia. Gvozdanovich, acting on instructions from the Minister of Justice, I. G. Shcheglovitov, also conducted an investigation, which essentially corroborated Weber's findings. TsGAOR SSSR, f. 102, op. 1905, d. 999, ch. 39, t. 2, pp. 65–66, 91–113. Additional information on the murder was divulged by one of the assailants, Aleksandr Polovnev, to the Provisional Government's investigatory commission in 1917. According to Polovnev, after the murder the conspirators returned to URP headquarters in St. Petersburg, where Dubrovin congratulated them for their excellent job. Chernovskii, *Soiuz russkogo naroda*, 54–55.

28. *Ibid.*, 97.

29. TsGAOR SSSR, f. 102, op. 1905, d. 999, ch. 39, pp. 120–121. In December 1907, an anonymous member of the Union, apparently as a matter of conscience, informed the procurator of the St. Petersburg district court that he had clear evidence that on 13 June 1906, Dubrovin, Iuskevich-Kraskovskii, Polovnev, and two other Union leaders met secretly and agreed on the plan for murdering Herzenstein. TsGAOR SSSR, f. 116, op. 1, d. 734, pp. 3–4.

30. Chrezvychainaia sledstvennaia komissiia, *Padenie tsarskago rezhima*, II, 352, 357.

31. The transcript of the early stages of the trial appear in *Pravo*, 1 July 1907, 1854–1867; 22 July 1907, 2004–2008; and 28 October 1907, 2793–2795. *Rech'* carried a detailed account and much of the transcript of the trial during August–October 1909.

32. Chernovskii, *Soiuz russkogo naroda*, 86–87. On the testimony, sentences, and pardons, see also TsGAOR SSSR, f. 102, op. 1905, d. 999, ch. 39, pp. 87, 117–124.

33. Witte, *Vospominaniia*, II, 336–338.
34. For accounts of the attempt on Witte's life, see Chernovskii, *Soiuz russkogo naroda*, 58–59; Witte, *Vospominaniia*, II, 380–381; TsGAOR SSSR, f. 102, op. 1906, d. 999, ch. 39, t. 2, p. 489; L. L'vov, "Sem' let nazad," *Russkaia mysl'* (February 1914), 48–51, 60–61.
35. *Russkiia vedomosti*, 15 March 1907, 2. In the mail Iollos had received a threatening letter, embellished with the emblem of the Union and a picture of a grave. Kizevetter, *Na rubezhe dvukh stoletii*, 456.
36. Chernovskii, *Soiuz russkogo naroda*, 60.
37. TsGAOR SSSR, f. 102, op. 1905, d. 999, ch. 39, pp. 128, 160; *Russkiia vedomosti*, 15 March 1907, 2–3; *Novoe vremia*, 15 March 1907, 2; Chernovskii, *Soiuz russkogo naroda*, 60; L'vov, "Sem' let nazad," 58.
38. Witte, *Vospominaniia*, II, 382; L'vov, "Sem' let nazad," 52–54, 58–59.
39. *Vestnik narodnoi svobody*, 30 August 1907, col. 1570.
40. TsGAOR SSSR, f. 102, op. 1905, d. 999, ch. 39, pp. 129–165.
41. *Rech'*, 28 June 1907, 1–2.
42. Witte, *Vospominaniia*, II, 382.
43. Not until 1917, when he appeared before the commission investigating the Union, did Stepanov tell his story. Chernovskii, *Soiuz russkogo naroda*, 58–62. It is consistent with Fedorov's account in L'vov, "Sem' let nazad," 48–94.
44. Useful information on the pogroms can be found in *Materialy k istorii russkoi kontr-revoliutsii* (St. Petersburg, 1908), I: *Pogromy po offitsial'nym dokumentam*; and Iu. Lavrinovich, *Kto ustroil pogromy v Rossii?* (Berlin, n.d.). S. A. Stepanov calculates that in October 1905 alone at least 1662 persons died in pogroms. This number included 711 Jews, 428 Russians, Ukrainians, and Belorussians, 47 Armenians, 32 persons of other nationality, and 404 whose nationality was unknown. Stepanov, *Chernaia sotnia v Rossii (1905–1914 gg.)*, 56–57.
45. Markov, *Istoriia evreiskago shturma Rossii*, 25.
46. S. M. Dubnow, *History of the Jews in Russia and Poland* (3 vols.: Philadelphia, 1916–1920), III, 127.
47. For excellent discussions of the pogroms during this period, see essays in John D. Klier and Shlomo Lambroza, eds., *Pogroms: Anti-Jewish Violence in Modern Russian History* (Cambridge, 1992), 195–289, 339–351.
48. TsGAOR SSSR, f. 102, op. 1905, d. 999, ch. 39, t. 2, pp. 151, 525.
49. *Ibid.*, pp. 157–167, 186–189. Court investigators in Elisavetgrad did not determine who killed the head of the Union's *druzhina*. A month later, on 27 March, assailants murdered another Unionist. Police arrested three prime suspects, none of them Jews, which suggests that the Union leaders had other than Jewish opponents. *Ibid.*, p. 326.
50. *Materialy k istorii russkoi kontr-revoliutsii*, I, 375–391. Friction continued between Russian and Jewish extremists in Gomel; and as the Union of the Russian People organized branches in the city and surrounding villages during 1906, it experienced a huge influx of members. In August 1906, the assistant gendarme chief for Mogilev province (in which Gomel was

located) warned the Department of Police in St. Petersburg that the tensions could result at any time in "a general slaughter." Fortunately, this did not occur. TsGAOR SSSR, f. 102, op. 1905, d. 999, ch. 39, t. 1, p. 164.

51. This document was published in *Rech'*, 3 May 1906, 2. Later, the Ekaterinoslav governor reported that, in December 1905, Budogovskii helped Aleksandrovsk residents form an armed *druzhina* to quell revolutionary disturbances in the city, and that he became closely associated with the local branch of the Union of the Russian People. The governor defended Budogovskii as an honorable and resolute police officer but admitted that he lacked sound judgment and in his fervor could "easily get carried away." TsGAOR SSSR, f. 102, op. 1905, d. 999, ch. 39, t. 2, pp. 7–9.

52. *Rech'*, 10 May 1906, 3.

53. Gosudarstvennaia Duma, *Stenograficheskie otchety: Pervyi sozyv*, II, 1583–1603. For a perceptive examination of spontaneity and planning in the pogroms, see Heinz-Dietrich Löwe, *Antisemitismus und reaktionäre Utopie. Russischer Konservatismus im Kampf gegen den Wandel von Staat und Gesellschaft, 1890–1917* (Hamburg, 1978), 87–98. Löwe acknowledges the role of rightist leaders in fueling antisemitic passions in Russia, but emphasizes the spontaneous nature of the pogroms, maintaining that the pogromists were not simply hooligans recruited by planners of these outrages against the Jews.

54. Belokonskii, "Chernosotennoe dvizhenie," 48–69.

55. *Materialy k russkoi kontr-revoliutsii*, I, cv–clxxxv; Robert Weinberg, "The Pogrom of 1905 in Odessa: A Case Study," in Klier and Lambroza, *Pogroms: Anti-Jewish Violence in Modern Russian History*, 248–289.

10: Rightists and the government

1. *Novoe vremia*, 19 February 1905, 1. On the genesis and significance of the manifesto, see Chapter 1. For a detailed and judicious examination of Nicholas's views and responses during the period 1905–1907, see Andrew M. Verner, *The Crisis of Russian Autocracy: Nicholas II and the 1905 Revolution* (Princeton, 1990).

2. *Moskovskiia vedomosti*, 15 January 1906, 2; *Russkoe znamia*, 9 January 1906, 3.

3. *Ibid.*, 4 June 1907, 1–2.

4. Witte, *Vospominaniia*, I, 245, 311–312; II, 81.

5. *Ibid.*, II, 80–81.

6. TsGAOR SSSR, f. 102, op. 1905, d. 999, ch. 39, t. 1, pp. 38–39, 44, 62; Gurko, *Features and Figures of the Past*, 435.

7. *Krasnyi arkhiv*, 32 (1929), 180. Emphases in the original document.

8. Gurko, *Features and Figures of the Past*, 437.

9. Kryzhanovskii, *Vospominaniia*, 102–104.

10. Reported in *Vestnik narodnoi svobody*, 30 August 1907, col. 1568.

11. *Vestnik Russkago sobraniia*, 3 March 1906, 3.

12. Kryzhanovskii, *Vospominaniia*, 100–101. M. S. Komissarov, assistant chief of the Okhrana in St. Petersburg from the end of 1906 to February 1909, testified in 1917 that Dubrovin received several payments of 5,000 rubles each from somewhere in the government through the Okhrana. Chernovskii, *Soiuz russkogo naroda*, 75.

13. Kokovtsov, *Iz moego proshlago*, II, 9–10.

14. Chernovskii, *Soiuz russkogo naroda*, 35–39. A URP official, A. I. Prusakov, also testified that the Union got money from the Ministry of Internal Affairs, the Department of Police, and the imperial court, although he did not specify the time period during which the money was received. *Ibid.*, 45.

15. Gurko, *Features and Figures of the Past*, 435–436.

16. Chernovskii, *Soiuz russkogo naroda*, 276.

17. TsGIA Leningrada, f. 569, op. 24, d. 2, p. 13. For a description of these tearooms, see Timofeev, "V chainoi Soiuza russkago naroda."

18. Alexander Gerassimoff, *Der Kampf gegen die erste russische Revolution. Erinnerungen* (Frauenfeld and Leipzig, 1934), 75–77; TsGAOR SSSR, f. 102, op. 1905, d. 999, ch. 39, p. 1.

19. *Ibid.*, pp. 5–6, 9, 71–72; op. 1906, d. 8, ch. 66, t. 2, pp. 131–132. In 1908, Dediulin bragged that he had practically created the Union of the Russian People, which he regarded in 1906 as a necessary instrument for dealing with the revolutionary crowds in the streets, even if the Union "was composed of hooligans." TsGAOR SSSR, f. 1467, op. 1, d. 853, pp. 29–30.

20. Still intent on carrying on the revolutionary struggle, the URP's *druzhina* began to look elsewhere for weapons. After January 1906, it got most of its revolvers clandestinely from dealers in Finland.

21. TsGAOR SSSR, f. 102, op. 1905, d. 999, ch. 39, pp. 27–34, 76; op. 1905, d. 999, ch. 39, t. 2, pp. 195, 222.

22. *Ibid.*, f. 1467, op. 1, d. 855, pp. 33–35.

23. See, for example, Ministry requests for local authorities to report on URP branches in Ekaterinoslav and Poltava, and on the Autocratic–Monarchist Party in Ivanovo-Voznesensk. *Ibid.*, f. 102, op. 1905, d. 999, ch. 39, t. 1, pp. 63, 401; t. 2, p. 173.

24. *Ibid.*, ch. 39, pp. 17–20, 23–26; t. 2, pp. 227–228.

25. In September 1907, the Bessarabian governor prevailed on Krushevan to remove I. I. Dudnichenko as chairman of the Orgeev sub-branch because of Dudnichenko's excessive intriguing and disregard for local authorities. TsGAOR SSSR, f. 1467, op. 1, d. 848, p. 17.

26. *Ibid.*, d. 847, p. 10; d. 853, p. 75.

27. Chernovskii, *Soiuz russkogo naroda*, 225.

28. TsGAOR SSSR, f. 1467, op. 1, d. 847, p. 10.

29. *Ibid.*, f. 102, op. 1905, d. 999, ch. 39, t. 1, pp. 287–288; t. 2, p. 154.

30. *Ibid.*, t. 2, pp. 236–237.

31. *Ibid.*, p. 75; *Polnoe sobranie zakonov rossiiskoi imperii. Sobranie tret'e*, 25, No. 27052 (16 December 1905).

32. *Vestnik Russkago sobraniia*, 30 March 1907, 1.

33. TsGAOR SSSR, f. 102, op. 1905, d. 999, ch. 39, t. 2, p. 402.
34. *Ibid.*, p. 93.
35. *Ibid.*, pp. 17, 25, 75.

11: Rightists and the Duma

1. Vostorgov, *Polnoe sobranie sochinenii*, III, 9.
2. For the texts of the 6 August 1905 electoral law and its 11 December 1905 amendments, see F. I. Kalinychev, ed., *Gosudarstvennaia Duma v Rossii v dokumentakh i materialakh* (Moscow, 1956), 39–54, 94–102. A detailed discussion of election procedures appears in Emmons, *The Formation of Political Parties*, 237–293.
3. In provinces having cities with separate representation, electors chosen by the workers were divided between the provincial assembly and the city assembly.
4. *Russkoe znamia*, 12 January 1906, 1; 27 February 1906, 3; 12 March 1906, 2; 17 March 1906, 2–3.
5. Levitskii, "Pravyia partii," 445; *Moskovskiia vedomosti*, 4 January 1906, 1.
6. See various issues of *Russkoe znamia* and *Moskovskiia vedomosti* from January through March 1906; *Vestnik Russkago sobraniia*, 16 February 1907, 3; 2 October 1908, 2–3; and Levitskii, "Pravyia partii," 358.
7. *Vestnik Partii narodnoi svobody*, 11 April 1906, 442–470; 19 April 1906, 545–546. Since many electors were imprecise about their political orientation, analysts at the time often had difficulty categorizing them. Some political observers also showed either a liberal or conservative bias. I have used statistics compiled shortly after the elections by Kadet analysts, who published the only comprehensive reports of First Duma returns. After the Second Duma elections, the Kadets again published statistics, based primarily on information from local newspapers and their own correspondents. The St. Petersburg newspaper *Novoe vremia*, which relied mainly on election data supplied by the semi-official St. Petersburg Telegraph Agency, also published detailed statistics. The two sets of statistics agree closely on landowner and urban electors; in identifying peasant electors, whose orientations were harder to determine, the Kadet analysts tended to list questionable electors as "progressives," while *Novoe vremia* more likely listed them as "moderates." The Kadet statistics seem more accurate: they provide a closer correlation than do the *Novoe vremia* statistics between the orientations of the electors and the known political affiliations of Second Duma deputies chosen by these electors. One may assume, therefore, that the Kadet statistics for the First Duma elections are also reasonably accurate. Consequently, I have used Kadet compilations for all three Dumas (with occasional corrections for miscalculations or misplaced figures).
8. Emmons, *The Formation of Political Parties*, 199; *Vestnik Partii narodnoi svobody*, 19 April 1906, cols. 544–546.
9. *Ibid.*, 11 April 1906, cols. 395–396; 19 April 1906, col. 543.

10. *Ibid.*, 11 April 1906, 434–439; M. M. Boiovich, ed., *Chleny Gosudarstvennoi Dumy. Portrety i biografii. Pervyi sozyv* (Moscow, 1906), 1–499.
11. S. M. Sidelnikov, *Obrazovanie i deiatel'nost' Pervoi Gosudarstvennoi Dumy* (Moscow, 1962), 94, 143.
12. These figures are based on Sidelnikov, *Obrazovanie i deiatel'nost'*, 192, although in contrast to Sidelnikov I find only six, not eight, deputies who can be specifically identified as rightists. Terence Emmons calculates that at the time of the elections, about 37 percent of the deputies belonged to the Kadet bloc and about 50 percent were non-party. Emmons, *The Formation of Political Parties in Russia*, 298–300, 355. Sidelnikov's figures, which Emmons cites, indicate that by the time the First Duma convened many non-party deputies, mainly peasants, had expressed progressive or leftist leanings.
13. *Russkoe znamia*, 23 March 1906, 2–3; 24 March 1906, 1; 14 May 1906, 2.
14. L-g, "Momenty kontr-revoliutsii," 60–61.
15. *Russkoe znamia*, 11 May 1906, 1–2; 11 June 1906, 2.
16. *Pravitel'stvennyi vestnik*, 6 May 1906, 3; 9 May 1906, 3.
17. For typical letters, see *Russkoe znamia*, 27 June 1906, 3; 7 July 1906, 1.
18. Information on the negotiations and the conversations with the tsar can be found in V. N. Kokovtsov, *Iz moego proshlago*, I, 194–219; Miliukov, *Vospominaniia*, I, 376–387; V. A. Maklakov, *Pervaia Gosudarstvennaia Duma; vospominaniia sovremennika* (Paris, 1939), 187–208; D. N. Shipov, *Vospominannia i dumy o perezhitom*, 446–460; and Alexander Izwolsky, *The Memoirs of Alexander Izwolsky* (London, 1920), 177–198. For a comprehensive account of the negotiations, see Ascher, *The Revolution of 1905: Authority Restored*, 180–192.
19. Gurko, *Features and Figures of the Past*, 483–485. There is evidence that members of the Permanent Council of the United Nobility met with Stolypin, as Minister of Internal Affairs, on 16 June, and urged him to persuade the tsar to dissolve the Duma; it is less certain that Stolypin acted on this request. See Manning, *The Crisis of the Old Order in Russia*, 250.
20. *Russkoe znamia* from April 1906 to February 1907 listed 171 new branches by name. Since some issues are missing, and the editors may not have included all the new branches, the total number was probably well over two hundred.
21. *Ibid.*, 27 July 1906, 1; 29 August 1906, 1; *Moskovskiia vedomosti*, various issues from April through November 1906; *Vestnik Russkago sobraniia*, 16 February 1907, 3; 3 March 1907, 3.
22. *Moskovskiia vedomosti*, 3–8 October 1906, various pages.
23. The data in these tables come primarily from *Rech'*, 6 February 1907, supplement. The same figures, compiled by Kadet analysts, appear in *Vestnik narodnoi svobody*, 8 February 1907, supplement; and A. Smirnov, *Kak proshli vybory vo 2-iu Gosudarstvennuiu Dumu* (St. Petersburg, 1907), 234–239. I have made some corrections based on provincial newspaper

reports of the elections as discussed in Chapters 6 and 7; and in some instances on statistics in *Novoe vremia*.

24. In St. Petersburg, the Russian Assembly and the Union of the Russian People revived their earlier coalition, this time adding the recently organized Party of Legal Order, which subscribed to a moderately rightist program. In Moscow, the Russian Monarchist Party and the Union of the Russian People again promoted a common slate of candidates, but the Union of Russian Men, which had entered the bloc in the first elections, campaigned separately. *Rech'*, 3 February 1907, 5; *Vestnik narodnoi svobody*, 18 January 1907, 197; 22 February 1907, 569; *Moskovskiia vedomosti*, 25–29 January 1907, various pages.

25. *Tul'skaia rech'*, 5 December 1906, 3; 14 December 1906, 3; 23 December 1906, 3. A liberal newspaper, *Tul'skaia rech'* was published from October 1906 to June 1907.

26. *Ibid.*, 13 February 1907, 3; *Vestnik narodnoi svobody*, 8 February 1907, supplement; *Rech'*, 4 February 1907, 3; Gosudarstvennaia Duma, *Ukazatel' k stenograficheskim otchetam: vtoroi sozyv, 1907 g.* (St. Petersburg, 1907), 23.

27. Kolesnichenko, *Trudoviki v period pervoi rossiiskoi revoliutsii*, 154. The Trudoviks originated as a leftist group in the First Duma, primarily among peasant deputies. The rightists in Tula province also encountered much opposition in the towns and cities from the Kadets. *Tul'skaia rech'*, 3 November 1906, 3; 17 November 1906, 3; 30 December 1906, 3.

28. *Ibid.*, 6 February 1907, 2.

29. *Tul'skii vestnik*, 8 February 1907, 2, designated the peasant curia deputy as a non-party leftist; other sources, including the official Duma register, listed him as inclined toward the Kadets. Most sources regarded the two generally elected peasants as rightists, except the Duma register, which indicated that in the Duma one of these peasants was simply non-party and the other tended toward the Kadets. *Rech'*, 21 February 1907, supplement; *Novoe vremia*, 12 February 1907, 2; M. M. Boiovich, ed., *Chleny Gosudarstvennoi Dumy. Portrety i biografii. Vtoroi sozyv* (Moscow, 1907), 358–362; Gosudarstvennaia Duma, *Ukazatel' ... vtoroi sozyv*, 23.

30. *Kurskaia byl'*, 23 January 1907, 3; 24 January 1907, 1; 25 January 1907, 1.

31. See, for example, *ibid.*, 28 January 1907, 1.

32. The Trudoviks were only loosely organized, but by this time they had established several branches in Kursk province. See Kolesnichenko, *Trudoviki v period pervoi rossiiskoi revoliutsii*, 154.

33. *Kurskaia byl'*, 24 January 1907, 3; 30 January 1907, 3; 6 February 1907, 3.

34. *Vestnik narodnoi svobody*, 8 February 1907, supplement; *Ukazatel' ... vtoroi sozyv*, 12.

35. Imperatorskoe vol'noe ekonomicheskoe obshchestvo, *Agrarnoe dvizhenie v Rossii v 1905–1906 gg.*, I, 49–58.

36. Belokonskii, "Chernosotennoe dvizhenie ili tainy rossiiskoi kontr-revoliutsii," 55–59.

37. *Kurskaia byl'*, 19 February, 1907, 1; *Utro*, 8 February 1907, 2. The peasant seats were divided among three Trudoviks, two SRs, one SD, one

moderate (who later joined the Trudoviks), and one non-party candidate inclined toward the left. Boiovich, *Chleny Gosudarstvennoi Dumy: Vtoroi sozyv*, 154–163. *Kurskaia byl'* identified the deputies as two Kadets, six Trudoviks, and two moderates, but probably the Trudoviks were actually members of a Trudovik-dominated bloc that included SRs and SDs. Possibly the Trudoviks in the bloc were outnumbered by SRs, since in the Duma the deputies from Kursk were listed as six SRs, one SD, one Trudovik, and two Kadets. *Kurskaia byl'*, 10 February 1907, 1; *Rech'*, 21 February 1907, supplement; Smirnov, *Kak proshli vybory*, 263–264; and *Ukazatel' ... vtoroi sozyv*, 12.

38. *Novoe vremia*, 6 February 1907, 3, citing reports from the St. Petersburg Telegraph Agency; *Orlovskaia rech'*, 15 February 1907, 3; *Ukazatel' ... vtoroi sozyv*, 15.

39. Imperatorskoe vol'noe ekonomicheskoe obshchestvo, *Agrarnoe dvizhenie v Rossii v 1905–1906 gg.*, I, 62–63; *Orlovskaia rech'*, various issues in December 1906 and January 1907; *Eletskii krai*, 11 April 1907, 4; TsGAOR SSSR, f. 102, op. 1905, d. 999, ch. 39, t. 2, pp. 402, 488.

40. *Orlovskaia rech'*, 7–10 February 1907, p. 3 in each issue. See also *Orlovskii vestnik*, 7–10 February 1907; *Rech'*, 10 February 1907, 3; Boiovich, *Chleny Gosudarstvennoi Dumy: Vtoroi sozyv*, 219–226; and *Ukazatel' ... vtoroi sozyv*, 15.

41. *Russkoe znamia*, various issues from March through December 1906; *Rech'*, 6 February 1907, supplement.

42. *Russkoe znamia*, 24 October 1906, 1; 3 December 1906, 1; *Rech'*, 6 February 1907, supplement.

43. *Moskovskiia vedomosti*, 7 April 1906, 3; *Russkoe znamia*, 8 May 1906, 1; 19 August 1906, 2; 15 December 1906, 1; *Vestnik narodnoi svobody*, 25 January 1907, col. 272; *Rech'*, 6 February 1907, supplement.

44. Zyrianov, *Pravoslavnaia tserkov' v bor'be s revoliutsiei*, 141; *Pochaevskiia izvestiia*, 11 January 1907, 1.

45. *Golos Volyni*, 17 January 1907, 3; 18 January 1907, 4; *Rech'*, 21 February, 1907, supplement; Boiovich, *Chleny Gosudarstvennoi Dumy: Vtoroi sozyv*, 40–52; *Ukazatel' ... vtoroi sozyv*, 6. In the Duma, 11 Volynian deputies joined the "non-party rightist" faction, an indication that the Pochaev organization operated autonomously enough that its adherents chose not to identify themselves with the Union of the Russian People.

46. *Bessarabskaia zhizn'*, 26 January 1907, 3; 31 January 1907, 3.

47. *Ibid.*, 31 January 1907, 3; 1 February 1907, 3; 2 February 1907, 3; *Vestnik narodnoi svobody*, 8 February 1907, supplement; *Ukazatel' ... vtoroi sozyv*, 4.

48. *Bessarabskaia zhizn'*, 7 February 1907, 1.

49. It seems likely that the Center Party candidates were incorrectly designated as moderates, because, when the Center Party polled heavily in the Third Duma elections later in 1907, Kadet analysts at that time listed no Bessarabian candidates as moderates but many as rightists, probably having decided to combine the Center Party and extreme rightists into a single category. See *Rech'*, 24 October 1907, 4. Further,

although Kadet compilers included all 12 Second Duma peasant electors from Akkerman district as moderates, a *Bessarabskaia zhizn'* article referred to peasant electors from this district as rightists. *Bessarabskaia zhizn'*, 8 February 1907, 3.

50. *Ibid.*

51. *Ibid.*; *Rech'*, 21 February, 1907, supplement; Boiovich, *Chleny Gosudarst-vennoi Dumy: Vtoroi sozyv*, 8–15; *Ukazatel'* ... *vtoroi sozyv*, 4.

52. *Minskoe slovo*, 4 February 1907, 1; 6 February 1907, 1.

53. Data in Tables 11–15 may be misleading. Local reports from Minsk indicate that many electors whom Kadet analysts listed as moderates, and perhaps even as progressives, were actually either RBU members or supporters, or, in the case of landowners, Octobrists. *Minskoe slovo*, 25 January 1907, 3.

54. *Ibid.*, 7 February 1907, 2; *Novoe vremia*, 7 February 1907, 2; *Ukazatel'* ... *vtoroi sozyv*, 13. In the Duma, the RBU peasant deputies added to the confusion over how to classify the RBU by designating themselves as non-party. In addition, the village clerk did the same, while the priest and one landowner affiliated with the rightists – a further reflection of the political fluidity in Minsk province. In any event, as explained in Chapter 7, the RBU can still be best characterized as "moderate rightist."

55. *Mogilevskii vestnik*, 23 January 1907, 3; 25 January 1907, 3; TsGIA SSSR, f. 1276, op. 2, d. 8, pp. 138–140; TsGAOR SSSR, f. 102, op. 1905, d. 999, ch. 39, t. 1, pp. 130–132; f. 588, op. 1, d. 1263, p. 32.

56. *Rech'*, 21 February 1907, 2; *Mogilevskii vestnik*, 7 February 1907, 1; 8 February 1907, 3; 9 February 1907, 2; *Ukazatel'* ... *vtoroi sozyv*, 13–14.

57. *Zakon i pravda*, 17 January 1907, 1; 26 January 1907, 3; 31 January 1907, 3; *Kievlianin*, 27 January 1907, 1.

58. *Zakon i pravda*, 31 January 1907, 3; *Vestnik narodnoi svobody*, 8 February 1907, supplement; *Kievlianin*, 7 February 1907, 2; *Ukazatel'* ... *vtoroi sozyv*, 10.

59. *Ukazatel'* ... *vtoroi sozyv*, 4, 6, 13. As indicated in n. 54, several Minsk deputies designated themselves as non-party, although they belonged to the Russian Borderland Union and should be classified as moderate rightists.

60. *Rodnoi krai*, 7 February 1907, 3; *Rech'*, 7 February 1907, 3.

61. *Rech'*, 11 February 1907, 3; 13 February 1907, 3; *Vestnik narodnoi svobody*, 22 February 1907, 550–551.

62. *Rech'*, 7 February 1907, 3; 8 February 1907, 3; 17 February 1907, 5. It should be noted that the rightist deputies, as compromise candidates, were not strongly committed, and in the Duma they gravitated toward the Octobrists.

63. *Rech'*, 7 February 1906, 2–3.

64. *Volgar'*, 9 February 1907, 3; 10 February 1907, 3.

65. While Table 18 summarizes political affiliations among Second Duma deputies, Table 17 above specifies these affiliations according to provinces and cities having separate representation. Data for these

affiliations at the time of the elections come from *Rech'*, 21 February 1907, supplement; *Russkiia vedomosti*, 11 February, 1907, 5; *Novoe vremia*, 9–22 February 1907, various pages; and provincial newspapers cited in Chapters 6 and 7. Data for political affiliations in the Duma itself come from Gosudarstvennaia Duma, *Ukazatel'* ... *vtoroi sozyv*, 3–33. In some instances where the *Ukazatel'* simply lists deputies as "non-party," I have determined political inclinations on the basis of information found in the issues of *Rech'*, *Russkiia vedomosti*, and *Novoe vremia* cited above. I have included the "non-party" deputies from Minsk province as "rightists" (and in Table 18 as "non-party rightists"), relying on provincial sources cited in Chapter 7. Information on the deputies in the Second Duma can also be found in Boiovich, *Chleny Gosudarstvennoi Dumy. Vtoroi sozyv*, 1–412; and Smirnov, *Kak proshli vybory*, 257–279. Table 18 includes deputies not only from European Russia but also from Poland, the Caucasus, Siberia, and Central Asia.

66. *Russkiia vedomosti*, 11 February 1907, 5; *Novoe vremia*, 9–22 February 1907.
67. Purishkevich's circular to the URP branches was reprinted in *Vestnik narodnoi svobody*, 29 March 1907, 858–859.
68. *Zakon i pravda*, 17 May 1907, 1.
69. *Vestnik Russkago sobranie*, 11 May 1907, 1–2; *Vestnik narodnoi svobody*, 24 May 1907, 1223–1224. Apparently, the Council of the United Nobility also discussed whether to call for the dissolution of the Duma, but it had not agreed on what position to take by the time that the dissolution came. See Manning, *The Crisis of the Old Order in Russia*, 320.
70. E. J. Bing, ed., *The Letters of Tsar Nicholas and Empress Marie*, 229.
71. Chrezvychainaia sledstvennaia komissiia, *Padenie tsarskago rezhima*, VII, 99–102.
72. For the text of the revised electoral law, see Kalinychev, *Gosudarstvennaia Duma v Rossii v dokumentakh i materialakh*, 357–381. For a detailed discussion of the law, see Alfred Levin, "June 3, 1907: Action and Reaction," in Alan D. Ferguson and Alfred Levin, eds., *Essays in Russian History* (Hamden, 1964), 247–255. In his testimony to the Extraordinary Investigatory Commission of the Provisional Government in 1917, Kryzhanovskii maintained that the imperial government changed the electoral law not to destroy the Duma but to preserve it; that is, the government saw the existing relationship between the Duma and the autocracy as intolerable, and it believed that only if a cooperative Duma could be arranged did the Duma have a chance of surviving as an institution. Chrezvychainaia sledstvennaia komissiia, *Padenie tsarskago rezhima*, VII, 417.
73. For a detailed account of the confrontation between the government and the Social Democrats in the Duma, see Alfred Levin, *The Second Duma* (2nd edn.: Hamden, 1966), 307–340.
74. *Russkoe znamia*, 4 June 1907, 1–2. Reprinted in *Rech'*, 6 June 1907, 1–2;

Vestnik narodnoi svobody, 21 June 1907, 1362; and *Pravo,* 10 June 1907, 1717.

75. Witte, *Vospominaniia,* I, 245.

76. *Russkoe znamia,* 4 June 1907, 1–2.

77. *Novoe vremia,* 5 June 1907, 2; 7 June 1907, 2.

78. Kadet analysts also calculated a 53 percent rightist vote in Kharkov province, but they had already observed before the elections that it was difficult to distinguish between moderate rightists and Octobrists among the Kursk electorate. *Vestnik narodnoi svobody,* 13 September 1907, cols. 1618–1619.

79. A close study of the election returns suggests that, while the revised electoral law may have ensured an overall loyalist victory, the rightist vote in several provinces exceeded what would have been anticipated from the law alone. The extent to which rightists won there apparently resulted not only because the new law further skewed the representation *between* curiae, giving the landowners a greater vote at the expense of the peasants, but because rightward shifts occurred *within* curiae. These shifts would in themselves have produced rightist majorities in seven provinces – Tula, Kursk, Tambov, Volynia, Podolia, Bessarabia, and Mogilev. Since these were all provinces in which rightist organizations had polled well in the second elections, the surmise is that continued campaigning contributed substantially to rightist gains in the third elections.

80. *Rech',* 24 October 1907, 4; *Novoe vremia,* 15 October 1907, 3; Gosudarstvennaia Duma, *Ukazatel' k stenograficheskim otchetam: Tretii sozyv, 1907–1908 gg.* (St. Petersburg, 1908), 13–16. According to the new electoral law, the city of Tula no longer had separate representation.

81. *Kurskaia byl',* various issues in August and September 1907. Like Tula, the city of Kursk had lost its separate representation.

82. The Duma register listed seven of these deputies as extreme rightists; the other four joined the moderately rightist National Group. Gosudarstvennaia Duma, *Ukazatel' ... tretii sozyv,* 13–14.

83. *Orlovskaia rech',* 19 September 1907, 1; 21 September 1907, 3; 15 October 1907, 2; Gosudarstvennaia Duma, *Ukazatel' ... tretii sozyv,* 13–17. Disconcertingly for staunch members of the Union of Law and Order, two of the three rightist deputies produced by the bloc were only moderate rightists.

84. Gosudarstvennaia Duma, *Ukazatel' ... tretii sozyv,* 13–14. *Rech'* and *Novoe vremia* both listed four of the deputies as members of the Union of the Russian People. One can assume that the Pochaev URP supported the other rightist deputies as well. *Rech',* 24 October 1907, 4; *Novoe vremia,* 16 October 1907, 2.

85. *Bessarabskaia zhizn',* 9 October 1907, 1; *Rech',* 24 October 1907, 4; and *Ukazatel' ... tretii sozyv,* 13–14. The city of Kishinev no longer had separate representation.

86. *Minskoe slovo,* 16 September 1907, 1; 16 October 1907, 1; *Rech',* 24 October

1907, 4; 26 October 1907, 3; 27 October 1907, 3; *Novoe vremia*, 15 October 1907, 2; *Ukazatel'* ... *tretii sozyv*, 13–16. Apparently, the Russian Borderland Union also made an impact in Grodno province. Probably many of the "non-party" electors listed in Tables 19–27 belonged to or were oriented towards the RBU, inasmuch as the provincial assembly chose almost all rightist deputies. *Rech'*, 16 October 1907, 1; *Ukazatel'* ... *tretii sozyv*, 13–17.

87. *Russkoe znamia*, various issues from April through August 1907; *Podoliia*, various issues from May through September 1907; *Pochaevskiia izvestiia*, 4 June 1907, 2.

88. *Rech'*, 24 October 1907, 4; *Ukazatel'* ... *tretii sozyv*, 13–14.

89. *Vestnik narodnoi svobody*, 8 November 1907, cols. 1879–1880; *Golos Moskvy*, 1 November 1907, 1; *Mogilevskii vestnik*, 15 October 1907, 2; *Ukazatel'* ... *tretii sozyv*, 13–14.

90. *Utro*, 14 February 1907, 4.

91. *Rech'*, 24 October 1907, 4; *Novoe vremia*, 15 October 1907, 2; *Golos Moskvy*, 1 November 1907, 1; *Ukazatel'* ... *tretii sozyv*, 13–17.

92. *Russkoe znamia*, 20 March 1907, 6; 26 July 1907, 1; 1 September 1907, 1.

93. *Simbirianin*, 16 October 1907, 1; *Rech'*, 19 October 1907, 5; 24 October 1907, 4; *Ukazatel'* ... *tretii sozyv*, 13–16.

94. See various issues of *Russkoe znamia* during 1907 for new URP branches in Tambov province; and *Tambovskii krai*, 16 October 1907, 2; 17 October 1907, 4, for election information.

95. *Kievlianin*, 19 October 1907, 3; 25 October 1907, 2.

96. *Rech'*, 24 October 1907, 4; *Novoe vremia*, 15 October 1907, 2; *Golos Moskvy*, 1 November 1907, 1; *Ukazatel'* ... *tretii sozyv*, 13–17. The Duma register indicates that the peasant deputy actually sided with the Kadets.

97. The unusually high rightist landowner vote in these elections probably depended on the large number of conservative clergy who participated among the small landowners, as they were admonished to do by the ecclesiastical authorities in Kiev province. For information and analysis, see *Vestnik narodnoi svobody*, 27 September 1907, cols. 1689–1690.

98. *Ibid.*; *Kievlianin*, 15 October 1907, 3; *Rech'*, 20 October 1907, 5; 24 October 1907, 4; *Ukazatel'* ... *tretii sozyv*, 13–16. *Golos Moskvy* reported that at the time of the elections three deputies were inclined toward the Octobrists. *Golos Moskvy*, 1 November 1907, 2.

99. Useful information on the rightist groups in the Third Duma can be found in Alfred Levin, *The Third Duma, Election and Profile* (Hamden, 1973), 112–121.

100. *Russkoe znamia*, 16 November 1907, 1.

101. For the role of the rightists in the Third Duma, see Robert Edelman, *Gentry Politics on the Eve of the Russian Revolution: The Nationalist Party, 1907–1917*. Government relations with the Third Duma are also

examined in A. Ia. Avrekh, *Tsarizm i tret'eiiun'skaia sistema* (Moscow, 1966).

Conclusion and epilogue

1. See, for example, S. Liubosh, *Russkii fashist: Vladimir Purishkevich* (Leningrad, 1925).
2. For an examination of some of these Russian fascist organizations abroad, see Erwin Oberländer, "The All-Russian Fascist Party," *Journal of Contemporary History*, 1 (January 1966), 158–173; and John J. Stephan, *The Russian Fascists: Tragedy and Farce in Exile, 1925–1945* (New York, 1978).
3. Hans Rogger, "Was There a Russian Fascism? The Union of the Russian People," 398–415.
4. See Edelman, *Gentry Politics on the Eve of the Russian Revolution: The Nationalist Party, 1907–1917.*
5. Interestingly, there has been a resurgence of rightist organizations in Russia following the demise of Soviet Communism in the early 1990s. See Laqueur, *Black Hundred: The Rise of the Extreme Right in Russia.*

Bibliography

Archives

Tsentral'nyi gosudarstvennyi arkhiv Oktiabr'skoi revoliutsii SSSR (TsGAOR SSSR) (now Gosudarstvennyi arkhiv Rossiiskoi Federatsii) (GARF)

Fond 102   Departament politsii

Fond 116   Vserossiiskii Soiuz russkogo naroda

Fond 434   Postoiannyi sovet Ob"edinennykh dvorianskikh obshchestv

Fond 588   B. V. Nikol'skii

Fond 1467   Chrezvychainaia sledstvennaia komissiia dlia rassledovaniia protivozakonnykh po dolzhnosti deistvii byvshikh ministrov i prochikh vysshikh dolzhnostnykh lits, 1917 god

Tsentral'nyi gosudarstvennyi istoricheskii arkhiv SSSR (TsGIA SSSR) (now Rossiiskii gosudarstvennyi istoricheskii arkhiv) (RGIA)

Fond 1276   Sovet ministrov

Tsentral'nyi gosudarstvennyi istoricheskii arkhiv Leningrada (TsGIA Leningrada) (now Tsentral'nyi gosudarstvennyi istoricheskii arkhiv S.-Peterburga)

Fond 253   S.-Peterburgskoe gubernskoe upravlenie

Fond 569   Kantseliariia Upravleniia S.-Peterburgskogo gradonachal'nika

Published documents

Arkhiv russkoi revoliutsii. 22 vols. Berlin, 1922–1937.

Bing, Edward J., ed. *The Letters of Tsar Nicholas and Empress Marie.* London, 1937.

Chernovskii, A., ed. *Soiuz russkogo naroda; po materialam chrezvychainoi sledstvennoi komissii Vremennogo Pravitel'stva 1917 g.* Moscow and Leningrad, 1929.

Chrezvychainaia sledstvennaia komissiia. *Padenie tsarskago rezhima.* 7 vols. Leningrad, 1924–1927.

Ermolov, A. S. "Zapiski A. S. Ermolova," *Krasnyi arkhiv,* 8 (1925), 49–69.

Gosudarstvennaia Duma. *Stenograficheskie otchety: pervyi sozyv.* 2 vols. St. Petersburg, 1906.

Ukazatel' k stenograficheskim otchetam: vtoroi sozyv, 1907 g. St. Petersburg, 1907.

Ukazatel' k stenograficheskim otchetam: tretii sozyv, 1907–1908 gg. St. Petersburg, 1908.

Ivanovich, V., ed. *Rossiiskiia partii, soiuzy i ligi.* St. Petersburg, 1906.
Kalinychev, F. I., ed. *Gosudarstvennaia Duma v Rossii v dokumentakh i materialakh.* Moscow, 1956.
Krasnyi arkhiv. 106 vols. Moscow, 1922–1941.
Levin, Sh. "Materialy dlia kharakteristiki kontr-revoliutsii 1905 g.," *Byloe,* 21 (1923), 156–186.
Materialy k istorii russkoi kontr-revoliutsii. Vol. I: *Pogromy po offitsial'nym dokumentam.* St. Petersburg, 1908.
Pervaia vseobshchaia perepis' naseleniia Rossiiskoi imperii 1897 g. 89 vols. St. Petersburg, 1899–1905.
Polnoe sobranie zakonov Rossiiskoi imperii. Sobranie tret'e. St. Petersburg, 1885–1916.
Revoliutsiia 1905–1907 gg. v Rossii: dokumenty i materialy. 15 vols. Moscow and Leningrad, 1955–1963.
  Revoliutsionnoe dvizhenie v Rossii vesnoi i letom 1905 goda, aprel'–sentiabr'. Chast' pervaia.
  Vserossiiskaia politicheskaia stachka v oktiabre 1905 goda. Chast' pervaia.
  Vserossiiskaia politicheskaia stachka v oktiabre 1905 goda. Chast' vtoraia.
  Vtoroi period revoliutsii, 1906–1907 gody. Chast' vtoraia.
  Vysskii pod"em revoliutsii 1905–1907 gg. Vooruzhennye vosstaniia, noiabr'–dekabr' 1905 goda. Chast' vtoraia.
Trudy pervago s"ezda upolnomochennykh dvorianskikh obshchestv 29 gubernii. 2nd edn. St. Petersburg, 1910.
Tsentral'nyi statisticheskii komitet Ministerstva vnutrennikh del. *Ezhegodnik Rossii 1904 g.* St. Petersburg, 1905.
  Ezhegodnik Rossii 1905 g. St. Petersburg, 1906
  Ezhegodnik Rossii 1906 g. St. Petersburg, 1907.
  Statistika zemlevladeniia 1905 g. 51 vols. St. Petersburg, 1906–1907.
Vodovozov, V. V., ed. *Sbornik programm politicheskikh partii v Rossii.* St. Petersburg, 1905.

Memoirs, diaries

Gerassimoff, Alexander. *Der Kampf gegen die erste russische Revolution. Erinnerungen.* Frauenfeld and Leipzig, 1934.
Gessen, I. V. "V dvukh vekakh," *Arkhiv russkoi revoliutsii,* 22 (1937), 5–414.
Gruzenberg, O. O. *Vchera: vospominaniia.* Paris, 1938.
Gurko, V. I. *Features and Figures of the Past: Government and Opinion in the Reign of Nicholas II.* Stanford, 1939.
Iliodor, *see* Trufanoff
Izwolsky, Alexander. *The Memoirs of Alexander Izwolsky.* London, 1920.
Kizevetter, A. A. *Na rubezhe dvukh stoletii: vospominaniia, 1881–1914.* Prague, 1929.
Kokovtsov, V. N. *Iz moego proshlago.* 2 vols. Paris, 1933.
Kryzhanovskii, S. E. *Vospominaniia.* Berlin, 1938.
Maklakov, V. A. *Pervaia Gosudarstvennaia Duma: vospominaniia sovremennika.* Paris, 1939.

Miliukov, P. N. *Vospominaniia, 1859–1917*. 2 vols. New York, 1955.

Nicholas II. *Dnevnik Imperatora Nikolaia II*. Berlin, 1923.

Nikol'skii, Boris. "Dnevnik," *Krasnyi arkhiv*, 63 (1934), 55–97.

Petrunkevich, I. I. "Iz zapisok obshchestvennago deiatelia: vospominaniia," *Arkhiv russkoi revoliutsii*, 20 (1934), 13–467.

Sheremet'ev, Pavel. *Zametki, 1900–1905*. Moscow, 1905.

Shipov, D. N. *Vospominaniia i dumy o perezhitom*. Moscow, 1918.

Tikhomirov, L. A. "25 let nazad; iz dnevnika L. Tikhomirova," *Krasnyi arkhiv*, 38 (1930), 20–69; 39 (1930), 47–75; 40 (1930), 59–96; 41 (1930), 103–147.

Trubetskaia, Olga. *Kniaz' S. N. Trubetskoi: vospominaniia sestry*. New York, 1953.

Trufanoff, S. M. (Iliodor). *The Mad Monk of Russia, Iliodor*. New York, 1918.

Urusov, S. D. *Zapiski gubernatora: Kishinev, 1903–1904 gg*. Moscow, 1907.

Witte, S. Iu. *Vospominaniia*. 2 vols. Berlin, 1922.

Newspapers and journals (1905–1907)

(Asterisks indicate periodicals published by or inclined toward rightist organizations.)

Bessarabets (Kishinev)
Bessarabskaia zhizn' (Kishinev)
Eletskii krai (Elets)
Glas naroda (Kharkov)*
Golos Moskvy (Moscow)
Golos Volyni (Zhitomir)
Grazhdanin (St. Petersburg)
Ivanovo-Voznesenskii vestnik (Ivanovo-Voznesensk)
Ivanovskii listok (Ivanovo-Voznesensk)*
Izvestiia Russkago sobraniia (St. Petersburg)*
Kievlianin (Kiev)
Kurskaia byl' (Kursk)*
Kurskii listok (Kursk)
Letopis' Russkago sobraniia (St. Petersburg)*
Minin (Nizhnii Novgorod)*
Minskoe slovo (Minsk)
Mogilevskii vestnik (Mogilev)
Moskovskiia vedomosti (Moscow)*
Novoe vremia (St. Petersburg)
Obrazovanie (St. Petersburg)
Orlovskaia rech' (Orel)*
Orlovskii vestnik (Orel)
Otchizna (St. Petersburg)*
Pakhar' (Moscow)
Pochaevskiia izvestiia (Pochaev Monastery)*
Podoliia (Kamenets–Podolsk)
Pravda i poriadok (Tula)*

Pravitel'stvennyi vestnik (St. Petersburg)
Pravo (St. Petersburg)
Pravo i poriadok (Kiev)*
Rech' (St. Petersburg)
Rodnoi krai (Kherson)
Russkaia mysl' (St. Petersburg)
Russkii narod (Iaroslavl)*
Russkii vestnik (St. Petersburg)
Russkiia vedomosti (Moscow)
Russkoe bogatstvo (St. Petersburg)
Russkoe delo (Moscow)
Russkoe znamia (St. Petersburg)*
Simbirianin (Simbirsk)
Tambovskii krai (Tambov)
Tovarishch (St. Petersburg)
Tul'skaia rech' (Tula)
Tul'skii vestnik (Tula)
Utro (Kharkov)
Vestnik narodnoi svobody (formerly *Vestnik Partii narodnoi svobody*) (St. Petersburg)
Vestnik Russkago sobraniia (St. Petersburg)*
Volgar' (Nizhnii Novgorod)
Zakon i pravda (Kiev)*
Zhurnal Soveta Otechestvennago soiuza (St. Petersburg)*

Books, articles, dissertations

Aksakov, I. S. *Sochineniia.* 7 vols. Moscow, 1886–1891.

Anan'ich, B. V., and others. *Krizis samoderzhaviia v Rossii, 1895–1917.* Leningrad, 1984.

Ascher, Abraham. *The Revolution of 1905: Russia in Disarray.* Stanford, 1988.
The Revolution of 1905: Authority Restored. Stanford, 1992.

Atkinson, Dorothy. *The End of the Russian Land Commune, 1905–1930.* Stanford, 1983.

Avrekh, A. Ia. *Tsarizm i tret'eiiun'skaia sistema.* Moscow, 1966.

Beliaeva, E. K. "Chernosotennye organizatsii i ikh bor'ba s revoliutsionnym dvizheniem v 1905 g.," *Vestnik Moskovskogo Universiteta. Seriia istorii.* No. 2 (1978), 32–44.

Beliaeva, L. N., ed. *Bibliografiia periodicheskikh izdanii Rossii, 1901–1916.* 4 vols. Leningrad, 1958–1961.

Belokonskii, I. P. "Chernosotennoe dvizhenie ili tainy rossiiskoi kontr-revoliutsii," *Obrazovanie* (January 1906), 48–69.

Bernstein, Herman. *The History of a Lie.* New York, 1921.

Bohon, John W. "Reactionary Politics in Russia, 1905–1907." Ph.D. dissertation, University of North Carolina, 1967.

Boiovich, M. M., ed. *Chleny Gosudarstvennoi Dumy. Portrety i biografii. Pervyi sozyv.* Moscow, 1906.

Chleny Gosudarstvennoi Dumy. Portrety i biografii. Vtoroi sozyv. Moscow, 1907.
Brock, John J. "The Theory and Practice of the Union of the Russian People, 1905–1907: A Case Study of 'Black-Hundred' Politics." Ph.D. dissertation, University of Michigan, 1972.
Bulatsel', Pavel. *Bor'ba za pravdu.* St. Petersburg, 1908.
Butmi, G. V. *Konstitutsiia i politicheskaia svoboda.* 5th edn. St. Petersburg, 1906.
Vragi roda chelovecheskago. 2nd edn. St. Petersburg, 1906.
Chermenskii, E. D. *Burzhuaziia i tsarizm v pervoi russkoi revoliutsii.* 2nd edn. Moscow, 1970.
Cohn, Norman. *Warrant for Genocide.* New York, 1966.
Curtiss, John Shelton. *An Appraisal of the Protocols of Zion.* New York, 1942.
de Jonge, Alex. *The Life and Times of Grigorii Rasputin.* New York, 1982.
Dubnow, S. M. *History of the Jews in Russia and Poland.* 3 vols. Philadelphia, 1916–1920.
Dubrovin, A. I. *Taina sud'by.* St. Petersburg, 1907.
Dubrovskii, S. M. *Krest'ianskoe dvizhenie v revoliutsii 1905–1907 gg.* Moscow, 1956.
Eldelman, Robert. "The Elections to the Third Duma: The Roots of the Nationalist Party," in Leopold H. Haimson, ed. *The Politics of Rural Russia, 1905–1914.* Bloomington, 1979.
Gentry Politics on the Eve of the Russian Revolution: The Nationalist Party, 1907–1917. New Brunswick, 1980.
Emmons, Terence. "The Beseda Circle, 1899–1905," *Slavic Review,* 32 (September 1973), 461–490.
The Formation of Political Parties and the First National Elections in Russia. Cambridge, 1983.
Fülöp-Miller, René. *Rasputin: The Holy Devil.* New York, 1929.
Ganelin, R. Sh. "Tsarizm posle nachala pervoi russkoi revoliutsii (Akty 18 fevralia 1905 g.)," in *Voprosy istorii Rossii XIX-nachala XX veka.* Leningrad, 1983.
Rossiiskoe samoderzhavie v 1905 gody: reformy i revoliutsiia. St. Petersburg, 1991.
Gratieux, A. *Le Mouvement Slavophile à la veille de la révolution: Dmitri A. Khomiakov.* Paris, 1953.
Gringmut, V. A. *Sobranie statei V. A. Gringmuta, 1896–1907.* 4 parts. Moscow, 1908–1910.
Hamm, Michael F., ed. *The City in Late Imperial Russia.* Bloomington, 1986.
Harcave, Sidney. *First Blood: The Russian Revolution of 1905.* New York, 1964.
Healy, Ann Erickson. *The Russian Autocracy in Crisis, 1905–1907.* Hamden, 1976.
Hosking, Geoffrey A., and Manning, Roberta Thompson, "What Was the United Nobility?" in Leopold H. Haimson, ed. *The Politics of Rural Russia, 1905–1914.* Bloomington, 1979.
Imperatorskoe vol'noe ekonomicheskoe obshchestvo. *Agrarnoe dvizhenie v Rossii v 1905–1906 gg.* 2 vols. St. Petersburg, 1908.
Iurekii, G. *Pravye v Tret'ei Gosudarstvennoi Dume.* Kharkov, 1912.
Judge, Edward H. *Plehve: Repression and Reform in Imperial Russia, 1902–1906.* Syracuse, 1983.

Kandidov, Boris, *Krestom i nagaikoi: Pochaevskaia lavra i chernosotennoe dvizhenie.* Moscow, 1928.

Klier, John D., and Lambroza, Shlomo, eds. *Pogroms: Anti-Jewish Violence in Modern Russian History.* Cambridge, 1992.

Kolesnichenko, D. A. *Trudoviki v period pervoi rossiiskoi revoliutsii.* Moscow, 1985.

Kol'tsov, D. "Rabochie v 1890–1904 gg.," in L. Martov and others, eds. *Obshchestvennoe dvizhenie v Rossii v nachale XX-go veka.* 4 vols. St. Petersburg, 1909–1914.

L-g. "Momenty kontr-revoliutsii," in *Itogy i perspektivy: sbornik statei.* Moscow, 1906.

Laqueur, Walter. *Black Hundred: The Rise of the Extreme Right in Russia.* New York, 1993.

Lavrinovich, Iu. *Kto ustroil pogromy v Rossii?* Berlin, n.d.

Levin, Alfred. "June 3, 1907: Action and Reaction," in Alan D. Ferguson and Alfred Levin, eds. *Essays in Russian History.* Hamden, 1964.

The Second Duma. 2nd edn. Hamden, 1966.

The Third Duma, Election and Profile. Hamden, 1973.

Levitskii, V. "Pravyia partii," in L. Martov and others, eds. *Obshchestvennoe dvizhenie v Rossii v nachale XX-go veka.* 4 vols. St. Petersburg, 1909–1914.

Lisenko, S. "Chernaia sotnia v provintsii," *Russkaia mysl',* 2 (1908), 20–28.

Liubosh, S. *Russkii fashist: Vladimir Purishkevich.* Leningrad, 1925.

Löwe, Heinz-Dietrich. *Antisemitismus und reaktionäre Utopie. Russischer Konservatismus im Kampf gegen den Wandel von Staat und Gesellschaft, 1890–1917.* Hamburg, 1978.

Lukashevich, Stephan. "The Holy Brotherhood, 1881–1883," *American Slavic and East European Review,* 18 (December 1959), 491–509.

L'vov, L. "Sem' let nazad," *Russkaia mysl'* (February 1914), 48–94.

Macey, David A. J. *Government and Peasant in Russia, 1861–1906: The Prehistory of the Stolypin Reforms.* DeKalb, 1987.

Maikov, A. A. *Revoliutsionery i chernosotentsy.* St. Petersburg, 1907.

Maklakov, V. A. *Vlast' i obshchestvennost' na zakate staroi Rossii.* Paris, 1936.

Manning, Roberta Thompson. *The Crisis of the Old Order in Russia.* Princeton, 1982.

Markov, N. E. *Istoriia evreiskago shturma Rossii.* Harbin, 1937.

Maslov, Petr. *Agrarnyi vopros v Rossii.* 2 vols. St. Petersburg, 1908.

Mech, V. *Sily reaktsii.* Moscow, 1907.

Oberländer, Erwin. "The All-Russian Fascist Party," *Journal of Contemporary History,* 1 (January 1966), 158–173.

Ol'denburg, S. S. *Tsarstvovanie Imperatora Nikolaia II.* 2 vols. Belgrade, 1939–1949.

Ostretsov, V. M. *Chernaia sotnia i krasnaia sotnia.* Moscow, 1991.

Otechestvennyi soiuz. *Zemskii sobor i zemskaia duma.* St. Petersburg, 1905.

Paustovsky, Konstantin. *The Story of a Life.* New York, 1964.

Rawson, Don C. "The Union of the Russian People, 1905–1907: A Study of the Radical Right." Ph.D. dissertation, University of Washington, 1971.

Rexheuser, Rex. *Dumawahlen und lokale Gesellschaft: Studien zur Sozialgeschichte der russischen Rechten vor 1917*. Cologne and Vienna, 1980.

Rogger, Hans. "The Formation of the Russian Right, 1900–1906," *California Slavic Studies*, 3 (1964), 66–94.

"Was There a Russian Fascism? The Union of the Russian People," *Journal of Modern History*, 36 (December 1964), 398–415.

"Russia," in Hans Rogger and Eugen Weber, eds. *The European Right*. Berkeley and Los Angeles, 1965.

Jewish Policies and Right-Wing Politics in Imperial Russia. London, 1986.

Senchakova, L. T. *Krest'ianskoe dvizhenie v revoliutsii 1905–1907 gg.* Moscow, 1989.

Seregny, Scott J. "A Different Type of Peasant Movement: The Peasant Unions in the Russian Revolution of 1905," *Slavic Review* (Spring 1988), 51–67.

Shanin, Teodor. *Russia, 1905–07: Revolution as a Moment of Truth*. Houndmills and London, 1986.

Shcherbatov, Aleksandr. *Zemel'nyi vopros*. Moscow, 1906.

Shelokhaev, V. V. *Partiia Oktiabristov v period pervoi rossiiskoi revoliutsii*. Moscow, 1987.

Sidelnikov, S. M. *Obrazovanie i deiatel'nost' pervoi Gosudarstvennoi Dumy*. Moscow, 1962.

Simmonds, George W. "The Congress of Representatives of the Nobles Associations, 1906–1916: A Case Study of Russian Conservatism." Ph.D. dissertation, Columbia University, 1964.

Smirnov, Aleksei. *Kak proshli vybory vo 2-iu Gosudarstvennuiu Dumu*. St. Petersburg, 1907.

Snow, George E. "The Peterhof Conference of 1905 and the Creation of the Bulygin Duma," *Russian History*, 2 (1975), 149–162.

Soiuz russkago naroda. *Rukovodstvo chernosotentsa-monarkhista*. Kremenchug, 1906.

K svedeniiu sluzhashchikh liudei. St. Petersburg, 1906.

Solov'ev, Iu. B. *Samoderzhavie i dvorianstvo v 1902–1907 gg*. Leningrad, 1981.

Samoderzhavie i dvorianstvo v 1907–1914 gg. Leningrad, 1990.

Spector, Sherman D. "The Doctrine and Program of the Union of the Russian People in 1906." Essay for the Certificate of the Russian Institute of Columbia University, 1952.

Spirin, L. M. *Krushenie pomeshchich'ikh i burzhuaznykh partii v Rossii (nachalo XX v.-1920 g.)*. Moscow, 1977.

Stephan, John J. *The Russian Fascists: Tragedy and Farce in Exile, 1925–1945*. New York, 1978.

Strel'skii, P. *Partii i revoliutsiia 1905 goda*. St. Petersburg, 1906.

Stepanov, S. A. *Chernaia sotnia v Rossii (1905–1914 gg.)*. Moscow, 1992.

Timofeev, P. "V chainoi Soiuza russkago naroda," *Russkoe bogatstvo* (February 1907), 57–81.

Verner, Andrew M. *The Crisis of Russian Autocracy: Nicholas II and the 1905 Revolution*. Princeton, 1990.

Veselovskii, B. B. *Krest'ianskii vopros i krest'ianskoe dvizhenie v Rossii, 1902–1906 gg*. St. Petersburg, 1907.

Viazigin, A. S. *V tumane smutnykh dnei: sbornik statei, dokladov i rechei.* Kharkov, 1908.

Vladimir Andreevich Gringmut: Ocherk ego zhizni i deiatel'nosti. Moscow, 1913.

Vostorgov, Ioann. *Pravoslavnomu russkomu narodu dobroe slovo.* Moscow, 1906.

Vostorgov, I. I. *Polnoe sobranie sochinenii.* 3 vols. Moscow, 1914–1915.

Weinberg, Robert. "The Pogrom of 1905 in Odessa: A Case Study," in John D. Klier and Shlomo Lambroza, eds. *Pogroms: Anti-Jewish Violence in Modern Russian History.* Cambridge, 1992.

Zaleskii, V. F. *Chto takoe Soiuz russkago naroda i dlia chego on nuzhen?* Kazan, 1907.

Zimmermann, Ernest Robert. "The Right Radical Movement in Russia, 1905–1917." Ph.D. dissertation, London University, 1967.

Zyrianov, P. N. *Pravoslavnaia tserkov' v bor'be s revoliutsiei 1905–1907 gg.* Moscow, 1984.

Index

Series list (continued)